SPIRITS OF FIRE

SPIRITS OF FIRE

English Romantic Writers
and Contemporary Historical Methods

Edited by
G. A. Rosso and Daniel P. Watkins

Rutherford • Madison • Teaneck
Fairleigh Dickinson University Press
London and Toronto: Associated University Presses

Associated University Presses
440 Forsgate Drive
Cranbury, NJ 08512

Associated University Presses
25 Sicilian Avenue
London WC1A 2QH, England

Associated University Presses
P.O. Box 488, Port Credit
Mississauga, Ontario
Canada L5G 4M2

Library of Congress Cataloging-in-Publication Data

Spirits of fire : English romantic writers and contemporary historical methods / edited by G.A. Rosso and Daniel P. Watkins.
    p.   cm.
  Includes bibliographical references.
  ISBN 0-8386-3376-5 (alk. paper)
  1. English literature—19th century—History and criticism—Theory, etc.   2. English literature—18th century—History and criticism—Theory, etc.   3. Romanticism—Great Britain.
  4. Historicism.   I. Rosso, G. A., 1954–   .   II. Watkins, Daniel P., 1952–   .
  PR457.S66   1990
  820.9'145—dc20   89-45548
                                                      CIP

IN MEMORY OF JOHN KINNAIRD

Teacher, Scholar, Beloved Friend
and Author of
William Hazlitt: Critic of Power

But the dens shook and trembled, the prisoners look up and assay
    to shout; they listen,
Then laugh in the dismal den, then are silent, and a light walks
    round the dark towers.
For the Commons convene in the Hall of the Nation; like spirits of
    fire in the beautiful
Porches of the Sun, to plant beauty in the desart craving
    abyss. . . .

        —William Blake, *The French Revolution*

Contents

Acknowledgments

We thank our contributors for their admirable patience and much-needed support over the past three years and especially for their excellent work. We also acknowledge the encouragement, sage advice, and friendship of Joe Wittreich, Tom Moylan, and Sam Tindall. Without the enduring support and warm friendship of Joanna Foster and Elizabeth Baxter this project would never have been realized; they know how much we owe to them. Finally, our greatest debt is to an anonymous friend whose labors in this volume are everywhere present and whose intellectual example has long served as an inspiration.

★　★　★

Four of the essays printed here have appeared previously in journals. We wish to thank the editor of *Critical Inquiry* for permission to reprint Jerome J. McGann's "The Meaning of The Ancient Mariner"; the editor of *Studies in Romanticism* for permission to reprint Stuart Curran's "The Political Prometheus"; the editor of *New German Critique* for permission to reprint Robert Sayre and Michael Löwy's "Figures of Romantic Anticapitalism"; and the editor of *Yearbook of English Studies* for permission to reprint Marilyn Butler's "Satire and the Images of Self in the Romantic Period: The Long Tradition of Hazlitt's *Liber Amoris*."

Finally, we are grateful to several presses for granting permission to quote from their copyrighted materials: the University of California Press for permission to quote from *The Complete Prose and Poetry of William Blake*, ed. David Erdman; Harvard University Press for permission to quote from *The Complete Poems of John Keats*, ed. Jack Stillinger; and Routledge and Kegan Paul for permission to quote from *Sir Walter Scott: On Novelists and Fiction*, ed. Ioan Williams.

Introduction

This anthology brings together some recent essays on romantic literature by practitioners of a resurgent historical criticism. We use this latter term merely as a convenient conceptual shorthand to refer to all critical methods, whether represented here or not, that subscribe to a fundamental materialist premise: that no aspect of the object of literary study—neither the letter of the text, nor generic forms, nor institutions, nor the minds of writer, reader, or interpreter—escapes the conditioning power of historical change.

Historical criticism thus comprises work of both Marxist and non-Marxist inspiration; carried on under a variety of preferred designations ("ideological criticism," "cultural materialism," "the new historicism," and so on); and including important tendencies within feminism and deconstruction. Within historical criticism, thus broadly conceived, our contributors neither club together in a single "school" nor pursue some shared, unitary method. What might fairly be called a classical method in literary history is represented here, but so too are methodologies that borrow elements from the international post-1960s renaissance in literary theory—including, notably, various kinds of borrowings, more or less eclectic, from the diverse intellectual tradition associated with the name of Marx. Even a partial list citing intellectual sources for the essays that follow—Lukács on "reification," the English Marxist historians, a specifically feminist-materialist deconstructive method, Marxist adaptations of hermeneutics, Jauss on "horizons of expectation," Habermas contra "technical reason," both Goldman and Gramsci on class-fractions and their intellectuals, historicist critiques of genre and representation—signals something of the plurality, and something of the mind-bending tangle of genealogies, within contemporary efforts to view literature *sub specie temporis.*

In these brief remarks, we are forced to forswear, as necessarily inadequate, any attempt to trace the branchings of these genealogies, or to scan, Satan-like, the still larger welter of contemporary theoretical debate. Our own broad allegiance to historical method is sufficiently indicated by our selection of these essays, and the day seems past when we might have needed to explain our fundamental proposition that literature is mortal. Whatever degree of specifically theoretical interest a given essay may have for a particular reader, this collection as a whole is addressed in the first instance to an audience of

students of romanticism, and for that audience each essay has been picked for
its ability to stand on the merits of its material argument.

Thus even the essays that make up the initial theoretical section of this
anthology, although they contribute a significant exchange on a crucial theoretical and methodological debate within (and beyond) historical criticism,
appear here primarily because of their bearing on the intractable debate as to
the nature of the phenomenon "romanticism" itself.

The first of these essays, by Robert Sayre and Michael Löwy, is that
miracle of rare device within contemporary criticism: a "strong" or avowedly
explanatory theory of romanticism on a pan-European or even global scale.
The authors begin by rejecting various earlier attempts to disallow the
"romanticism" problem as misconceived, or to offer summary solutions:
Lovejoy's application of the solvent of nominalism to dissolve the supposed
entity "romanticism" into bundles of attributes; the Procrustean, or academic, strategy of squeezing the bewildering range of romantic cultural
phenomena down to fit the narrower frame of the history of a literary school;
romanticism as "feminine" incoherence, as conservatism, as an anti-Enlightenment *Weltanschauung*, and so on. Instead, Sayre and Löwy posit an
"essence" of romanticism that is itself historical—in the sense of originating
as a "response" to a locatable, and durable, historical phenomenon of com-
paratively recent date.

That phenomenon is capitalism, whose specific essence Sayre and Löwy
see as an inner dynamic that drives that system to subdue an ever-widening
range of phenomena, including eventually even the human soul, to the power
of its quantifying relations. Sayre and Löwy are here clearly indebted to the
concept of "reification," which Lukács derives from the classical Marxist
tradition (see Marx on the "fetishism of commodities" in *Capital I*). Yet as
they also note, a similar phenomenon, under other theoretical descriptions,
appears in thinkers from other traditions (for example, Weber's "disenchantment of the world"). The reaction against this phenomenon is first visible
within circles of artists and intellectuals associated with the aristocracy; but
as the experience of "reification" is registered by an expanding number of
social groups (writing in the Marxist tradition, Sayre and Löwy necessarily
see a cultural phenomenon like romanticism as a product of groups rather
than of remarkable individuals), the subvarieties of romantic response increase, and so too do the bewildering number of thematic and formal characteristics of romantic art.

But it is important to note that in Sayre and Löwy's model (presented here
in an extremely schematic form, and without their richness of illustration),
there is thus no "essence" of romanticism that can be defined in purely formal
terms. What *is* essential about "romanticism," for Löwy and Sayre, is not a
set of formal attributes but the fact that it is a "worldview" characterized by
this shock of recoil, the "opposition to capitalism in the name," originally, "of

precapitalist values." This opposition, in the form of "hostility to a present reality" (which is recognized, however obliquely, as capitalist), can help interpret many thematic elements that have been recognized as belonging to romanticism: nostalgia for a past (or future, or imaginary) state of society; romance (the narrative of some world qualitatively different from this one); the isolated individual (shaken loose from a society of fixed "stations" that no longer exists); and so on through an extensive list. Yet unlike the well-known studies of Lucien Goldmann, to raise an important related point, Sayre and Löwy do not attempt to find strictly *formal* "homologies" between the situation of the social groups they consider and formal features of romantic art itself.

Similarly, the rough-sketch "typology" of romantic "figures," or subvarieties, that Sayre and Löwy introduce (the early "restitutionist" romanticism, the "conservative," the "resigned," even a "Nazi" romanticism—counterbalanced by varieties of "revolutionary" romanticism running from "Jacobin" through "Marxist") needs to be understood in terms of its intent. It is not meant as an architectonic guide to the formal features of romantic art—and still less, as the authors warn, as a tool for the close reading of individual texts or the oeuvres of individual authors. Instead, it comes closer to being an abstract developmental schema of how, over time, the worldviews of an ever longer list of identifiable social groups begin to register the effects of the capitalist demiurge that was remaking the world—and thus also of how the potential social basis for later varieties of romanticism has expanded until it now approaches universality.

And this developmental model (again, presented in high abstraction here) in turn explains the differences between Sayre and Löwy's conclusions and those of even the earlier writers on romanticism for whom they feel the strongest affinities. Thus, for example, there can be no question for Sayre and Löwy of establishing a concluding date for romanticism—in "1848," or thereafter. Just as capitalism has persisted, so too (as Marx predicted) have romantic responses to it, even down to the present. Nor can Sayre and Löwy pass the kind of simple evaluative judgment on romanticism that comes more easily to proponents of different explanatory schemes. In their eyes, the romantic response persists in a range of art good and bad, and from the most austere to the most collusively popular (they mention *E.T.* and *Return of the Jedi*). But the variety of non-artistic expressions is comparably wide: the Nazi dream of a neomedieval Europe, for instance, but also such contemporary romantic-utopian movements as "ecology, feminism, pacifism, and the theology of liberation," all of them oriented not toward the past but toward a future that might realize romantic aspirations.

Michael Ferber's response to the Sayre and Löwy essay, in fact, begins by paying tribute not only to the range, learning, and audacity of its authors but also to their evident belief that romanticism can yet serve "a wider and deeper social vision." Nevertheless, Ferber offers some pointed criticisms of their argument, and because his remarks on individual points in their essay are integrally related to his contention that Sayre and Löwy's totalizing intellectual method and theoretical categories are radically flawed, it is this latter challenge that we must consider first.

For Ferber, first of all, it is not necessarily the case that the existence of various manifestations of "romanticism" implies the existence of a romantic "essence," historical or otherwise. To assume otherwise courts circularity. Ferber therefore criticizes as too hasty Sayre and Löwy's dismissal of attempts by Lovejoy and others to specify, in formal or thematic terms, a set of common properties for romanticism, arguing rather that the Lovejoy-Wellek-Peckham tradition of attempts to find a "definition" of romanticism, for all its vicissitudes, remains an inspiration to methodologically sharper and more localized research programs that might still be formulated. The Sayre-Löwy model, Ferber claims, slights or omits a number of elements that are significant for romanticism (for instance, its religious definition); but its greater problem is overinclusiveness, which accounts for its inability to establish *differentia specifica* or to handle finer-grain distinctions between periods and putative "romantic" manifestations.

The problems that Ferber sees in Sayre and Löwy's definition of romanticism reoccur in their treatment of "capitalism," thus setting up a problem that threatens the causal element in Sayre and Löwy's model, and so the intelligibility of their entire argument. As with romanticism itself, where Sayre and Löwy see a historical "essence," Ferber sees Wittgensteinian "family resemblances"—between forms of capitalism that change over time, and between the economy of capitalism and such economic phenomena as medieval usury, which predate it. Behind Ferber's objections to both these points lie his methodological (and ultimately philosophical) scruples about Sayre and Löwy's use of such concepts as an "essence" of capitalism, or the "worldview" conceived as a "collective mental structure."

Throughout, where Ferber cites difficulties, he also suggests emendations; in particular, he includes a list of proposed topics ("archaic" anger at capitalism; opposition to church and state; the marriage market; and so on) that could be used to open up the Sayre-Löwy reification thesis to empirical investigation. (Ferber acknowledges its potential value, and is unwilling to deny it outright.) He concludes by suggesting that the romantic tradition may be exhausted as a possibility for serious art—even as it survives within emancipatory movements that suggest the possibility of a "postcapitalist" romanticism.

In their reply to Ferber, Sayre and Löwy concede the limitations of their essay's treatment of particular points, starting with the religious dimension of romanticism, which they believe Ferber rightly emphasizes. On philosophical grounds, however, they decline to draw an absolute distinction between "definition" and a causation they see as effected by real entities (for example, capitalism, reification) cited in their original formulation. For them, the elements Ferber separates need to be preserved in a "dialectical unity." Taken together, these three essays illuminate the problems of intellectual method that inhere in any serious attempt to address the "romanticism problem."

This theoretical debate is followed by a section of practical critical essays on the rhetoric and traditions of English romantic literature. David Sebberson recuperates the history behind the rhetoric of Wordsworth's 1800–1802 "Preface," and in particular that history's relation to Wordsworth's assumption of a polar opposition between "great national events" and the privatized "essential passions of the heart." The more systematic "rhetorics" of Wordsworth's contemporaries provide a valuable analogue to Wordsworth's poetic program. For Sebberson, the disappearance of the face-to-face classical polity is reflected in the degraded categories of such eighteenth-century rhetoricians as Campbell and Priestley, whose art, to put matters severely, teaches the student writers tricks designed to speed the ingress of one's message into the isolated Lockean mind of an individual reader, this rhetoric's only "audience." In the "Preface," Wordsworth's own intellectual starting points similarly reproduce the results of this long process. Wordsworth's "feeling is an explicitly empiricist concept, and his rationale for a "poetry of feeling" follows the example of eighteenth-century rhetoric in abdicating the world of knowledge and action (the rhetorician's *logos* and *praxis*), this time as a possible subject for poetry.

Michael Scrivener closely studies the dialectic between the "Prefatory Memoir" to John Thelwall's *Poems* (1801) and the historical conjuncture within which Thelwall lived out his life as Enlightenment rationalist, radical democratic tribune, and minor romantic poet and man of letters. Scrivener finds that Thelwall's attempts to theorize and practice literature (the parallelism to his material circumstances and political ideas here is marked) were ground between the upper millstone of a politically conservative aristocratic taste and the nether millstone of a more pious wider public that denied him his chosen role of representative bard. Thus situated by Scrivener's "Gramscian" analysis, Thelwall (who ended his days as a jackleg "Professor of Elocution") appears less as the figure of fun he has sometimes seemed in unsympathetic accounts, and more as an alert lower-middle-class intellectual gamely responding to the limitations and possibilities of a structural situation not of his making.

Daniel Cottom uses the case of the avowedly supernatural elements in Scott's novel *The Monastery* (1820), a rare commercial failure for its author, to explore the early nineteenth-century emergence of a dominant realist aesthetic for the novel—and so, more obliquely, the riot of crossed textual purposes, discordant discourses, and low-intensity class warfare that this aesthetic, in its heyday, frequently manages to finesse. One essential early step in this process, Cottom notes, was the positing of a normative definition of the novel (as opposed to the romance) as a tale that observes probabilities and remains true to "natural reality." Writing after the fact, Scott attributed some part of *The Monastery's* failure with the public to the presence of its out-and-out unexplainable apparition, whose hijinks broke with this emerging protocol. But as Cottom finds in his subtle examination of Scott's published utterances on the literary supernatural, Scott in his own way is perfectly aware of the arbitrariness of the exclusionary tactics demanded by the new, novelistic "nature"; and of the uneasiness of the coexistence of his Enlightenment principles and retrograde politics; and even of the uncanny aspects of the practice of writing books, and reading them—what now might be called "the darkness of figuration itself."

Marilyn Butler produces what is virtually a new text of Hazlitt's *Liber Amoris* by the simple expedient of rejecting its familiar designation as romantic self-portraiture, and reading it instead as an example of the seldom-discussed genre of romantic satire—here, as directed against the self-absorbed, rather De Quinceyan persona of that work's artist-narrator, whose own relentless self-mythologizing establishes him as a satirical object. Butler suggests that the cultural dominance of romantic conventions over later nineteenth-century literature may encourage us to impose them, mistakenly, on an earlier literature (*Alastor, Endymion,* even "Resolution and Independence") that actually expresses ethical and intellectual misgivings about the novel and extreme self-referentiality of a work such as *The Excursion.* For Butler, the balance of the available internal and external evidence establishes *Liber Amoris* as such a "satirical counterportrait," rather than as the naked confession it has almost invariably been taken for. Insofar as Butler is right, the later reputation of *Liber Amoris* thus represents yet one more unkind trick played on Hazlitt by the merry muse of History: a mislaying of the subtle anatomist of one historical moment as a result of the duller, yet ultraromantic spirit of the succeeding one.

The final section of essays moves to consider issues of politics and gender in certain romantic texts. G. A. Rosso extends the insights of Frye and Abrams on the "internalized" romantic apocalypse, contending that Blake's vision in *The Four Zoas* contains an inherent political dimension. Recalling the radical social tradition of early Christian apocalyptic, Blake, Rosso shows, imagines a revolutionary future in terms of both individual and collective transformation. This political interest is directly connected to Blake's larger vision of history. Rosso enters the labyrinthian final nights of Blake's unfinished epic and attempts to pull together the various symbolic threads of this historical vision. Rosso discovers that Blake's symbolism allows him to mediate apocalypse through poetic structure and to invoke the "End" without foreclosing on history's future. Rosso's central assertion, then, is that Blake's apocalypse takes on its political meaning in the gap between fiction and the world and opens into history by virtue of its transactive focus.

In her essay, Catherine L. McClenahan uses a number of poems from the Pickering Manuscript, written during the politically harrowing nodal year of 1795, to examine the difficult question of how, or whether, Blake's later thought moves in the direction of political disengagement and a retrograde conservatism on the politics of gender. Evidence for a pessimistic, affirmative answer here has been seen in the later prophecies. By focusing instead on the Pickering Manuscript's condensed, enigmatic dramas of domestic life, McClenahan glimpses a different Blake—one who is conscious of the peculiar tunnel vision that arises when each gender remains in the straitened walk of life that has been assigned to it. In her reading of "William Bond," McClenahan argues that that poem's "Mary" heroine, whose actions and attitudes seem so mad and disturbing to others, reflects Blake's admiration for Mary Wollstonecraft's attempts to effect an enlargement of social vision.

Jerome J. McGann's *de novo* reinterpretation of *The Ancient Mariner* finds a key to understanding Coleridge's intentions in the successive frames of interpretation through which this poem's narrative (here we suspend our disbelief) purports to pass: a supposititious fifteenth-century mariner, whose story is told by a balladeer contemporary, and then glossed by a seventeenth-century commentator (all of them arising in the mind of a late-eighteenth and early nineteenth-century poet), only to be glossed and reinterpreted yet again by the narrative's later readers. For McGann, this passage of a significant message through successive maculate filters irresistibly suggests a model Coleridge would have known of from his reading in his contemporary Geddes, a pioneer translator of the German Higher Criticism that Coleridge himself was later to adapt and champion in England. Coleridge's own conception of the *Mariner* may thus prefigure the labors of interpretation that became the major ideological task of his later life—rather as this challenging rereading further extends the new lead McGann sought to give to romantic studies in his own *The Romantic Ideology.*

Daniel Watkins argues that the figuration of Keat's *Urn*, "Attic shape" and poem both, is itself the bearer of an unwelcome counterstatement to the vision of art's plenitude that is the *Urn*'s "official" message. As Benjamin's famous aphorism has it, a subtextual record of ancient and continuing oppressions persists within the very idiom in which all actually existing societies (from the original Arcady through Keat's Regency and beyond) have recorded their real and ideal accomplishments. In the *Urn*, Keats registers the pathos of a mutable human world, but one heartened by an art whose icon in this poem is a utopian vision of a once and future resurrected human community. Yet even this attractive vision, Watkins argues, must necessarily employ representations shaped by a system of masculine values older than any surviving urn and so remain haunted by a pathos arising not simply from human limitation, or from the nature of figuration itself, but from the brute crimes of real history and the silences of all official discourse. Even Keats's ideal "realms of gold" need to be tested, as do ideals of our own, against the yet-to-be-transacted agenda that opens toward a more fully human future.

Stuart Curran notes that it was the political somnolence of the Causabon-like British mythographers he once studied, when set against Shelley's Promethean "avatar of revolution," that originally set him looking for the very different possible source material he discusses in his essay. Besides classical sources and translations (for example, the English Aeschylus craze of Shelley's Oxford year), Curran finds in works that Shelley may have known representations of Prometheus as American, Black African, French (Napoleon as living Promethean icon), and even—in a Blake illustration that Shelley almost certainly never saw—as a woman. Curran's most fascinating exhibit is Salvatore Viganò's *Prometeo*, a politically charged ballet that seems to have approached to the status of *Gesamtkunstwerk*, and which was certainly still being talked about in Milan when Shelley arrived there a few years after its performance. (Shelley saw other Viganò work, possibly saw the Promethean medal struck to commemorate the earlier production, and may even have known its libretto.) Curran's larger object of study here is the revolutionary cultural moment that gave birth to English romanticism (see his reference to Jauss), and as such his investigation has a value independent of and different in kind from that of yet another attempt to establish one more indisputable source. For it is such conditioning cultural moments, rather than fabulous lightnings leaping directly between authorial minds, that communicate all literary "influence."

SPIRITS OF FIRE

Part 1
Romanticism as a Historical Phenomenon

Figures of Romantic Anticapitalism

Robert Sayre and Michael Löwy

There has recently been a renewed interest in Europe and the United States in romanticism and romantic ideas. This tendency has been particularly evident in West Germany, a paradigmatic case of advanced capitalist society. Several recent essays and collections deal with the history of romanticism and with typically romantic subjects of interest like mythology, political theology, literary utopia, dionysian religion, etc.,[1] and these publications have aroused considerable discussion among German critics and historians.

But the phenomenon goes well beyond the limits of academia. A neo-romantic dimension is present in much of contemporary German artistic production, from literature to cinema. A novel by Michael Ende, *Die unendliche Geschichte* (Stuttgart: K. Thienemanns Verlag, 1979)—a kind of neoromantic fairy tale, a magical journey of initiation—has sold more than one million copies in the Federal Republic of Germany and has recently been made into a film. The author, who is the son of a surrealist painter, does not hide his affinity with the romantic tradition, and his contempt for capitalism and modern industrial society.

Moreover, there is also a very essential romantic component in certain large-scale social movements like ecology, pacifism, and the antinuclear coalitions, which have changed the political map of the country. The romantic longing for a harmonious relationship between man and nature is one of the main driving forces of such movements, and one of the main tenets of their counterculture.

Although these developments may be particularly intense in West Germany, they are not a specifically German trend. As can easily be seen, they are to be found in most contemporary industrial/capitalist societies. One cannot therefore avoid facing the hypothesis that, *far from being a purely nineteenth-century phenomenon, romanticism is an essential component of modern culture,* and its importance is in fact growing as we approach the end of the twentieth century. We must therefore go beyond the traditional view of romanticism as a purely literary trend located at the beginning of the 1800s.

But what exactly is romanticism? An undecipherable enigma, a labyrinth with no exit, the romantic phenomenon seems to defy scientific analysis, not only because its rich diversity apparently resists all efforts to reduce it to a common denominator, but also and above all because of its extraordinarily contradictory character, because it is a *coincidentia oppositorum:* at the same time (or alternately) revolutionary and counterrevolutionary, cosmopolitan and nationalist, realist and fanciful, restorationist and utopian, democratic and aristocratic, republican and monarchist, red and white, mystical and sensual. These are contradictions that inhabit not only the romantic movement as a whole but often also the life and work of a single author and sometimes even a single text.

The apparently easiest way out of this difficulty is to solve the problem by eliminating the term itself or by reducing it to a nominalist *flatus vocis.* The best known representative of this attitude (which goes back to the nineteenth century) is Arthur O. Lovejoy, who proposed that critics should abstain from using a term that lends itself to so much confusion: "The word romantic has come to mean so many things that, by itself, it means nothing. It has ceased to perform the function of a verbal sign. . . . The one really radical remedy— namely, that we should all cease talking about Romanticism—is, I fear, certain not to be adopted."[2] However, such efforts to cure the romantic fever by breaking its terminological thermometer remain relatively marginal. Most of the investigators start from the more reasonable hypothesis that there cannot be smoke without fire. But what kind of fire is it? What fuels it? And why does it extend in all directions?

Another expeditious method for getting rid of the contradictions of romanticism is to explain them away by reference to the incoherence and frivolity of romantic writers. The most eminent representative of this school of interpretation is Carl Schmitt, author of a well-known book on political romanticism. According to Schmitt, "the tumultuous multiplicity of color (*tumultuarische Buntheit*) in Romanticism dissolves itself into the simple principle of subjectivist occasionalism, and the mysterious contradiction between the various political orientations of so-called political Romanticism can be explained by the moral inadequacy of a lyricism for which any content whatsoever can be the occasion for an aesthetic interest. For the essence of Romanticism, it is unimportant whether the ideas which are being romanticized are monarchist or democratic, conservative or revolutionary; they are only occasional starting points for the productivity of the Romantic creative ego." Schmitt also insists on the "passivity," the "lack of virility," and the "feminine exaltation" (*feminine Schwärmerei*) of authors like Novalis, Schlegel, or Adam Müller, but this would-be "moral inadequacy" can hardly replace a social and historical explanation of the phenomenon.[3] Other authors also stress the "femininity" of romanticism. This is the case, for instance, with Benedetto Croce, who attempts to account for some of the contradictions by reference to the "feminine, impressionable, sentimental, incoherent and voluble" nature of the romantic soul.[4] There is no need to dwell on the superficiality and sexism of such remarks, in the context of which "feminine" is synonymous with degradation or intellectual inferiority, and which claim that coherence is an exclusively male attribute.

As a matter of fact, for a large part (if not the majority) of the critics who deal with romanticism, the problem of the antinomies of the movement does not arise at all, insofar as for them the phenomenon is stripped of its entire political and philosophical dimension and reduced to a simple literary school, the most visible traits of which are then described in a more or less superficial way. In its most shallow and mediocre form, this approach opposes romanticism to "classicism." For instance, according to the well-known French encyclopedia, *Larousse du XXe Siècle*, "one designates as *Romantics* the writers who, at the beginning of the 19th century, emancipated themselves from the classical rules of composition and style. In France, romanticism was a profound reaction against the national classical literature, while in England and Germany it expresses the primitive foundations of the indigenous spirit." For some authors it is a basic psychological attitude that belongs to all ages, while for others it corresponds to the "inborn dispositions" of this or that nation.[5]

On the other hand, most of the works that examine the *political* aspect of romanticism neglect its cultural and literary dimension and try to solve the contradictions by stressing exclusively the conservative, reactionary, and counterrevolutionary aspect of the movement, by purely and simply ignoring the revolutionary romantic currents and thinkers. In their most extreme forms, these interpretations perceive the romantic political thinkers mainly as forerunners of Nazism. In a book significantly titled *From Luther to Hitler*, William McGovern explains in all seriousness that Carlyle's works "appear to be little more than a prelude to Nazism and Hitler." How does one include Rousseau in such a narrow analytical framework? According to McGovern, the fascist doctrine of absolutism "is little more than an expansion of the ideas first laid down by Rousseau."[6] In a more serious work, devoted to the analysis of pre-fascist thought (*stricto senso*) in Germany—Lagarde, Langbehn, and Moeller van der Bruck—Fritz Stern nevertheless links these authors to what he calls a "formidable tradition": Rousseau and his followers, particularly in Germany, who criticized the Enlightenment as a naively rationalist and mechanistic form of thought. He also mentions here, pell-mell, Carlyle, Burkhardt, Nietzsche, and Dostoevsky.[7] The most discerning historians—like John Bowle—limit themselves to taking notice of the fact that the "Romantic reaction" is born simultaneously under the sign of revolution—Rousseau—and of counter-revolution—Burke—but they are unable to identify what is common to these antinomic poles of the romantic spectrum, except a vague "awareness of community" and a talent for "phrase-making."[8]

More interesting are the works—mainly German—that consider romanticism as a *Weltanschauung* and try to grasp the spiritual essence that is common to literary, artistic, religious, and political romantics. Most of them define the romantic worldview by its opposition to the *Aufklärung*, i.e., by its rejection of the abstract rationalism of the Enlightenment.[9] But these authors can hardly explain why romanticism appeared at a certain historical moment, what its social significance is, and why it takes such contradictory forms.

A characteristic common to most of the non-Marxist essays on the subject (however respectable their historiographical, philological, and analytical contribution may be) is the refusal to situate the phenomenon in relation to social and economic reality—which makes it difficult, if not impossible, to produce a real understanding or explanation of the romantic enigma. Some authors purely and simply ignore the concrete social conditions and consider only the abstract sequence of literary styles (classic—romantic) or philosophical ideas (rationalism—irrationalism); others link romanticism in a superficial and external way to this or that historical, political, or economic fact: the French Revolution, the Restoration, the Industrial Revolution. A typical example: A. J. George, author of a book with the promising title *The Development of French Romanticism: The Impact of the Industrial Revolution in Literature*, presents romanticism as a way of "adjusting to the effects of the Industrial Revolution." According to him, the Industrial Revolution simply "functioned as one of the prime sources of Romanticism" by furnishing it with "an imagery closer to reality and presensational forms tailored for modern conditions"; it helped also "focus attention on prose, thereby aiding the shift from the romance to the novel. . . . To both prose and poetry it gave new and striking images. In short, it was a major factor in the development of French Romanticism."[10] Far from grasping the deeply antagonistic relationship of romanticism to industrial society, this incredibly superficial analysis does not conceive their relationship otherwise than in terms of "modernization" of literature and a renewal of its imagery.

Of course, the non-Marxist critical literature *has* made some remarkable contributions to knowledge of this field, in the form of literary history, detailed studies of specific writers, and in some cases the analysis of *Weltanschauung*. It has identified some important traits that are to be found in most, if not all, romantic authors. But one searches in vain for a global approach that might reveal the internal coherence of these elements, the underlying unity of these *membra disiecta*, and their sociocultural meaning.

The merit of the Marxist studies—whatever their limitations and simplifications (they are sometimes extremely arbitrary and one-sided)—is that most of them have been able to grasp the *essential* dimension of the phenomena, by designating the common thrust, the unifying element of the romantic movement in its principal manifestations throughout the key European countries (Germany, England, France, Russia): *opposition to capitalism in the name of precapitalist values.*

The concept of "Romantic anticapitalism" first appears with Lukács, but one can find its antecedents in Marx and Engels's writings on Balzac, Carlyle,

Sismondi, etc. These writings reveal (in spite of the criticism) the very high esteem in which the authors of the *Communist Manifesto* held those authors who, although *laudatores tempis acti,* were able to strike at the heart of capitalism through their criticism.[11]

Unlike Marx and Engels, most of the Marxist authors of the twentieth century (or those influenced by Marx) considered romanticism—particularly the German strand—as an essentially reactionary and counterrevolutionary tendency. In France this orientation is exemplified by the historian Jacques Droz. His remarkable works on political romanticism in Germany show very accurately the general character of the phenomenon (its unity as a *Weltanschauung*) and its anti-capitalist dimension. However, he sees the movement as being, in the last analysis, the reaction of the German intelligentsia against the "principles of the French Revolution and of the Napoleonic conquest," a reaction that longs for the restoration of medieval civilization, and that is located without any doubt "in the camp of counterrevolution"; in short, a movement that expressed "the consciousness of the old ruling classes of the danger which threatened them." This position implies that Hölderlin, Büchner, and the other romantics who favored the French Revolution are excluded from the framework of analysis and that the Jacobin and prorevolutionary period of numerous writers and poets, whose romantic character is beyond question, remains an inexplicable accident. Referring to Friedrich Schlegel, Jacques Droz acknowledges that his transformation from republican into conservative is "difficult to explain," and he ends by attributing it (following Carl Schmitt's thesis, which he criticizes elsewhere in his book as wrong) to the "occasionalist dilettantism" of the poet.[12]

Lukács himself is also one of those Marxist authors who consider romantic anticapitalism mainly as a reactionary current, tending toward the Right and fascism. He has, however, the merit of having formulated the concept itself to designate the whole range of forms of thought in which the criticism of bourgeois society is inspired by reference to the precapitalist past. He was also able to grasp the contradictory character of the phenomenon, even though he insisted that romanticism leads more easily to reaction than to the Left and revolution.[13] Finally, one can find in at least *some* of his works, such as his writings on Balzac during the years 1939–41, a much deeper and more subtle analysis (precisely inspired by Marx and Engels' above-mentioned writings), where he stresses that the hatred of the author of the *Comédie Humaine* for capitalism, and his romantic rebellion against the power of money, are the main sources of his realist clear-sightedness.[14]

Balzac is indeed at the center of the debate among Marxists on the problem of romanticism. Engels hailed in Balzac—in his famous letter to Miss Harkness—the "triumph of realism" over his own political prejudices, i.e., his legitimist loyalties.[15] A vast critical literature has devotedly and dogmatically followed this scant indication, and the mysterious "triumph of realism" has become the principle commonplace of numerous Marxist studies on Balzac. Other authors have questioned this analytical framework in order to show that the writer's critical realism does not contradict his world-view. Unfortunately, their solution consists in arguing that Balzac's political ideology has a "progressive," "democratic," or even "leftist" character. For instance, the Czech historian Jan O. Fischer, author of an excellent book on romantic realism that has many interesting insights into the double nature (sometimes turned toward the past, sometimes toward the future) of romantic anticapitalism, tries in vain to prove that Balzac's legitimism was "objectively democratic" and that the "true content" of his monarchism was democracy. The arguments he puts forward are not very convincing: Balzac aimed for the "well-being of the people" and of the nation; he "sympathized with the common people" and their social needs—these are all in fact philanthropic tendencies typical of monarchist paternalism and have nothing whatsoever to do with democracy.[16] One finds a similar approach in some of the writings of Pierre Barbéris, one of the best contemporary French Marxist critics. In one of his essays, he suggests that one can find in Balzac—particularly in his youthful writings—"a leftist Romanticism" which is "Promethean" and inspired by the "cult of progress."[17] Lukács himself also claims that Balzac was a "great progressive artist," but he recognizes that the author of *Illusions perdues* was a realist not in spite of but *because of* his Romantic and "pessimistic" anticapitalism.[18]

In our view, this last remark opens the way for the most adequate interpretation of Balzac and of many other romantic anticapitalist authors. Their critical lucidity is not at all contradicted by their "reactionary," past-oriented, legitimist or Tory ideology. It is vain (and useless) to dress them up with nonexistent "democratic" and "progressive" virtues. It is *because* they turn their gaze toward the past that they are able to criticize the present with such acumen and realism. Of course, this criticism can be made (and better so!) from the standpoint of the *future*, as with the utopians and the revolutionaries. But it is a prejudice—inherited from the Enlightenment—that existing social reality can be criticized only from a "progressive" perspective.

Moreover, it seems to us that the category of "realism" itself is too narrow to embrace the richness of the romantic anti-capitalist contribution. Too many Marxist works have as their only criterion the "realist" or "nonrealist" character of a literary or artistic work, and some rather byzantine debates have opposed "socialist realism," "critical realism," and "realism without frontiers." Many romantic and neoromantic productions are deliberately *nonrealistic:* fantastic, fairylike, magical, oniric, and more recently, surrealist. Yet this does not at all reduce their relevance and importance, both as critiques of capitalism and as dreams of *another world*, quintessentially opposed to bourgeois society. It would perhaps be useful to introduce a new concept—"critical unrealism"—to designate the creation of an imaginary, ideal, utopian, or fantasy universe radically opposed to the gray, prosaic, and inhuman reality of industrial capitalist society. Even when it apparently takes the form of a "flight from reality," this "critical unrealism" may contain a powerful negative load of (explicit or implicit) protest against the established order. It is because of their "critical unrealist" character that not only poets and writers like Novalis and E. T. A. Hoffmann but also utopians and revolutionaries like Fourier and William Morris have brought to romantic anticapitalism an essential dimension, as interesting from a Marxist standpoint as the ruthlessly realist clear-sightedness of a Balzac or a Dickens.

Some Marxist studies do exist, however, that embrace, in a dialectical way, both the contradictions and the essential unity of romanticism, and that do not neglect its revolutionary potential. Ernst Fischer, for instance, defines romanticism as "a movement of protest—of passionate and contradictory protest against the bourgeois capitalist world, the world of 'lost illusions', against the harsh prose of business and profit. . . . Again and again, at each turning-point of events, the movement split up into progressive and reactionary trends. . . . What all the Romantics had in common was an antipathy to capitalism (some viewing it from an aristocratic angle, others from a plebeian). . . ."[19]

One can find similar analyses in certain writings of Lukács, of his Hungarian disciples (Ferenc Fehér, György Marcus), and of other critics influenced by the Lukácsian approach (Norman Rudich, Paul Breines, Andrew Arato, Adolfo Sanchez Vazquez), as well as in several of Herbert Marcuse's works and those of Americans influenced by him (Jack Zipes). Outside of this specifically German cultural tradition, it is among English Marxists that we find the most insightful studies of romantic anticapitalism: E. P. Thompson and Raymond Williams (for the Anglo-Saxon cultural sphere) and Eric Hobsbawm (for the romantic movement in the first half of the nineteenth century).

Raymond Williams's contribution is particularly significant. His remarkable book *Culture and Society* (1958) is the first critical assessment, from a socialist standpoint, of the whole English romantic anti-capitalist tradition, from Burke and Cobbett to Carlyle, from Blake and Shelley to Dickens, from Ruskin and William Morris to T. S. Eliot. While recognizing the shortcomings of the romantic attitude toward modern society, he vindicates the positive aspects of its defense of art and culture as the embodiment of "certain human values, capacities, energies, which the development of society towards an industrial civilization was felt to be threatening or even destroying," of the struggle for "a mode of human experience and activity which the progress of society seemed increasingly to deny." The possibility of mobilizing this tradition for socialism is illustrated by William Morris, who was able to link the cultural values of romanticism to the organized movement of the working class.[20]

In Eastern Europe there is no lack of studies on romanticism, but only a few of them escape the dogmatic official framework and develop a fruitful analysis, as in the case of Jan O. Fischer in Prague and Claus Träger in the German Democratic Republic. Finally, in France, Pierre Barbéris is the most important critic examining romanticism from an "open" Marxist viewpoint.

Most of the above-mentioned studies, however, are limited in scope: they restrict themselves to a single author, or a single country, or one historical period (generally the beginning of the nineteenth century); they consider mainly the literary and artistic aspect of the phenomenon; and finally, they have little to say about its social basis. There seems to be a gap that needs to be filled; for nowhere has there been attempted, as far as we know, an overall analysis, from a Marxist perspective, of romanticism as a *Weltanschauung*, in its full historical extension and in terms of its sociological foundations.

In what follows we will attempt first of all to define romanticism as a *Westanschauung*, or world view, i.e., as a collective mental structure characteristic of certain social groups. Such a mental structure can be concretized in many, diverse areas of culture: in literature and the other arts, in philosophy and theology, in political, economic, and legal thought, in sociology and history, etc. Consequently, the definition that we will propose here is limited neither to literature and art alone nor to the historical period in which the artistic movements termed "romantic"" developed. We consider as romantics—or at least as having a romantic dimension—not only a Byron, a Vigny, or a Novalis in literature, but also, for example, Sismondi in economic theory, Schleiermacher in theology, Edmund Burke, Proudhon, and Marcuse in political philosophy, Simmel, Tönnies, and Max Weber in sociology.[21]

The modern conception of worldview has been elaborated most thoroughly by the sociologist of culture Lucien Goldmann, who has developed—and carried to a higher level—a long tradition in German thought (especially W. Dilthey). However, in spite of the fact that he took into consideration principally the worldviews of the modern period, and that he explored in detail a number of the most significant among them, romanticism is not one of those treated by Goldman. If we enumerate in historical order the worldviews analyzed by him—the tragic worldview in its Jansenist and Kantian forms, the rationalist worldview in Cartesian and Enlightenment guise, the dialectical worldview in its varied manifestations, and finally existentialism and structuralism[22]—we cannot fail to notice a gap, mainly in the nineteenth century; for it can hardly be claimed that dialectical thought (and the positivism that continues the rationalist trend) represent the only predominant worldviews of the period. One of the missing elements, at least, is precisely romantic anticapitalism, or the worldview of which we will attempt a preliminary analysis.

Since what is involved is an *historical* worldview—one localized in time rather than a universal tendency of the human mind—we must first define the boundaries of the historical field in which it manifests itself. As regards the origin, or genesis of the phenomenon, we must reject as overly restrictive the hypothesis according to which romanticism is "the fruit of disillusionment with the unfulfilled promises of the bourgeois revolution of 1789," or "a series of questions and answers directed at postrevolutionary society."[23] According to this conception, romanticism as a mental structure does not exist before the French Revolution, having been generated by the disillusionment that follows the full coming to power of the bourgeoisie. In this perspective, it is a transformation on the political level that becomes the catalyst for the romantic groundswell. In our view, however, the phenomenon is to be understood as a response to that slower and more profound transformation that takes place on the socioeconomic level: the rise of capitalism. This hypothesis would lead us to expect manifestations of romanticism *before* 1789, since of course the development of capitalist economic structures well precedes restructuration on the political level.

In fact we do find a certain number of cultural phenomena well before the Revolution that correspond to our conception of romanticism. Indeed, Pierre Barbéris has demonstrated a filiation leading to romanticism from the social criticism of La Bruyère, Fénelon, and Saint-Simon at the end of the seventeenth century.[24] Here, however, we can only speak of precursors, for the above writers are far from articulating a full set of romantic attitudes. The real beginnings of romanticism are rather to be found in the latter half of the eighteenth century, as a reaction against the Enlightenment on the one hand, but also often *bound up with it in a complex way.* Many of the most important manifestations of nascent romanticism—especially Rousseau in France and the *Sturm und Drang* movement in Germany—by no means totally negate the Enlightenment perspective. On the contrary, rather than simply turning away from the far-reaching cultural critique undertaken in a rationalist vein by the philosophers of the *Aufklärung,* many eighteenth-century romantics can be seen as *extending* this critique, widening and developing it further in a new register. Thus, for instance, to the Enlightenment's indictment of aristocratic privilege—judged in the light of Reason—is added a revulsion of the whole affective being against the bourgeois mentality and the capitalist social relations that are increasingly predominating. In this period we often find a subtle admixture of classic Enlightenment attitudes, along with something quite new and different that later comes to be called romanticism; and in certain cases the two elements do not coexist in contradictory juxtaposition, but rather the second represents a kind of radicalization from within the

Enlightenment nucleus. This characteristic of early romanticism makes it abundantly clear that as a whole romanticism cannot be defined as the antithesis of Enlightenment. As we will see, at least one strand of romanticism is the direct heir of the latter, and several others (the revolutionary/ utopian forms in general) have significant ties with it.[25]

Concerning the alleged "end" of romanticism, none of the dates often put forward as marking its termination are viable in terms of our conception; neither 1848 nor the turn of the century witness its disappearance or even marginalization. What is true of the Romantic anticapitalist worldview in general holds also for its artistic expressions more specifically. Although twentieth-century artistic movements are generally not termed romantic, nonetheless trends as important as Expressionism and Surrealism are profoundly impregnated with the romantic spirit. If our hypothesis—that the romantic worldview represents in essence a reaction against the conditions of life in capitalist society—is justified, it would follow that the romantic stance should continue to retain its vitality as long as capitalism itself persists. And indeed, although the latter has undergone considerable modifications since its beginnings, it has kept its essential characteristics, the same characteristics that stimulated the earliest romantic revolt. According to Max Milner, the first romantic wave continues to have something to say to us because "the crisis of civilization associated with the genesis and development of industrial capitalism is far from having been resolved."[26] And, as already mentioned, a number of the most crucial sociocultural phenomena of recent times are impossible to understand adequately without reference to the romantic anti-capitalist worldview.[27]

In what follows we will attempt to sketch an analytic definition of that worldview, presenting it as a series of themes, logically related and formulated at a level of generality sufficient to allow us to include all of the diverse manifestations of the phenomenon throughout the historical span that we have just indicated. The first element is the source of all the others, and they are wholly dependent on it. At the root of the romantic worldview is a hostility toward present reality, a rejection of the present that is often quasi-total and heavily charged with emotion. This severely critical attitude toward the here and now determines the other elements of romantic thematics. In the past, romanticism has often been defined by way of an enumeration of themes presented in an abstract and atemporal manner, without any awareness that its seemingly most spiritual or intellectual aspects are closely bound up with temporality. Romanticism issues from a revolt against a concrete, historical present. In the dictionary of the brothers Grimm, *romantisch* is defined (in part) as "belonging to the world of poetry . . . in opposition to prosaic reality"; and Chateaubriand and Musset contrast the overflowing plenitude of the heart with the dismaying "emptiness" of the real world around it.[28] According to Lukács's formulation in the *Theory of the Novel*, the "Romanticism of disillusionment" is characterized by a lack of correspondance between reality and the soul, in which "the soul is broader and more vast than any destiny that life can offer it."[29] Balzac grouped together a number of works published in 1830 (among them Stendhal's *Le Rouge et le noir*), and called them the "school of disenchantment"; this term could in fact be applied to the whole of the romantic worldview. Referred to in France as "*le siècle*" (cf. the expression "*mal du siècle*"), in England and Germany as "civilization" (in opposition to "culture"), modern reality produces disenchantment. For Max Weber, capitalism represents the "disenchantment of the world" (*Entzauberung der Welt*), and conversely Tieck has defined romanticism as "the enchanted night in the glow of the moon" (*die mondbeglänzte Zaubernacht*). An important aspect of romanticism, then, is the *re-enchantment* of the world through imagination.

Moreover the romantic sensibility perceives in present reality—more or less consciously and explicitly—essential characteristics of modern capitalism. What is rejected, in other words, is not the present in the abstract but a specifically capitalist present conceived of in terms of its most important defining qualities. Although there is sometimes an awareness of the exploitation of one class by another (as, for example, in the portrayal of the industrialist John Bell in Vigny's *Chatterton*), this awareness is by no means always present in romanticism. *All* of the diverse currents of romantic anticapitalism, on the other hand, in one way or another point to and protest against *those characteristics of capitalism whose negative effects are felt throughout the social classes*, and which are experienced as misery everywhere in capitalist society. What is involved is the all-powerfulness in this society of exchange value—of money and market relations—i.e., the phenomenon of reification. And, as a corollary of generalized reification, social fragmentation and the radical isolation of the individual in society. For a society based on money and competition separates individuals into egotistical monads that are essentially hostile or indifferent to each other.[30] Romantic anticapitalism revolts most particularly against these traits—the deepest principles of oppression at work *throughout* the social fabric.

The experience of a loss is linked to this revolt; in the modern world something precious has been *lost*, on the level both of the individual and of humanity as a whole. The romantic vision is characterized by the painful conviction that present reality lacks certain essential human values, values that have been "alienated." This sharp sense of alienation in the present is often experienced as an *exile*. In defining the romantic sensibility, A. W. Schlegel speaks of the soul "under the weeping willows of exile" (*unter den Trauerweiden der Verbannung*).[31] The soul, which is the seat of the human qualities in man, lives in the here and now far from its true home and true fatherland (*Heimat*); indeed, for Arnold Hauser "the feeling of homelessness (*Heimatlosigkeit*) and isolation became the fundamental experience" of the early nineteenth-century romantics.[32] And Walter Benjamin—whose own sensibility is thoroughly impregnated with the romantic worldview—sees in the German romantics' fascination with dream an indication of the obstacles laid out in real life on the "road that returns to the soul's maternal home" (der Heimweg der Seele ins Mutterland).[33]

The romantic soul longs ardently to return home, and it is precisely the nostalgia for what has been lost that is at the center of the romantic anti-capitalist vision. What the present has lost existed once before, in a more or less distant past. The determining characteristic of this past is its difference from the present; it is the period when the alienations of the present did not yet exist. Since these alienations stem from capitalism such as the romantics perceive it, the nostalgia is for a precapitalist past, or at least for one in which the capitalist system was less developed than at present. Therefore this nostalgia for the past is—as Marx points out in relation to the English romantics—"closely linked" to the criticism of capitalism.[34] The past that is the object of nostalgia can be entirely legendary or mythological, as in the case of Eden, the Golden Age, or the lost Atlantis. But even in the many cases in which it is quite real, the past is always idealized. The romantic vision takes a moment of the real past in which the negative traits of capitalism were lacking or were attenuated, and in which human values crushed under capitalism existed still, and transforms it into a utopia, making it an incarnation of romantic aspirations. It is this which explains the apparent parodox that the romantic orientation toward the past can be—and is in general in a certain sense—a look into the future; for the image of a dreamed-of future beyond capitalism is inscribed in the nostalgic vision of a precapitalist era.

In the term "romantic," such as it was understood in the beginnings of the movement designated by that name, there is a reference to one particular past: the Middle Ages. For Friedrich Schlegel, what is involved is the "period of the knight, of love and of the fairy-tale, from which the phenomenon and the word itself derive."[35] One of the principal origins of the word is the medieval courtly romance. But romantic anticapitalism as we conceive it looks backward toward many other pasts than the Middle Ages. Primitive societies, ancient Greece, the English Renaissance, and the French ancien régime have all served as vehicles for this worldview. The choice—but even more the interpretation—of the past is made according to the different romantic tendencies (of which we will attempt to outline a typology in the following section).

The nostalgia for paradise lost is most often accompanied by a quest for what has been lost. It has often been noticed that at the heart of romanticism lies an active principle taking many forms: restlessness, questioning, perpetual becoming, searching, struggle. In general, then, the second moment of the phenomenon involves an active response, an attempt to rediscover or recreate the lost paradise (there also exists, however, a "resigned" romanticism, which we will discuss in the next section). For the young Lukács, the romantics' Golden Age is not only of the past: "It is the goal, and the duty of each person is to reach it. It is the 'blue flower'!"[36]

The quest may be undertaken, however, in several different ways: in imagination or in reality, and aiming for accomplishment in the present or in the future. An important orientation of romanticism attempts to recreate paradise in the present on the level of imagination, by poeticizing or aestheticizing the present. For Novalis, for example, "the world must be romanticized" through a "heightening" (*Potenzierung*) of banal, habitual reality.[37] More generally, romantic artistic creation can be seen in this light, as a utopian projection realized in the present through imagination. A second tendency consists in rediscovering paradise in the present, but in this case on the level of the real. What is involved here is flight to "exotic" countries, that is, countries ouside the pale of capitalist reality, flight to an "elsewhere" that preserves a more primitive past in the present. The strategy of exoticism is thus to seek the past in the present through a simple movement in space.

But there exists a third tendency that considers the other two to be illusory or at least only partial solutions, and that orients itself toward the rebuilding of paradise in a *real future*. In this perspective—which was shared by Benjamin and Marcuse, for example—memory of the past serves as a weapon in the struggle for the future. A well-known poem by Blake expresses the notion with great power. The poet first wonders whether the divine presence once manifested itself in England "in ancient time," before her hills were covered with "these dark Satanic mills"; then he asks that weapons be brought to him, and declares: "I will not cease from Mental Fight / Nor shall my Sword sleep in my hand / Till we have built Jerusalem / In England's green and pleasant Land."[38] In this form of romanticism the quest is aimed at the creation of a new Jerusalem in the future.

Experience of a loss in the capitalist present, nostalgia for what has been lost, localized in a precapitalist past, and quest for what has been lost in present or future: such are the principal components of the worldview we are exploring here. But *what* exactly has been lost? The question of the content of the alienation, of the nostalgia and of the quest, remains to be raised. What, in other words, are the *positive values* of romantic anticapitalism? They are an aggregate of *qualitative* values—ethical, social, and cultural—in opposition to the mercantile rationality of exchange value. In our view they are concentrated around two opposing but not contradictory poles. The first of these primary values, although often experienced in terms of loss, in fact represents a new acquisition historically, or at the very least a development that can only come to full fruition in the modern context. We are referring to *individual subjectivity*, to the development of the self in all the depth, breadth, and complexity of its affectivity, and also in the free play of its imaginative capacities.

The development of this individual subject is in fact directly linked to the history and "prehistory" of capitalism: the "isolated" individual develops with and because of it. This phenomenon is the source, however, of a significant contradiction in capitalist society; for this very individual created by the latter cannot but live frustrated within its constraints, and is eventually led to revolt against it. Capitalism calls forth the independent individual to fulfill certain socioeconomic functions; but when this individual transforms itself into a full-fledged subjectivity, and begins to explore the internal universe of its particular constellation of feeling, it enters into contradiction with a system based on quantitative calculation and standardization. And when it begins to want to freely exercise its powers of fantasy, it comes up against the extreme mechanization and platitude of the world created by capitalist relations. Romanticism represents the revolt of the repressed, manipulated, and deformed subjectivity, and of the "magic" of imagination banished from the capitalist world.

The other, dialectically opposed value of the worldview is *unity,* or *totality:* unity of the self with two encompassing totalities—the universe of nature, on the one hand, and, on the other, the human community. While the first romantic value constitutes its *individual*—even individualistic—moment, the second is *transindividual* or collective. And while the first is in fact modern despite its being experienced as a nostalgia, the second represents a true return (in the case of romantics oriented toward the future, what is involved is not a simple return to the past but a recreation of past unity on a higher level).

The two forms of nostalgic yearning for unity are defined specifically in opposition to the capitalist status quo. Hauser rightly comments that the romantics' enthusiasm for nature is "unthinkable without the isolation of the town from the countryside."[39] The capitalist principle of domination and exploitation of nature is absolutely antithetical to the romantic quest for the integration and harmony of mankind in the universe. And the impulse to recreate the human community (conceived of in various ways: as authentic communication with other selves, as participation in the organic whole of a people, *Volk,* and in its collective imagination as expressed through mythology, folklore, etc., as social harmony or a future classless society, etc.) is the counterpoint to the rejection of social fragmentation and the isolation of the individual under capitalism. Thus Brentano describes his reactions on visiting Paris in 1827: "All the people I saw were walking in the same street, beside each other, and yet each one seemed to be following his own solitary course; no one greeted anyone else, and each pursued his personal interest. All these comings and goings seemed to me the very emblem of egoism. Each person is thinking only of his own interest, like the number of the house towards which he is hurrying."[40] Protest against capitalism and the positive romantic values are thus two sides of the same coin: what is rejected in capitalism is the exact antithesis of the values that are sought because they have been lost.

The worldview that we have very briefly outlined above is, in our estimation, a kind of lost continent on the map of the human sciences, since it entirely escapes notice in the context of their habitual categories and frames of reference. Literary and artistic studies generally give a far more limited extension to romanticism, and do not relate it to capitalism. And as far as the other disciplines are concerned—like history, sociology, political science, economics, etc.—romanticism is usually not recognized as a perspective that can structure mentalities in their areas of competence. Since it doesn't fit into the usual categories (in philosophy: rationalism, empiricism, idealism, etc.; in history and politics: Left/Right, conservative/liberal, progressive/reactionary, etc.), it slips through their conceptual grid and most often remains invisible in their analyses. Yet, as we hope to demonstrate in the typology of varieties of romanticism that follows, this little-studied and ill-understood worldview has in fact played an absolutely crucial role in many different respects, on a worldwide scale and over the course of two centuries.

* * *

It would seem that a typology of the figures of romantic anticapitalism might serve as a useful tool, both to account for the rich diversity of specific trajectories within a common matrix and to explicate more precisely the universe of concrete works. There are obviously several criteria that could be used in making a classification: style (realist or nonrealist), national culture (German, French, etc.), intellectual field (politics, literature, etc.), historical period ("preromanticism," late romanticism, neoromanticism, etc.). However, having defined romanticism as a reaction to capitalism and bourgeois society, it seems to us more logical to define the types *in terms of their relation to capitalism*, according to the particular manner in which they envisage the relationship. This does not mean a political typology in the limited sense, but rather a framework that brings together the economic, the social, and the political. The different categories are, of course, *ideal types* in the Weberian sense, and they are generally to be found combined, juxtaposed, or blended in the work of a particular author. We will say that a given author belongs to a given type when the latter constitutes the *dominant* element in his writings.

What follows is a list of what we consider to be some of the principal types of romantic anticapitalism:

1) *"Restitutionist"* romanticism, which explicitly aims to reestablish precapitalist sociocultural formations that have disappeared (most often medieval). This concept is not identical with "reactionary," a term that refers directly to counterrevolutionary reaction, which is not necessarily romantic (the term "restitutionist," which we have borrowed from the sociologist of religion Jean Seguy, seems preferable to the pejorative terms "retrograde" and *"passéiste"* that one of us, Michael Löwy, has used in several earlier works).

2) *Conservative* romanticism, which does not wish to reestablish a more or less distant past but to *maintain* society and the state as they exist in countries untouched by the French Revolution (England and Germany at the end of the eighteenth, and beginning of the nineteenth century), and to restore the French *status quo ante* of 1788. In both cases, what is involved is *a particular juxtaposition of capitalist and precapitalist formations.*

There also exists, however, a *nonromantic* conservatism that justifies the capitalist order and defends it against all criticism, whether it be in the name of the past or the future. One may speak of conservative *romanticism* only when some measure of criticism of capitalism, from the point of view of organic values of the past, is present in the discourse. This obviously holds true for the other types we will discuss further on: liberal and socialist romanticism, etc.

3) *Fascist* romanticism, a very specific modern form in which neoroman-ticism transforms itself into Nazi or fascist ideology with the rise of those movements between the two wars. There are doubtless elements of the fascist ideologies that are foreign or even hostile to romanticism—one need only think of Italian Futurism, for example—but nonetheless one of their pre-dominant themes is hatred of the modern world and nostalgia for an organic community of the past.

4) *"Resigned"* romanticism, which realizes that the reestablishment of a precapitalist structure is impossible and which considers, although deeply regretting it, that the advent of industrial capitalism is an irreversible fact to which one can only resign oneself. In some cases, this type of romanticism can give rise to a tragic worldview (the insurmountable contradiction between values and reality); in other cases, it produces a reformist point of view that aims to remedy some of the most glaring evils of bourgeois society, with precapitalist institutions playing a regulative role.

5) *Liberal* romanticism, which seems to be a contradiction in terms, be-cause classical liberalism and anticapitalist romantic revolt would appear to be mutually exclusive. But one is obliged to recognize the existence of such a phenomenon—especially in the early nineteenth century—in which roman-ticism and its opposite are an unstable compound, the former on the point of negating itself. The type is essentially based on a misunderstanding, since for liberal romanticism the paradise lost is not entirely incompatible with the capitalist present; all that would be necessary would be to cure the most flagrant ills of that order by social and moral reform.

6) *Revolutionary and/or utopian* romanticism, in which the nostalgia for a precapitalist past is projected into the hope for a post-capitalist future. Rejecting both the illusion of a pure and simple return to organic commu-nities of the past and a resigned acceptance of the bourgeois present, it aspires—more or less radically and explicitly, depending on the case—to see

the abolition of capitalism and the creation of a utopian future possessing some traits or values of precapitalist societies.

Within revolutionary romanticism there are a number of currents that constitute quite distinct types, which should consequently be examined in their specificity:

I—*Jacobin-democratic* romanticism, which adopts a critical stance toward both feudalism and the new aristocracy of wealth, in the name of the egalitarian values of the radical wing of the French Revolution. Most often its precapitalist reference points are the Greek polis and the Roman Republic.

II—*Populist* romanticism, which opposes industrial capitalism as monarchy and serfdom, and which aims to salvage, reestablish, or develop in some way as a social alternative the forms of production and of peasant and artisan community life of the precapitalist "people."

III—*Utopian-humanist* socialism, by which term we designate those socialist currents and thinkers who aspire to a collectivist (postcapitalist) utopia, but who do not see the industrial proletariat as the historical agent of this project. Their discourse is addressed to humanity as a whole (or to suffering humanity in particular). They might also be designated by the term "utopian socialists," but this would be ambiguous since most forms of revolutionary romanticism are utopian in the etymological sense of the word: the aspiration for a not-yet-existing society (utopia: in no place).

IV—*Libertarian*, or anarchistic romanticism, which draws on the precapitalist, collectivist traditions of peasants, artisans, and skilled workers in their revolutionary struggle against capitalism and the modern state in all its forms. What distinguishes this current from other similar ones is its irreconcilable opposition to the centralized state, perceived as the quintessence of all the oppressive characteristics of capitalist modernity, and its intention to create a decentralized federation of local communities.

V—*Marxist* romanticism. One can find a romantic anticapitalist dimension in the works of Marx, but it is far from being the dominant one. However, it becomes dominant in the thought of certain authors, in whom the nostalgia for a precapitalist *Gemeinschaft* (or for its values, its culture, etc.) plays a central role, both as a motivating force for the critique of industrial capitalism and as a crucial element in the socialist utopia of the future.

This typology is to be used with caution, not only because the work of an author generally does not correspond exactly to any of the ideal types, but also because of the shifts, transformations, disavowals, and reversals of position that are so common to romanticism, to say nothing of the movements of a single author from one position to another within the spectrum of romantic anticapitalism. We have only to recall, just to cite a few examples, the itinerary of Friedrich Schlegel and of Görres from Jacobin republicanism to the most conservative monarchism, that of Georges Sorel from revolutionary syndicalism to the Action Française (and vice versa), that of Lukács from tragic, resigned romanticism to revolutionary bolshevism, that of William Morris from romantic nostalgia for the Middle Ages to Marxist socialism, that of Robert Michels and Arturo Labriola from revolutionary syndicalism to fascism, etc.

In some cases, this kind of change eventually leads to a break with romanticism and a reconciliation with the bourgeois order. But those cases are exceptional. For the most part, what occurs are changes of position *within the same intellectual field*, developments within the same sociocultural matrix, romantic anticapitalism. It is precisely the *homogeneity of the ideological space* that allows us to comprehend these metamorphoses that are seemingly so bizarre. The fundamentally ambiguous, contradictory, and as it were "hermaphroditic" character of this *Weltanschauung* allows for the most multifarious of solutions, and the passage from one to another without the author having broken with the basic framework of his earlier problematics. This unity-in-diversity manifests itself also in the existence of certain cultural movements like Symbolism, Surrealism, and Expressionism, which traverse the different types and cannot be pinned down to any one of the categories mentioned. The same holds for certain social movements calling for a return to nature, like the *Jugendbewegung* at the beginning of this century, or more recently the ecological movement.

In the following pages we will attempt to examine in more detail each of the types of romantic anticapitalism, principally through exemplary authors whose work—in the internal coherence of its basic structure—most nearly approaches the ideal characteristics of each type.

1) "Restitutionist" Romanticism

Within the constellation of romantic anticapitalisms, the "restitutionist" vision occupies a privileged place, and consequently constitutes a logical point of departure in discussing the types. For this articulation of the worldview is both qualitatively and quantitatively the most significant. On the one hand, it is clear that by far the largest number of important romantic writers and thinkers are to be situated principally in this category. On the other hand, we might say that the "restitutionist" perspective is of all the types the closest to the *essence* of the overall phenomenon. For at the heart of the general worldview we have found a nostalgia for the precapitalist past; and the restitutionist type is defined precisely by the desire to restore or recreate such a past state in the present. Restitutionism is neither resigned to the degraded present out of disenchanted realism nor oriented toward the future, toward transcendance of both past and present, but rather calls for an actual return to the past that is the object of nostalgia. This past is sometimes a traditional

agrarian society (as with the Russian Slavophiles, for example, or the Southern "Agrarian School" in the United States between the two wars), but most
often restitutionism looks to the Middle Ages. This concentration of the
restitutionist ideal in the medieval past, especially in its feudal form, might
perhaps be explained on the one hand by the relative proximity in time of the
Middle Ages (compared with antiquity, prehistoric times, etc.), and on the
other by its radical difference from what is rejected in the present: it is close
enough for its restoration to be conceivable, yet totally opposed in its spirit
and in its structures to the capitalist system.

Another characteristic of the restitutionist trend is that its most notable
exponents are in the majority *literary*. Although one also finds it in philosophy
(Schelling) and in political theory (Adam Müller), for example, it is especially
artists who have discovered an affinity for it. It seems plausible that the
predominance of artists can be explained principally by the growing
awareness of the unrealistic—or even *entirely unrealizable*—character of the
project to recreate a period of the past that is gone forever. And yet the dream
of a return to the Middle Ages (or an agrarian society) continues to have great
suggestive power for the imagination, and lends itself to visionary projections. Consequently it stands to reason that it should particularly attract
sensibilities oriented toward the symbolic and aesthetic dimension.

If one passes in review the major writers who share this vision, it also
becomes clear that one of its principal focuses is Germany. Restitutionism
appeared very early there—in the last years of the eighteenth century—and
an intellectual milieu of artists and thinkers grew up in which it was developed. Yet at the outset the German *Frühromantik* enthusiastically took
sides with the French Revolution and the values and hopes it incarnated, a
fact that demonstrates very clearly that restitutionism by no means always has
its roots in a reactionary or right-wing ideology. However, disillusioned by the
direction taken by the Revolution in its later years, and even more so by the
Napoleonic period following it, the German romantics turned toward the
ideal of a medieval restoration, its primary values being the hierarchical order
of the *Stände*, person-to-person feudal bonds, and the communion of the
whole social body in religious faith and love for the monarch. Elaborated in
the realm of politico-economic thought against the liberalism of Adam Smith
by Baader, Görres, and Adam Müller, and in the realm of theological and
philosophical speculation by Ritter, Schleiermacher, and the Schlegel brothers, this vision of an idealized Middle Ages first found literary expression in
Tieck, Wackenroder, and Novalis. The latter provided the classic formulation
in his essay "Europe, or Christendom" (1800), in which he contrasts not only
the sterile rationalism of the *Aufklärung* with the lost religious sense of
marvel, but also the "commercial life" (*Geschäftsleben*), characterized by
"egotistical preoccupations" (*eigennützige Sorgen*) and "man avid for posses-

sions" (*habsüchtiger Mensch*), with medieval culture united in the spiritual community of the Church.[41] Later we find the restitutionist vision in E. T. A. Hoffmann, Eichendorff, and Kleist and in the operas of Wagner; it reappears again in the neoromantic currents of the end of the nineteenth and beginning of the twentieth centuries, for example in Paul Ernst, a friend of Lukács' in his youth,[42] in the Viennese theoretician Othmar Spann, and in Stefan George and his circle.

In England the same reversal occurred in the first romantic generation: after an initial *parti pris* for the French Revolution and its values, Wordsworth and Coleridge became disillusioned and turned—especially Coleridge—to medieval restitutionism. The later perspective was soon articulated again in the novels of Walter Scott and the essays of Carlyle; it resurfaced later in the century in Ruskin and the Pre-Raphaelites. As for France, the ideological reversal within romanticism was exactly the opposite: the original perspective—more or less impregnated with restitutionism—of Chateaubriand, Vigny, Lamartine, Lamennais, and Hugo gave way under the pressure of events to more liberal and democratic positions, and ones more oriented to the future.

At the end of the nineteenth century and throughout the twentieth, although restitutionism tends to a certain extent to be replaced by resigned, revolutionary, or fascist romanticism, it remains nonetheless a current of the first order of importance. To give an idea of its persistence at least up to World War II, we might mention its influence on Barrès and the French Right, on Oswald Spengler and the right-wing *Kulturpessimisten* in Germany, and on Yeats, T. S. Eliot, and G. K. Chesterton in Ireland and England. It has in fact survived up to the present, the most illustrious recent case of it being that of Solzhenitsyn.

To demonstrate its continued vitality in the twentieth century, we will take as an example of the restitutionist perspective a French novelist from the period between the two wars: Georges Bernanos. His case is particularly interesting because he appears to give literary voice to the worldview of a significant sector of French youth at the beginning of the twentieth century. For in his youth before World War I, Bernanos was active in a far right-wing student organization the very name of which reveals its restitutionist character: the Camelots du Roi. Between the two wars, along with other members of the Camelots, Bernanos joined the Action Française; but, whereas a large portion of the latter organization, and of the French Right in general, moved progressively closer to fascism, Bernanos remained faithful to his original ideal: the medieval Christian monarchy. Consequently, in spite of the anti-Semitism that disfigures some of his earlier works, his vision differs totally from that of the romantic anticapitalists who were attracted by fascist ideology, and he remains a particularly pure case of restitution.

The title of one of Bernanos's works, *Les Grands Cimetières sous la lune* (The Great Cemeteries in Moonlight), conveys metaphorically his conception of modern society: everything is stricken with spiritual death in a world illuminated only by the value of money (the moon). In this same work he cries out against "the extreme solitude to which [modern man] is abandoned by a society that hardly knows any longer other relations between human beings than those based on money."[43] His best-known novel, *Journal d'un curé de campagne* (Diary of a Country Priest), develops the same conception through portrayal of the social microcosm represented by the priest's parish. As one of the characters says: "The gods who protect the modern polis, we know who they are! They dine in town, and are called bankers." The representatives of true spiritual values in the novel oppose to this thoroughly debased world the ideal of medieval Christendom; if it had survived into the present, "we would have torn the feeling of solitude from the heart of Adam."[44]

The spiritual adventure embarked upon by the priest—a kind of modern saint—is to attempt to awaken his parish to the true values and thereby to create a favorable terrain for the restoration of the lost Christendom. His vocation is surprisingly similar, *mutatis mutandis*, to that of the German restitutionists, as defined by Friedrich Schlegel in 1805: "It is the express purpose of the new philosophy to restore the ancient German constitution, that is to say, the system based on honor, freedom and loyalty, by working to bring into being the state of mind on which the true, free monarchy depends, the state of mind that . . . [is] the only one having a saintly character."[45] One could not better summarize the restitutionist project, in its continuity from early German romanticism to the period between the two wars in France. But in Bernanos's novel the project is condemned to failure. The modern malady is too deep, and the priest's struggle to save the soul of his parish is totally hopeless. The relative optimism of the German romantics is replaced by a radical pessimism in Bernanos. And yet in spite of that, Bernanos never becomes "resigned." In his novelistic universe the only valid attitude remains to accept the necessity of an *absurd* struggle—one that is *lost from the outset— to restore the lost paradise. Such is the despair that tends to take hold of restitutionism in late capitalism.*

2) Conservative Romanticism

Conservative romanticism in the strict sense manifests itself mainly in the work of *political* thinkers, who legitimate the established order by interpreting it as a "natural" result of historical evolution (for example, the "Historical School of Law" of Hugo and Savigny, the positive philosophy of the State of Friedrich Julius Stahl, and the Tory ideology of Disraeli). Among the important romantic philosophers, Schelling is probably closest to the conservative position, and in political economy Malthus is not without some affinities with it.

Its borderline with restitutionist romanticism is fluid and imprecise: authors like the French ultras Joseph de Maistre and Louis de Bonald seem to be situated somewhere in a transitional area. One of the characteristics that allows us nonetheless to distinguish between the two types is the acceptance or nonacceptance of elements of the capitalist order. The total rejection of modern industry and of bourgeois society is essential to the restitutionist type, whereas full acceptance of them implies a nonromantic form of thought (whatever the importance given to tradition, religion, authoritarianism, etc.), as in the case of Auguste Comte's positivism. It is rather the intermediate position, which corresponds to the combination of feudalism and capitalism characteristic of that period in Europe (end of the eighteenth century, first half of the nineteenth), that is typical of conservative romanticism.

A concrete example that may help to clarify these traits is the thought of Edmund Burke. His work belongs without any doubt to romanticism: passionately hostile to the Enlightenment ("this literary cabal"), in his famous pamphlet against the 1789 Revolution, *Reflections on the Revolution in France* (1790), Burke opposes the "old feudal and chivalrous spirit of *fealty*" to the new age of "sophists, economists and calculators." He opposes wise and ancient prejudices, product of a "gothic and monkish education," to the barbarous philosophy produced by "cold hearts," and venerable landed property, heritage of our ancestors, to the sordid speculations of Jews and jobbers.[46] This is the reason why his book made such an impact in Germany, where it helped to develop the themes of political romanticism.

However, unlike the restitutionist romantics, Burke is not a truly antibourgeois thinker; for his doctrine also has a "liberal" dimension typical of the Whig party to which he belonged. His earlier political interventions in favor of conciliation with the rebellious American colonies, and of parliamentarian principles against George III's royal absolutism, won him a reputation of liberalism to an extent that Thomas Paine believed that he would join the camp of the English partisans of the 1789 revolution.

Burke's political and social ideology is in fact an expression of the compromise between bourgeoisie and landowners that had ruled the political life of England ever since the Glorious Revolution of 1688 (of which he was a fervent admirer). In a very revealing passage of *Reflections on the Revolution in France*, Burke regrets that in France, unlike England, the mutual convertibility of land into money and of money into land has always been difficult. This tradition, as well as the great mass of landed property held by the French crown and Church, "kept the landed and monied interests more separated in France, less miscible, and the owners of the two distinct species of property not so well disposed to each other as they are in this country."[47]

In spite of his admiration for the hereditary aristocracy and the great landowners, Burke did not at all intend to reserve for them the monopoly of power. Political power must be given to all property owners, or rather to what he calls the "natural aristocracy," which includes not only the nobility but also magistrates, professors, and "rich traders," who "possess the virtues of diligence, order, constancy, and regularity."[48]

The dimension of nostalgia for the "chivalrous" Middle Ages is not lacking in Burke's writings, but the past does not play the same role as with the restitutionist romantics; it serves much more as the legitimation of the (English) present than as a criticism of it. The laws, customs, institutions, and social hierarchies of England in 1790 are justified as both the natural and the providential result of an organic growth, as an ancestral heritage transmitted over the centuries by each generation, as a part of what he called "the whole chain and continuity of the Commonwealth."[49]

The influence of Burke is not limited to the German romantics; his adoption by antirevolutionary bourgeois liberalism, from his time up to today, is an indicator of the specific character of conservative romanticism. It is revealing that a contemporary American political scientist, William McGovern, for whom Rousseau, Carlyle, and all the German romantics are forerunners of the totalitarian doctrines of the twentieth century, insists on the other hand that "the political philosophy of Burke was truly liberal" and that "Burke was anti-despotic, and to this extent a believer in democracy."[50]

3) Fascist Romanticism

In dealing with the fascist type of romantic anticapitalism, it is important to emphasize at the outset that in our view what is involved is one type among many, and one that is far from the most important or essential vis-à-vis the overall phenomenon. In this respect, we wish to distinguish ourselves very clearly from those—both anti-fascists and fascists—who have seen the entire history of romanticism as a prelude to fascism, and romanticism as indissolubly linked with fascist ideology. As the discussion of the other elements of the typology should unambiguously demonstrate, this is by no means the case. The romantic anticapitalist worldview manifests itself in many diverse perspectives that are totally foreign to fascism. It is doubtless also true that starting with the first romantic movement one already finds elements of what will become fascist ideology much later. In his *Discourse to the German Nation* of 1808, Fichte develops the idea that the German people is superior because it is ancient (an *Urvolk*), and that its duty is to guard its racial purity; one also finds expressions of anti-Semitism in von Arnim. It is equally undeniable that fascism drew quite extensively on the thematics of certain neoromantics: those of Wagner, Nietzsche, Gobineau, and Moeller van den Bruck, for example. But in all these cases only *partial elements* are involved; these are reintegrated into and reinterpreted within the fascist ideology, without their being an overall correspondence between the worldviews of the neoromantic authors and that of fascism.

One may only characterize an author as a fascist romantic if he has adopted the *totality* of the fascist perspective. Since what is involved is a very specific sociopolitical movement, this implies that the author has explicitly manifested his approval of that movement. Consequently this type of romanticism comes into being only with the rise of fascism between the two world wars. To the extent that fascist movements—or ones with a fascist tendency—continue to appear up to the present day, this type of romanticism also continues to subsist today. For there to be a true case of fascist romanticism, two conditions must in fact be fulfilled: not only must there be expression of approval of the movement, but also adoption of the fascist perspective. The second condition eliminates several writers—such as Paul Ernst, Ernst Jünger, and Montherlant, for instance—who on the one hand have neoromantic sensibilities, and on the other collaborated or compromised with fascism. For their vision is much closer to restitutionism than to fascism, and they remain foreign bodies when attached to the latter.

However, in spite of all the above limitations on the concept of fascist romanticism, one is obliged to recognize that it exists, and even that it represents a relatively important tendency. On the one hand, there have been numerous—and some notable—cases of neoromantic writers both supporting fascism and embracing its worldview; on the other hand, romantic themes play an absolutely essential role in fascist ideology as it is expressed in the culture of the mass movements themselves. This joining of romanticism with fascism is particularly noticeable in the case of Nazism. For while the nostalgic reference to Roman antiquity gives a definitely romantic dimension to Italian fascism, a contradictory theme tends to predominate—the one that is articulated by the Futurists: glorification of urban, industrial, and technological life, and the call to go further still in the direction of modernity. Nazi ideology, on the other hand, is more thoroughly nostalgic: for the old tribal and feudal Germany, for traditional peasant life in opposition to the frenzied pace of the big city, for the ancient *Gemeinschaften* in contrast with today's *Gesellschaft*. These nostalgias figure in the architecture, the plastic arts, and the cinema of the Nazi period, as well as in its literature.[51]

What is specific to romantic anticapitalism in its fascist form? First of all, the rejection of capitalism is blended with a violent condemnation of parliamentary democracy as well as of Communism. In addition, anticapitalism is often colored with anti-Semitism; the capitalists, the rich, and those who incarnate the spirit of the city and of modern life appear in the guise of the Jew. Thirdly, the romantic valuation of subjectivity is carried to its farthest limits, becoming glorification of the irrational in its pure form, of brute instinct in its most aggressive manifestations. Thus the romantic cult of love becomes its opposite—praise of force and cruelty. Finally, in its fascist version, the individualistic pole of romanticism is greatly attenuated or entirely suppressed; in the fascist movement and state, the suffering romantic "I" is obliterated. The periods of the past that are most often the subject of nostalgia are a prehistory peopled with barbarous, instinctive, and violent savages; Greco-Roman antiquity in its elitist, slave-owning, and martial aspects; the Middle Ages (in Nazi paintings Hitler sometimes appears as a medieval knight); and the rural *Volksgemeinschaft* already mentioned.

In addition to the rather substantial number of mediocre or worthless neoromantic authors who become the official bards of Nazism or of fascism (the expressionist Hanns Johst, for example), a certain number of writers of quality joined the movement as well. Among those whose work exhibits, in one way or another, the fusion of romantic anticapitalism with fascism, one might mention Drieu la Rochelle and Brasillach in France, Malaparte and D'Annunzio in Italy, Ezra Pound, Wyndham Lewis, and Lovecraft in England (and the United States), Knut Hamsun in Norway, and H. H. Evers in Germany. But the case we will focus on especially is that of Gottfied Benn, since he illustrates in a particularly striking way the nature of the fascist romantic type.

Benn, one of the most notable representatives of German expressionism, publicly supported the Hitlerian regime from the moment it took power. Unlike many others, though, he very rapidly grew disillusioned. Benn actively gave his support to Nazism only during a period of two years, from 1933 to 1935. There is, however, an essential continuity over the whole of his work, and one finds the same themes—with the exception of the explicit reference to fascism—before he espouses that cause. In his earlier works he expresses his hatred of the modern world—in its bourgeois and capitalist, urban and scientific, but also democratic and socialist aspects—and dreams of a primitive, instinctual past (see, for example, "Primal Vision," 1929). During his short period within the Nazi orbit, Benn wrote some ten prose texts that unambiguously reflect fascist ideology. In two of them in particular, the romantic anticapitalist element of his vision appears most clearly.

The first, and least important, is a favorable review of a work by another fascist romantic, Julius Evola, entitled *Erhebung wider die moderne Welt* (Revolt Against the Modern World). Benn summarizes—and accepts—the main theme of the book, which is a definition and glorification of what Evola calls the *Traditionswelt:* the world of primitive societies during the period from Homer to Greek tragedy, in the Orient and the Nordic countries as well as in Greece. What follows this period is decay (*Verfall*) and the rise of the degenerate modern world. According to Evola (and Benn agrees), fascism and Nazism for the first time allow modern peoples to reestablish contact with the lost *Traditionswelt.* For Benn, however—and this holds for fascist romanticism in general—it is not a question of simply returning to the *Traditionswelt*. In another text from his fascist period he declares that in his view "only today begins the history of man, his danger, his tragedy,"[52] suggesting thereby that man is soon to reach a higher stage of development. Indeed, the fascist perspective is oriented toward the future as well as the past, as is indicated by some of its slogans, such as "New Order," "New Europe," etc.

The past of which Benn dreams is amply developed in a long essay entitled "Dorische Welt." The Doric world, i.e., the Greek states up until the fifth century B.C., is Benn's chosen *Traditionswelt*. In the picture he sketches of it the following are considered to be essential and necessary traits: war, sport that prepares for war, slavery without scruples, "antifeminism," racism and xenophobia, elitism and a powerful state. The image Benn gives of the Doric world in fact makes it resemble National Socialist society quite closely. But he also emphasizes another characteristic of the Doric as he interprets it: there is no private property in the modern sense, since land is *inalienable*. Moreover there is not really any money, only a very ineffective kind of iron coin. Consequently "gold is not desired, but rather sacred things, magic weapons. . . ."[53] Benn's ideal past is thus specifically anticapitalist. In this context, it is interesting to note that in the first text in which Benn declares his disillusionment with the Nazis—"Art and the Third Reich," written in 1941—he accuses them of wanting to enrich themselves, and therefore of not providing a true alternative to the bourgeois world. This reveals the essential continuity of the romantic anticapitalism of Benn, who thought—like a considerable number of others, unfortunately—that he had found in fascism the realization of his hopes.

4) "Resigned" Romanticism

Resigned romanticism emerges mainly from the second half of the nineteenth century onward, when capitalist industrialization appears more and more as an irreversible process, and the hope for a restoration of precapitalist social relations—still strong at the beginning of the century—tends to disappear. Its grudging acceptance of capitalism brings this variety of romanticism close to the conservative type, but its social criticism of industrial civilization is much more significant and intense. One might consider many of the writers whose works belong to what Lukács calls "critical realism" as belonging to it: for instance, Dickens, Flaubert, and Thomas Mann (Balzac would probably fall in the no-man's-land between restitutionist and resigned romanticism). But it is in Germany at the turn of the nineteenth century that one finds the most characteristic expressions of this current, mainly among the academic mandarinate and the first great German social scientists. Its major ideological nucleus was the *Verein für Sozialpolitik*, founded by Gustav Schmoller,

Adolph Wagner, and Lujo Brentano, and later joined by Ferdinand Tönnies and Max Weber; its social philosophy was the so-called *Kathedersozialismus*. Other German academics of this period can also be considered as close to resigned romanticism: Werner Sombart, Alfred Troeltsch, Max Scheler, Georg Simmel, Karl Mannheim, etc. Max Weber probaby expressed an attitude common to many of them when he wrote, in an article in 1904 for the journal *Archiv für Sozialwissenschaft und Sozialpolitik,* that we must accept capitalism "not because it seems to us better than the old forms of social structure, but because it is practically inevitable."[54]

Some of these authors were rather traditionalist (Adolph Wagner), while others were more modernizing (Lujo Brentano, Max Weber), some going so far as to support the trade unions and social democracy (Tönnies). In spite of its reformist bent, this current has a profoundly *tragic* dimension, insofar as its precapitalist social and cultural values appear as condemned to decline and extinction.[55] Simmel's work is where this tragic dimension manifests itself in the most systematic way, particularly in the important essay "Der Begriff und die Tragödie der Kultur" (*Logos,* Bd. II, 1911–12) and in his *Philosophie des Geldes* (The Philosophy of Money) of 1900.

The most typical representative of the contradictions within resigned romanticism is probably Ferdinand Tönnies, who is considered to be the founding father of German sociology. In his famous work *Gemeinschaft und Gesellschaft* (Community and Society, 1887), he contrasts two kinds of sociability: on the one hand, the "community" (family, village, small traditional town), its universe governed by harmony, custom, religion, mutual help, and *Kultur;* on the other hand, "society" (the large city, the national state, the factory), its world ruled by calculation, profit, the struggle of each against all, and *Zivilisation* as technical and industrial progress. Tönnies's book is intended to be an objective and "value-free" comparison between these two structures, but his nostalgia for the rural, "organic" *Gemeinschaft* is evident: "Community is the true and lasting common life; society is only transitory and superficial. One can, to a certain extent, understand community as a living organism, and society as an artificial and mechanical aggregate." While domestic economy "relies on pleasure, particularly the pleasure and love of production, creation and conservation," the big city and the *Gesellschaft* in general "represents the corruption and death of the people."[56] *Gemeinschaft,* of course, refers to precapitalist communities and forms of life (not necessarily medieval), while *Gesellschaft* embodies all the traits of industrial/capitalist society. The opposition between two forms—or the contrast between *Kultur* and *Zivilisation*—became one of the main themes of romantic anticapitalism in Germany at the turn of the century.

What characterizes Tönnies as a "resigned" romantic author is the tragic conviction that return to the *Gemeinschaft* is an illusion, and that social decadence is inevitable, like the decline of a living organism that cannot return to its youthful days.[57] Tönnies looked with sympathy on the trade unions and consumers' cooperatives and neocommunitarian organisms that corrected the excesses of modern industrial society, but he did not believe in the possibility of restoring the authentic *Gemeinschaft* of the past.

5) Liberal Romanticism

The first problem one encounters in attempting to deal with the phenomenon of liberal romanticism is that at the beginning of the nineteenth century, the period in which the most noteworthy cases of the type are concentrated, there existed a considerable confusion in terminology. The term "liberal"—as well as "democratic," "republican," and "socialist," for example—was given vague and multifarious meanings; moreover, the distinctions between the different terms were far from being precise. Thus Victor Hugo defined his political position after 1830 as *at the same time* liberal, socialist, and democratic.[58] At that time, the term "liberal" possessed at least two different meanings: on the one hand, a political tendency linked to a party that reflected the interests of the rising bourgeoisie against ecclesiastical and aristocratic reaction; on the other, a considerably broader movement of opinion and ideas that today would be called "progressive" in the largest sense of orientation toward change and the future.

This terminological confusion means that it is impossible to arrive at a coherent definition of the phenomenon if one relies on what the authors of the period said about their own politics. However, even if we admit that, and even if we also admit that in many concrete instances a precise categorization is extremely difficult to make, it does nonetheless seem clear that a liberal romanticism exists and more specifically that a meaningful distinction can be made between it and "Jacobin-democratic" romanticism. We will define liberal romanticism as the perspective that, while critical of the modern bourgeois world, does not draw the radical conclusions following from this criticism, and is content simply to call for reforms rather than for more fundamental change. These romantics, then, make their peace with the status quo, at least to some degree, and they back off when faced with the perspective of social upheaval. While they, like the Jacobin-democrats, take as their point of reference the French Revolution and its values, they look to its most moderate elements—the Girondists rather than the Jacobins—for their ideal. Most often their revolutionary ardor is expressed in vague, sentimental, and mythical terms, and they tend to leave aside the question of class exploitation.

The liberal romantics are not to be confused, however, with pure and simple liberals. The latter—for example, Victor Cousin and Paul-Louis Courier in France, and Bentham and the Utilitarians in England—are totally lacking in the critical dimension and the nostalgia for the past that characterize the romantic vision. In them we find simply a celebration of the new bourgeois order and of its victory over the forces of the past. The romantic anticapitalist liberals, on the other hand, constitute an astonishing contradiction, for they are at one and the same time critical and noncritical vis-à-vis the present. In our view, this paradox might be explained by two factors, one historically contingent and the other essential to romanticism. In the first place, this contradictory type arises out of the historical situation of the early nineteenth century, most particularly that of the Restoration in France. In that context, it quite easily could appear that the source of the evils of the present—and consequently the principal enemy to be combated—was not the bourgeois order but aristocratic reaction and all that remained of the Old Regime. Moreover, there did not yet exist a clear awareness of the new social forces at work, of the splitting up of the Third Estate into two antagonistic classes. And beyond the horizons of past and present the possibility of a future *tertium datur* was not yet visible. Under these conditions the choice could seem to be the following: to keep the purity of one's revolt against the present by opting for the past, that is, for restitutionism (Balzac being an excellent case in point); or, to accept a compromise with the present, while hoping to reform it—to eliminate or diminish its most flagrant wrongs.

However, although this type of romanticism is found mainly in the above historical situation, it nonetheless represents a possible permutation of romantic anticapitalism at any moment in its development by virtue of an aspect of its very nature. For we have claimed that one of the two poles of value for romanticism is the subjective self. And, although in the final analysis there is a profound and explosive conflict between this subjective self and individualism in the socioeconomic realm, this conflict often remains latent and hidden. This allows for a possible affinity between the cult of the romantic individual and the individualism of bourgeois liberalism; it is at this precise point that romanticism joins, and runs the risk of being transformed into, its opposite.

These two factors—probably with different relative importance in each case—contributed to make of Michelet, Lamartine, Sainte-Beuve, and Hugo the hybrid phenomenon we are terming liberal romantics. The latter two are instructive to compare, since they illustrate two modalities of this contradictory state of being. It is Pierre Barbéris who has provided us with the most incisive analyses of French liberal romanticism in general, and more specifically of Sainte-Beuve and Hugo. In an excellent study of *Joseph Delorme*, Barbéris demonstrates that in Sainte-Beuve the coexistence of liberalism and romantic revolt takes the form of a split between two kinds of writings: the articles and the literary works. In the former, "on the level of clear consciousness and abstract analysis," Sainte-Beuve shows himself to be a classic liberal, whereas only in literary creation does his unhappy, problematic, and rebellious cosciousness express itself. This may explain the violent condemnation of *Joseph Delorme* by the liberals; and, as Barbéris points out, the fact the Sainte-Beuve chose to reissue the book after 1830 would indicate that its real subject is not the Restoration but the bourgeois order.[59]

In the case of Hugo, on the other hand, the contradiction is internal to the literary production. In a detailed analysis of the "Châtiments," Barbéris reveals a bourgeois ideology at work that is critical only of "preliberal oppression" and that sees in the progress of science and technology the future solution for the ills of the present, whereas in the same poem one also finds nostalgia for the old France of countryside and handicraft. Barbéris concludes that "with Hugo . . . the juxtaposition remains unresolved of a non-capitalist worldview . . . and a grandiose vision of the new industrial society—but at the price of refusing to see what *kind* of industrial society is being set up."[60] The date of the "Châtiments" (1853) indicates that liberal romanticism by no means disappears after the Restoration; in certain cases, the illusion of harmony between romanticism and liberalism subsists long afterward. In other works by Hugo, of course, and most particularly in *Les Misérables*, there is a more pronounced antibourgeois dimension. Yet in spite of the fact that he was a political chameleon, and that in certain respects he might seem to be close to the "Jacobin-democrats" or even to humanitarian socialism, Hugo's work in general, after an early monarchist period, seems to correspond to the paradoxical phenomenon of liberal romanticism: Hugo, for whom the writer's role is to give full expression to his epoch, in fact expressed both its contradictory sides—not only its revolt but also its integration.

6) I—Jacobin-democratic Romanticism

The very existence of a type of Romantic anticapitalism that can be termed "Jacobin-democratic" is eloquent proof against the affirmation that there is an absolute opposition between romanticism and Enlightenment. Far from there being a necessary contradiction and conflict between the two movements, an important component of the former is the spiritual heir of the latter, the filiation most often passing through Rousseau, who is to be located at the junction between the two. What characterizes this type of romanticism—and what distinguishes it from the liberal type—is that it mounts a radical critique *both* of oppression by forces from the past—the monarchy, the aristocracy and the Church—and of the new bourgeois oppression. This double critique is made (except of course in the case of writers—particularly Rousseau—who preceded it) in the name of the French Revolution and of the values represented by its most radical wing, Jacobinism. The Jacobin allegiance is sometimes accompanied by Bonapartism, to the extent that Napoleon is seen as an effective and heroic extension of Jacobinism; the admiration for Bonaparte often stops, however, at the 18th Brumaire. In contrast to liberals, the Jacobin-democrats do not call for slow evolution, compromise, and moderate solutions, but for revolutionary turning points and profound upheavals.

We are placing Jacobin-democratic romanticism first among the "revolutionary/utopian" types because it comes first chronologically. This current, which is clearly distinguishable from the purely rationalist form of radicalism (e.g., Godwin) is to be found in all the principal countries of the first wave of romanticism. And naturally it manifests itself in the country of the Revolution. Following Rousseau, the Jacobins themselves may be included in the French line of development, since their impassioned idealization of antiquity represents a clearly romantic nostalgia. It is to be noted, however, that the most radical version of Jacobinism—that of Buonarroti and Babeuf—comes close to communism and thus tends to fall outside the bounds of the type under consideration. In the years following the Revolution, among those who were both Jacobins and Bonapartists we might mention Stendhal and Musset—the Musset of the introduction to *Confession d'un enfant du siècle*. In Germany, where the first romantics were briefly Jacobin-democrats before becoming restitutionists, several important writers—Hölderlin, Büchner, and Heine—never abandoned their original perspective.

Heine, an antiromantic who finally admitted to being at heart a romantic, saw the French Revolution as the agent for the redemption of humanity: "Freedom is a new religion, the religion of our age. . . . The French . . . are the chosen people . . . Paris is the new Jerusalem, and the Rhine is the Jordan which divides the consecrated land of liberty from the land of the Philistines."[61] At the end of his life, after a number of shifts to the left and to the right of this position, Heine reaffirmed as the unifying principle of his thought "an unchanging devotion to the cause of humanity, to the democratic ideas of the Revolution."[62] The case of Heine is particularly interesting with respect to the past for which he is nostalgic. In his "aveux de l'auteur" (author's confessions), which conclude *De l'Allemagne*, he reveals that, although once a philhellene (like most Jacobin-democrats), he has recently turned back to his Judaic antecedents; and he affirms that the true prefiguration of the French Revolution is neither ancient Greece with its slavery, nor Rome with its legalistic chicanery, but rather Mosaic law and the customs of ancient Judaism.

In England also there is a significant tradition of Jacobin-democrats. The first to be mentioned is Blake, whose poem *The French Revolution* (1790–91) is written from a Jacobin point of view, and who continued in later poems to represent in mythical form the struggle of the principle of liberation that the Revolution had momentarily brought to life. Subsequently there was the Jacobin episode of Coleridge and of Wordsworth—to which we have already alluded—and lastly the more durable radicalism of the second generation of English romantics, notably that of Byron and Shelley.

Jacobin-democratic romanticism, then, is rather narrowly circumscribed in time: beginning with Rousseau, it is concentrated mainly in the Revolutionary period and its immediate aftermath. Its last great representative is perhaps Heine. This current of thought is limited in time by its very nature, which is to make a radical indictment of the present in the name of the values of the French Revolution; for with its transformation into a founding myth of the victorious bourgeoisie, the Revolution can no longer serve as sole reference point for a radical critique of the present (and of the past—oriented, that is, toward the future) if the critique is to remain radical. With the birth of the socialist and labor movements, the authentic critique must change if it is not to negate itself.[63] Heine, who, especially during the period of his association with Marx, was fascinated and tempted by communism without ever committing himself to it, and also Shelley represent the extreme limits of Jacobin-democratic romanticism, beyond which it becomes transformed into other "revolutionary/utopian" types. With Heine and Shelley the worldview is at the point of mutation, and this characteristic differentiates them from earlier representatives of the type. Lukács notes this difference between Hölderlin and Shelley, and (rightly) affirms that "a Hölderlin of a later time who did not follow the path of Shelley, would not have been a Hölderlin, but rather a narrow, classicist liberal."[64]

The difference is so striking that some have gone so far as to portray Shelley as a socialist. In particular, Marx's daughter and son-in-law—Eleanor Marx Aveling and Edward Aveling—attempted to demonstrate just that in an essay entitled "Shelley's Socialism."[65] In this text they claim that there is a fundamental difference between the essentially bourgeois radicalism of Byron and that of Shelley, who speaks in the name of the proletariat. But while the dissimilarity between Byron and Sheley is real enough, in our opinion what is involved is a variation *within the same type*, and the identification of Shelley with socialism is untenable. For in spite of the fact that in several poems— especially "The Mask of Anarchy" (1819)—he makes himself the advocate of rebellious workers and violently condemns the condition of the working class as a kind of slavery, Shelley never goes so far as to place private property in question, and his ideological reference point always remains Jacobin-democratic radicalism.

His political perspective is unaltered, in fact, from the early poem "Queen Mab" (1812) to "Ode to Liberty" (1820) and "Hellas" (1821), written the year before his death. Shelley's historical, social, and political vision is perhaps most fully expressed in these last two works. Unlike Rousseau, Shelley experiences no nostalgia for primitive man; for according to him, although liberty was inscribed in the world itself by God at the creation, it succeeds in manifesting itself for the first time, after a long initial period of barbarism, only in ancient Greece: "Let there be light! said Liberty . . . / Athens arose!"[66] After a brief continuation of its reign in Rome, liberty suffers a long eclipse, at first due to the tyrannies of throne and altar, and later to the greed for money. In the modern era of revolution, liberty is preparing to return to earth, but this time at a higher level, and definitively. For Shelley, "The coming age is shadowed on the Past / As on a glass," and "The world's great age begins anew, / The golden years return." But in ancient Greece only "Prophetic echoes flung dim melody," and the world to come will be "A brighter Hellas." It will constitute a return, but the return will be to the mythical and utopian age of Saturn rather than to an actual state of Greece in antiquity: "Saturn and Love their long repose / Shall burst . . . / Not gold, not blood, their altar dowers, / But votive tears and symbol flowers."[67] For Shelley the future will not be the simple recreation of a real past, but rather the coming to full flower of all its qualities, qualities that were only in bud in the past era; the future will thus represent a total fulfillment such as never existed before, a utopia of love and beauty.

6) II—Populist Romanticism

Sismondi's work inaugurates populism as an economic doctrine, but it is in Russia that this trend—for reasons which have to do both with the social structure of the country and the situation of its intellectuals during the second half of the nineteenth century—is most fully developed as a social philosophy and as a political movement. Economists such as B. Efroussi, V. Vorontsov, and Nicolai—on (pseudonym for N. Danielson, who corresponded for many years with Marx and Engels), all more or less influenced by Sismondi, sociologists like Mikhailovsky, and above all "nihilist" revolutionary philosophers like Herzen are the main representatives of romantic populism. They saw in the traditional Russian rural community (*obchtchina*) the foundation for a specifically Russian road to socialism, and rejected both czarist autocracy and Western capitalist civilization. The political manifestation of populism was the movement *Narodnaya Volya* (The Will of the People), which wanted to "go to the people" and win the peasantry to the new revolutionary ideas. Of all the great Russian writers, Tolstoy is certainly the one with the greatest affinity for the populist cult of the peasantry.

J. C. Sismonde de Sismondi was far from being a revolutionary, but his rigorous and radical criticism of capitalism elicited the admiration of Marx, who considered him in certain respects superior to Ricardo. In opposition to classical economy, his analysis of economic reality is inspired by a moral principle: "I will always struggle against the industrial system which has made cheap of human life."[68] Sismondi rejects wealth as an end in itself— what he calls "Chrematistics"—and the reduction of men to the condition of machines. Marx, in the *Communist Manifesto*, although criticizing Sismondi for being a utopian and a "petty-bourgeois socialist," pays him homage for having provided an irrefutable demonstration of the deadly consequences of machinism, division of labor, overproduction, crises, etc.

The criticism of the capitalist system is romantic, since it refers constantly to a precapitalist Golden Age—especially to the Italian republics of the Middle Ages—and dreams of a patriarchal society of small artisans and small peasant landowners, associated in corporatist or communitarian structures. In a characteristic passage from his major work, *The New Principles of Political Economy* (1819), he writes: "In the countries where the farmer is owner, and where the fruits of the earth belong entirely to the people who do all the labor—countries whose form of exploitation [of the land] we will designate as patriarchal—one sees everywhere signs of the cultivator's love for the house he lives in and the land he takes care of."[69] Sismondi refuses, however, to be considered as "an enemy of social progress" and insists that his desire is not to restore what used to be, but to create "something better than that which is now" through certain social reforms: the partition of large landed properties and of enterprises, etc.

The continuity between the economic ideas and those of the Russian populists almost a hundred years later is undeniable, even though the latter gave a much more revolutionary coloring to the same program. In 1887, Lenin wrote a pamphlet entitled *A Characterization of Economic Romanticism (Sismondi and Our National Sismondists)*, in which he sharply attacked the populists and totally condemned the work of Sismondi as reactionary. Rosa Luxemburg, however, in her book *The Accumulation of Capital* (1911), defends Sismondi against Lenin's criticism and praises his criticism of capitalism as well as his having raised some essential questions for the development of Marxist political economy.

6) III—Utopian-Humanist Socialism

The romantic authors related to this current build imaginary models for a socialist alternative to industrial/bourgeois civilization, using as reference points certain social paradigms and certain precapitalist ethical or religious values. Their criticism of capitalism is not formulated in the name of one class—the proletariat—but in the name of *humanity* as a whole, and it is addressed to all men of goodwill. Those who are usually designated as "utopian socialists" are not always romantics. Owen and Saint-Simon, for instance, are above all men of the Enlightenment, favoring industry and progress. Among those who do belong to the romantic socialist type we might mention French authors like Fourier, Cabet, Enfantin (and most of the Saint-Simonians), Leroux, and (to a certain extent) George Sand. In nineteenth-century Germany, there is the so-called "true socialism" (Karl Grün and

Moses Hess); and, in the twentieth century, expressionist writers like Ernst Toller, Marxist-humanist philosophers like Erich Fromm, etc.

A very illuminating example of this kind of socialism is the work of Moses Hess—in particular his youthful writings (1837–45). His first book, *The Sacred History of Humanity* (1837), is probably the one in which the presence of the romantic *Weltanschauung* goes deepest. In it, Hess develops a political-messianic interpretation of history, and looks back to antiquity as an era of social harmony based on the common ownership of goods. Private property destroyed this original equilibrium, permitting the rise of industry and commerce, accompanied by inequality, egoism, and social injustice. The messianic task of the future is to suppress inheritance and private property "in order that the primitive equality among men may be re-established," opening the way for the advent of a New Jerusalem, a New Eden, the establishment of the Kingdom of God on earth.[70] Strongly influenced by Fourier, whose concept of social harmony is the central theme of the book, Hess outlines a radical critique of capitalism, of the new aristocracy of wealth and industry, which is only increasing the riches of the few at the expense of the misery of the majority.[71]

While this work evoked little response, the next book published by Hess, *The European Triarchy* (1841), had a considerable impact on the critical intelligentsia (particularly the neo-Hegelians) in Germany. Hess proposes the constitution of Europe as a unified "organism," based on a spiritual alliance between France, Germany, and England, which will bring the Kingdom of God to earth. In a typically romantic short cut between the past and the future, he writes: "What the Holy Jewish State in antiquity, or the Holy Roman Empire of the Middle Ages used to be, Roman-German Europe will be in the future: the pupil in the eyes of God, the central point from which the world is led."[72]

The socialist ideas implicit in these books become progessively clearer in a series of essays and articles by Hess during the years 1842–45, in the *Rheinische Zeitung*, the *Deutsch-Französische Jahrbücher*, the *Neue Anekdoten*, and the *Rheinische Jahrbücher*. These pieces oppose the communist principle of Humanity to the principle of Egoism, the Spirit of Mammon, and the socialist community of the future to the egotistical, "inorganic" individual of bourgeois society. The most important of these essays is probably "The Essence of Money," written in 1843 and published in 1845, which exerted a very significant influence on the young Marx. This text passionately criticizes the monetary alienation, the domination of the god-money over people, and the system of selling human freedom that characterizes our society. For Hess, the modern mercantile world (*moderne Schacherwelt*), of which money is the essence, is worse than ancient slavery because it is "unnatural and inhuman that people sell themselves voluntarily." The task of communism is to abolish money and its malefic power, and to establish an organic community (*organische Gemeinschaft*) of authentically human life.[73]

6) IV—Libertarian Romanticism

Libertarian or anarchist (or anarcho-syndicalist) romanticism, which opposes to industrial capitalism and the centralized state the utopia of a federation of small communities (consisting mainly of peasants and artisans), which lays claim to values or traditions of the precapitalist "people," reached its zenith at the end of the nineteenth and beginning of the twentieth centuries. One also finds in anarchism a rationalist, *Aufklärer* tendency that is rather foreign to romanticism. But most of the "classic" libertarian thinkers like Proudhon, Bakunin, Kropotkin, Elisée Reclus, etc., are without doubt romantic anticapitalists. This applies equally to the revolutionary syndicalist circle connected with the journal *Mouvement Socialiste* in France (Georges Sorel, Hubert Lagardelle, Edouard Berth), to Jean Grave and his symbolist friends, and to the Jewish anarchist Bernard Lazare (a friend of Charles Peguy). In Germany, one might mention Gustav Landauer, his friend the poet Erich Mühsam, and to a certain extent Martin Buber. Some writers also can be associated with this worldview: Strindberg, Oscar Wilde, and Kafka.

Perhaps the most typical representative of libertarian romanticism is Gustav Landauer. Writer, literary critic, social philosopher, leader of the Munich Commune of 1919 (he was killed by the counterrevolution after the defeat of the Bavarian Councils Republic), Landauer was influenced in his youth by Wagner and Nietzsche, before he became an anarchist. However, from the beginning he distinguished himself from the author of *Zarathustra* not only by his revolutionary orientation but also by his interest in religious spirituality (in 1903 he published a translation of the mystical writings of Master Eckart). Landauer shares with "classical" German romanticism a deep nostalgia for medieval Christianity: "Christianity, with its gothic towers and battlements, . . . with its corporations and fraternities, was a *Volk* in the most powerful and elevated sense of the word: an intimate fusion of the economic and cultural community with the spiritual bond (*Geistesbund*)."[74]

On the contrary, modern, capitalist England, "with its sterile industrial system, its desolation of the land, its uniformization of the masses and of misery, with its production for the world market instead of true needs," is for him the sinister image of contemporary civilization. He bitterly reproaches Marx, "that son of the steam engine," for admiring the technical achievements of capitalism. For him the task of socialism is not to perfect the industrial system but to help mankind *rediscover* culture, *Geist*, freedom, and community.[75]

Radically hostile to the state and bourgeois society, Landauer exhorted the socialist to withdraw from this decadent and corrupt social universe, and to establish autonomous rural communities united in a free federation. Rather than a general strike or insurrection, the road that leads to libertarian socialism is the abandonment of the capitalist economy and the building of a socialist *Gemeinschaft, hic et nunc,* in the rural areas of Germany.[76]

However, it would be wrong to present Landauer as a partisan of the pure and simple restoration of past social and cultural forms. He acknowledges the importance and value of certain achievements of civilization: the *Aufklärung,* the abolition of superstitions, the development of science. He aspires to create a *new society* with both modern *Zivilisation* and precapitalist *Kultur* as its basis, a society that would be authentically communitarian, free, and egalitarian, without State or social classes.[77]

6) V—Marxist Romanticism

The romantic element that is unquestionably present in the works of Marx and Engels—one need only recall their sympathy with the Russian populists and their hope that the traditional rural district *(obchtchina)* would serve as the germ of a future socialist Russia—has been denied by official Marxism (strongly influenced by evolutionism, positivism, and Fordism) and by the Second and Third Internationals. In the writings of Kautsky, Plekhanov, and Bukharin—not to mention Stalin—one looks in vain for any trace of the romantic heritage. The first important attempt at a neoromantic reinterpretation of Marxism is that of William Morris at the end of the nineteenth century. Morris's perspective has recently been taken up again and developed by the British historians E. P. Thompson and Raymond Williams. But it is principally in the area of German culture—and entirely unrelated to the English developments—that one finds authors who consider themselves Marxists but at the same time as strongly marked by the romantic critique of capitalism. The work of these authors constitutes perhaps the summit of the twentieth-century Marxist philosophy: the young Lukács, Ernst Bloch, and the Frankfurt School (particularly Benjamin and Marcuse). One also finds in certain Third World countries—especially among the founders of the communist movement in the 1920s—thinkers who look to precapitalist social traditions in their countries as a possible sociocultural basis for the revolutionary movement: José Carlos Mariategui in Peru, and Li-Ta-Chao in China.

What distinguishes this trend from other socialist or revolutionary currents exhibiting a romantic sensibility is the central preoccupation with essential problems of Marxism: class struggle, social revolution, the role of the proletariat as universal class and agent of emancipation, the possibility of using modern productive forces in a socialist economy—even if the conclusions drawn are not necessarily identical with those of Marx and Engels.

Ernst Bloch's writings are probably the most important example of Marxist romanticism in the twentieth century. He has been called a "Marxist Schelling"—and indeed, in an autobiographical interview, he recalled that the four volumes of Schelling's *Philosophie der Mythologie und Offenbarung* were among the first philosophical books he read with awe and fascination.[78] A student of Georg Simmel—at whose seminar he first met Lukács—and a member of Max Weber's circle in Heidelberg, Bloch broke with his masters because of their support for the "German Fatherland" in 1914, but he nonetheless incorporated some elements of their criticism of modern bureaucratic *Zivilisation* into his worldview.

Written during the war, *Geist der Utopie* (1918–23) owes much of its power of attraction up to the present day to its remarkable fusion of anticapitalist romanticism and apocalyptic, revolutionary Marxism. Typically romantic, for instance, is its rapturous paean to Gothic art, whose "central fire" contains both the "deepest organic and the deepest spiritual being," and whose "alchemical measure" was not the sun, or astrology, but "Man, Man in his deepest interiority, as Christ."[79] In the first edition of the book he goes so far as to call for a utopian society composed only of peasants, artisans, "a nobility without serfs and without war," and "a spiritual aristocracy," i.e., "a humanity which is *ritterlich* and pious once more."[80] Explaining this astonishing formulation, Bloch told one of the present authors (M. Löwy) in an interview in 1974: "The new aristocracy I was talking about was, therefore, *not profitable* economically, that is, not founded on exploitation, but on the contrary it had ascetic and chivalrous virtues"; and he added that Marx's own criticism of capitalism as an "unfair" system is based on a standard of values that "goes back to the Code of the Knights, to the Code of King Arthur's Round Table."[81] In the second edition of the book (1923) this passage disappears and is replaced by a Marxist definition of social utopia: from each according to his capacities, to each according to his needs. He now criticizes the "Romanticism of the new reaction," which is "without spirit and unchristian *(geistlos und unchristlich)*," but clings to the "truly Christian" medieval idea of humanity.[82] The romantic reference to precapitalist values is still essential to his *Weltanschauung*, although he distinguishes between two different traditions, going back respectively to Thomas Münzer and to his enemies, the "heraldic robbers."

In *Thomas Münzer, the Theologian of Revolution* (1921), he sees the Bolsheviks as the inheritors of the first tradition, which he traces back—as the "underground history of the Revolution"—to the Cathars and the Russites, Münzer and the Anabaptists, Meister Eckart and Sebastian Frank, Rousseau and Tolstoy. Bloch wrote an afterword for the 1960 republication of the book, in which he himself refers to its spirit as "Romantic revolutionary." It is interesting to notice that among the precapitalist *Gemeinschaften* which appear as the most positive moments of the past, there is precisely the period that the *Aufklärung* and modern historiography consider to be a regression to barbarism and a Dark Age of decline: the centuries following the fall of the Roman Empire, the Low Middle Ages. Bloch hails the falling apart of the ancient abstract-bureaucratic form of state, and of the money economy, and their replacement by the Germanic vestiges of agrarian communism, i.e., by a society based on fidelity *(Treue)*, tradition *(Herkommen)*, piety *(Pietät)*, warmth, and patriarchal simplicity.[83]

Romantic anticapitalism remains a crucial component of Bloch's later Marxist philosophy, aesthetics, and politics. It is at the root of his defense of expressionism against Lukács' criticism in the 1930s, as well as of his political analysis, in *Heritage of Our Times* (1935), of the rebellion against capitalist rationality by the "nonsynchronic" classes of Germany.[84] The same applies to his magnum opus *Das Prinzip Hoffnung* (1953–59), in which he calls for the uniting of rational Marxist analysis—'*der kälteste Detektiv*'—with the warm spirit of the *Märchen* and with the dream of the Golden Age.[85] Nostalgia for the past, imaginary representation of a different world, and hope for a better future are intimately linked in Bloch's peculiar understanding of historical materialism and revolutionary praxis.

One of the characteristic aspects of Bloch's romantic Marxism is the reference to religious traditions—Jewish and Christian, heretical and mystical, from the Biblical prophets to the Kabbalah, and from Joachim di Fiore to Karl Barth. Of course it is an "atheistic religion," or a secularized one, but it gives his theory of socialist revolution a uniquely millenarian quality.[86]

★   ★   ★

Having attempted to define romantic anticapitalism as a whole and then to sketch out a typology of its principal variants, it remains to raise the question of the sociological explanation of the phenomenon. What are the social bases of romanticism? Is it possible to link that worldview to one or several social groups? Although Marxist analyses do not, generally speaking, offer very well-developed hypotheses on this point, one does find a certain number of sociological explanations in them, albeit schematic and limited in scope. On the whole, these explanations seem inadequate to fully comprehend romanticism.

Among the explanations proposed, the one that in our view is the most erroneous sees in romanticism an essentially bourgeois phenomenon. Thus, for Leo Löwenthal romanticism is a form of "bourgeois consciousness," and according to Arnold Hauser the fact that its public is composed of members of that class reveals the "essentially bourgeois [character] of the movement" and of its ideology.[87] This reduction of romanticism to a bourgeois ideology—illustrated here by critics whose work in other respects is of high quality—is in fact the dogmatic commonplace of those who violently deny the affinities between the Marxist and the romantic worldviews. The error of this position is to ignore the *essence* of the romantic phenomenon. For in spite of the fact that a part of its authors and public belong to the bourgeoisie, romanticism represents a deep-seated revolt against this class and the society that it rules. If romanticism is in its essence anticapitalist, it is the antithesis of a bourgeois ideology. Doubtless, we ourselves have pointed out possible *rapprochements* with a bourgeois state of mind and a bourgeois status quo— particularly in the cases of "conservative" and "liberal" romanticism. But in our view these are precisely extreme cases in which romanticism is in danger of negating itself and of becoming its opposite.

Sometimes Marxist analyses associate romanticism with other social classes, however, in particular with the aristocracy and the *petite bourgeoisie.* According to Jacques Droz, although most German romantics belong to the latter class, they express the ideology of the former: they "in fact only served the interests of the old ruling classes, i.e., the nobility, the corporations and the Churches"; their work was "the expression of the old ruling classes' consciousness of the danger that awaited them."[88] Conversely, for the East German critic G. Heinrich the very same German romanticism articulates "the class interests of certain strata of the *petite bourgeoisie*," and Ernst Fischer finds that, more generally, "the Romantic attitude could not be other than confused, for the petty bourgeoisie was the very embodiment of social contradiction. . . ."[89] In our opinion, however, both these interpretations are one-sided; neither one is entirely false, but each gives only a partial explanation and needs to be integrated into a more complete explanatory framework.

Barbéris's work on romanticism has the merit of offering a multidimensional explanation. He sees at the sources of French romanticism an historical conjunction of the aspirations and interests of several different social groups marginalized by Capital: in particular, "aristocrats dispossessed" by the bourgeoisie and the younger generations of bourgeois "without endowment, which ran up against the barrier of money and found no way of employing themselves. . . ."[90] In spite of its merits, however, this more complex sociological analysis remains too limited. In the first place, it seems insufficient to stop at mention of the aristocracy and *petite bourgeoisie* alone (or young bourgeois who have not yet "arrived"), at least if one wishes to take into account the overall phenomenon of romantic anticapitalism as we conceive it. In addition, although Barbéris is well aware that the flood tide of romanticism swells with *diverse victims* of the bourgeoisie and its social order, most often he conceives of the oppression as operating only at the economic level. Thus, he seems to see the romantic revolt of young petty bourgeois mainly as a reaction to frustrated ambition and insufficient employment opportunities. But although this motive doubtlessly played some role in the genesis of romanticism, it cannot by itself explain the latter. It cannot adequately account for the force and depth of the critique of a whole socioeconomic order. Far more important, in our view, is the *experience of alienation and reification*, and sociological analysis must pose the problem in terms of differential sensitivity to this experience within the social totality. In conclusion, then, we will put forward a number of propositions that take that direction.

First of all, most of the usual analyses of the social framework of romanticism fail to take into consideration an essential category for the understanding of the phenomenon: the *intelligentsia*, a group made up of individuals coming from varied social backgrounds but which possesses a unity and (relative) autonomy due to its position in the process of the production of culture. One of the exceptions is Karl Mannheim, who demonstrates in his remarkable essay on conservative thought in Germany that those who represent the romantic movement are essentially *freischwebende Intellektuelle*.[91] Generally speaking, it is clear that the *producers* of the romantic anticapitalist worldview are *certain traditional sectors of the intelligentsia* whose culture and way of life are hostile to bourgeois industrial civilization: independent writers, ecclesiastics or theologians (many romantics are ministers' sons), poets and artists, academic mandarins, etc. What is the social basis for this hostility?

The traditional intelligentsia (we might recall the "Cénacle" in Balzac's *Illusions perdues*) inhabits a mental universe governed by *qualitative* values, by ethical, aesthetic, religious, cultural, or political values. All of their social activity of "spiritual production" (the term is used by Marx in *The German Ideology*) is inspired, motivated, oriented, and molded by these values, which constitute their *raison d'être* as intellectuals. But the central characteristic of capitalism is that its functioning is entirely determined by *quantitative* values: exchange value, price, profit. There is a fundamental opposition, then, between these two worlds, an opposition that creates contradictions and conflicts.[92] Naturally, the intelligentsia of the old type cannot escape certain constraints of the market as industrial capitalism develops—the need to sell its "spiritual products," for example. A part of this social group ends up accepting the hegemony of exchange value, yielding internally (sometimes even with enthusiasm and fervor) to its demands. Others, remaining faithful to their precapitalist cultural universe of qualitative values, refuse what Balzac's Cánacle called "the decision to do business with one's soul, one's mind, one's thought"; these become the seedbed for the production of the romantic anticapitalist worldview.

While the *creators* of the various figures of romantic anticapitalism, and the "carriers" of romantic movements, issue from the "classic" intelligentsia as distinct from the modern type—scientists, technicians, engineers, economists, administrators, media personnel, etc.—the *audience* of the worldview, its *social base* in the full sense, is far more vast. It is potentially composed of all classes, fractions of classes or social categories for which the rise of industrial capitalism spells decline or creates a crisis in their economic, social, or political status and/or negatively affects their way of life and the cultural values to which they are attached. For example, depending on circumstances and the historical period involved, they can include groups like the aristocracy, landowners, the "old" urban and rural *petite bourgeoisie*, the intelligentsia, the clergy, students, etc. What is involved, of course, is only an *objective possibility*, a probable behavior as Max Weber would say, the actual realization of which depends on a whole series of concrete sociohistorical conditions.

In this sense, the analyses that designate the old ruling classes, or the aristocracy, or the precapitalist petty bourgeoisie as the social base of romanticism are not false but rather too limited; restricting themselves to a single class or fraction of a class, they are unable to account for the vast extension and complexity of the aggregate of social forces that identify themselves with this worldview at different historical moments.

Is it possible also to define the social bases specific to *each of the types* of romantic anticapitalism? Generally speaking, one might advance the hypothesis that the utopian-revolutionary forms draw their audience mainly from among nondominant social strata; but any attempt at a more precise determination seems problematic—particularly since, as we have seen, a single individual frequently passes from one position to another within the romantic spectrum.

The attempt at a sociological analysis that we have outlined here has, nonetheless, a limitation: it tends to reduce the audience of romantic anticapitalism—its *social public*—to certain archaic, precapitalist "pockets of resistance," groups that are tradition-bound or marginal to modern society. If this were true, the romantic worldview would be a phenomenon in decline, one condemned to disappear by the very development of industrial civilization. But that is far from being the case. A significant part of contemporary cultural and literary production is deeply influenced by it, from Tolkien to Borges and from Agnon to Michael Ende. Even the movie industry increasingly includes romantic and critical ingredients in its ideological makeup: *The Return of the Jedi* and *E.T.* are typical examples. Moreover, several of the most important recent social movements—ecology, feminism, pacifism, the theology of liberation—express feelings and aspirations strongly colored by romantic anticapitalism. Pacifism and ecology, which are partially convergent, are the most massive ones, and also the most heterogeneous. They include the most diverse forms of romanticism, from conservative or restitutionist to the most radical revolutionary utopianism, and they refer to different kinds of precapitalist values: religious ethics, grassroots *Gemeinschaft*, natural equilibrium. Nuclear weapons and nuclear energy, the most advanced point of modern industrial *Zivilisation*, appear in their eyes to be the worst expression of a kind of technological progress that has grown out of control and threatens to destroy humankind.

On the whole, these social movements tend towards the Left of the political spectrum, but the issues they raise cut through the traditional party lines. The German Social Democratic Party, for instance, is deeply divided between a modernist, rational/pragmatist, and neoliberal wing (Helmut Schmidt), and a moralist/romantic one, religiously inspired, ready to support the pacifist and ecological campaigns (Erhard Eppler). Utopia, rather than regression, is their dominant note, although it is difficult to identify one particular kind of romantic anticapitalism as being the hegemonic tendency. Humanist socialism (of Christian inspiration) and neopopulism are probably among the best represented among the activists and rank and file in both pacifism and ecology, but it would be wrong to reduce the latter to this political dimension. In any case, it is significant that they have achieved their greatest successes precisely in the (technologically) most advanced societies of *Spätkapitalismus,* like the United States and West Germany. It would seem as if industrial capitalist civilization has reached a stage in its development where its destructive effects on the tissue of society and on the natural environment have attained such proportions that certain themes of romantic anticapitalism (and certain forms of nostalgia for a precapitalist past) exert a diffuse influence far beyond the classes and social categories traditionally associated with the worldview.

Notes

1. See, for example: *Mythos und Moderne: Begriff und Bild einer Rekonstruktion,* ed. Karl Heinz Bohrer (Frankfurt am Main: Suhrkamp, 1983); Manfred Frank, *Der kommende Gott: Vorlesungen über die neue Mythologie* (Frankfurt am Main: Suhrkamp, 1982); *Religionstheorie und politische Theologie,* ed. Jacob Taubes (Munich: Wilhelm Fink Verlag, 1983); *Romantische Utopie—utopische Romantik,* ed. Gisela Dischner and Richard Faber (Hildesheim: Gerstenberg Verlag, 1979), etc.

2. A. O. Lovejoy, "On the Discriminations of Romanticism," in *Romanticism: Problems of European Civilization* (Boston: D. C. Heath, 1965), 39.

3. Carl Schmitt, *Politische Romantik,* 2d ed. (Munich and Leipzig: Verlag von Duncker und Humbolt, 1925), 162, 176, 227. We might add that Schmitt converted to Nazism in 1933 and in 1934 published an essay entitled "Der Führer schützt das Recht."

4. B. Croce, "History of Europe in the 19th Century" (1934), in *Romanticism,* 54.

5. See, for example, Fritz Strich, *Deutsche Klassik und Romantik* (Bern: Francke, 1962; 1st edition, 1922), for whom romanticism is the expression of the "deepest inborn tendencies of the German soul."

6. William McGovern, *From Luther to Hitler* (Cambridge: Riverside Press, 1941), 200, 582.

7. Fritz Stern, *The Politics of Cultural Despair: A Study in the Rise of the Germanic Ideology* (University of California Press, 1961), xvii.

8. J. Bowle, *Western Political Thought* (London: University Paperbacks, 1961), 422, 434.

9. See, for example, Anna Tumarkin, *Die romantische Weltanschauung* (Bern: Paul Haupt, 1920), although it is a rationalist study rather hostile to romanticism; see also the essays of H. A. Korff, G. Hubner, W. Linden, M. Honecker, and others, collected by Helmut Prang in *Begriffsbestimmung der Romantik* (Darmstadt: Wissenschaftliche Buchgesellschaft, 1968).

10. A. J. George, *The Development of French Romanticism: The Impact of the Industrial Revolution in Literature* (Syracuse, N.Y.: Syracuse University Press, 1955), xi, 192.

11. On this subject, see M. Löwy, *Marxisme et romantisme révolutionnaire* (Paris: Sycomore, 1979). By giving the title "Against Romanticism" to a section of his collection of texts by Marx

and Engels on literature and art, Jean Fréville takes a completely one-sided position that does not correspond to the texts and that illustrates the impoverishment of Marxism by the Stalinist perspective: *Sur la litterature et l'art* (Paris: Éditions Sociales Internationales, 1936).

12. Jacques Droz, *Le Romantisme allemand et l'Etat, Resistance et collaboration en Allemagne napoléonienne* (Paris: Payot, 1966) 50, 295; and *Le Romantisme politique en Allemagne* (Paris: A. Colin, 1963), 25, 27, 36, etc. The opposite position, asserting the essentially *revolutionary* character of romanticism, is presented (in a perspective close to Marxism) in the interesting and original study by Paul Rozenberg: *Le Romantisme anglais* (Paris: Larousse, 1973). However, this analysis also seems one-sided, since it appears to exclude from romanticism all forms of counterrevolutionary thought (e.g., Burke).

13. See his article on Dostoevsky in 1931, where the term "romantic anticapitalism" appears for the first time: "Über den Dostojewski Nachlass," *Moskauer Rundschau*, March 1931. In his history of German literature, Lukács refuses to consider Hölderlin as a romantic writer: cf. *Brève Histoire de la littérature allemande* (Paris: Nagel, 1949), 57.

14. G. Lukács, *Ecrits de Moscou* (Paris: Editions Sociales, 1974), 159.

15. Marx-Engels, *Über Kunst und Literatur* (Berlin: Verlag Bruno Henschel, 1948), 104.

16. Jan O. Fischer, *"Epoque Romantique" et réalisme: Problèmes méthodologiques* (Prague: Univerzita Karlova, 1977), 254–55, 258, 260, 266–67.

17. Pierre Barbéris, "Mal du siècle, ou d'un romantisme de droite à un romantisme de gauche," in *Romantisme et politique, 1815–1851* (Paris: A. Colin, 1969), 177.

18. Lukács, *Ecrits de Moscou*, 150.

19. Ernst Fischer, *The Necessity of Art: A Marxist Approach* (London: Penguin, 1963), 52, 55.

20. Raymond Williams, *Culture and Society, 1780–1950* (London: Penguin, 1976), 53, 56, 153. In a recent interview with *New Left Review,* Williams makes a critical reassessment, from a Marxist standpoint, of the limitations and shortcomings of this book (first published in 1958): *Politics and Letters: Interviews with New Left Review* (London: Verso, 1981), chap. II, 1.

21. For a descriptive presentation that gives a similar extension to the romantic phenomenon, see Paul Honigsheim, "Romantik und neuromantische Bewegungen," in *Handwörterbuch der Sozialwissenschaften* (Stuttgart: Gustav Fischer, 1953).

22. For a typology and discussion of the worldviews studied by Goldmann, see S. Naïr and M Löwy, *Lucien Goldmann ou la dialectique de la totalité* (Paris: Seghers, 1973); and R. Sayre, "Lucien Goldmann and the Sociology of Culture," in *Praxis* 1 (1976): 2.

23. Claus Träger, "Des Lumières à 1830: Héritage et innovation dans le romantisme allemand," in *Romantisme* 28–29 (1980): 90; H. P. Lund, "Le Romantisme et son histoire," in *Romantisme* 7 (1974): 113.

24. See P. Barbéris, *Aux sources du réalisme: aristocrates et bourgeois* (Paris: 10/18, 1978), 330–40.

25. Werner Krauss has developed the idea—which goes a step further than we do and in our view represents an exaggeration—that romanticism *as a whole* can best be seen as an extension of the *Aufklärung:* see his "Französische Aufklärung und deutsche Romantik," in *Wissenschaftliche Zeitschrift der Karl-Marx Universität Leipzig* No. 12 (1963); for a discussion of his thesis, see *Literaturwissenschaft und Sozialwissenschaften 8: Zur Modernität der Romantik*, Dieter Bäusch, ed. (Stuttgart: Metzler, 1977), 12ff.

26. M. Milner, *Le Romantisme I (1820–1843)* (Paris: Arthaud, 1973), 242.

27. Cf. H. Kals, *Die soziale Frage in der Romantik* (Cologne and Bonn: P. Hanstein, 1974), 7–15.

28. *Deutsches Wörterbuch von Jacob Grimm und Wilhelm Grimm* (Leipzig, 1893), 8:1156; Chateaubriand, *Génie du Christianisme*, II, iii, 9; Musset, *La Confession d'un enfant du siècle*, chap. 2.

29. Lukács, *La Théorie du roman* (Paris: Gonthier, 1963), 109.

30. See R. Sayre, *Solitude in Society: A Sociological Study in French Literature* (Cambridge: Harvard University Press, 1978).

31. *European Romanticism: Self-Definition*, ed. L. Furst (London: Methuen, 1980), 36.

32. A. Hauser, *Sozialgeschichte der Kunst und Literatur* (Munich: Beck, 1953), 2:182.

33. W. Benjamin, *Gesammelte Schriften*, 3 (Frankfurt: Suhrkamp, 1978), 560.

34. Marx-Engels, *Sur la littérature et l'art*, 287.

35. *European Romanticism*, 9.

36. Lukács, "La Philosophie romantique de la vie," in *L'Ame et les formes* (Paris: Gallimard, 1974), 84.

37. *European Romanticism*, 3; cf. Wordsworth's conception of poetry, 11–12.

38. W. Blake, *Poems and Prophecies* (London: Dent, 1975), 109–110.

39. A. Hauser, *The Social History of Art* (New York: Vintage, 1951), 3:208.

40. Cited by Träger in *Romantisme* 28–29: 99. This passage strikingly resembles another—on London—by Engels in *The Condition of the Working Class in England in 1844* (New York: J. W. Lovell Co., 1887), 17: "The hundreds of thousands of all classes and ranks crowding past each other, are they not all human beings with the same qualities and powers, and with the same interest in being happy? . . . And still they crowd by one another as though they had nothing in common, nothing to do with one another. . . . The brutal indifference, the unfeeling isolation of each in his private interest becomes the more repellent and offensive, the more these individuals are crowded together within a limited space."

41. Novalis, *Werke* (Stuttgart: Hädecke Verlag, 1924), 313–14.

42. See M. Löwy, *Pour une sociologie des intellectuels révolutionnaires* (Paris: P.U.F., 1976), 52–54.

43. G. Bernanos, *Les grands Cimetières sous la lune* (Paris: Plon, 1938), 27.

44. Bernanos, *Journal d'un curé de campagne* (Paris: Plon, 1936), 21, 212. On the subject, see the chapter on Bernanos in R. Sayre, *Solitude in Society*.

45. In *Philosophical Lectures*, cited by J. Droz, *Le Romantisme politique et Allemagne*, 19.

46. Edmund Burke, *Reflections on the Revolution in France* (London: University Tutorial Press), 56, 78–81, 90, 104, 109, etc. Anti-Semitic comments are frequent in Burke, as they are in many other romantic anticapitalist authors—socialists (e.g., Proudhon) as well as conservatives.

47. Ibid., 114.

48. Cited by R. Kirk, *The Conservative Mind* (Chicago: H. Regnery Co., 1954), 55.

49. Burke, *Reflections on the Revolution in France*, 99.

50. W. McGovern, *From Luther to Hitler*, 111–12. See also C. W. Parkin, "Burke and the Conservative Tradition," in David Thomson, ed., *Political Ideas* (London: Penguin, 1969), 128: "In the era of worldwide Marxism, Burke's polemic against the revolutionary idea . . . has not lost its relevance or cogency." Concerning Burke's "belief in democracy" (McGovern *dixit*), let us simply recall that for this declared enemy of popular sovereignty "a perfect democracy is the most shameless thing in the world" (*Reflections*, 97).

51. See Jean-Michel Palmier, *L'Expressionnisme comme révolte* (Paris: Payot, 1978) on the subject of Nazi art and culture.

52. Cited by Palmier, *L'Expressionnisme comme révolte*, 373.

53. G. Benn, *Essays. Reden. Vorträge* (Wiesbaden: Limes Verlag, 1959), 280.

54. Weber, *Gesammelte Aufsätze zur Wissenschaftslehre* (Tübingen: Mohr, 1922), 159.

55. Cf. Kurt Lenk, "Das tragische Bewusstsein in der Deutschen Soziologie," in *Studien und Materialien zur Soziologie der DDR* (Köln: West deutscher Verlag, 1964).

56. F. Tönnies, *Communauté et société* (Paris: P.U.F., 1944), 5, 236–37.

57. Tönnies responded to young disciples who favored the reestablishment of community by saying that one cannot combat the process of aging. Cf. J. Leif, *La Sociologie de Tönnies* (Paris: P.U.F., 1946), 71.

58. See D. O. Evans, *Le Socialisme romantique: Pierre Leroux et ses contemporains* (Paris: Marcel Rivière, 1948), 174.

59. "Signification de *Joseph Delorme* en 1830," in P. Barbéris, *Lectures du réel* (Paris: Éditions Sociales, 1973).

60. Ibid., p. 182.

61. In *Englische Fragmente*, cited in W. Rose, "Heine's Political and Social Attitude," in *Heinrich Heine: Two Studies of his Thought and Feeling* (Oxford: Oxford University Press, 1956), 16.

62. In the preface to the French edition of *Lutezia*, cited in ibid., 86.

63. The only exception would appear to be the Third World, where retarded socioeconomic development has allowed an authentic Jacobin-democratic romanticism to persist until recently, for example in the case of José Marti, Fidel Castro in his first period, etc.

64. Lukács, *Werke*, 7:182.

65. First limited edition, 1888; republication by Journeyman Press, London, 1962–1975.

66. Shelley, *Selected Poetry* (London: Oxford University Press, 1968), 292.

67. The quotation "Prophetic echoes flung dim melody" is from "Ode to Liberty," and all the others are from "Hellas."

68. Sismondi, *Études sur l'économie politique* (Paris: Trenttel et Wurtz, 1837), 1:209.

69. Sismondi, *Nouveaux Principes de l'économie politique* (2d ed.; Paris: Delaunay, 1827), 1:165–66.

70. Moses Hess, *Die heilige Geschichte der Menschheit, von einem Jünger Spinozas* (Stuttgart, 1837; reprint, Hildesheim: Gerstenberg, 1980), 249. Cf. also 235–37, 249, 257, etc.

71. Ibid., Cf. also A Cornu, *Karl Marx et Friedrich Engels* (Paris P.U.F., 1955), 1:237–38.

72. M. Hess, *Die europäische Triarchie* (1841), in *Ausgewählte Schriften* (Köln: Melzer Verlag, 1962), 91.

73. M. Hess, "Über das Geldwesen" (1845), in *Sozialistische Aufsätze 1841–47*, ed. Theodor Zlocisti (Berlin: Welt-Verlag, 1921), 168, 185. It is interesting to note that Hess appends to his essay a long quotation from *Queen Mab*, in which Shelley expresses horror at the modern idolatry of money.

74. Gustav Landauer, "Volk und Land: Dreissig sozialistische Thesen" (1907), in *Beginnen: Aufsätze über Sozialismus* (Köln: Marcon-Block-Verlag, 1924), 8–9.

75. Landauer, *Aufruf zum Sozialismus* (Berlin: Paul Cassirer, 1919), 47–48.

76. Landauer, "Der Bund," in *Beginnen*, 91–140.

77. Landauer, *Aufruf*, 100–102.

78. See *Tagträume vom aufrechten Gang: Sechs Interviews mit Ernst Bloch*, ed. Arno Münster (Frankfurt am Main: Suhrkamp, 1978), 27–28.

79. Ernst Bloch, *Geist der Utopie*, 2d ed., 1923 (Frankfurt: Suhrkamp, 1973), 37, 39.

80. Bloch, *Geist der Utopie*, 1st ed., 1918 (Frankfurt am Main: Suhrkamp, 1971), 410.

81. See M. Löwy, "Interview with Ernst Bloch," in *New German Critique* 9 (Fall 1976): 42.

82. Bloch, *Geist der Utopie* (1923), 294–95.

83. Bloch, *Thomas Münzer als Theologe der Revolution* (Frankfurt am Main: Suhrkamp, 1972), 156, 228, 230.

84. For Bloch "the fact that it was the Nazis and not the Left who gave political form to the utopian substance embedded in the Romantic anti-capitalism of the German peasantry and *Mittelstand*, does not reduce the authentic impulses to be discovered there." Anson Rabinbach, "Ernst Bloch's *Heritage of Our Times* and the Theory of Fascism," in *New German Critique* 11 (Spring 1977): 11.

85. Bloch, *Das Prinzip Hoffnung* (Frankfurt am Main: Suhrkamp, 1973), 3:1621.

86. On the mystical and apocalyptic aspects of his early work, see Arno Münster, *Utopie, Messianismus und Apokalypse in Frühwerk von Ernst Bloch* (Frankfurt am Main: Suhrkamp, 1982).

87. L. Löwenthal, *Erzählkunst und Gesellschaft* (Neuwied am Rhein: Luchterhand, 1971); Hauser, *Sozialgeschichte*, 2:185.

88. Droz, *Le Romantisme allemand et l'Etat*, 295; see also *Le Romantisme politique en Allemagne*, 28–29.

89. Gerda Heinrich, *Geschichtsphilosophische Positionen der deutschen Frühromantik* (Berlin: Akademie-Verlag, 1976), 60; E. Fischer, *The Necessity of Art*, 53.

90. Barbéris, "Mal du siècle," in *Romantisme et politique*, 165, 171.

91. K. Mannheim, "Das konservative Denken" (1927), in *Wissenssoziologie* (Neuwied am Rhein: Luchterhand, 1964), 452–54.

92. On this subject, see Lucien Goldmann, *Pour une sociologie du roman* (Paris: Gallimard, 1964), 31ff.

Romantic Anticapitalism: A Response to Sayre and Löwy

Michael Ferber

Sayre and Löwy have ventured bravely into two fields most scholars have learned to avoid as graveyards of reputations: the *definition* of romanticism, where the dragon of Lovejoy still lurks, and the *cause* of romanticism, which is even more perilous, being littered with fallen vulgar Marxists and other reductionists. With what success Sayre and Löwy have emerged from the enchanted land is the subject of this essay and, I hope, of essays by many other scholars, but I want to begin by paying tribute to the energy and ambition with which they have undertaken their mission. It is inspiring work. Their range of reference in three literatures over two centuries, their six types of romanticism and five subtypes, and their succinct descriptions of heterogeneous thinkers establish a full curriculum, a lifetime reading plan, indeed a whole program of scholarly research. To introduce "reification" into the subject, however well it may ultimately stand up, is a worthy contribution. Most important, they do their subject (and us) the honor of taking it seriously, of assuming the continuing relevance of romanticism and engaging it in dialogue. Whether they have correctly defined and explained romanticism matters less than their effort to retrieve it and enlist it in the service of a wider and deeper social vision.

The errors of great theories are more fruitful than the truths of little ones, as Nietzsche almost said, and that might serve as an epigraph to this response, in which I will try to restate Sayre and Löwy's key arguments and put them to various tests.

The main problems of their essay have to do with the definition of romanticism, and they are obvious enough. The romantic worldview, a "collective mental structure" shared not only by Shelley and Novalis but by Weber, Marcuse, and T. S. Eliot, is much broader than what is usually meant by "romanticism." Even those who have argued that the term is meaningless have ordinarily confined themselves to the "romantics" as commonly understood, or misunderstood: to certain major writers and artists of the late eighteenth and early nineteenth centuries. It is not to deny the value of Sayre and Löwy's construction of this worldview to point out that by casting their net so wide they have landed some fish few scholars would consider romantic, and that they have landed others they themselves would have to exclude by their own definition. For many of the characteristics they describe, such as disenchantment, reenchantment through the imagination, a feeling of exile, nostalgia, flight to the exotic, frustration of individual subjectivity, and even opposition to the "mercantile rationality of exchange value," could be found singly and in clusters before industrial capitalism began to dominate western Europe, and surely before "reification" began to pervade society. We can extend the worldview backward not only deep into the eighteenth century, with the English "preromantics" or poets of sensibility and the German *Sturm und Drang*, but into seventeenth-century England with its radical Protestant sects, perhaps into sixteenth-century Germany with its Anabaptists, and back through various Christian heresies to gnosticism, Neoplatonism, and the pastoral daydreams of the great ancient cities. Of course the number of decisivie features of the romantic worldview drops off as one goes back in history, but before we rule out any of these early movements we may ask why Novalis's attack on commercial life and greed or Bernanos's denunciation of money and bankers should be cited as distinctive; as Sayre and Löwy presented them, at least, they sound archaic, reminiscent of medieval diatribes against usury and cupidity, or of the tale of Timon of Athens.

What sets a limit to the earliest date of the romantic worldview is the key definition, "opposition to capitalism in the name of precapitalist values," and the elaboration that it is not necessarily capitalist *exploitation* that the romantics opposed but *reification*, whose effects penetrate all social classes. This may eliminate gnosticism and the Protestant sects, but it still raises important questions about eighteenth-century writers, and it seems to confuse the definition of romanticism, as a describable cultural phenomenon, with its cause, reification. In order to test the Sayre and Löwy thesis, then, we must look closely at reification and try to set some reasonable dates.

Definitions of Romanticism

Before turning to reification, however, I would like to take up something I found irritating at the opening of the essay: the dismissal of Arthur Lovejoy with the proverb "no smoke without fire." Lovejoy's arguments deserve, and have received, much more thoughtful replies than that. But the proverb itself is questionable in two respects: it is the wrong kind of proverb, and it is mistaken about smoke. Lovejoy was mainly concerned with the *definition* of romanticism, with identifying a common set of features, and he concluded that none existed. "No smoke without fire," on the other hand, is a little *explanation* of smoke, not a definition of it. Assuming that we can remold the smoke-and-fire proverb to make it a definition (I am not sure how), or that we can restate Lovejoy's project as the search for a common cause or source, the proverb is still too smoky in itself. For in fact there is no smoke *without at least one* fire. Lovejoy's main point, in these terms, was that the smoke was due to several different fires, burning different kinds of things, producing several different kinds of semantic smoke. Sayre and Löwy think there is only one kind of smoke and one fire—a drought of reification, perhaps, or an incendiary Luddite. They may be right, but they have not offered much of an argument.

They would have made a stronger argument, and shown a greater respect for previous scholarship in English (I am less competent to judge their use of French and German secondary works), had they frankly faced up to the problem of defining and then explaining romanticism in the narrow sense, before they folded it into their broad worldview type. They might have avoided the implication that the early romantics (such as Blake and Novalis) were responding to the same capitalism that the later Romantics (such as Weber and Marcuse) were. They say that capitalism has kept "its essential characteristics" from well before 1789 to the present day, but that is certainly debatable. We need a stronger sense of the particularities of "romanticism proper," from Herder to Hugo, say, and a closer look at contemporary capitalism. Then the more general type might be erected and tested against a changing capitalist "base," changing ideological expressions among changing social classes, and the influence of the original romanticism itself on the oppositional culture.

Let me briefly sketch the history of the debate on romanticism, familiar to English scholars, and suggest a way to proceed with it that might do justice to the complexity of romanticism and still connect compatibly with Sayre and Löwy's project. Lovejoy has of course been answered, though not to everyone's satisfaction, by René Wellek in a series of essays that survey English, German, and French literature and recent scholarship in all three languages, as Sayre and Löwy do, though they do not mention Wellek. He sees in period terms like "romanticism" not arbitrary labels but names for "systems of norms" (conventions, themes, philosophies, styles, and the like) "which dominate literature at a specific time," and he offers his now well-known set of three norms for romanticism: "imagination for the view of poetry, nature for the view of the world, and symbol and myth for poetic style."[1] Though one can chip away at each of these legs, I think the tripod stands up fairly well, as an abstract basis for defining the subject.

Morse Peckham offered another tripod, which he cleverly educed from Lovejoy's own book, *The Great Chain of Being:* organicism, dynamicism, and diversitarianism. Underlying these three is "dynamic organicism." Peckham later withdrew much of this claim, having discovered that organicism is an idea of the Enlightenment.[2]

Both Wellek and Peckham responded to Lovejoy's assertion that there is no "least common denominator" among the phenomena that are widely considered to be romanticism. The sets of least common denominators (LCDs) they proposed have not convinced everyone largely because they are so abstract, and anyone can think of difficult cases that squirm out from under the abstractions. The difficulty lies partly in the LCD approach itself. It may be truer to the widely felt diversity of romanticism to try a different kind of definition, Wittgenstein's notion of "family resemblances." Under this procedure, Wellek's and Peckham's three categories might be placed at the top of a longish list of frequently recurring traits. Just as two members of the same family may share no distinctive features, but each may share several features with several other members, so no single criterion will be decisive for determining if a work or author is romantic, but two works or authors that have nothing (nontrivially) in common may still be brought into the fold when they are matched against a rich matrix of characteristic traits. To decide which features to adduce, which are most important, how many are needed to certify a work as romantic—these decisions will still give us plenty to argue over, but this approach ought to be more hospitable to the variety of current research on romanticism than the LCD approach.

A list of Romantic "family resemblances," then, might begin like this:

imagination for the view of poetry
nature for the view of the world
symbol and myth for poetic style
organicism
dynamism
diversitarianism
"a profound change, not primarily in belief, but in the spatial projection of
    reality" (Northrop Frye)
"internalization of quest romance" (Harold Bloom)
"natural supernaturalism" (Carlyle, and M. H. Abrams)
"spilt religion" (T. E. Hulme)

These last four all have to do with what Feuerbach called the anthropological "secret" of Christian theology and man's recovery of his projected or alienated essence.[3] This key religious dimension of romanticism could be stated in many other ways (Fairchild called it "a tissue of heresies"),[4] but these four will do. (It is surprising that Sayre and Löwy neglect this side of romanticism, since it is very prominent in German thought as well as English.) The list might continue with less inclusive features, such as these:

new emphasis on lyric, including lyrical drama and epic
rise of autobiography, including *Bildingsroman* and *-gedicht*

a distinctive kind of irony, the "romantic comic" which "annihilates the finite," including itself (Jean Paul)

the fragment as typical form

foregrounding of epistemology, of interaction between mind and nature, as central theme

new sense of history; uniqueness of historical periods and national cultures

dislike of science (or Newtonian science) and utilitarianism

privileging of art, or aesthetic perception, or "play," as highest human product or faculty

typical themes: the unique world of the child

primitives, solitaries, noble savages, outcast poets

ideal community, fraternity

Prometheus

incest

ruins

typical metaphors: lamp, as opposed to mirror (Abrams)

correspondent breeze, Aeolian harp (Abrams)

birds (as poets)

And so on.

No doubt each of these features can be found in nonromantic writers, but as more and more features are invoked they should eliminate more and more writers until only romantic writers remain. There is in the end something circular about this procedure, of course, just as there is with Sayre and Löwy's general type: having defined romanticism as opposition to capitalism in the name of precapitalist values, and produced an impressive roster of such "romantics," they can then show that what they all have in common is opposition to capitalism in the name of precapitalist values, which then appears to be the least common denominator of romanticism. But these circles are no more vicious than the "hermeneutical circle" that governs any cultural inquiry.

In their opening paragraphs, Sayre and Löwy casually name several items of the sort that could join a list of distinctive features of romanticism in the narrow sense, such as mythology, Dionysian religion, and "a longing for a harmonious relationship between man and nature." These could have served as the start of a definition, but definitions are left behind as Sayre and Löwy rather enigmatically decide that romanticism is an "undecipherable enigma, a labyrinth with no exit," and so on, even though they already know what romanticism is. They refer, for example, to studies that have "identified some important traits which are to be found in most if not all romantic authors," implying that they know that some authors are romantic even though they lack these important traits. Sayre and Löwy seem impatient with the original, historically specific phenomenon of romanticism (or phenomena: they use both singular and plural) and so, after curtly putting down Lovejoy and Schmitt, they pass to their *Weltanschauung* type and the question of reification.

Reification and Romanticism

Reification, the illusory objectivity of the products of our work, brought about by the fragmentation of the labor process and the transformation into commodities of, ultimately, everything, including human labor and time itself: when did this effect of capitalism arise and begin to dominate or pervade social relationships? It is not the kind of process to which one can set a date, but if we are to take romanticism as a response to it then we are looking at the middle of the eighteenth century, and that strikes me as too early. One can reply, certainly, that artists are the antennae of the race, and Sayre and Löwy do mention seventeenth-century French forerunners, but what I miss in their theory is a sense of how capitalism made itself felt—unevenly, at varying tempos in different countries and regions—outside the workplace and marketplace, and then a sense of how the various responses to it began to cohere into something we can identify as the romantic worldview.

All typologies and epochal categories meet difficulties when origins and histories are looked into, and the difficulties this one meets may be no worse than those encountered by, say, "possessive individualism," or by any other. If romanticism is a collective mental structure, it obviously arose *somehow*, among a few individuals at particular times and places. But the problem of "genetic structuralism" (Lucien Goldmann's difficult phrase) as applied to the romantic worldview is compounded by Sayre and Löwy's typological or epochal view of capitalism itself. They say that capitalism "has kept its essential characteristics, the same characteristics that stimulated the earliest romantic revolt," ever since that early revolt. We may wonder if the essential characteristics of late or postindustrial capitalism, which are evidently stimulating many romantic responses today, are the same as those of two centuries ago. Is it only a question of degree, of intensity, of depth of social permeation? Is it only industrial capitalism we are talking about, as opposed to mercantile and finance capitalism? In which case we need to make comparisons with the noncapitalist industrialized nations of the twentieth century (unless we widen the definition of "capitalism" to include them as well): it is possible we are seeing in romanticism a reaction more to industrialization than to capitalism itself.

I raise these questions not to refute the reification thesis but to open it up for investigation. Indeed I think the thesis sets a fascinating series of subjects for many scholars to pursue, and it could transform the field of romantic studies, not to mention socialist studies. In the remainder of this essay, then,

I will bring up some specific problems, not very systematically, as points of departure for further work (or perhaps work already done: one of the virtues of the reification thesis is that its interdisciplinary demands make one feel a lot more ignorant than one did).

Capitalism in some of its forms is very old, and so is opposition to it. The Old Testament prohibition of usury and John of Patmos's "mark of the beast" (a license to buy or sell) are early examples; so is the contrast between usury and inherited or landed wealth as found in Horace and other classical writers. *The Merchant of Venice* presents a threefold opposition among inherited wealth (Portia), finance capital or usury (Shylock), and mercantile capital or merchant-adventuring (Antonio); the retreat to Belmont at the end is certainly "romantic" in one old and persistent sense. Buying and selling, getting and spending, are targets of much of the moral and religious literature of the West since ancient times, and it would be interesting to trace the connections between this tradition and romanticism, with its less specific target, the social consequences of the unleashed market.

Within the early romantic period we find intense protests against the pervasive effects of capitalism, but some of them vent an "archaic" anger. Blake's "London," for instance, engraved in 1792, begins with an evocation of the complete permeation of London by commercialism, by "chartering":

> I wander thro' each charter'd street,
> Near where the charter'd Thames does flow.
> And mark in every face I meet
> Marks of weakness, marks of woe.

Reification would seem to be in command. But Blake does not speak of alienation and fragmentation, the lonely crowd or loss of *Gemeinschaft:* he sees the evil as a kind of commercial slavery, the buying and selling of people. The chimney sweeper whose cry appalls the church (which has done nothing to relieve his condition) has been sold by his father, as we learn in another Blake poem, to a master who will exploit him. The hapless soldier whose sigh turns to blood on the palace walls has been impressed into service and paid his shilling. The third young victim is a harlot, who is bought or rented for a night's exploitation, and who sends a curse or blight on marriage, which, as Blake makes clear elsewhere, is a twin of harlotry, a commercial transaction like any other. Church and state create these commodities in youthful human flesh and are in turn marked or infected by them: the whole society is trapped, manacled, enslaved from infancy to death. The poem's unrelieved bleakness and the sense of thoroughness or totality have a modern ring, but the evils Blake names are very old. It is not surprising that a poet, especially one steeped in religious language as Blake was, should rely on traditional imagery as he gropes to understand an overwhelming modern experience; on the other hand, Blake's example might remind us that the effects of reification in 1792 were not yet felt by sensitive antennae as outweighing other miseries, brought about by money, markets, and greed.

As for the marriage market, it would also be interesting to trace romanticism's affiliations to the protests or compensatory daydreams of women locked in loveless marriages. From at least as far back as the courtly love poems (the provenance of the word "romance"), there is a fitful tradition of protest by these slaves of patriarchal commercial or legal transactions. It revives strongly among male romantic writers in England (Blake and Shelley notably), but the romantic period is also the era of Mary Wollstonecraft, Mary Shelley (whose *Frankenstein* is a central romantic document), and Madame de Staël.

Another problem in chronology that the Sayre and Löwy theory must cope with is the early appearance of romanticism in Germany, at least as early as in England (and earlier if we take *Sturm und Drang* as romanticism), despite Germany's famous economic backwardness. It complicates matters interestingly that the *Sturm und Drang* and later *Romantik* had an "English" cast, in the influence of Edward Young's *Conjectures* (translated in 1760) and then Macpherson's "Ossian" songs and Percy's *Reliques*, not to mention Shakespeare. Raymond Williams has shown that the terms in which Young dismisses imitation in art, as "a sort of *manufacture*, wrought up by those *mechanics*, *art* and *labour*, out of pre-existent materials not their own," anticipated the industrial processes about to transform English society.[5] The songs of Ossian and the ballads Percy collected can be taken as a search for an earlier culture, prebourgeois, preurban, even pre-English. This English "prescience" before its own industrial revolution may have stimulated German culture, but the early flowering of romanticism in Germany (which then had a major influence on English romanticism) and its growth into the most intense and most medievalist of romanticisms, remains a difficulty for the response-to-capitalism thesis.

At what point did reification begin to dominate the various European (and American) societies? When, in Lukács's words, was the "commodity structure" able "to penetrate society in all its aspects and to remould it in its own image"? For it was not enough that factories reduced the inherent, qualitative, "organic" rhythms of labor to mechanical, clock-regulated fragments, for there were factories and mineworks in ancient times and of course there are many nonmechanized laborers even today. The whole of society, according to Lukács, had to be transformed by the commodity structure before the factories themselves could reach their potential. Karl Polanyi has an interesting argument that ought to be useful in establishing a chronology. It was only by gradual stages over many centuries that money, land, and labor were brought under the category of commodity and allowed to enter the market. Of these three "fictitious commodities" (as opposed to the true commodities of goods and services), money and land were released from most restrictions, such as the laws of usury and entail, well before the industrial revolution; it was only labor that could not be mobilized according to the dictates of the market. The Speenhamland system of grants in aid of wages (tied to the price of bread), established in 1795, was only the latest of many laws that subsidized the poor and tied them to the parish, thus interfering with the market's setting of wages and the movement of laborers to the site of employment. The Anti-Combination Acts of 1799–1800 removed the right of workers to form unions (repealed, but with some restrictions left, in 1824), and then in 1834 the New Poor Law abolished the remaining protections for the laboring population (except for deliberately dreadful workhouses) and exposed them to the full force of the market mechanism.[6] It created what Weber would call "formally free labor" and completed the legal basis of Britain's march into pure commodification. No single date, of course, can have anything more than symbolic significance for a process as vast and cumulative as commodification, but 1834 is still a date inconveniently late for romanticism.

The Division of Labor

The moral consequences of the division of labor, particularly the division of manual labor, until the well-rounded skill of the craftsman was degraded to the repetitive machine-driven responses of a factory "hand," were searchingly explored by theorists we consider classic liberals, such as Adam Ferguson and Adam Smith, before being taken up by the romantics. In *The Wealth of Nations* Smith wrote,

> The man whose whole life is spent in performing a few simple operations, of which the effects too are, perhaps, always the same, or very nearly the same, has no occasion to exert his understanding, or to exercise his invention in finding out expedients for removing difficulties which never occur. He naturally loses, therefore, the habit of such exertion, and generally becomes as stupid and ignorant as it is possible for a human creature to become.[7]

Schiller's famous version of this is in *The Aesthetic Education of Man*, Sixth Letter:

> Eternally chained to only one single little fragment of the whole, Man himself grew to be only a fragment; with the monotonous noise of the wheel he drives everlastingly in his ears, he never develops the harmony of his being, and instead of imprinting humanity upon his nature he becomes merely the imprint of his occupation, of his science.[8]

Schiller's wheel finds an analogue in Blake's "intricate wheels invented, wheel without wheel"—cogs in great machines—invented to perplex and bind English youth

>   that they may grind
> And polish brass & iron hour after hour laborious task!
> Kept ignorant of its use, that they might spend the days of wisdom
> In sorrowful drudgery, to obtain a scanty pittance of bread:
> In ignorance to view a small portion & think that All,
> And call it Demonstration: blind to the simple rules of life.
>   (*Jerusalem* 65.23–28)

Hölderlin's Hyperion, visiting Germany after an adventurous life in Greece, concludes,

> I can think of no people more at odds with themselves than the Germans. You see artisans, but no men, priests, but no men, masters and servants, but no men, minors and adults, but no men—is this not like a battlefield on which hacked-off hands and arms and every other member lie pell-mell, while the life-blood flows from them to vanish in the sand?[9]

This romantic theme is another continuity with the Enlightenment tradition, which Sayre and Löwy remind us had a complex influence on the romantics. The Enlightenment attack on priesthood, which it inherited from Protestantism, is almost a special case of its critique of the division of labor, the first division of labor being the separation of priests from the laity. That also represented the first self-alienation or "self-diremption" of humanity, as it projected its human essence onto the heavens. So the characteristic romantic project of recovering humanity's upward projection of its spirit gave terms for understanding the continued division and redivision of manual (and mental) labor under the relentless mechanization of industry. Sayre and Löwy put it well in saying that romanticism shows "a kind of radicalization from within the Enlightenment nucleus." This somewhat resembles Geoffrey Hartman's formula (though with a parenthetical hedge), "Romanticism seems to me a viable *poetic* form of enlightenment (or postenlightenment) thought."[10] These are suggestive ways to study the development of romantic thought up to modern times in tandem with the mechanization and "Taylorization" of labor.

Utilitarianism

Romanticism tended to wage war with the ideologies of the times, with the mind-forged manacles, more than with the social conditions or economic structures that nurtured them, though, as we have seen, romantic heads were not always in the clouds. Systems of thought, such as utilitarianism or

Newtonianism, are the main antagonists in romantic writings. Though Sayre and Löwy can find a few representatives, it was not easy for romantics to be liberals; they tended to go far to the left of it or to react against it to the right. Though they may have welcomed some of the political reforms liberals brought about, they shrank from "this eternal whirlpool of universal utility," as Schleiermacher put it, "in which everything good is allowed to go down."[11] It is as if they took utility, which of course in Mill's and Bentham's theories had a broad, even humane, content, as a cloak for the economic category of exchange-value, now compelling all thought to conform to its structure. Dickens's *Hard Times* and Dostoevsky's *Notes from Underground* are classic later attacks on it, but it is the early romantics who draw the battle lines. The young Shelley, for instance, under the influence of Godwin, praises utility as morality itself (in his Notes to *Queen Mab*), but in a few years he is widening "true utility" to include "the delight of love and friendship, the ecstasy of the admiration of nature, the joy of the perception and still more of the creation of poetry" (*Defence of Poetry*), as if to smuggle the highest precapitalist values into a capitalist ideology.

Reification and Form

Have romantic artists, whether of the first generation or of its many successors, resisted reification in the *form* of their works? David Punter has claimed that Blake did so, largely by being difficult. Invoking Marcuse and others on the one-dimensionality of thought in an age of reification, Punter argues that "Blake writes difficult poetry because to write with ease and facility is itself delusive in a situation where language is tainted with domination."[12] I think this is right, though not the whole story, for Blake also seems to have feared prosecution if he said what he honestly thought. He was indicted for sedition (though acquitted) for something he said to a soldier, and a few years later he wrote, in *Jerusalem*, "deep dissimulation is the only defence an honest man has left."

Theodor Adorno is the great analyst of how reification inscribes itself in art, and how some art resists it. To resist it, art must strive to make itself irreconcilable or indigestible to the commercial purveyors and most "consumers" of art—by its autonomy, asceticism, irony, defamiliarization, and absolute devotion to the inherent logic of its formal means. Hence Schönberg and Beckett, whom no one would call romantic, are Adorno's touchstones, and he criticizes Stravinsky and Wagner in part for their neoromantic regression to (falsely) primeval "pre-individual" music. Meanwhile the lyrics of popular songs, kitsch, nature paintings, and Muzak all thrive on recycled bits of high romanticism. There are utopian moments in romantic literature, especially the lyric poetry, with its expression of loneliness (in a society that papers it over with phony *Gemütlichkeit*) and reconciliation with nature (in a society that declares "natural" what it feels like doing, such as exploiting nature).[13] But the question of romanticism's resistance to, vulnerability to, and even collaboration with commodification remains (I think) to be explored.

One might begin by studying the "consumer revolution" of eighteenth-century England, the dramatic and sustained rise in material consumption and prosperity, noticed by many observers of the time, which *preceded* many of the events that we think of as definitive of the industrial revolution. As early as 1690, economists were praising the power of consumer desire to drive the economy upward, and it "is not Necessity that causeth the Consumption," according to Nicholas Barbon. "Nature may be Satisfied with little; but it is the wants of the Mind, Fashion and the desire of Novelties and Things Scarce that causeth Trade." Wants of the mind are engendered by emulation of one's betters, by "keeping up" with and surpassing one's peers.[14] Thus the romantics' turn toward nature, or toward Bohemia, may be seen in part as a withdrawal from peer pressure to consume, and the "simplicity" and "sincerity" of many of their works, especially lyrics and ballads, as a conscious rejection of the fashionable gewgaws that emulative eighteenth-century poetry had felt obliged to acquire.

Form is not considered by Sayre and Löwy, neither the form of individual works nor—and this is more fundamental to their project—the form of the romantic worldview itself. The features of this worldview that they list, such as social fragmentation, homelessness, quest for a lost totality, and so on, are mainly themes, elements of the worldview's content, not form. On the other hand, Lucien Goldmann, whose path they are following, investigated form as well as content in his ambitious and controversial project of finding "homologies" between worldviews and the social structures that generate them and between both of these and the economic infrastructures that support them. Sayre and Löwy do have some interesting passages on how capitalism both summons individual subjectivity into existence and then frustrates its free expression, and (at the end) on the possible social bases of romanticism's different varieties. It may have been wise not to press any further the question of just how the romantic response to capitalism arose and spread, but it is disappointing that they have not taken up the full implications of Goldmann's work—not only homologies, but the difference between ideology and worldview, and the idea of the "possible consciousness" of a social class or group.

Romanticism Today

"Romanticism is an essential part of modern culture." Sayre and Löwy cite the best-selling *Dei unendliche Geschichte*, now a best-seller in the United

States as well, and Tolkien, *E.T.*, and *Star Wars*. But if these are instances of contemporary romanticism, then the question arises whether it has anything left to teach us. I do not find anything very radical, searching, or thought-provoking in these works, either in their content or their form, whereas I am continually drawn to the early romantic period for sustenance and challenge. For all their charm and wit, these twentieth-century works reduce the intelligence, subtlety, and fundamental seriousness of "high" romanticism to magic and entertainment. In fact, they belong less to the line of romanticism than to the archaic tradition of romance; they are re-externalizations of the quest romance that romanticism had internalized (to use Harold Bloom's terms). The Jedi doctrine of "the Force," which slightly resembles the Zen discipline of a samurai swordsman, becomes megalomaniacal claptrap when it is enlisted as an aid in destroying an enormous high-technology empire. The truths of E.T., lovable though he may be, we can find better expressed inside fortune cookies.

No doubt, if we work at it, we can find a utopian moment in the disdain for mighty imperial powers, or for the adult world of police and hospitals, and in the pastorialism of quiet little planets, children in the suburbs, forests full of Ewoks, and shires full of Hobbits. But these books and movies (especially *Star Wars*) positively discourage the kind of thinking needed to translate their terms to contemporary society and to make comparisons; there is barely time to think at all and little reason to do so. We need not take as severe a stance as Adorno takes toward modern art to see these works, for the most part, as products of reification and the regression of attentiveness by their "consumers." And it may be that, as serious art, the romantic tradition is exhausted, its emancipatory moment lost in its susceptibility to being ransacked for effects, for quotable bits, as it devolves into manipulatory Muzak and kitsch. Only, perhaps, through the alienation-effects of modernism, now themselves growing too familiar, can the revolutionary *sincerity* of romanticism be rescued, as in, say, Azdak's anarchistic tribunal in Brecht's *Caucasian Chalk Circle*, or the fitful yearnings and dreamings of the lost characters in Beckett's plays.

I think Sayre and Löwy are right, however, that as an ingredient in the peace, ecology, and feminist movements romanticism remains alive and brings something valuable to them. It helps sustain them in bleak environments not only by offering visions of a future world at peace, its people living in balance with nature and in democratic nonpatriarchal relations with each other, but also by nurturing an alternative culture here and now. As it grows more and more obvious that unbridled capitalist (and state socialist) rapacity and technology have brought us to the brink of disaster, whether by the hydrogen bomb, biological warfare, nuclear power plant accidents, the depletion of the ozone layer, the greenhouse effect, or a massive break in the food chain, more and more people abandon their faith in material progress and turn to other images and values. No doubt much of the response is merely escapist (not that I question the motive to escape)—into "art," into neoromance—but some of it is tough-minded and activist. In societies that practice thorough ideological control of their populations (that is, all modern industrial societies), to believe in an alternative, even to conceive of an alternative, is an act of resistance. To borrow E. P. Thompson's phrase for William Morris's purpose, romanticism's role could be the "education of desire,"[15] without which we are either resigned or feckless.

We should remember, too, that the religious revival America has undergone over the past fifteen years or so has had a left thrust as well as a right. At the center of the resistance to America's low-intensity wars in Central America, to the nuclear arms race, to the spread of poverty and hunger are the churches. In Germany and Holland, too, the churches have anchored the great opposition to the cruise and Pershing missiles. Something within Christianity (and American Judaism), or within their institutions, remains partly unassimiliated into the dominant culture, resistant to commercialism, the relativism of moral values, the blandishments of power. Right-wing romantics used to enter the church; today the church may be the last home of left-wing romanticism.

One large question remains. If the motivating ideal of the most progressive social movements is in large part hostility to "progress," we may wonder if the key term "precapitalist" is not misleading. That romanticism is a rebellion against capitalism in the name of precapitalist values suggests that there is another kind of rebellion in the name of postcapitalist values. What might these values be? A belief in "progress" underlies these terms, a belief in the vector of history passing inevitably through capitalism to scientific socialism. Most of those who have held this belief have also held values that seem to be neither precapitalist nor postcapitalist (whatever the latter might be) but precisely capitalist: more material goods, more comforts, expanding control of nature, "modernization," and so on. It was not perverse of Simone Weil to describe Marxism as "the highest spiritual expression of bourgeois society";[16] it may have been the utopian and romantic side of Marx that kept him revolutionary, not his analyses of capitalism.

Strictly speaking, there is only one value in capitalism, exchange value. All other values, "use values," are as various as there are uses of things, as various as life, but they do not enter the world of capitalism except as a "return of the repressed" to cause a crisis. What capitalism represses are not precapitalist values per se, though early capitalism waged explicit warfare against feudalism, but all values other than exchange value. In seeking pockets of resistance against capitalism, where else can we look but at survivals of older traditions, religious, ethnic, aesthetic, or whatever? A postcapitalist society exists only in our imaginations, and we must draw from precapitalist societies, as the only other societies ever to exist (not counting the very problematic "actually existing socialist" societies), for evidence that it is possible. It does not follow that we must adopt any particular precapitalist practice, or that we must deny the free market's historic power to emancipate individuals from traditional bonds. The values in whose name we oppose capitalism are transhistorical, if not transcendental: nonviolence, participatory democracy, the dignity of the individual, equal rights, respect for the natural environment, sustainable economic systems, and so on. Versions of these values have been found in many cultures for thousands of years. Perhaps only in postcapitalist (or postindustrial) conditions will it be possible to achieve societies with such ideals. Perhaps, too, we will want to preserve some measure of capitalism, of small-scale free enterprise, for example, as an institution that promotes some kinds of freedom. (Goldmann, in *The Philosophy of the Enlightenment*, 1968, is aware of the deep connection between production for market exchange and the values of the Enlightenment—freedom, equality, toleration—that any future socialist society should want to preserve.) But to decide such questions, those who try to reconstruct society will have to appeal to values, and these values may be found anywhere, not least as they are embodied in the great romantic literature of the last two centuries.

Notes

1. René Wellek, "The Concept of Romanticism in Literary History," *Comparative Literature* 1 (1949): 1–23, 147–72; reprint in Wellek, *Concepts of Criticism* (New Haven: Yale University Press, 1963). This replies to A. O. Lovejoy, "On the Discrimination of Romanticisms," *PMLA* 39 (1924): 229–53; reprint in Lovejoy, *Essays in the History of Ideas* (Baltimore: Johns Hopkins University Press, 1948). See also Wellek, "Romanticism Re-examined," in *Romanticism Reconsidered*, ed. Northrop Frye (New York: Columbia University Press, 1963) and in Wellek, *Concepts of Criticism*.

2. Morse Peckham, "Toward a Theory of Romanticism," *PMLA* 61 (1951): 5–23; and "Toward a Theory of Romanticism: Reconsiderations," *Studies in Romanticism* 1 (1961): 1–8.

3. Northrop Frye, "The Drunken Boat: The Revolutionary Element in Romanticism," in *Romanticism Reconsidered*, ed. Northrop Frye; reprint Frye, *The Stubborn Structure* (Ithaca: Cornell University Press, 1970); see also Frye, *A Study of English Romanticism* (New York: Random House, 1968), chapter 1; Harold Bloom, "The Internalization of Quest Romance," in *The Ringers in the Tower* (Chicago: University of Chicago Press, 1971); M. H. Abrams, *Natural Supernaturalism* (New York: Norton, 1971); T. E. Hulme, "Romanticism and Classicism," in *Speculations* (New York: Harcourt, 1936); Ludwig Feuerbach, *The Essence of Christianity*, trans. George Eliot (1841; London: n.p., 1854).

4. Hoxie Neale Fairchild, *Religious Trends in English Poetry* 3: 1780–1830, *Romantic Faith* (New York: Columbia University Press, 1949).

5. Raymond Williams, *Culture and Society, 1780–1950* (London: Chatto and Windus, 1958), pt. 1, ch. 2.

6. Karl Polanyi, *The Great Transformation* (New York: Rinehart, 1944), pt. 2.

7. Adam Smith, *The Wealth of Nations*, ed. Edwin Cannan (1776; New York: Modern Library, 1937), 734.

8. Friedrich Schiller, *On the Aesthetic Education of Man*, trans. Reginald Snell (1795; London: Routledge, 1954), "Sixth Letter."

9. Friedrich Hölderlin, *Hyperion*, trans. Willard Trask (1797–99; New York: New American Library, 1965), 164.

10. Geoffrey Hartman, *The Fate of Reading* (Chicago: University of Chicago, 1975), 277.

11. Friedrich Schleiermacher, *On Religion: Speeches to its Cultured Despisers*, trans. John Oman (1799; New York: Harper, 1958), 21.

12. David Punter, "Blake: Creative and Uncreative Labour," *Studies in Romanticism* 16 (1977): 535–61.

13. Theodor W. Adorno, *Philosophy of Modern Music*, trans. Anne G. Mitchell and Wesley V. Blomster (1948; New York: Seabury, 1973); Adorno, "Lyric Poetry and Society" (1957), trans. Bruce Mayo, *Telos* 20 (1974): 56–71.

14. Neil McKendrick, John Brewer, and J. H. Plumb, *The Birth of a Consumer Society: The Commercialization of Eighteenth-Century England* (Bloomington: University of Indiana Press, 1982), esp. ch. 1.

15. E. P. Thompson, *William Morris: Romantic to Revolutionary*, rev. ed. (New York: Pantheon, 1977), pt. 4.

16. Simone Weil, "Fragments 1933–38," in *Oppression and Liberty*, trans. Arthur Wills and John Petrie (London: Routledge, 1958), 131.

The Fire Is Still Burning: An Answer to Michael Ferber

Robert Sayre and Michael Löwy

We are well aware of the limitations of our paper, and the kind of criticism offered by Michael Ferber is welcome; it will help us to rethink, reformulate, and develop our analysis. We agree with a number of his suggestions: it is true, as he contends, for instance, that the *religious dimension* of romanticism must be dealt with more thoroughly, since it is one of the most significant expressions of the romantic desire for a "re-enchantment of the world" and for the restitution of an all-embracing, spiritual *Kultur.* We will bring up some other of Ferber's interesting contributions further on in this answer. Even when we do not agree with him, we find his critical remarks stimulating and productive.

There are, however, a certain number of major points that we wish to debate. Our first disagreement relates, of course, to the issue of *definition.* Ferber is unhappy ("irritated") with our dismissal of Arthur Lovejoy, who in his opinion deserves a more thoughtful reply. What we meant by our "smoke-and-fire" metaphor was only this: the widespread use of the term "romanticism" to designate very different cultural phenomena is an objective social and historical fact ("smoke"). Instead of telling people that they should stop using the word (Lovejoy's method), one should attempt to discover the reason that lies behind this fact (the "fire"). Lovejoy's approach seems to us sterile. It could in fact be applied to almost any term in politics ("Left" and "Right," for instance), in literature ("realism"), or in economics ("feudalism") without increasing our understanding in the slightest. Let us take the concept of "capitalism." It is easy to show the enormous difference between the English economy of the nineteenth century and the U.S. economy today, or between the German economy around 1900 and the Mexican economy today. A purely empirical approach would suggest that there is no sense in using the same term to define such different realities. And some liberal political economists have indeed proposed that the concept should not be used at all. This having been said, though, we acknowledge that Lovejoy deserves a more thorough and systematic refutation.

In our opinion, Wellek, Peckham, and other proponents of "least common denominators" do not offer a convincing alternative to Lovejoy's nominalism. Ferber's use of the Wittgensteinian notion of "family resemblances" is more interesting and flexible, but shares the same methodological approach. In our view, the main shortcoming of all such lists of features is *empiricism;* they remain on the surface of the phenomena. As descriptive surveys of the romantic cultural world, they may be helpful, but their cognitive value is limited. First of all, they are inevitably *arbitrary:* why select this and not that other trait? To qualify as romantic, must a work exhibit all the features, or are some of them sufficient? Above all, these lists leave unanswered *the* main question: what holds all this together? Why are these elements associated? What is the unifying force behind all these traits?

What is needed is a different method than one that looks for another and still another "denominator" or "resemblance" to add to a list that is necessarily infinite. One must attempt to discover the *concept,* the *Begriff* (in the Hegelian-Marxist sense of the term), of romanticism, which can explain its innumerable forms of appearance, its diverse and manifold empirical traits. Our own hypothesis may be wrong, but it is an attempt to go beyond the empiricist approach, using a dialectical method of definition/explanation. Of course we do not deny the usefulness of empirical and descriptive studies of romanticism and its various characteristics (we paid homage to the German tradition in this area); but in order to understand romantic culture one has to grasp its inner core, its essential principle.

It is not that we were "impatient" with the "original" romanticism, but rather that we took notice of a much broader cultural and social use of the concept, and tried to find the reason behind it. We did not invent the terms "political romanticism," "economic romanticism," or "neoromanticism"; they are commonly used and show that we are dealing with a phenomenon much broader than an early nineteenth-century literary school. We think that our definition makes it possible to better understand *both* the artistic movement "from Herder to Hugo" *and* the other cultural forms usually designated as romantic. If our *Weltanschauung* approach is correct, any definition that returns to the traditional, purely literary (and historically limited) concept would be a methodological regression. Of course, concrete studies in the early romantic literature are essential to grasp the genesis and meaning of the phenomena, but to *reduce* romanticism to this dimension alone is in our opinion unjustified. One of the main advantages of a dialectical approach to cultural phenomena is precisely that it breaks down the artificial barriers set up by the academic "disciplines" between literature, politics, philosophy, religion, etc.

Ferber also criticizes us for not following Goldmann's program, which calls for finding "homologies" between worldviews and social structures. But our definition of romantic anticapitalism takes as one of its starting points a very important idea from Goldmann's sociology of the novel. The novel is seen as a form of resistance to bourgeois society and the market; as such, it represents the feelings and aspirations of "problematic" individuals—artists, writers, philosophers, theologians, etc.—who remain oriented in their behavior by qualitative values opposed to reification and the absolute reign of exchange value. We broadened this hypothesis and reformulated it (although without using the more debatable concept of "homology"). Goldmann hesitates in defining the social basis for this opposition, attributing it either to certain sections of the middle classes (from which writers are recruited) or to a diffuse aspiration toward qualitative values, related to human nature per se. We attempted to suggest a more specific analysis of the social categories and groups tending toward the romantic worldview.

Another major area in which Ferber raises doubts about our analysis concerns the question of the root cause or causes of the romantic phenomenon. Early on in his text Ferber introduces the theme by suggesting that we in fact confuse the definition of the latter with its cause. His remarks seem to advocate a clean separation between definition and cause. But surely an approach that wishes to be both dialectical and materialist must reject any such absolute dichotomy between the description of a thing and the relating of it to a concrete socioeconomic context. And indeed, although we do not in fact *confuse* definition and cause (the definition is not exhausted by simple reference to the cause), the two are integrally linked in our essay. The "cause" or source of romanticism is *contained within* its definition, since romanticism is seen as a particular kind of response to the development of capitalism, a response whose general characteristics we attempt to outline.

Ferber identifies our principle of causality as "reification," and although he finds our hypothesis interesting he hesitates throughout to accept its validity. At one point, he entertains the question whether romanticism as a whole may not be a reaction to industrialization rather than to capitalism and reification. At other points, he seems to suggest that while reification may be at the heart of *some* manifestations of romanticism, others involve rather the perception of social misery and oppression (Blake), the consequences of the division of labor (Schiller, Hölderlin), etc. And in several places he questions our basic premise that the "essential characteristics" of capitalism remain the same throughout its entire evolution.

Here again it seems that Ferber is separating factors that should be dialectically conceived as a *Gesamtkomplex*. In our view, the category of totality is crucial. Seen from that perspective, capitalism is a multifaceted whole, all of the aspects of which cohere indissolubly together. The market, money, free labor, the intensified division of labor, industrialization, "reification," and the fragmentation of social relations: all these elements or dimensions of capitalism mentioned by Ferber, seemingly as separate entities, must be understood as integral parts of a common matrix. It is this matrix—capitalism—that represents for us the root source underlying the romantic consciousness in its diverse forms over the entire course of its history. The conception of capitalism as a totality, and as possessing the same "essential characteristics" now as in its early stages (in spite of important transformations within the basic frame), is of course not peculiar to us, but is rather that of Marxism in general.

The question of the nature of the "cause" is related to another theme running through Ferber's remarks—that of the origin, or genesis, of romanticism on the one hand and of the phenomenon to which it is causally related on the other. As Ferber rightly points out, elements of both romanticism and capitalism can be traced all the way back to antiquity. Yet as a *Gesamtkomplex* each is a specifically modern development. It is of course impossible to establish an absolute date for either, but in both cases the essential "qualitative leap" does seem to occur at approximately the same time (and in the same places)—in the second half of the eighteenth century with the industrial revolution on the one hand, and on the other with the appearance of the first authors and literary/intellectual trends that can be considered fully romantic.

Ferber seems to believe that reification, as an isolatable factor, appears considerably later than this period, citing 1834 as a "symbolic" date for its emergence. But if capitalism is a totality, reification should be part and parcel of it from its inception. Indeed, even before capitalism as such is fully constituted, societies in which money and the market play a significant role can call forth protests—more limited in their scope than truly romantic ones—against the reification of human relations. And protests by early romantics, both those mentioned by Ferber (like Blake) or unmentioned by him (like Rousseau), against the observed and felt effects of early industrial capitalism are certainly as much or more a response to reification as to other aspects of capitalism. This would appear clearly in the case of Blake, for example, if one looked at other texts than the single poem quoted by Ferber.

But Ferber is quite right when he says that he misses in our piece a treatment of exactly "how capitalism made itself felt—unevenly, at varying tempos in different countries and regions—outside the workplace and marketplace," and "how the various responses to it began to cohere into something we can identify as the romantic worldview." It is true that we do not attempt any detailed historical analysis of the advent of romanticism, as we likewise do not attempt to trace with any comprehensiveness its later development. For we were principally concerned with creating a general model and a typology of varieties of romanticism. Within the limits of an essay, all we could hope to do was to propose a theoretical framework that might serve as a groundwork for future reflection and research. We entirely agree with Ferber that an historical approach (both to the genesis and to the later evolution of the phenomenon) sensitive to particularities and modifications within the matrix of the romantic worldview will be necessary to develop our first, schematic mapping of the territory.

Another, more specific problem involving the origins of romanticism also certainly deserves further study: the early appearance of the latter in Germany. Ferber is doubtlessly also right in insisting that a theory purporting to explain romanticism as opposition to capitalism needs to explain why some of the first and strongest manifestations of romanticism occur in a relatively backward country. Ferber's own comments are certainly relevant in this regard, since he alludes to the "English cast" of German romanticism, strongly influenced by works coming from the most "advanced" country at the time. But the problem still remains, and should be studied carefully. We might offer, though, a tentative hypothesis: is it not true that often the most virulent reactions to capitalism come from its periphery rather than its center? After all, the first socialist revolution came not in a leading industrial country but in Russia. And indeed, an antimodern and anticapitalist romanticism dominates Russian literature of the nineteenth century. By contrast, countries on the cutting edge of development—England and France—spawned alongside romanticism intellectual currents reflecting enthusiasm for the new order: Utilitarianism and Positivism. On the other hand, it should be added that in some "peripheral" countries romanticism often seems to be at least as much antifeudal and nationalistic as anticapitalist. The answers are in all probability not simple, and we feel that study of the "periphery" in the light of our theory is an important priority.

Ferber also raises questions involving the other end of romanticism's chronological span: the twentieth century up to the present. He discusses our assertion that "Romanticism is an essential part of modern culture" by criticizing Tolkien, *E.T.*, and *Star Wars*. For him "these twentieth-century works reduce the . . . fundamental seriousness of 'high' romanticism to magic and entertainment." We might reply that some nineteenth-century critics probably would have written the same about E. T. A. Hoffmann. But more important, we feel that there has been some misunderstanding here. When speaking of romanticism in modern (twentieth-century) culture, we were thinking of such "fundamentally serious" movements as Expressionism and Surrealism, of writers such as Kafka, Thomas Mann, Gottfried Benn, Georges Bernanos, W. B. Yeats and T. S. Eliot, and of philosophers such as Ernst Bloch and Walter Benjamin (all mentioned in our paper).

A similar point could be made about contemporary developments (roughly the second half of the century). We mentioned best-selling authors like Ende and Tolkien to illustrate the *mass appeal* of neoromantic literature. But we do not share Ferber's completely negative assessment of these authors. For as Jack Zipes has stressed in his fine essay, "The Utopian Function of Fairy Tales and Fantasy," Tolkien's books, whatever their obvious ideological and political shortcomings, are important because they point to "the widening gap between a technologically constraining society and its alienated individuals in search of authentic community."[1]

The same applies, to an even greater extent, in the case of Michael Ende. In an interview with a French journalist he explained his aim in writing *Die unendliche Geschichte:* "I was not attacking individuals, but a system—call it, if you will, capitalist—which is leading us (as we will discover in ten or fifteen years) directly to the abyss. . . . I do not hide the fact that in this book I was trying to link up again with certain ideas of German romanticism. Not in order to return to the past, but because there are, in that movement which failed, some seeds that are ready to germinate."[2]

Among contemporary writers we referred also to Borges. We could have added many others: Ernesto Sabato, Allen Ginsberg, Heinrich Böll, Christa Wolff, Peter Weiss, etc. Philosophers like Herbert Marcuse and Henri Lefebvre represent a crucial link between the romantic critique of civilization of the 1930s and the new cultural upsurge in the 1960s and 1970s. All of this is certainly more than mere entertainment. If we mentioned some movies (like *E.T.* and *The Return of the Jedi*), it was only to show that *even* the film industry cannot ignore, in producing its commodities, the social demand for a romantic critique of industrial capitalist civilization. We are not unaware of the reified character of *all* products of the culture industry, but we believe, as Fredric Jameson has shown in an important essay, that they may also include utopian strands, notably in the case of certain contemporary films.[3]

In brief, the romantic fire *is* still burning. It is alive not only in social movements (pacifism, ecology, feminism), as Ferber himself recognizes, but at the same time in new religious currents ("liberation theology") and in the present literary and cultural production (part of which, by the way, is influenced by the same social movements).

A final question raised by Ferber involves the nature of the positive values projected by romantic anticapitalism. At the conclusion of his essay he wonders if to call them "precapitalist" may not be "misleading." He goes on to argue that the values in the name of which authentic opposition to capitalism is voiced are "transhistorical"; but this opposition must necessarily look to the precapitalist past for concrete models, he suggests, thereby implying (though he does not explicitly say so) that all authentic anti-capitalism is romantic in the sense of our definition.

We do not believe this to be true. There is surely an intellectual stance that is quite authentically opposed to the capitalist value system (which amounts to the rule of exchange value, as Ferber rightly remarks), but in the name of certain "modern" values: rationalism, scientific and technological advance, "progress" in general, etc. The case of Lenin, who once defined socialism as "soviets plus electrification," is exemplary. Who would seriously claim that Lenin was not a sincere enemy of the rule of exchange value on the one hand, or that he was in any significant way a romantic on the other? The difference between the two forms of anticapitalism is clearly visible also if we put side by side the indisputably romantic worldview of Shelley and the thoroughgoing rationalism of his mentor, Godwin.

We maintain, then, that values are always anchored in history (arising as they do at specific sociohistorical conjunctures), and that opposition to capitalism can be based both on values drawn from the past and on those drawn from the modern world. Romantic values are largely drawn from the past (although not exclusively, since the value of the individual subjectivity is in fact modern, albeit *experienced* as a nostalgia), and represent only one strand of anticapitalism. But it should also be clear from our essay that we consider the principal values of the romantic worldview to be *essential ones* without which the movement to transcend the present economic order is severely impoverished. In our view, far from being an "infantile disorder" of socialist thought, as has often been affirmed by revolutionary purists, the romantic protest brings a fundamental and irreplaceable dimension to the anticapitalist struggle. This perspective on romanticism we fully share, it would seem, with Michael Ferber.

Notes

1. See Jack Zipes, *Breaking the Magical Spell: Radical Theories of Folk and Fairy Tales* (Austin: University of Texas Press, 1979), 158–59.

2. *Le Monde*, 16 March 1984.

3. Fredric Jameson, "Reification and Utopia in Mass Culture," *Social Text* 1 (Winter 1979).

Part 2
Romantic Literary Practice: Rhetoric and Tradition

Practical Reasoning, Rhetoric, and Wordsworth's "Preface"

David Sebberson

1

In the "Preface" to the *Lyrical Ballads* Wordsworth states that he wishes to produce "a class of Poetry . . . not unimportant in the multiplicity, and in the quality of its moral relations."[1] The poet, then, must have a means of articulating the moral, a means of practical reasoning that can comprehend the "quality" and "multiplicity" that a poetry of "moral relations" requires. While Wordsworth declines to develop a "systematic defense of the theory" informing the practice of his poetry, the "few words of introduction" that he does provide introduce far more than a text of poems "materially different" from what his readers were accustomed to. Introduced as well is a response to the crisis in practical reasoning historically determined by the empiricist hegemony of prudence. Embedded in the response, however, is the ideological reproduction of the crisis itself.

Briefly stated, the crisis in practical reasoning occurs with the establishment of empiricism as the theoretical basis of all valid knowledge. Aristotle had distinguished between different types of knowledge, including *phronesis*, which is "concerned with the affairs of men and with things that can be the object of deliberation," and *episteme*, which is concerned with the necessary and eternal things that are the object of demonstration.[2] With empiricism, however, the theoretical distinction between types of knowledge is dismissed and practical reason is transformed into an instrumental or technical reason that aspires to the certainty of science. The result of such a transformation is that human affairs are subjected to the same ends of control that physical nature is. Political and ethical action is conceived in terms of behavior that can be manipulated.[3]

Although the ends of empiricism and the Enlightenment were to free humanity from superstition, the radical subjection of political and ethical action to the reductive rigors of scientific method creates a crisis that threatens human autonomy insofar as human qualities motivating the political and the ethical are reduced to the subjective and denied their validity in the realm of knowledge. As such, questioning the hegemony of scientific method over practical reasoning is a topic in current philosophical debate.[4] But it can also be seen as a topic in romantic studies. Indeed, when the relation between romanticism and the Enlightenment is explored as a moment in the history of practical reason, we can enter a new dimension of undertanding the nature of romanticism, an understanding that breaks what Jerome McGann has identified as the romantic ideology.[5]

That Wordsworth was responding to a crisis in practical reasoning becomes clear when we read *Wordsworth's Second Nature* by James K. Chandler. Chandler creates an explanatory framework that comprises, on the one hand, qualities usually associated with the Enlightenment such as rationality, reason, abstract theory, and scientific method and, on the other hand, qualities of Burkean "second nature" such as habit, prejudice, feelings, and tradition.[6] Within this framework Chandler sees Wordsworth first accepting Enlightenment principles, rejecting them in a state of crisis, and finally embracing "second nature" as a foundation for moral reasoning.[7] While Chandler is correct to ascertain the Burkean elements in Wordsworth, I would like to argue that in terms of practical reasoning Wordsworth also reproduces the Enlightenment ideology in the "Preface" to the *Lyrical Ballads* by incorporating assumptions of empiricist rhetorical theory that had adopted Enlightenment premises.

Such a critique of Wordsworth depends on elements common to romantic criticism but addresses them differently. Issues regarding imagination and consciousness or language and rhetoric, to name but two, are recast when considered as part of the transformation of practical reason into technical reason.

For example, C. M. Bowra argues in *The Romantic Imagination* that the characteristic distinguishing the English romantics from eighteenth-century poets is the former's attitude toward the imagination and "the special view which they held of it."[8] Yet the preoccupation with "imagination" itself is a trait common to both the Enlightenment and romanticism and is part of the instrumentalization of reason where the ethical and political are considered in terms of subjectivity. Similarly, Geoffrey Hartman's phenomenological study of the development of Wordsworth's consciousness in *Wordsworth's Poetry, 1787–1814* focuses on what Hartman call's "humanizing the imagination" as Wordsworth attempts "to direct its great but uncertain powers toward the things of this world."[9] Consequently, Hartman's study can be seen as an extended parable reinforcing the theoretical opposition between subjective imagination and objective nature that underlies technical reason as well as the "Romantic ideology." By reading Wordsworth in the context of the transformation of practical reason, however, we can come to understand a moment in what Jurgen Habermas has called the "dimension of moral-practical consciousness,"[10] which governs our ability to comprehend and to act.

Furthermore, it is a truism that philosophy of language underlies contemporary literary theory. Approaching language issues in the context of rhetoric, and viewing rhetoric in terms of the history of practical reason, however, can lead to a different articulation and understanding of those issues. A word needs to be said about the way I use "rhetoric" and the way it is commonly used in literary criticism. For example, those texts of criticism that hover around principles of deconstruction typically define "rhetoric" in the strictly textual terms of "figures" or "verbal devices." Paul De Man, in *Allegories of Reading*, defines "rhetoric" as "the study of tropes and of figures . . . and not in the derived sense of comment or of eloquence or persuasion"; Hartman, while addressing Derrida in *Saving the Text*, defines "traditional" rhetoric "as the art of persuasion, [which] relies on a smooth consensual calculus of means and ends. Specific verbal devices are isolated as if they effectively corresponded to specific mental or affectional states." And as a final example, Arden Reed, in introducing the essays that constitute *Romanticism and Language*, states that they tend to "take a rhetorical as opposed to a mimetic approach to Romantic literature and attempt to record linguistic play that resists reduction to a single meaning."[11]

Such definitions are themselves instances of the reduction of rhetoric from the practical to the technical.[12] By recasting as the ends of rhetoric "linguistic play" and "the study of tropes and figures" (itself a derivation), De Man and Reed reiterate the undermining of the critical, ethical, and political dimensions of rhetoric inherent in the rhetorical theories of Plato and Aristotle. Moreover, Hartman's claim that traditional rhetoric "relies on a smooth consensual calculus of means and ends" is a more accurate description of eighteenth-century empiricist rhetoric (and that of the sophists whom Plato and Aristotle opposed) than of traditional rhetoric. But approaching rhetoric as a means of practical reasoning rather than as a series of (purely) linguistic devices allows for a critique of the manner in which the ethical and political are articulated. As such, rhetoric is not concerned so much with linguistic play as with human action and the language that governs it. To this end will I be examining Wordsworth's "Preface."

Thus my argument will consist first of a discussion of eighteenth-century empiricist rhetorical theory—Campbell's—showing its technical ground in contrast to the practical ground of Platonic and Aristotelian rhetoric. This theoretical discussion will provide the framework for showing, in Section 3, the relation between Priestley's rhetorical theory—also empiricist—and Wordsworth's "Preface." By pointing out the relationship, I hope to show how the stage of development in the transformation of practical reason into technical reason limits Wordsworth from ultimately overcoming the crisis in practical reasoning and explains his development of a subjectivist poetic of "moral relations" that reproduces the ideology he wished to break.

2

Just as the classical doctrine of politics aimed at the good life, so too did rhetoric. During the eighteenth century, however, there was a significant shift in rhetorical theory, a shift that is parallel to the transformation in the realm of politics from practical reasoning to technical reasoning that Habermas has identified.[13] Thus it would be helpful to examine the basic difference between Aristotelian rhetoric, which was preeminently practical, and the empiricist, technical rhetoric of the eighteenth century, particularly that developed in *The Philosophy of Rhetoric* by George Campbell.

For Aristotle, rhetoric is "an offshoot of Dialectic and of Ethics which may reasonably be called Politics."[14] Furthermore, rhetoric gives direction to speech, which is "designed to indicate the advantageous and the harmful, and therefore also the right and the wrong; for it is the special property of man in distinction from the other animals that he alone has perception of good and bad and right and wrong and the other moral qualities."[15] The human being is at once *zoon politikon* and *zoon logon;* as such he or she articulates the moral, engaging in *praxis* toward the end of *eudaimonia*, living well.

As a form of *praxis*, Aristotelian rhetoric had four uses: exposing fraud and injustice, educating citizens in matters of policy and justice, providing a precaution against fallacious reasoning, and providing a defense superior to force.[16] To achieve these ends in a particular situation, the rhetorician had to discover all possible means of persuasion and engage three interrelated types of proof: *logos, ethos,* and *pathos* (*Rhetoric* 1356a). Now *logos*, with its multiple meanings of speech and reason, reflection and account, the subject of speech and the ground of reason, can be defined as the articulation of the real; it is a term comprising language, thought, and reality, and acknowledging the ontological depth of the human world. A concept of *logos* that acknowledges the complexity of the human world enables us to address complexity—to speak about it, understand it, reflect upon it, reason about it. Logical proof, then, cannot be reduced to simple accounts of mere facticity, but rather must account for complexity.[17] *Ethos* is also a complex term, which Aristotle defines as comprising three qualities: good sense, virtue, and goodwill (*Rhetoric* 1378a). Taken together, these qualities combine the capabilities of judgment and understanding with the notion of virtue.[18] Thus ethical proof consists of judgments about values and how such judgments bear on our understanding of a situation. While proofs drawn from *ethos* address the relation between values and understanding, proofs drawn from *pathos* address the relation between emotions and understanding. For Aristotle it was imperative for the rhetorician not to "warp . . . feelings, [not] to arouse . . . anger, jealousy or compassion, which would be like making the rule crooked which one intended to use" (*Rhetoric* 1354b), but rather to understand how "opinions vary, according as men love or hate, are wrathful or mild, and things appear either altogether different, or different in degree" (*Rhetoric* 1377b). Consequently, the end of proof based on *pathos* is not to manipulate the feelings and emotions of the audience but rather to understand how emotions could affect the audience's judgment, to determine whether or not a particular emotion is appropriate for a particular circumstance. Arguments drawn from the emotions are rational, not blind impulses.[19]

Implicit in both the uses of rhetoric and the rhetorical proofs is a view of rhetoric that is not only ethical but also critical. In order to engage in rhetoric as a *praxis* leading to *eudaimonia*, the Aristotelian rhetorician could not accept received opinion as a given. Moreover such acceptance would preclude the possibility of doing the job at hand—discovering all possible means of persuasion. Such discovery requires critical judgments regarding rhetorical proof. In any given situation the following questions arise: What assumptions about reality and its articulation are being made—are the rhetorician's statements true? What values are either implicitly or explicitly being brought to bear in the argument—is the rhetorician's speech truthful? What emotions are being aroused or allayed in the speech and how do they affect understanding—are the rhetorician's statements appropriate?[20]

Such a critical theory of rhetoric is at odds with both Enlightenment theories of rhetoric and the traditionalist response to Enlightenment philosophy made by Wordsworth, for neither is Enlightenment rhetoric ethical nor the traditionalist response critical. I would like first to outline the basic tenets of the empiricist rhetoric of George Campbell and then to suggest that "habit" and "feeling," central to Wordsworth's "second nature" and understandable in terms of *ethos* and *pathos*, are not so much a response to the Enlightenment as a reproduction of Enlightenment ideology.

While Campbell does not use the terms, *ethos*, *pathos*, and *logos*—the notion of "artificial" proofs is, after all, in direct opposition to Enlightenment (and romantic) thought—they are strong explanatory terms that can help in analyzing not only discourse but also rhetorical theory itself. Thus bringing the concepts of *logos*, *ethos*, and *pathos* to bear on Campbell's rhetorical theory provides a means of judging how his theory addresses the articulation of reality *(logos)*, the manner in which the ethical dimension of speech is developed *(ethos)*, and the role of emotions in affecting judgment *(pathos)*. Basically, Campbell reduces the practical dimensions of rhetorical proof to techniques of manipulation and control, for the end of the empiricist rhetorician, as Campbell states it, is not *eudaimonia* but rather "to operate on the soul of the hearer."[21]

The subject of Campbell's rhetorical theory is psychology. As such, it assumes a Cartesian dualism, which is based on a radical division between the subjective and the objective and adopts scientific method as the arbiter of all that is knowable and true. Consequently, there is a large schism in Campbell between arguments drawn from *logos* and those drawn from *ethos* and *pathos*. For Campbell, *logos* is reduced to qualities that complement scientific method. Reality is reduced to what can be observed and classified. Furthermore, experience is based solely on retention and association, and what distinguishes humans from beasts is not that humans have the capability of speech—which for both Aristotle and Habermas implies the judgment of truth and falsehood, right and wrong—but rather the ability to classify (*PR* 48). Thus Campbell believes that moral reasoning can best be exemplified by a botanist faced with the problem of classifying a newly discovered plant (*PR* 51). Like Hobbes before him, Campbell has sacrificed *phronesis* for *episteme*, the practical for the scientific, and in doing so reduces the two principal dimensions of *logos*, speech and reason, to description and classification, neither of which is ethical or critical.

Pathos also undergoes a transformation from the practical to the technical. While Aristotle's rhetoric moved beyond a concept of *pathos* that entailed no more than the manipulation of emotions, Campbell's notion of "discourse . . . addressed to the emotions" is nothing if not manipulative, for such discourse is like a "magical spell [that] hurries them, ere they are aware, into love, pity, grief, terror, desire, aversion, fury, or hatred" (*PR* 4). Furthermore, Campbell's notion of *pathos* allows the rhetorician to dominate his audience as he imposes his reason with a power "superior even to what despotism itself can bestow" (*PR* 5). Now the schism between *logos* on the one hand and *ethos* and *pathos* on the other helps to explain Campbell's reduction of *pathos* from *praxis* and means of understanding—a "moral psychology" to use Fortenbaugh's phrase (see n19)—to the technical manipulation of emotions. For the reduction of *logos* to little more than the methodology of science precludes a concept of *pathos* that is anything other than manipulative. Since emotions are viewed as strictly subjective, they bear no validity in the determination of understanding. There is the truth of scientific reason on the one hand—the proper realm of thought—and emotional reaction on the other, which, in its "vehemence," produces "irresistible power over . . . thoughts" and "defiance of every obstruction" (*PR* 4–5). As such, *pathos*, like *logos*, can be neither critical nor ethical, but only a technique "to operate on the souls of hearers."

Perhaps the most radical reduction from the practical to the technical takes place in the area of *ethos*. As with *pathos*, the rhetorician informed by Campbell's philosophy has no means to articulate the ethical or to sustain a critical judgment. Everything ethical is reduced to psychological processes and discussed in terms of the individual imagination, which "terminates in the gratification of some internal taste: as a taste for the wonderful, the fair, the good; for elegance, for novelty, for grandeur" (*PR* 3). In Campbell, arguments addressing the "fair" and "the good" bear little relation to the Aristotelian qualities of good sense, virtue, and goodwill, which constitute a critical and ethical concept of *ethos*. Instead of articulating and assessing the values that help us understand a given situation and providing reasons for action, the Campbellian rhetorician addresses the imagination or fancy[22] for the end of creating pleasure or producing sympathy. Thus the rhetorician turns away from a concern with human action informed by ethical deliberation to controlling psychological processes that will produce desired effects in the audience's mind; action is sacrificed to behavior, good sense and virtue to pleasure, goodwill to sympathy. As such, *ethos* is reduced to a technique where values or "moral sentiments," as Campbell calls them, are nothing but "auxiliaries to keep passions alive" (*PR* 91) and do no more than "justify . . . passion" (*PR* 92).

In the course of transforming ethical reasoning into a matter of controlling psychological responses, Campbell claims that both virtues and passions "necessarily imply an habitual propensity to a certain species of conduct, an habitual aversion to the contrary: a veneration for such a character, an abhorrence of such another" (*PR* 80). The notion of "habitual" takes on particular significance when considered in the context of *ethos* and its development as a term for practical and rhetorical reasoning that is critical in nature.

Originally, "*ethos*" carried the meaning of habit and as such was noncritical. Similarly, Eric A. Havelock argues that before Socrates, "*psyche*," or soul, was also noncritical and meant "ghost-like wraith."[23] Together these two concepts informed the uncritical, imagistic basis of mimesis, which served as the foundation for practical reasoning in a culture dependent on oral tradition. Thus Havelock describes the Homeric Greek as having an image of Achilles, say, doing something brave, and imitating that image accordingly when he wished to act bravely. By mimesis and repetition the *ethos* or habit of bravery would be developed in the individual. But as Havelock argues, it is just this notion of mimesis that Plato opposed, causing him to develop the concept of soul as critical and self-reflective, not mimetic and habitual—in short as the "ghost that thinks." Following Plato, Aristotle develops the concept of *ethos* far beyond the notion of habit to include, as Jaeger argues, moral culture "based on the harmony of intelligent insight and habit," a development that "became the foundation of all modern systems of 'ethics.'"[24] Keeping in mind that Aristotelian *ethos* comprises good sense (constituted by understanding and judgment), virtue (informed by intelligence), and goodwill, we can see the (Platonic and) Aristotelian transformation of *ethos* from a concept of habitual action informed by the "spell" of "rhythmic narrative," to use Havelock's words, to a concept that, while possibly retaining the notion of habit, breaks any "spell" by reconstituting the *praxis* of *ethos* as one of critical endeavor. Consequently, Campbell's invocation of the "habitual" reduces and constrains the rhetorician's ability to reason ethically. By associating virtue and passion, Campbell sees *ethos* not as a means of critical, ethical thought, but rather as a means of manipulation. The rhetorician need only play on the audience's "habitual propensity to a certain species of conduct," not examine, question, understand, or judge it. The rhetorician need only cast a spell of pre-Socratic darkness to usher in the Enlightenment of scientific method.

This brief analysis of Campbell's rhetorical theory suggests that basic foundations of second nature—habits, feelings—on which Wordsworth wishes to counter Enlightenment thought are part and parcel of the Enlightenment thought itself. To explore more fully the similarity between Enlightenment notions of moral reasoning and Wordsworth's thinking behind his new class of poetry and the "quality of its moral relations," I would like to turn to another eighteenth-century rhetorician—and Enlightenment scientist—Joseph Priestley. For it is in comparing Priestley's rhetoric to Wordsworth's notions of poetry outlined in the "Preface" that we can clearly see how Wordsworth embraces Enlightenment ideology to articulate his response to the Enlightenment.

3

Priestley dedicates *A Course of Lectures on Oratory and Criticism* to the Lord Viscount Fitzmaurice, to whose education it is his "earnest wish to contribute." In doing so, he clearly states a position that reflects Enlightenment goals: "The same maxims of good sense which regulate all other things, will finally new-arrange whatever belongs to the affairs of society and government; and those distinctions which mere *force*, mere *superstition*, or mere *accident* will be found to have established, and to which *public utility* does not give its sanction, will gradually sink into *public disesteem:* and this, long continued, will make part of that *spirit of men* of *nations*, and *times*, which must finally bear down every thing that opposes it."[25] It is precisely the "new-arrangement" of society and government that, according to Chandler, Wordsworth opposes. Furthermore, it is the methodology of science that will liberate humanity.[26] Yet an examination of Priestley's rhetoric and Wordsworth's "Preface" indicates that Wordsworth articulates the means of moral reasoning in the same manner as Enlightenment rhetoricians do.[27] Just as evidence of Burke's anti-Enlightenment second nature can be found in Wordsworth, so too can Priestley's pro-Enlightenment principles of empiricist rhetoric.

Like Campbell's, Priestley's rhetoric is based on empiricist principles. Although he does not organize his rhetoric around faculties of mind as Campbell does, he does state explicitly that his theory differs from earlier ones in that it is based on principles of association (*CLO* i). Furthermore, while Priestley claims that he has "arranged" his subject differently from previous rhetoricians, he makes the same division between the *logos* of scientific method on the one hand and *ethos* and *pathos* on the other,[28] and in doing so, he also associates virtue and passion.

This basic division is explicit in the "Preface" as well when Wordsworth distinguishes between poetry and science. The manner in which Wordsworth makes the division is complex. At first, Wordsworth seems to reestablish the Aristotelian distinction between *episteme* and *phronesis,* recovering the latter from the sacrificial altar of the former. The Poet's knowledge "cleaves to us as a necessary part of our existence, our natural and unalienable inheritance," as it results in the Poet "singing a song in which all human beings join with him" in the "impassioned expression" that is the "rock of defence for human nature; an upholder and preserver carrying everywhere with him relationship and love" (*PWW* 141). On the other hand, the Man of Science "seeks truth as a remote and unknown benefactor," attained in "solitude" and "by no habitual and direct sympathy connecting us with our fellow-beings" (*PWW* 141). Here Wordsworth appears to differentiate between absolute, scientific knowledge, which is the object of demonstration, and practical, contingent knowledge in the realm of human action, about which people deliberate.

At this point, the poet (unlike his contemporary rhetorician) appears to regain the practical from the technical. But Wordsworth goes on to say that the poet "follow[s] in the footsteps" of the Man of Science by "carrying sensation into the midst of the objects of Science itself. The remotest discoveries of the Chemist, the Botanist, or Mineralogist, will be as proper objects of the Poet's art as any . . . [as] the Poet will lend his divine spirit to aid the transfiguration" of science into "flesh and blood" (*PWW* 141). And here we return to the same dichotomy drawn by both Campbell and Priestley. The poet, on behalf of science, carries out the job of *pathos* by "open[ing] a speedy passage to the heart" (Campbell's words) and through "the medium of imagination or the passions" (Priestley's words). First there is reason (*logos*); then there is "impassioned expression" (*pathos, ethos*). Or, to join Priestley's metaphor (see n.28) with Wordsworth's, there is the truth of method—the "bones, muscles, and nerves of a composition" (*logos*)—and the "flesh and blood" of the "graceful attitude" of "the external lineaments, the colour, the complexion" (*pathos, ethos*). The dichotomy exists for both Priestley and Wordsworth; the only difference is that Priestley prefers the side of "bones, muscles, and nerves," Wordsworth that of "flesh and blood."

Campbell's division between *logos* on the one hand and *ethos* and *pathos* on the other reduced rhetoric from practical reasoning to technical manipulation of psychological processes. In that reduction is the initial transformation of ethical reasoning into private, subjective behavior. Values such as the good and the just were no longer in the public domain of politically and ethically validated knowledge: instead they were somehow a function of psychology, stimulants of passions. Now this is not to say that rhetoricians or anyone else quit their concerns with ethical reasoning; the nature of that reasoning, however, had been transformed, a transformation whose development can be seen by reading Wordsworth against Priestley in terms of *ethos* and *pathos*.

When *ethos* and *pathos* are joined in contradistinction to *logos*, the distinctions between *ethos* and *pathos* themselves, between the ethical and the emotional, tend to disappear, particularly as the effectiveness of both *ethos* and *pathos* becomes a matter of creating pleasant sensations and feelings for the individual mind. Priestley writes that "discourse . . . must either be *interesting* by exciting those gross and more sensible feelings we call *passions*, or must awaken those more delicate sensations, which are generally called *pleasures of the imagination*" (*CLO* 72). Consequently, the privatization of *ethos*, of values, is carried one step further by the association of values with feelings. For the empiricist rhetorician, thinking about values becomes little more than thinking about a stimulant for pleasure—especially the "delicate" pleasure of the imagination. And here Priestley's rhetorical theory and Wordsworth's poetics converge. For Priestley, *ethos*, now considered in terms of imagination, finds its end in pleasure. Likewise, Wordsworth writes that the purpose of poetry is "to produce excitement in coexistence with an overbalance of pleasure" (*PWW* 147). It is on this foundation that *ethos* is made subjective and, ultimately, private. *Ethos*, as an articulation of values, had been the heart of practical or moral reasoning. And Wordsworth's new class of poetry was to point the way to moral relations. It is significant that both Priestley and Wordsworth develop their concepts of moral reasoning in terms of pleasing the imagination.

In the passage just quoted from Priestley, the only distinction made between the grosser passions and the more delicate sensations was one of degree, relating the emotional to the ethical, values to feeling. Wordsworth also develops his concept of moral reasoning in terms of the gross and the delicate:

> The human mind is capable of being excited without the application of gross and violent stimulants. . . . [T]o produce or enlarge this capability is one of the best services in which, at any period, a Writer can be engaged; but this service, excellent at all times, is especially so at the present day. For a multitude of causes . . . are now acting with a combined force to blunt the discriminating powers of the mind, and unfitting it for all voluntary exertion, to reduce it to a state of almost savage torpor. The most effective of these causes are the great national events which are daily taking place, and the increasing accumulation of men in cities, where the uniformity of their occupations produces a craving for extraordinary incident. . . . (*PWW* 129)

I have quoted this rather remarkable passage at length because it shows the striking similarity between Priestley and Wordsworth in their attitude toward the delicate sensations necessary for pleasing the imagination. Indeed, it gets at the heart of ethical reasoning based on private subjectivity. When Wordsworth invokes the modern world with its "almost savage torpor" and the congestion of cities, he is responding to the alienated life, its commodification noted in the "degrading thirst after outrageous stimulation" remarked on later in the same passage, that was resulting from the rise of capitalism generally and the industrial revolution specifically. Certainly there was cause for concern with "the great national events . . . daily taking place." But consider the theoretical response to these events: a turning inward to the individual imagination in an attempt to refine its capabilities. This was the special power of the poet, for as Wordsworth states later, the poet creates, "by his own choice, or from the structure of his own mind . . . without immediate external excitement" (*PWW* 138). The poet's power, then, rests on the privatized subjectivity of the individual.

By equating the emotional with the moral and locating both in the private, subjective imagination, Priestley, as a rhetorician concerned with affecting his audience, focuses on the manner in which the imagination is pleased:

> One property essential to every thing that gives us pleasure is, that it occasions a *moderate exercise of our faculties.* Pleasure consists of sensations moderately vigorous. It is, therefore, capable of existing in any degree between the two extremes of perfect languor and tranquillity of mind on the one hand, and actual pain and uneasiness on the other. It is observable, likewise, that the more moderate any pleasure is, the longer continuance it is capable of; and that the more intense the pleasure, or the more nearly it approaches to a state of pain, the less capable it is of a long duration. Immoderate pleasure, as it were, oppresses, fatigues, and exhausts the mind. (*CLO* 136)

In this passage we see a sort of nascent behaviorism based on pleasure and pain. If the rhetorician is to be effective and enduring, he must make sure that emotional responses are made psychologically pleasant by moderation. Now I am not arguing for immoderation, nor would Aristotle. But it is significant that the articulation of moral reasoning, with the conflation of the ethical and emotional, is cast in terms of psychological pleasure and pain. The good, or freedom, or justice can only be conceived of and argued for in terms of what is psychologically pleasing to the faculty of imagination. The possibility that such values have a historical, ethical, and political reality independent of the individual mind and outside the emotional poles of tranquillity and pain does not exist. The empiricist rhetorician does not concern himself with the substance of moral reasoning but rather with the psychology of the process and the effects it produces.

The limited range for articulating moral reasoning in terms of argument that occurs in Priestley is identical to that of Wordsworth in his definition of poetry as "the spontaneous overflow of powerful feelings":

it takes its origin from emotion recollected in tranquility: the emotion is contemplated till, by a species of reaction, the tranquility gradually disappears, and an emotion, kindred to that which was before the subject of contemplation, is gradually produced, and does itself actually exist in the mind. In this mood successful composition generally begins, and in a mood similar to this it is carried on; but the emotion, of whatever kind, and in whatever degree, from various causes, is qualified by various pleasures, so that in describing any passions whatsoever, which are voluntarily described, the mind will upon the whole be in a state of enjoyment. . . . [T]he Poet ought . . . to take care, that whatever passions he communicates to his Reader, those passions . . . should always be accompanied with an overbalance of pleasure. (*PWW* 1 : 150–51)

Wordsworth has simply turned a psychological process that Priestley thought the rhetorician should consider in terms of affecting the audience into the process of poetic composition itself. The reasoning that the poet uses to explore "moral relations" takes place within the same emotional range of tranquillity and pain moderated by pleasure. Again, the whole theoretical articulation of moral reasoning is in emotional terms, and again the emphasis is on psychological process.

It is the concern with the individual mind—its emotions, its psychological processes—that governs the privatization of subjectivity in moral reasoning. For neither Priestley nor Wordsworth does the moral reasoner look outward with a critical eye on the values institutionalized by ethical and political structures constituting society and shaping the individual. Instead, both the Enlightenment rhetorician and the romantic poet must look inward to private feelings. There is no social practice, only sympathy. Priestley tells us that "from the principle of *sympathy*, which is natural to the human mind, we universally feel ourselves disposed to conform to the feelings, the sentiments, and every thing belonging to the situation of those we converse with" (*CLO* 109). Priestley also tells us that "no form of expression can appear natural, unless it correspond to the feelings of the person using it" (*CLO* 83). Similarly for Wordsworth, "to excite rational sympathy, [the poet] must express himself as other men express themselves" (*PWW* 1 : 143). This, Wordsworth believed, would allow the sharing of passions between the poet and his readers, would break the tyranny of Enlightenment rationality so that "the feeling . . . gives importance to the action and situation, and not the action and situation to the feeling" (*PWW* 1 : 129). But the tyranny cannot be broken on these terms, only made more subtle, for the terms belong to Priestley and the Enlightenment as well as to Wordsworth and romanticism.

4

The similarity between Priestley's theory of rhetoric and Wordsworth's notion of poetry takes on a particular significance for practical reasoning when considered in conjunction with the development of technical reasoning and Burkean influences on Wordsworth. What becomes clear is how the power of Enlightenment ideology distorts not only our ability to reason ethically and critically but also our ability to articulate a way to reason. For Wordsworth represents a moment when the historical structure of Enlightenment thought assimilates the reaction against it.

While Wordsworth tries to explain the creation of a new class of poetry that expands the concept and realization of moral relations, he can only articulate those moral relations, ultimately, by structurally opposing reason and moral sentiments, the latter of which are dominated by feelings. Yet this is the same structure of opposition manifest in the rhetoric of technical control developed by Campbell and Priestley. Consequently, Wordsworth's response to the Enlightenment—his reliance on second nature, for example, to "recollect emotions in tranquility" or to reconstruct reality in the privacy of imagination—reproduces the drive of technical reason to reduce the legitimacy of compassionate and ethical reasoning by relegating both to the realm of the subjective, where moral knowledge and moral action can occur only with feeling and "without," as Priestley puts it, "the slow intervention of reason" (*CLO* 80). And it is here, with Priestley's phrase, that the domination of Enlightenment and the response of second nature are merged in a single, overriding expression of ideology.

Drawing out the similarities between eighteenth-century rhetorical theory and Wordsworth's poetic theory of "moral relations" not only underlines the continuation of Enlightenment ideology in Wordsworth but also raises a question in the metadiscourse of romantic criticism regarding the philosophy of language. The differing positions taken by Aarsleff and Scholes are paradigmatic.

Hans Aarsleff argues that Wordsworth's philosophy of language embodies the typically romantic notion of expressive language while rejecting the eighteenth-century ideal of imitative language.[29] This position is in direct opposition to Robert Scholes, who argues that Wordsworth presents an "atomistic and ontological view of language (individual words representing things in reality)," while it is Shelley who presents a "view that is contextual and epistemological (combinations of words representing mental processes)" and therefore expresses the "modern view of language."[30] These opposing views toward Wordsworth's philosophy of language reproduce the very problem of Enlightenment ideology itself, for both rely on an abstract notion of language that can do little more than iterate either the subjective or objective; as such there can be no hope for anything but an arbitrary resolution. A rhetorical approach to language, however, is concerned more with the praxis of articulation than with the objects of iteration. Thus by examining Wordsworth's poetics in the light of Priestley's rhetoric, we can make a judgment about the manner in which Wordsworth articulates the "moral relations" that inform his poetry rather than bicker about whether his language iterates external objects or internal ideas. Judgment in the light of rhetorical praxis revolves around not whether Wordsworth exemplifies "the modern view of language"—itself a problematic position that remains unilluminated without a critique of rhetoric in relation to practical reason—but rather the adequacy of a position that further articulates the foundation of "moral relations" in increasingly subjectivist terms.

Notes

1. W. J. B. Owen and Jane Worthington Smyser, eds., *The Prose Works of William Wordsworth* (Oxford: Oxford University Press, 1974), 1:121. All references to the "Preface" are from passages and revisions included by 1802 and are cited parenthetically in the text as *PWW.*

2. Aristotle, *The Nicomachean Ethics,* trans. H. Rackham (1926; reprint, Cambridge: Harvard University Press, 1962), 1141b, 1139b.

3. For a discussion of the ideology of control, see Max Horkheimer and Theodor W. Adorno, *The Dialectic of Enlightenment,* trans. John Cumming (New York: Herder and Herder, 1972). For a discussion of the transformation of practical reason into technical reason, see Jurgen Habermas, "The Classical Doctrine of Politics," in *Theory and Practice,* trans. John Viertel (Boston: Beacon Press, 1973). According to Habermas, Aristotle's theory of politics aimed at *eudaimonia,* living well, rather than at mere survival, which is the end of Hobbes's political theory. With the shift in ends from living well to survival, political doctrine came to be articulated in terms of instrumental reason, necessary for the control of nature, rather than in terms of practical reason, which sustains as valid the purely human quality of value.

4. The debate has many participants expressing a broad range of views. Those whom I have found to offer especially helpful insights are, in addition to Horkheimer and Adorno and Habermas (noted above), Richard Bernstein, *Beyond Objectivism and Relativisim; Science, Hermeneutics, and Praxis* (Philadelphia: University of Pennsylvania Press, 1985); Roy Bhaskar, *The Possibility of Naturalism: A Philosophical Critique of the Contemporary Human Sciences* (Atlantic Highlands, N.J.: Humanities Press, 1979); and Charles Taylor, *Human Agency and Language; Philosophical Papers 1* (Cambridge: Cambridge University Press, 1985), and *Philosophy and the Human Sciences; Philosophical Papers 2* (Cambridge: Cambridge University Press, 1985).

5. Like McGann, I attempt "to situate Romanticism and its works in the past in order to make them present resources by virtue of their differential; and, on the other, to free present criticism from the crippling illusion that such a past establishes the limits, conceptual and practical, of our present and our future." Jerome J. McGann, *The Romantic Ideology: A Critical Investigation* (Chicago and London: University of Chicago Press, 1983), 3.

6. To underline the difference between Enlightenment and traditionalist thought, Chandler cites Hans-Georg Gadamer, who calls traditionalism the " 'romantic critique of enlightenment,' . . . which he associates with Burke." Chandler continues, "Gadamer defines traditionalism straightforwardly as 'the critical attitude that again addresses itself to the truth of tradition and seeks to renew it. In contrast to the enlightenment's belief in perfection, which thinks in terms of the freedom from "superstition" and prejudices of the past, we now find that olden times, the world of myth, unreflective life, not yet analyzed away by consciousness . . . acquire . . . a priority of truth.' " The key term in Gadamer is "unreflective" with its connotations of the noncritical. James K. Chandler, *Wordsworth's Second Nature: A Study of the Poetry and Politics* (Chicago and London: University of Chicago Press, 1984), 181.

7. Chandler argues convincingly that Wordsworth's progression from Enlightenment principles to a state of second nature takes place early in his career, thereby explaining what to many has been Wordsworth's unaccounted for shift from young radical to old conservative; he had already adopted Burke's conservative principles of "second nature" by the late 1790s.

8. C. M. Bowra, *The Romantic Imagination* (New York: Oxford University Press, 1961), 1.

9. Geoffrey H. Hartman, *Wordsworth's Poetry, 1787–1814* (1964; reprint, New Haven and London: Yale University Press, 1971), xii.

10. According to Habermas, "The species learns not only in the dimension of technically useful knowledge decisive for the development of productive forces, but also in the dimension of moral-practical consciousness crucial for structures of interaction. The rules of communicative action, to be sure, evolve in reaction to changes in the domain of instrumental and strategic behavior; but in doing so they develop their own logic." Jurgen Habermas, *Communication and the Evolution of Society,* trans. Thomas McCarthy (Boston: Beacon Press, 1979), 148. While Hartman's work is helpful in understanding the development of Wordsworth's consciousness as an individual, my purpose is, in effect, to examine the "rules of communicative action" at that stage of historical development—romanticism—where the reaction to the "domain of instrumental and strategic behavior" is particularly strong.

11. Paul De Man, *Allegories of Reading: Figural Language in Rousseau, Nietzsche, Rilke, and Proust* (New Haven and London: Yale University Press, 1979), 6; Geoffrey H. Hartman, *Saving the Text: Literature / Derrida / Philosophy* (Baltimore and London: Johns Hopkins University Press, 1981), 120; Arden Reed, ed., *Romanticism and Language* (Ithaca: Cornell University Press, 1984), 20.

12. While it would not be appropriate here to give a comprehensive history of the transformation of rhetorical theory from the practical to the technical, the general outline of the transformation of rhetoric from *praxis* to *techne* would include the technical refinements that reduce types of proof to rhetorical devices, carried out in classical and medieval times; the reduction of rhetoric to matters of style carried out by Ramus in the seventeenth century; and the theoretical recreation of rhetoric based on empiricism and natural law carried out in the eighteenth century.

13. See note 3 on Habermas. I am indebted to Steve Badrich, who first pointed out the applicability of Habermas's essay for understanding the transformation of rhetoric from *praxis* to *techne.*

14. Aristotle, *The Art of Rhetoric,* trans. John Henry Freese (1926; reprint, Cambridge: Harvard University Press, 1975), 1356a. Subsequent references to this work are cited parenthetically in the text as *Rhetoric.*

15. Aristotle, *Politics,* trans. H. Rackham (1932; reprint, Cambridge: Harvard University Press, 1977), 1253a.

16. See Edward Meredith Cope, *An Introduction to Aristotle's Rhetoric with Analysis Notes and Appendicies* (London and Cambridge: Macmillan, 1867), 144 *passim.*

17. For both Plato and Aristotle, *logos* comprised more than mere accounts of facticity. See, for example, *Theaetetus* 207a–208b and *The Republic,* 531e–532c. More to the point of Aristotle's *Rhetoric,* see 1396a–1396b, where Aristotle says that "in regard to the subject of our speech or reasoning, whether it be political or of any other kind, it is necessary to be also acquainted with the elements of the question . . . for if you know none of these things, you will have nothing from which to draw a conclusion." Aristotle then gives examples of "elements," which can range from empirical data to considerations of justice and the good. That Aristotle can range freely from the factual to the value-laden indicates a theory of *logos* that can articulate and speak to a complex and comprehensive reality.

18. In *The Nicomachean Ethics,* Aristotle draws the relation between "judgment" and "understanding" as constituents of good sense in the realm of practical reasoning: "When we . . . judge what another person says about matters that are in the sphere of Prudence, we are said to understand (that is, to judge rightly, for right judgment is the same as good understanding)" (1143a). He then goes on to state that good sense or intelligence is required for virtue, that, indeed, "without Intelligence [virtuous natural dispositions] may manifestly be harmful. . . .If a man of good natural disposition acquires Intelligence, [however,] then he excels in conduct, and the disposition which previously only resembled Virtue, will now be Virtue in the true sense" (1144b).

19. For a discussion that supports this view of *pathos,* see William W. Fortenbaugh, "Aristotle's Rhetoric on Emotions," in Keith V. Erickson, ed., *Aristotle: The Classical Heritage of Rhetoric* (1970; reprint, Metuchen, N.J.: The Scarecrow Press, 1974), 205–34. Fortenbaugh remarks, for example, that "the *Rhetoric* makes clear that emotions can be reasonable and that emotional appeal need not be a matter of charms and enchantments. . . . [Aristotle's] emphasis upon cognition helps to distinguish emotions from bodily drives and so helps to develop an adequate moral psychology" (205–6).

20. I have used the terms "truth," "truthfulness," and "appropriate" deliberately to draw a parallel between Aristotelian rhetoric and the validity claims that Habermas argues are raised every time we speak. See, for instance, Habermas's essay, "What is Universal Pragmatics?" in *Communications and the Evolution of Society.*

21. George Campbell, *The Philosophy of Rhetoric,* ed. Lloyd F. Bitzer (1776; reprint Carbondale: Southern Illinois University Press, 1963), xliii. Subsequent references to this work are cited parenthetically in the text as *PR.*

22. Campbell does not distinguish, as Coleridge would, between imagination and fancy, but uses the terms interchangeably throughout his work.

23. Throughout *Preface to Plato,* Havelock is addressing the transition from an oral tradition to a written one for the transmission of culture. His insights have particular significance for the subject at hand:

> [For the Homeric Greek an] over-all body of experience . . . is incorporated in a rhythmic narrative or set of narratives which he memorises and which is subject to recall in his memory. Such is poetic tradition, essentially something he accepts uncritically, or else it fails to survive in his living memory. Its acceptance and retention are made psychologically possible by a mechanism of self-surrender to the poetic performance, and of self-identification with the situations and the stories related in the performance. Only when the spell is fully effective can his mnemonic powers be fully mobilised. His receptivity to the tradition has thus, from the standpoint of inner psychology, a degree of automatism which however is counter-balanced by a direct and unfettered capacity for action, in accordance with the paradigms he has absorbed. "His is not to reason why." (198)

It is against this "self-surrender" and "automatism" that Socrates introduces a new concept of the soul:

> Scholarship has tended to connect [the] discovery [of souls] with the life and teaching of Socrates and to identify it with a radical change which he introduced into the meaning of the Greek word *psyche.* In brief, instead of signifying a man's ghost or wraith, or a man's breath, or his life blood, a thing devoid of sense and self-consciousness, it came to mean "the ghost that thinks," that is capable both of moral decision and of scientific cognition, and is the seat of moral responsibility, something infinitely precious, an essence unique in the whole realm of nature. (197)

See Eric A. Havelock, *Preface to Plato* (Cambridge: Harvard University Press, 1963).

24. Werner Jaeger, *Paideia: The Ideals of Greek Culture,* trans. Gilbert Highet (New York: Oxford University Press, 1939–44), 3:227–28.

25. Joseph Priestley, *A Course of Lectures on Oratory and Criticism,* eds. Vincent M. Bevilacqua and Richard Murphy (1777; reprint, Carbondale: Southern Illinois University Press, 1965). This passage is taken from the Dedication, which has no page numbers. All subsequent citations of Priestley are taken from the *Course of Lectures* and are noted parenthetically in the text as *CLO.*

26. Priestley believes that "Truth, whether geometrical, metaphysical, moral, or theological, is of the same nature, and the evidence of it is perceived in a similar manner by the same human minds" (*CLO* 45). Similarly, Priestley argues that "the *analytic* method [emphasis his unless otherwise noted] of communicating any truth is . . . nothing more than a copy of the method of its *investigation*" (*CLO* 56), and the method is that of natural science.

27. H. W. Piper argues convincingly that there is a basis for understanding Wordsworth in the light of Priestley, but Piper emphasizes Priestley's metaphysics rather than his rhetoric. See *The Active Universe: Pantheism and the Concept of Imagination in the English Romantic Poets* (London: University of London/Athlone Press, 1962). Similarly, Alan Grob discusses Priestley, but focuses on him as a proponent of Hartley rather than as a rhetorician. See *The Philosophic Mind: A Study of Wordsworth's Poetry and Thought, 1797–1805* (Columbus: Ohio State University Press, 1973). And although Priestley's *Course of Lectures* is noted by W. J. B. Owen in his extended study of the "Preface," no theoretical implications are drawn out. See *Wordsworth as Critic* (Toronto: University of Toronto Press, 1969). Hans Aarsleff, too, acknowledges the influence of Priestley on Wordsworth, but sees Condillac as a more appropriate source for Wordsworth's philosophy of language. See "Wordsworth, Language, and Romanticism," in *From Locke to Saussure* (Minneapolis: University of Minnesota Press, 1982).

28. Separate from the methodology of truth and science is that of style, which

comprehends whatever is *ornamental* in a discourse or composition. . . . The subject of this last part is calculated to attract and engage the attention, by the grace and harmony of the style, the turn of thought, or the striking or pleasing manner in which sentiments are introduced and expressed. We have hitherto examined [under the category of method] what we may call the bones, muscles, and nerves of a composition; we now come to the covering of this body, to describe the external lineaments, the colour, the complexion, and graceful attitude of it. (*CLO* 71–72)

It is in the context of style, of ornamentation, that Priestley develops his separation of *logos* from *ethos* and *pathos*, in terms, like Campbell's, of the imagination and passions:

The pleasure that a discourse may give to the *imagination*, or the emotion it may raise in the *passions*, are things that are brought about more indirectly, being effected by the *manner* in which things that tend ultimately to *convince* and *persuade* are expected. The orator may, indeed, intend to please or affect his hearers; but, if he understands himself, he only means to influence their judgments, or resolutions, by the medium of imagination or the passions. (*CLO* 68)

29. Aarsleff, *From Locke to Saussure*, 372–81.
30. Robert Scholes, *Structuralism in Literature: An Introduction* (New Haven and London: Yale University Press, 1974), 173.

The Rhetoric and Context
of John Thelwall's "Memoir"

Michael Scrivener

A hostile landlord and the disastrous harvest of 1800 ended John Thelwall's three and a half years as a farmer on this thirty-five acres in Lyswen, Brecknockshire, a remote and isolated Welsh village. He could have found another farm, but he decided instead to reactivate his career as a public writer with *Poems chiefly written in Retirement.*[1] Earlier in 1801 the liberal publisher Phillips had paid him desperately needed cash for the hastily written but fairly well received novel *The Daughter of Adoption* by John Beaufort. The pseudonym is interesting, first for its necessity (Thelwall's name was too notorious for the novel-reading public) and its defiance (his most famous political lectures were delivered from the Beaufort Buildings). With the 1801 *Poems,* he reduced the risk of publishing in his own name by relying on subscription rather than the anonymous market. It went without saying that he could not write about politics because of the political repression (even moderates like Gilbert Wakefield, Joseph Johnson, and Benjamin Flower were being legally prosecuted) and the dramatic change in the public's attitude. By 1801 the anti-Jacobin reaction had thoroughly discredited democratic cultural tendencies of any sort for most of the book-buying public; the New Philosophy had been subjected to a devastating flood of sermons, pamphlets, novels, satires, burlesques, caricatures, and critiques in the latter part of the 1790s. This was also a time when former enthusiasts of the French Revolution and radical reforms in England were recanting or moderating their ideas. Thelwall was in a tiny minority of middle-class intellectuals who neither recanted nor moderated their earlier radicalism. Nevertheless, he wanted to make a living as an intellectual and was necessarily dependent on an anti-Jacobin public.

The 1801 *Poems* is Thelwall's attempt to rehabilitate his status as an intellectual. Although the book sold well (1,500 copies by subscription, and there was a second edition), he in fact used the occasion of the book's relatively favorable reception to become a self-nominated Professor of Elocution, lecturing around England and Scotland, finally settling in London after he had succeeded so well elsewhere. He eventually became prosperous from his elocution and speech therapy business, but his financial success had not changed his politics or his devotion to poetry: he continued to write and sometimes publish his poetry, and in 1818, during the revival of democratic politics, he bought the moderate-reform *Champion* and turned it into a radical-reform periodical; he also fully participated in London reform politics at public meetings. In one way, the 1801 *Poems* achieved an important purpose because he was able thereafter to publish in his own name and resume his role as an intellectual. In other ways, however, the book failed: he was unable to make a living and support his family as a *literary* intellectual, clearly his first preference. One could say, of course, that Thelwall's poetry was not good enough to merit the fame he desired, but this is an inadequate explanation. There were far worse poets than Thelwall who were popular at the time, and in terms of quality, although he wrote no great poems, he did write numerous good ones and many more interesting and promising poems that initiated experiments the more famous romantic poets would use more skillfully.[2] Had he been given more encouragement and opportunities, he surely would have developed more as a poet. He turned professionally from poetry to elocution because the literary public would not grant him the power of poetic representation he asked for, and the public's refusal was ultimately political.

Thelwall had been a poet both before and during his tumultuous political career, so that his credentials as a serious poet were well established. Nevertheless, some kind of special appeal to the reader was necessary because of his radical reputation. The "Prefatory Memoir" to the *Poems* is a forty-eight-page text fascinating not only in its own right but also as it frames the subsequent poems, as it narrates his life, as it reflects on his other writings, as romantic autobiography, and as a cultural document relevant to the period's politics and literary assumptions. The preface was a genre Thelwall seems to have been fond of since he wrote so many, but this is an extraordinary one because the immediate rhetorical task is so difficult: to ask the literary public to read his poetry without political prejudice. Other than Paine, who had left England in 1792, there was probably no one who evoked the image of intransigent democratic radical more than Thelwall, not simply because he had been tried for treason in 1794, but because he was so closely associated with the most discredited "Jacobin" idea, social equality. After his acquittal, he lectured on politics to ever larger audiences of laborers, artisans, and tradesmen. Once the 1795 "Gagging Acts," enacted in part because of Thelwall, prohibited political lecturing, he lectured on classical history first in London and then in various towns around England where organized groups of anti-Jacobins disrupted the lectures. More than once he feared for his safety, even his life. When he retired from politics in 1797, he did so because he had little choice.[3] That he lectured to the "lower orders" during a time of intense political conflict to encourage radical democracy was unforgivable because it violated one of the most basic hegemonic assumptions of the literary culture, namely, the dichotomy between the "judicious" and the "uneducated" reader. The former was educated enough to read potentially subversive texts without danger because his learning permitted him to interpret and discriminate. The latter, however, was like an empty vessel that a subversive text filled without any act of interpretation; this passive reader, then, was unable to make proper use of such a text and would turn against established authorities if exposed to it. For example, in the sedition trial for Paine's *The Rights of Man, Part II*, attorney general Archibald Macdonald prosecuted the case only because Part II was published in a cheap edition and distributed so widely among poor people. The "judicious reader" could "refute" Paine "as he went along," but the text was placed in the hands of those incapable of interpretation, "that part of the public whose minds cannot be supposed to be conversant with subjects of this sort, and who cannot therefore correct as they go along."[4] These passive readers have "minds perhaps not sufficiently cultivated and habituated to reading," so that they are "ignorant," "credulous," and, when politicized, "desperate" (383). Thelwall was worse than Paine in one respect: one did not even have to read his words but only to listen to them.[5]

Near the end of the "Memoir," Thelwall complains that "he has to encounter prejudice and hostility in those classes of society, who alone can be expected to have a taste for such [poetic] compositions, or to give them extensive encouragement" (xliii). Although this seems to be a version of the judicious/uneducated dichotomy, it reflects more the economic reality of the poetry business: the book-buying public was socially different from the public that attended his political lectures. Nevertheless, the kind of poetry Thelwall writes presupposes not just the money to buy books but also the leisure to read it and other texts that provide the literary conventions by which his poetry is meaningful. He is in an awkward situation because he does not believe in the judicious/uneducated dichotomy, which he attacks directly in one section of the "Memoir," yet he has to depend on the genteel public if he is to earn money as a literary intellectual. How can he appeal to this public without betraying his former political public? The "Memoir" tries to remove the prejudice and hostility of the literary public while at the same time *not* recanting his politics. The rhetorical strategies he uses in the "Memoir" are inevitably complex, but they can be characterized as vindication of his "character," his moral qualities.

The timing of his public reappearance does not seem accidental. Thelwall's retirement from and return to public life roughly coincides with the activity of the Foxite Whigs. On 26 May 1797, Grey's motion for parliamentary reform was overwhelmingly defeated, leading to the Foxite Whig secession from Parliament and political retirement to their country estates. On 4

February 1800, Fox returned to Parliament, and a year later Pitt resigned; moreover, peace negotiations that would result in the treaty of Amiens in March 1802 were under way in 1801. That Thelwall's political retirement (even the choice of a rural retreat is Whiggish) and reentry into public life coincided with the moves of the Foxite Whigs could be mere coincidence, but it more likely indicates the degree to which, consciously or unconsciously, his decisions as an intellectual were influenced by the most liberal wing of a social group to which he did not belong.[6] The "Memoir," however, portrays a chain of disasters that forced Thelwall to reenter public life in order to take care of his family.

The parallel with Fox raises the issue of Thelwall's political ideology and his social role as intellectual. Although everyone is an intellectual, according to Gramsci, not everyone has the "function" of the intellectual, which is to give homogeneity to a social group's awareness of itself economically, socially, politically, and culturally. A social group draws upon "traditional" intellectuals or generates its own "organic" intellectuals. As a group in their own right, intellectuals tend to seek as much autonomy as they can and also tend to idealize their autonomy, disguising their dependence on the social group they ultimately serve.[7] During his most radical period (1793–97), Thelwall was an organic intellectual for the educated artisans and "middling classes." As the London Corresponding Society's most prominent orator, Thelwall spoke to a fairly homogenous audience of educated artisans and the politicized lower-middle class before being arrested in 1794 for treason.[8] After being acquitted, he launched another series of lectures only after resigning from the LCS, the Society for Constitutional Information, and the Friends of the People so as not to involve these organizations in the legal trouble he anticipated. At this, his most famous series of lectures, he discovered that the audience was no longer socially homogenous but included far more poor people (*Life*, 358–59). The specific social group from which he came, with which he identified, and to whom he spoke in most of his lectures was "the second and third rate class of tradesmen," those of the "middling classes" who were socially above laborers but well below the genteel middle class (*Life*, 21). According to an historian of the period, "There was often no great gap between journeyman and small master or shopkeeper, tradesman, self-employed engraver, printer, apothecary, teacher, journalist, surgeon or Dissenting clergyman."[9] This social group filled the ranks of the LCS, which was influential with the urban poor and which, according to one of its famous members, Francis Place, was just as valuable for social and educational reasons as political. Many former LCS members, according to Place, became "respectable" and prosperous businessmen, just as Place and Thelwall did, and they assisted one another in ways typical for union members but not competing businessmen.[10] Nevertheless, because this social group was not powerful enough to contest for power on its own, there were enormous pressures on Thelwall to serve, as an intellectual, a social group other than his own.

The political ideology to which Thelwall subscribed was a typical synthesis and revision of the reform ideology formulated at least by the 1760s. His social group, then, illustrates its weakness by relying so heavily on an ideology that was already established. Although Thelwall had little faith in the Foxite Whigs, whose timidity rarely failed to disappoint him, he nevertheless maintained an ideological affinity with them by asserting political concepts he liked to call True Whig principles, rooted in the Commonwealthman tradition, the "Norman yoke" myth of Saxon democracy, and classical republicanism. The democratic reforms he promoted were not "innovations" but restorations of ancient and natural rights that a fraudulent aristocracy had taken away. When the earliest parliamentary reformers in the 1760s advocated universal suffrage and annual parliaments, they did not think that property would be in jeopardy or that the "labouring poor" and "middling classes" would pursue a politics independent of "respectable" politicians because they were so confident that the "lower orders" would defer to their "superiors." They actually envisioned an assault on "Old Corruption," the network of interlocking alliances, monopolies, and patronage created and sustained by the crown and aristocracy. The bourgeois utopia was to be economic (scientific, technological) development and free trade, low taxes, peace, complete civil liberties for Dissenters, and a minimal state with moral legitimacy (hence the centrality of the reform issue of abolishing the slave trade).[11] The middle-class reformers were a part of a much broader ideological configuration that was sponsored ultimately by the Whig magnates who contested for power against George III, who, unlike the first two Georges, tried to revive royal prerogatives. According to Marilyn Butler, the Whig oligarchy from the 1760s to the early 1790s promoted a libertarian cultural insurgency that entailed an extraordinary degree of experimentation. Like the reformers, the liberal Whigs were confident that libertarian rhetoric and cultural innovation would not undermine but expand their power.[12] Pocock has written about the English Enlightenment enjoying so much establishment tolerance, haunted as the ruling class was by the specter of religious irrationality and revolutionary disorder.[13] The Enlightenment ideological consensus that had been so confident was destroyed by the LCS, Thelwall's own lectures, the widespread popularity of Paine's *The Rights of Man, Part II,* and of course revolutionary Paris. As the sternest critics of Enlightened culture had been warning, political reforms and cultural innovation could indeed threaten the power of the propertied classes to "represent" their society. As the Enlightenment synthesis crumbled, political repression supplanted tolerance, and anti-Jacobin cultural reaction replaced libertarian experimentation.[14]

Thelwall, who came to intellectual maturity before the cultural reaction, never abandoned the Enlightenment assumptions he had acquired. He tried to make these assumptions fit the new ideological situation, but he did not, like Coleridge, articulate a new synthesis. Thelwall's literary romanticism was completely unmarked by any counter-Enlightenment concepts or by any disillusionment with the French Revolution or English democratic politics. Rather, his romanticism was an inevitable aspect of Enlightened culture, compatible with its other components: materialism, democracy, scientific reason, and antireligious secularism. Revising and experimenting with primarily sentimental conventions, he never felt compelled to dissociate this literary romanticism from other aspects of Enlightened culture.[15]

The "Memoir"'s difficult rhetorical task, then, is to make Enlightened assumptions fit the new cultural situation. The "Memoir" begins appropriately enough with an insistence that Thelwall will not discuss politics; rather, "he is desirous that the politician should be forgotten; and that, till the prejudices of party shall subside into the candour of unimpassioned appreciation, he should henceforth be known and noticed (as here he is introduced) only as a candidate for poetical and moral reputation" (ii). Using the third person is an obvious way to add objective credibility to the "Memoir," especially because in the first paragraph he claims that he is slightly revising the article on himself in Phillips's *Public Characters*, as if someone other than himself had written it.[16] Being able to separate private and public, the aesthetic and the political, was part of the Enlightenment structure of feeling. The famous episode related by Boswell in which Samuel Johnson dined very amicably with his political enemy John Wilkes is a good example of the older tolerance Thelwall is trying to rehabilitate. That "poetical" is linked so closely with "moral" is no accident because the *kind* of literature he is offering to the public is such that the author's morality is an issue. The romantic bard, to have representative power, has to be morally impeccable, according to the myth, and the author of highly personal lyrics must also maintain an image of moral rectitude in order to fulfill his role in the author-reader contract for that genre.

One purpose of the "Memoir" is to establish a moral character that would supplant his public persona as a radical politician. As a democratic "tribune," appealing to a very different audience, he also felt it was necessary to establish his moral credentials. Early in one particular speech, he declares:

I have renounced myself those pursuits of taste and literature to which, from my boyish days, I have been so fondly devoted, as to sacrifice to them the flattering prospects of affluence and worldly ambition, which a lucrative profession presented before me; and have devoted myself, whole and entire, to the service of the public . . . whose happiness alone I look forward to as my dearest, and my ultimate reward.[17]

Just as the romantic bard must renounce worldly ambition, so the tribune must also prove his disinterestedness—and in this case, by renouncing his role as poet! Whether in politics or literature, the intellectual has to assert his autonomy and the special qualities that place him above those he serves. In the "Preface" to *The Tribune*, Thelwall asserts his "higher motives" in publishing his lectures, higher, that is, than fame or profit.[18] Indeed, he claims he is sacrificing both fame and profit by conducting and then publishing his lectures, but he is willing to undergo the sacrifice for the sake of "the oppressed and industrious orders of society" (vii). In fact, even before the 1795 lectures, as I have already noted, he effaced himself and added to his authority as a tribune by resigning from the political organizations to which he belonged. By Volume 3 of *The Tribune*, he writes of having "sold myself to the public," of no longer having personal interests: "I am no longer my own property" (2). As tribune, he becomes subject to the conventions of that role, which require a disinterested motive in politically educating his immediate audience and representing their interests to the wealthier public that purchased *The Tribune*. These conventions, which reassure the audience and provide a norm by which tribunes are judged, obviously obscure the tribune's own interests, material and otherwise, which no human being can ever fully repress.

To return to the "Memoir," after reassuring his readers that they will not have to approve his politics, he writes about his ancestors, grandfather and father, highlighting the "respectable" aspects of his family and in fact generating a narrative in which three generations of Thelwall sons are defrauded of a rightful patrimony. His grandfather Walter was cheated of his rightful property because as a naval surgeon he treated not just the British but the Spanish as well, thus committing an unforgivable political misdeed that disqualified him from laying "claim to the inheritance of his fathers" (iii). This is the stuff of sentimental fiction, whether it happened or not, because an act of "benevolence" leads to a melodramatic social punishment. The patrimony eludes Thelwall's father as well due to the "selfish apathy of certain relations" (iii). Whatever property Walter had accumulated was squandered in his grandmother's second marriage. His father, a London silk mercer who died when Thelwall was ten years old, is represented in an idealized way (his older brother assumes the role of tyrant). His father "formed great expectations" for his son John, hoping to make him "an historical painter" (vii), but this plan was undermined after his father's death by the family's failure to follow the father's will in selling the silk shop. Instead, they continued the business and Thelwall was forced "against his own inclination, and in violent opposition to every indication of his mind" to work "behind the shop counter" until he was sixteen, after which he was apprenticed to a London tailor. Before being apprenticed, he tried to become a painting student but "the mistaken economy of his mother made the premium and expences an insurmountable bar" (viii). Had the family followed the paternal will by selling the business, John would have had enough money to pay "a painter of some eminence" (viii) for instruction. He next tried to apprentice himself to the theater, for which he had enthusiasm but little self-confidence.

The ever elusive patrimony and Thelwall's intellectual ambitions are interesting in this respect: structurally, the way he portrays his father and his own identity is homologous with his political ideology, which assumes the existence of a democratic constitution that has been fraudulently destroyed by a self-aggrandizing aristocracy; by following his own desire for intellectual distinction, he is in fact fulfilling the true wishes of the absent and now powerless father; he has formed an alliance with his dead father against the various tyrants who try to coerce Thelwall away from his true identity.

His schooling was unexceptionally miserable except for what must have been a remarkable three months during which he was taught by a clergyman named Harvey (tributes to whom are in his 1787, 1793, and 1801 poetry). Harvey's libertarian teaching methods "sowed" in Thelwall's mind "the seeds of literary ambition" (vi). The teacher was so good because he was friendly, informal, encouraging, and permitted a degree of student initiative. In his political lectures, he adopts Harvey's pedagogic style: conversational, informal, personal, encouraging initiative on the part of his audience. So much of his poetry, too, represents an amiable persona. In describing both his father and Harvey, the "Memoir" notices as most endearing those qualities not traditionally masculine, especially for the lower middle class: his father was "mild and gentle" and "the enemy of no human being" (iv); Harvey was a "conversational champion," "remarkably lax" in discipline. The qualities of his ideal males are significant when one notices Thelwall's emphasis on his own sickliness, weakness, and "want of figure" (viii). Physical weakness as a sign of spiritual strength was a sentimental convention. Whether the young John had read sentimental fiction as a sickly youth hardly matters because he would have been acquainted with the sentimental conventions in some way; those conventions, a version of which was the bardic myth, gave Thelwall a way to articulate his unhappiness with lower-middle-class life.

Except for Harvey, Thelwall represents himself as primarily self-taught, learning the most when stealing some moments for reading books from the hours of labor. One of the things he shared with the audience of his political lectures and fellow "citizens" of the LCS was the pride of the autodidact. As an apprentice, he found himself among men of a slightly lower social stratum but found them more intellectually compatible than the shopkeepers he had grown up with. He makes a sociological reflection to emphasize the point:

> . . . the manufacturing and working classes . . . are much better informed than the thriving shopkeepers. . . . The former have their common hive, as it were, to which each brings his stock, however small, of intellectual

attainment, where it grows by copartnership, and is enjoyed in common; while the other secluded, for so many hours of the day, from all conversation, but what relates to the mere object of barter, toils, insulated, like the *Solitary Bee*, storing up his profits in his particular cell. . . . (x)

Although he has agreed to refrain from discussing politics, in this and other passages he vindicates the social group for which and with which he worked as "tribune." He is also idealizing the journeymen and artisans by highlighting their desire for knowledge and giving to the shopkeepers the stereotypical qualities associated with laborers, intellectual dullness and caring only for "low" pleasures ("the pipe, the bottle, or the bowl"). He is also undermining the dichotomy between the judicious and the uneducated reader by showing that formal education is not a prerequisite for intellectual culture.

During the year and a half he was a tailor's apprentice, he associates his literary ambition with his physical illnesses because when he was too sick to work he could read "at his mother's country house" (xiii). His particular ailments were asthma and "inflammations of the lungs," both of which could be representative of his repressed desire for literary fame as actor or poet speaking a language that transcends commerce. Work literally made him sick, which in turn permitted him to fulfill his desire for literature. Being too sensitive for the business world was already a cliché in Thelwall's time as novels and poems portrayed gentlemen too exquisitely sensitive to fare well in the harsh, greedy world (Mackenzie's *The Man of Feeling* is a perfect example of this; the hero literally dies because of his sensitivity). The romantic myth of the poet, including a sickly, alienated childhood, is governed ultimately by sentimental conventions that established a huge gap between literary and material-economic realities.

After insisting that his master-tailor cancel his indentures, to which his master agreed, Thelwall for three and a half years was a law apprentice. His "objections to the profession itself were radical and insurmountable" because as a lawyer he could not "give unreserved utterance to the existing convictions of his heart" (xvii). There was only one profession that might permit such free expression, and finally, at age twenty-two in 1786, now free of his law indentures, he began his career "as a literary adventurer" with serious disadvantages: no profession, fortune, or literary friends; "without the advantages of a regular education"; having to support an aged mother and a sick brother he disliked. Despite these obstacles, he published by subscription *Poems on Various Subjects* in 1787, which was noted favorably by the *Critical Review* and which led to his meeting new people and forming "truly valuable friendships" (xix), only one of which he mentions by name. (Coleridge insisted that Thelwall omit any references to him in the "Memoir" as he was afraid this would damage his reputation and ability to provide for his family.)[19] In his early years as a literary intellectual he lived in Lambeth with his mother and ailing brother, earned around fifty pounds a year, edited the *Imperial and Biographical Magazine*, wrote for other periodicals, and was engaged as a teacher. By 1791, his prospects were good enough—two to three hundred pounds a year from various sources—to marry and move to a presumably better neighborhood where he expanded his intellectual contacts. In the narrative of his early years as a literary intellectual, there is a recurrent pattern of Thelwall's success being sabotaged by factors out of his control. For example, he proudly relates his success among the medical professors at Guy's Hospital and in the Physical Society, of which he was a member and to which he delivered several lectures, the last of which led to his expulsion from the Society (xxii–xxiii). According to Thelwall, the only factor in his expulsion was political prejudice because his first lecture, which was well received, maintained the same ideas as the second, which was judged so offensive, namely, that mental "phenomena" could be "explained upon principles *purely* Physical." He portrays himself as a well-intentioned intellectual performing his work honestly, but he is continually undermined by prejudice, "calumnies," and "misrepresentations." In truth, his medical lecture was not quite as innocent as he claims.

A similar narrative accompanies his prospects as a dramatist. Thomas Holcroft was so impressed by the 1793 *Peripatetic* that he urged Thelwall to concentrate solely on drama for the London theater, in which Holcroft was a prominent playwright (xxi). According to the "Memoir," after the treason trials (during which, of course, Holcroft was indicted too), Thelwall could have enjoyed great literary success, but instead he ruined his literary prospects by concentrating on politics (xxix). As he complains in 1801, he is excluded from the literary genre for which he seems most suited—apparently drama (xliii). The London theaters were indeed sensitive to ideological heresy, eventually driving Holcroft from the stage, but the "Memoir" makes it appear as if Thelwall's theatrical career were prevented from prospering solely as an *individual* instance of prejudice, a personal attack, as if it had happened to a hero in a sentimental novel. Rhetorically, the victimized individual is more appealing than a victimized ideology and political-social movement.

He cannot avoid discussing his political career, but he does so without discussing the content of his politics, which he had promised to do. First, he portrays his acquisition of democratic "principles" as an organic, natural process that follows the dictates of his reason and "heart," and all he ever gets from politics are "anxieties and misfortunes" (xxiii). He makes it seem as if his democratic ideology happened *to* him so that any sort of blame would be beside the point. Second, his political narrative emphasizes civil liberties, political procedures (rather than ideas), and ordinary fairness. His entry into politics, for example, was precipitated by the rigging of the Westminster election in 1790, and his earliest political awareness was acquired by participating in a debating society that had no political agenda. He was instrumental in getting the debating society to concentrate solely on history and politics, but, in consequence, he was excluded from the Coachmaker's Hall. After the society was expelled from its second location, Thelwall tried to find—without success—a room anywhere in the City of London where "the right of magisterial interference with the freedom of popular discussion" might be debated (xxv). After finding a room in the borough for a debate, he had to prevent a riot when the police came (xxv). As a consequence of this near riot, he could find no one to debate him, and so began his career as a political lecturer (xxvi).

Thelwall's account of becoming a tribune is rhetorically effective because he omits from the narrative all things that would have disturbed his readers. By late 1792 or early 1793, the political situation was so highly charged and polarized that democratic ideas could not be debated in a gentlemanly, Enlightenment manner: 21 May 1792, there was the Royal Proclamation against Seditious Writings; November 1792, the Association for Protecting Liberty and Property against Republicans and Levellers was established; 11 December 1792, a Manchester Church and King riot attacked French Revolution sympathizers; 13 December 1792, there were Cambridge loyalist riots; 21 January 1793, King Louis XVI was executed; February 1793, war was declared between France and England. Thelwall's lectures were bold political actions, not mere exercises in abstract civil liberties, as his audience swelled from a lowly sixty at a Compton Street newspaper room to an impressive 750 at the Beaufort Buildings (xxvi). What was politically terrifying to anti-Jacobins—democratic orators lecturing to large audiences of the "uneducated"—the "Memoir" turns into a story of entrepreneurial success, adherence to abstract rights, and personal courage.

One way Thelwall treats the most significant event in his political life—his seven weeks at Newgate Prison, five months in solitary confinement in the Tower, the treason trial—is to protest against the seizure and loss of his literary manuscripts, books, engravings and notes that were unrelated to politics. He transforms this episode into an allegory directly related to the "Memoir"'s purpose of vindicating his own literary reputation: "in the fiercest warfare of opinion, the Temple of the Muses should still be sacred: confiscation should not extend to intellect and the arts: there should be no war against the mind" (xxvii–xxviii). Of all the things he could have represented, he chooses to highlight the loss of his literary manuscripts. Of the trial itself, he refers the reader to his lawyers' speeches in court, especially the famous Erskine's, and alludes to his own published defense in a manner that disguises its apologetic ethos (xxviii–xxix). The only representation of his experiences he selects for mention is the 1795 *Poems written in close confinement in the Tower and Newgate*, "the first published attempts . . . at correct composition" (xxix). In deferring to his lawyers' representations and highlighting the literary correctness of his prison poetry, Thelwall once again appeals to his readers' predilections.

After leaving prison Thelwall resumed his lecturing activities, publishing his lectures—taken down in shorthand, as a legal precaution against the state's "arts of Misrepresentation" (xxix)—in the periodical *The Tribune*, to which I have already alluded. "Representation," like "constitution," was a key word for Thelwall, the democratic movement, and the hegemonic culture. Politically, Thelwall supported radical parliamentary reform, universal manhood suffrage, and annual parliaments, but spoke against direct democracy (appropriate only for a small state), the hegemonic concept of "virtual representation" (for which Burke provided one of the most effective defenses), and moderate reform (property qualifications for suffrage and less frequent elections). As a tribune, he was supposed to represent the "people." As a literary writer, he was engaged in representation of a very complicated sort. In fact, the entire 1801 volume is ultimately a sentimental performance, an appeal to the reader on the basis of feeling and sensibility to grant the author representative power in at least the nonpolitical realm. He seeks election, if not as a tribune for political ideas and interests, then as a bard representing the culture's inner life. Thelwall cannot get elected because he cannot or will not represent the feelings his public would like represented. Since the literary public defines itself now *against* the radical ideas Thelwall refuses to recant or moderate, it cannot permit Thelwall to become its bard.

There is a logical sequence in the 1801 *Poems* from the "Memoir," through the lyrical drama *The Fairy of the Lake* and the autobiographical lyrics ("Effusions," as they were called), to the concluding national epic, *The Hope of Albion*. The "Memoir" is a sentimental narrative showing the development of someone who ultimately becomes a "man of feeling" and literary intellectual; the unfeeling world drives the hero into exile where he is still hounded by persecution; additionally, he is a victim of bad luck (the unfortunate 1800 harvest) and loses his firstborn child, his beloved daughter, to a fatal illness; driven to desperation, he is forced to leave his isolated farm and settles in what he calls a more civilized town (apparently Hereford), where at least he can feel safe, even if his notoriety ruins any chance for a social life that he sorely misses. His suffering can be alleviated only if the reader accepts the narrative and all its conventions, which would lead at least to his losing a pariah status and at best to his gaining literary encouragement.

The lyrical drama, however unorthodox, is designed for the stage and illustrates the dramatic talent he would like to employ. *The Fairy of the Lake* is a treatment of the Arthurian legend that focuses on the destruction of one order and the emergence of another, with the central force of power being represented as a feminine entity very much like the romantic Muse or Nature so common in Thelwall's other poetry. Despite the nationalistic appeal, the poem is too experimental and, at a structural level, too "Jacobin" in its celebration of old authority being overthrown to appeal to the public.[20]

The autobiographical "Effusions" are introduced by a note that declares the poems here "are not presented as specimens of Poetical Talent. They have . . . a higher interest. They are the effusions, not of the Poet, but of the Father. . . . If fiction be essential to Poetry, there is little here. . . ." (94). Actually, most of the poems in this section are neither paternal nor connected with his daughter's death, but they are similar in that they try to represent Thelwall's own private rather than public consciousness. The best of these are what we would now call conversation poems, which did not enjoy the same generic prestige then as they do now. The overall purpose of the "Effusions," however, is to illustrate Thelwall's moral character and establish his authority as a sentimental writer.

The most ambitious text is the national epic, *The Hope of Albion*. As becomes clear in his introductory note, these "specimens" (parts of the first two books) are designed as a test: if the public approves these fragments, then the poet will devote the time and effort to complete the work; without encouragement, the epic will not be completed because it entails the kind of labor he cannot undertake without the patronage of the literary public. A lyrical "effusion" requires no study or arduous rewriting, but a national epic does because it represents the spiritual concerns of the nation, without whose support the epic is meaningless, at least within Enlightenment assumptions. Thelwall lacks the individualistic confidence of a Blake, who could compose national epics without any social encouragement. One should note, however, Wordsworth's painful progress with his own epic, *The Recluse*, which also needed a long "prefatory memoir" to justify his character as a bard.

Although neither the lyrical drama nor the epic provoked a positive enough response, even a hostile reviewer, Francis Jeffrey, had some favorable words for the "Effusions." The literary public could grant Thelwall authority to represent his feelings but not society's broader cultural concerns, which now lay outside Enlightenment assumptions. That he structured the 1801 *Poems* as a sentimental narrative could not have been accidental because the genre contained those conventions derived from Enlightenment culture that could vindicate his private character. He uses the conventions, however, to prepare the reader to accept him as a public poet. For example, the "Memoir" represents Thelwall as being unable to work in the theater and on his epic because of public persecution: at Lyswen farm, he had no access to any library, public or private, and was forced to purchase all his books, and even the post was subject to state inspection and interference; one parcel of materials was intercepted and sent to the Privy Council. Although the parcel was returned, he again became an object of politicl notoriety, which stirred up the neighborhood and thus distracted him from work on the epic (xxxix). He also complains that social isolation hampers his work as a poet: "Whatever may have been said by visionary enthusiasts, continued solitude is the grave, rather than the nurse, of mind" (xlvi–xlvii). In order for Thelwall to succeed as a public poet, as the voice of more than private feelings, he has to be accepted into society. (He was too much within Enlightenment culture to revise the bardic myth in the direction of an utterly isolated poet whose autonomous imagination required no social support.)[21] Moreover, the "Memoir," far from being remorseful, constructs a situation whereby the *public* ought to be guilt-ridden for so mistreating a potential bard. Thelwall thus leaves only one way in which the reader can resist the narrative's logic: to impugn his character, to interpret the "growth" of his mind not as a sentimental tragedy of repression but as a sentimental farce of presumptuous arrogance.

Francis Jeffrey does precisely this in his review of the 1801 volume in the *Edinburgh Review*.[22] "In every page of this extraordinary Memoir," Jeffrey writes, "we discover traces of that impatience of honest industry, that presumptuous vanity, and precarious principle, that have thrown so many adventurers upon the world, and drawn so many females from their plain work and embroidery, to delight the public by their beauty in the streets, and their novels in the circulating library" (200). This sentence is informed by the anti-Jacobin assumptions that even a liberal Whig periodical now takes for granted: whatever reforms of public policy might be desirable, the idea of social equality must be ruthlessly beaten down. The analogy between Thelwall and a streetwalking, novel-writing woman suggests that both are guilty of disturbing a natural order in which women perform menial tasks and men from the "middling classes" stay behind the shop counter; also, Jeffrey draws an implicit contrast between a legitimate literary culture unconnected with buying and selling and a presumptuous democratic culture marked entirely by the most immoral kind of economic exchange, prostitution. (One liability of the bardic myth of literature's unworldly origins is that it is not dissimilar to the reactionary idea that only "gentlemen" who do not have to work for a living can create and properly judge literature; Jeffrey employs this idea with great zeal.) Yet he also draws another implicit comparison: for just as the English Jacobins upset the natural political order by promoting social equality, so various literary pretenders from the lower classes try to gain recognition as poets and serious writers, upsetting the literary order. Jeffrey groups Thelwall with ploughboys, carpenters, hairdressers, valets, waiters, shoemakers, and tailors, all of whom have tried to acquire literary "distinction" (197). Robert Bloomfield, who was both a "ploughboy" and a "shoemaker," was a spectuclar poetic success (he also attended the debates at the Coachmaker's Hall where Thelwall received such an important education).[23] There were other poets, not nearly as successful, from the "lower orders": Joseph Blackett, Kirke White, and Ann Yearsley, to name three. Jeffrey represents them all as social bounders who are trying to avoid the hard work that destiny has given them.

The Thelwall-Jeffrey controversy did not end with the review. Shortly after the review, Thelwall's lecture on elocution in Edinburgh was disrupted by hecklers, who were orchestrated, according to Thelwall, by Jeffrey (also in attendance). Thelwall published an attack on Jeffrey, an anonymous reply by Jeffrey (or a very close friend) attacked Thelwall, and finally Thelwall wrote a reply to this.[24] Thelwall's pamphlets express an anxiety over his inability to make a living and support his family because in Edinburgh he could neither lecture nor sell any literature. If his career as elocution professor was to be subject to the same persecution as his political career, he could not live as an intellectual. Jeffrey's hostility, however, was actually moderate in comparison with anti-Jacobin diatribes typical of an earlier period (1791–1800). The anonymous pamphlet replying to Thelwall is marked by a sneering contempt for Thelwall, whose politics are unforgivable but no longer dangerous. The critique of Thelwall, not so much political as social, finds especially offensive Thelwall's portrait of himself as an emergent literary intellectual. According to the pamphlet, Thelwall is lazy, lacks integrity, and is willing to sell himself to anyone who will buy; he has "broken his indentures to three regular professions, purely because he had an 'abhorrence' of 'trade,' and 'a distaste for drudgery;' and who has since lived as an Itinerant Lecturer on Politics, History, and Elocution" (13). The adjective "itinerant" has a rich resonance for Thelwall because as a poet he portrays himself as a "peripatetic," a wanderer in nature and with an imagination that could not follow a regular course but rather pursued its own objects; moreover, he took pride in writing verse that wandered away from the preestablished literary rules. Also, his literal wandering from place to place was governed by political repression and persecution. Jeffrey's use of "itinerant," however, evokes dangerous vagrants, beggars, rabble-rousing democratic orators, and religiously suspect Dissenting ministers, as well as peddlers, gypsies, and others without a fixed place or station.[25]

Both men won the debate but in different ways: Thelwall's defenses of himself were successful enough to permit his elocution business to flourish, but Jeffrey's attacks were consonant enough with public feeling that Thelwall's *literary* career went nowhere. Moreover, Jeffrey's attack and Thelwall's reception in Edinburgh served as a warning that Thelwall hardly needed: if he was tempted to inject radical politics into his elocution business, he would be punished without mercy.

Thelwall's becoming an elocution and speech entrepreneur was hardly an accident. He went from democratic tribune speaking on politics to lecturing on classical history, which ended with his forced political retirement. After a long public silence because of political repression, he lectures on the *process* of lecturing; all content has been omitted and what remains is pure technique. Although his elocution writings are apolitical, they are also entirely without Enlightenment assumptions: he draws upon his medical materialism to reduce speech problems to their purely physical operations; he asserts that anyone, regardless of birth, can become a fine public speaker; he emphasizes the importance of public speaking in a vital political culture. In fact, however, market considerations worked against any democratic tendencies because it was more profitable to sell speech techniques to the wealthy. By 1813 he was so successful that his library had between three and four thousand volumes, he lived in a spacious mansion (even though the rooms were used also to house students), and he had been able to send his son to Cambridge.[26] In 1818 he could *buy* a newspaper and run it in the way he wanted.

Although Thelwall bristled at Jeffrey's calling him a prostitute, he undoubtedly turned to elocution in order to make money and provide a comfortable existence for his family. He was hardly naive about the cultural cash nexus, as is evident in his political lectures. In Volume 2 of *The Tribune*, he attacks the power of wealth to determine the ideological meanings of literary culture, showing that literary representation is also tied to power:

> These privileged classes though not themselves very famous for works of genuis, have, in a considerable degree held not only the sword but the pen. For money will make the pen to go as well as the mare: nay, power and patronage will command it without the assistance of money; and therefore it is, that more than one half of the romances which are sent into the world under the denomination of histories, political surveys, views of society and *morals*, topographical descriptions, and the like, are stuffed with nothing but servile adulations and time-serving misrepresentations, to gloss over the conduct and characters of the higher, and calumnious abuse and false descriptions of the lower orders—calculated to steel the hearts of the readers against them. (326)

In another passage, he further develops the theme:

> . . . the powerful orders have the opportunity of painting the common people in whatever light it suits them; and to the disgrace of literature it has hardly ever happened that any man of considerable talents has had the disinterestedness and independence of mind to enlist himself in the service of the latter. (327)

Thelwall realizes that power is not exerted just in government and wealth but in literary culture in the form of what Gramsci would call hegemony. These passages also illustrate the extent to which they bear the weight of cultural hegemony even while protesting against it: "direct" literary democracy is not considered because the writer is stuck between the "people" and the literary public; the "people" cannot represent themselves. The literary tribune, unlike the aristocratic writer, accurately represents the interests of those who cannot represent themselves.

Jeffrey's hostility to Thelwall's "Memoir" and bardic ambitions was part of a much broader cultural rehabilitation of traditional authority, so weakened by Enlightenment culture. Coleridge's *Biographia Literaria* and the *Lay*

Sermons are good examples of defending weakened authorities without being utterly reactionary and by integrating some aspects of Enlightenment culture. Moreover, Coleridge could write with the authority of a former "Jacobin." By that time, 1816–17, however, there was a new democratic cultural insurgency led by Hunt, Hazlitt, Keats, Shelley, and Byron that accompanied the revival of democratic politics. Although Thelwall's role in the new democratic movement was not nearly as central as it was in the 1790s—Cobbett was the new democratic tribune—he nevertheless partici-pated actively in the reform politics, this time, however, trying to promote radical reform among an increasingly skeptical middle class. The lower classes were already in favor of radical reform, he reasoned, so the wealthier classes needed the political education. Several years after *The Champion* folded (as was predictable, given the middle-class hostility to universal suf-frage), he edited the *Monthly Magazine*, a periodical that had published Thelwall's own work even during his "exile" and whose publisher, Phillips, had published his novel in 1801 when he needed the money. In its prime, the *Monthly Magazine* had been the most advanced periodical for middle-class reformers, scientists, and Dissenting intellectuals, but by the time Thelwall became editor the cultural situation was altogether different: although he had not changed, middle-class culture had left behind its most radical past. Appropriately enough, Phillips sold the journal to owners who eventually fired Thelwall, who, in his sixties, still found himself victimized for his politics and adherence to Enlightenment cultural values.[27]

Notes

1. John Thelwall, *Poems chiefly written in Retirement* (Hereford: W. H. Parker, 1801). This work, along with several others by Thelwall, has been reprinted, with an introduction by Donald H. Reiman, in *Ode to Science, John Gilpin's Ghost, Poems, The Trident of Albion* (New York and London: Garland Publishers, 1978). All parenthetical references to Thelwall poems in the text are to this later edition.

2. Reiman, "Introduction" to *Ode to Science*, v–x. See also Vernon Owen Grumbling, "John Thelwall: Romantic and Revolutionist" (Ph.D. diss., University of New Hampshire, 1977), especially chaps. 3–5.

3. For Thelwall's political career in the 1790s, see Grumbling, "John Thelwall," chaps. 1 and 2; E. P. Thompson, *The Making of the English Working Class* (New York: Vintage, 1963), especially 156–60, and "Disenchantment or Default? A Lay Sermon," in *Power and Con-sciousness*, ed. Conor Cruise O'Brien and William Dean Vanech (London and New York: University of London Press and New York University Press, 1969), 156–62.

4. Quoted in T. B. Howell, *A Complete Collection of State Trials*, (London: Hansard, 1817), 22:381.

5. Godwin attacked Thelwall's political lecturing for not promoting rational public education but instead creating potential social disorder. *Considerations on Lord Grenville's and Mr. Pitt's Bills* (London: Joseph Johnson, 1795), reprinted, with an introduction by Jack W. Marken and Burton R. Pollin, in *Uncollected Writings by William Godwin* (Gainesville: Scholars' Facsimiles and Reprints, 1968). Cf. Coleridge's famous political dictum of always speaking *for* but never *to* the poor.

6. Grumbling disputes the emphasis Charles Cestre, *John Thelwall, A Pioneer of Democracy in England* (London and New York: Swann Sonneschein and Charles Scribner's Sons, 1906), places on the Whig influence on Thelwall's political thought, which, according to Grumbling, was also influenced by Toryism, which provided "a concern for economic and human ties as well as simply political ones" (84). Grumbling also sees Thelwall's political ideology as closer to socialism than to bourgeois liberalism (99).

7. Antonio Gramsci, *Selections from the Prison Notebooks*, trans. and ed. Quintin Hoare and Geoffrey Nowell Smith (New York: International Publishers, 1971), 5–9.

8. Mrs. [Cecil Boyle] Thelwall, *The Life of John Thelwall* (London: John Macrone, 1837), 354–55. Subsequent references to this volume will be given parenthetically in the text.

9. Iorwerth Prothero, *Artisans and Politics in Early Nineteenth Century London: John Gast and His Times* (Folkestone: William Dawson and Son, 1979), 20.

10. Mary Thale, ed., *The Autobiography of Francis Place, 1771–1854* (Cambridge: Cambridge University Press, 1972), 198–200. Place and Thelwall were friends, and very probably Place wrote the economic articles in Thelwall's *Champion*. For Place, see Thompson, *Making of the English Working Class*.

11. For middle-class reformism before 1832, see Thompson, *Making of the English Working Class;* Carl Cone, *The English Jacobins, Reformers in Late Eighteenth Century England* (New York: Charles Scribners' Sons, 1968); J. E. Cookson, *The Friends of Peace, Anti-War Liberalism in England* (Cambridge: Cambridge University Press, 1982).

12. Marilyn Butler, *Romantics, Rebels and Reactionaries* (Oxford: Oxford University Press, 1981), 1–38.

13. J. G. A. Pocock, "Post-Puritan England and the Problem of the Enlightenment," in Perez Zagorin, ed., *Culture and Politics, from Puritanism to the Enlightenment* (Los Angeles: University of California Press, 1980), 91–112.

14. Marilyn Butler has written persuasively on this phenomenon in *Romantics, Rebels and Reactionaries* and in other studies, especially *Jane Austen and the War of Ideas* (Oxford: Clarendon Press, 1975).

15. Cf. Butler's treatment of Blake, Wordsworth, and Shelley and his circle, which provocatively emphasizes the Englightenment and neoclassical continuities with romanticism (*Romantics, Rebels and Reactionaries*, chaps. 2 and 5).

16. All of the information and most of the wording in the *Public Characters* sketch are contained in the "Memoir," which, however, is approximately eight times longer. It seems obvious that Thelwall himself composed the *Public Characters* sketch. *Public Characters of 1800–1801* (London: Richard Phillips, 1801), 3:177–93.

17. John Thelwall, *Political Lectures*, no. 1 (London: Eaton, 1794), 2. The central text for Thelwall's own version of the bardic myth was James Beattie's *The Minstrel*, which, according to *The Peripatetic* (London: Thelwall, 1793; reprinted with an introduction by Donald Reiman, New York and London: Garland Publishers, 1978), was the poem in which he discovered his identity as a poet: "I traced in the youthful manners and dispositions of Edwin, the faithful delineation of my boyish years; and beheld, as in a mirror, the reflection of those features that so evidently marked my own eccentric mind" (1:97).

18. *The Tribune* (London: Eaton, Smith, Burks, 1795), 1:vi.

19. See S. T. Coleridge to John Thelwall, 23 April 1801, in Earl Leslie Griggs, ed., *The Collected Letters of Samuel Taylor Coleridge, 1801–1806* (Oxford: Clarendon Press, 1956), 2:724.

20. Grumbling points out the political allegory of *The Fairy of the Lake*. See "John Thelwall: Romantic and Revolutionist," 183.

21. Butler, *Romantics, Rebels and Reactionaries*, emphasizes how "social" the English romantics actually were, despite the romantic assertions of autonomy. In chapters 5 and 6, she portrays a cultural battle between the Shelley circle and the Lake poets.

22. *Edinburgh Review* 2 (April 1803): 197–202.

23. In Capel Lofft's Preface to *The Farmer's Boy* (1800), there is a brief portrait of Robert Bloomfield's life in which the Coachmaker's Hall debates are discussed. See Robert Bloomfield, *Collected Poems (1800–1822)*, ed. Jonathan N. Lawson (Gainesville: Scholars' Facsimiles and Reprints, 1971).

24. John Thelwall, *A Letter to Francis Jeffray [sic], Esq., On Certain Calumnies and Misrepre-

sentations in the Edinburgh Review (Edinburgh: Thelwall, 1804); Anon., *Observations on Mr. Thelwall's Letter to the Editor of the Edinburgh Review* (Edinburgh: D. Willison, 1804); John Thelwall, *Mr. Thelwall's Reply to Observations on Mr. Thelwall's Letter to The Editor of the Edinburgh Review* (Glasgow: W. Lang, 1804).

25. Especially in *The Peripatetic*, there are recurrent representations of various "itinerants," including vagrants, beggars, peddlers, gypsies, and even the unconfined insane, with all of whom the wandering and "eccentric" poet feels an affinity. The novel's narrator, Sylvanus Theophrastus, is especially drawn to gypsies, who perform no productive labor but who enjoy a "savage liberty" and who are remarkable for "their eternal propensity for conversations" (1:47), thus suggesting parallels between the "eccentric" poet and the gypsies.

26. This information is contained in John Thelwall, *Plan and Objects of Mr. Thelwall's Institution* (London: McCreery, 1813).

27. After losing the *Monthly Magazine*, he established his own *Panoramic Miscellany*, which lasted less than a year. See Geoffrey Carnall, "The *Monthly Magazine*," *Review of English Studies*, n.s., 5 (1954): 162–63.

Sir Walter Scott and the Spirit of the Novel

Daniel Cottom

> The only supernatural Agents which can in any Manner be allowed to us Moderns are Ghosts; but of these I would advise an Author to be extremely sparing. These are indeed like Arsenic, and other dangerous Drugs in Physic, to be used with the utmost Caution; nor would I advise the Introduction of them at all in those Works, or by those Authors to which, or to whom a Horse-Laugh in the Reader, would be any great Prejudice or Mortification.
>
> —Fielding, *Tom Jones*

Destiny is unpredictable, Sir Walter Scott used to insist; and it is no wonder he sometimes found the course of the novel as bewildering as the adventures of his heroes. Although texts we now call novels were written in the eighteenth century and earlier, the genre had floundered about, uncertain of its identity, until the nineteenth century. Through a popular fiction of its own history, the novel then began to number fictional histories and many other forms of narrative in its lineage. Mock autobiographies like *Moll Flanders*, *Clarissa* (which Samuel Richardson had said was not "a *light Novel, or transitory Romance*"),[1] the comic epic of *Joseph Andrews*, and the ironic romance of *Don Quixote* could then be made ancestral to contemporary novels. Uncertainties and conflicts in eighteenth-century classifications were suppressed in favor of this genealogy, which invented a tradition of the novel by rewriting the relationship between the novel and the romance. Whereas the novel had generally been seen in the eighteenth century as a kind of romance, by the nineteenth it was no longer a subordinate species. It was even possible then for writers to see the romance as a kind of novel, thus reversing the earlier form of definition.[2]

As the Author of Waverley recognized, names are powerful talismans; and in this time the name of the novel seemed to shatter the spell of romance. The plot of *Waverley* dramatizes this power of disenchantment, which was associated with a new rigor in generic definition. In the preceding century, "Feign'd

131

Stories" might be an adequate description of the substance of the novel, which might also be identified simply as a "short Romance."[3] By the early nineteenth century, a more elaborate formula had appeared. The distinction between romance and novel that Clara Reeve had offered as an innovation in *The Progress of Romance* (1785) had become conventional by the time George Eliot was writing in the second half of the nineteenth century, and Scott was one of those who helped standardize it. His 1824 article for the *Encyclopaedia Britannica* echoed Reeve in defining "a *Romance*" as

> "a fictitious narrative in prose or verse; the interest of which turns upon marvellous and uncommon incidents;" being thus opposed to the kindred term *Novel*, which Johnson has described as a "smooth tale, generally of love;" but which we would rather define as "a fictitious narrative, differing from the romance, because the events are accommodated to the ordinary train of human events, and the modern state of society."[4]

Through definitions like this the novel was identified with natural reality. Scott called *Tom Jones* "the first English novel" and said that until it appeared the public "had not yet seen any works of fiction founded upon the plan of painting from nature." Fielding's novel, he went on to say, "is truth and human nature itself, and there lies the inestimable advantage which it possesses over all previous fictions of this particular kind" (*SWS*, 52).[5] No fan of Scott's poetry or politics, Hazlitt nonetheless followed this tradition in calling Scott, as a novelist of Scottish life, "the amanuensis of truth and history." Hazlitt continued, "It is impossible to say how fine his writings in consequence are, unless we could define how fine nature is."[6]

Of course, quarrels over what this natural reality was and how it ought to be represented were frequent, sometimes bitter, and practically interminable. Nevertheless, a common ground was staked out. Writers generally committed themselves to this reality by omitting supernatural machinery from the representation of life. Any study of the history of realist aesthetics will show other aspects, but this omission is among the most important. Providence might be allowed as a rule in the novel, but not as a meddler. Discoveries might so upset expectations as to seem miraculous, but they would not violate common sense. Some improbabilities might be tolerated, but not impossibilities. As Robert Bisset said in his preface to *Douglas; or, The Highlander* (1800), "I can promise my readers no ghosts, for I know nothing about them myself: I can promise them flesh and blood, for this is a subject of which I do know something."[7] Whatever one might think of the relation between mundane events and supernatural designs, spirits would not be allowed an immediate presence. This tradition led Georg Lukács to write, "The novel is the epic of a world that has been abandoned by God."[8] Even if Scott's themes "are very often drawn from the 'age of heroes,' from the infancy of mankind," Lukács wrote, his works "are real and genuine novels" because "the spirit of his writing is . . . that of man's maturity, the age of triumphing prose."[9] Mikhail Bakhtin's characterization is similar: "Prophecy is proper to the epic, prediction proper to the novel."[10]

By the second half of the nineteenth century, narratives that broke faith with this conception of natural reality were often called by the old term of romance, which had a different meaning now that it stood in contrast to the dominance of the novel.[11] Later still, the general category of the novel would maintain its sovereignty even as critics spoke of subgenres such as the "antinovel." In most forums the absence of the supernatural from the drama of the novel remains a normative principle, though this situation may not last much longer. In magazines with intellectual pretensions, reviewers now feel called upon to note that a work is a "traditional novel," as if the untraditional had become the unremarkable norm.

But whatever surprises the future may hold in store, this tradition was not clear-cut even when it was invented in the nineteenth century. For instance, Scott frequently failed to distinguish between generic terms, as when he began his introduction to *Guy Mannering* (1829) by referring to the "Novel, or Romance, of *Waverly*" (*GM*, 1 : xxvii). Most novelists did not fuss over-much about writing to rule, leaving others to tell them the name and principles of the tradition to which they were contributing. In this century the novel became a dominant genre, as writing became a profession, without pausing to search through the historical conditions of its practices. In itself this situation is ordinary enough, but its inevitable result was a disturbance in the spirit of the novel that is neither incidental nor accidental. In showing that tradition *is* an invention, a historical fiction, this disturbance reveals historical conflicts from which we can claim a better understanding of genre.[12]

To put it simply, the tradition of the novel is maintained by saying that many works that look like novels, act like novels, and are constantly seen in the company of novels are nevertheless *not* novels. They are trash masquerading as novels, illegitimate novels, simulacra of novels, or some kind of burlesque. In this regard, Scott's dismissal of E. T. W. Hoffmann ("In fact, the inspirations of Hoffmann so often resemble the ideas produced by the immoderate use of opium that we cannot help considering his case as one requiring the assistance of medicine rather than of criticism" [*SWS* 352]) is comparable to the line Lukács drew between the novel and the thing he described as "a caricatural twin almost indistinguishable from [it] in all inessential formal characteristics: the entertainment novel, which has all the outward features of the novel but which, in essence, is bound to nothing and is based on nothing, i.e. is entirely meaningless."[13] Similarly, in following the work of Lukács and René Girard on the novel, Lucien Goldmann set "the authentic novel form" aside from "secondary novel forms."[14]

These comparisons may be unfair, for the invention of tradition is a far more complicated process than they indicate. But any study of literature that does not blindly reproduce tradition should show that descriptions like those I have quoted from Lukács, Bakhtin, and Goldmann are tautologous. Criticism that turns history into rational teleologies or categories may still have great value, as with the work of these writers; but it ignores most literary materials and obscures many aspects of the works it does canonize. As this brief account indicates, critics go awry in defining generic terms because these terms are subject to the historical invention of tradition, which has implications for the definition of rationality and criticism, among other things. The fact that the critics I have cited were all Marxists very much concerned with the relation between literature and history should emphasize the importance of this recognition, which is not simply a call to round up the usual suspects: idealists, elitists, aesthetes, Leavisites, New Critics, and other figures beyond the leftist pale. As Scott's novels demonstrate, the spirit of tradition is as tricky as it is powerful, and it is apt to show itself in unusual places and startling forms.

So a commitment to natural reality is important in the nineteenth-century tradition of the novel but is not at all definitive of the novel's history unless one arbitrarily excludes many works from that history. The significant fact remains that the relation between natural and supernatural agency seemed vital to the question of this genre in the early nineteenth century, in which its tradition was being invented. This question of the sources and responsibilities of power nagged at Scott throughout his novels and critical writings. As one can see from his struggles with this issue, it represented to him historical changes affecting the institution of literature, the position of the artist, the character of the public, and the nature of representation. In Scott's writings as in the works of others in this time, the attempt to define the novel as a genre was an attempt to come to terms with these changes. It was also an attempt to harmonize the clashing images of the literary text that accompanied them: the text as emblem of taste, source of pleasure, economic commodity, expression of spirit, incarnation of tradition, representation of knowledge, site of common feelings or exclusive identity, useful tool, or dangerous drug. To define a genre is to establish an authentic text and thus necessarily to diagnose proper and perverse readings: these practices, too, are involved in Scott's deliberations on the question of the supernatural. And all these issues are involved as well in *The Monastery* (1820), in which this question reached a symbolic crisis because in the novel Scott decided to represent a spirit.

Scott's novels teem with supernatural spirits, but almost always in places an enlightened modern would find appropriate. They appear in legends, tales, folklore, metaphor, hearsay reports, equivocal events, the unsubstantiated accounts of individuals, and allusions to Biblical times, when "the ordinary laws of nature were occasionally suspended," though "few Protestants are disposed to bring [the age of miracles] down beneath the accession of Constantine, when the Christian religion was fully established in supremacy" (*LDW* 59, 66). The one exception to this rule is *The Monastery*, in which a spirit, the White Lady of Avenel, plays a dramatic role. In Scott's estimation, this was the first of the Waverley Novels to be a failure, and he cast most of the blame on this spirit. Because Scott frequently returned to the issue over which he had stumbled in this novel and because it is such an oddity in his oeuvre, *The Monastery* is a valuable work for considering literary tradition and the spirit of the novel.

Scott's writings on superstition include passages in the Introduction to *Minstrelsy of the Scottish Border* and in his introductions to individual poems in this collection, such as "The Young Tamlane"; passages in the introductions and notes to his own poems and in the prefatory material and introductions to the Waverley Novels; comments in essays on other writers such as Hoffmann, Ann Radcliffe, and Horace Walpole; and his *Letters on Demonology and Witchcraft*, which he wrote and published in 1830, shortly before his death, but which he had been contemplating for years, in one form or another.[15] In almost all these writings, Scott seems a perfectly representative man of the Enlightenment. In the *Letters on Demonology and Witchcraft*, for instance, he discusses superstitious beliefs in witches, ghosts, fairies, and the like and then calls on rational explanations to make the creatures of superstition vanish (as the contemporary trope would have it) like shadows before the light of day. Scott discovers a major source of superstition in an innate consciousness of God and the afterlife, but his flexible analysis also finds many other influences. These include group psychology; emotional, intellectual, and organic disturbance or trauma; irrational, primitive, and pagan habits of thought; sensory illusions; deliberate deceptions; drug-and alcohol-induced hallucinations; and excessive passion or religious devotion.

In short, Scott uses Enlightenment assumptions about human nature, scientific explanation, and historical progress to maintain a picture of a world run by orderly natural laws.[16] In this world, as he puts it, we

> discover that the most remarkable phenomena in Nature are regulated by certain fixed laws, and cannot rationally be referred to supernatural agency, the sufficing cause to which superstition attributes all that is beyond her own narrow power of explanation. Each advance in natural knowledge teaches us that it is the pleasure of the Creator to govern the world by the laws which he has imposed, and which are not in our times interrupted or suspended. (*LDW* 154)

Although Scott does note that "no man, unless very peculiarly circumstanced, can extricate himself from the prejudices of his nation and age" (*LDW* 213), this comment seems conventional, like the easy ironies of *The Persian Letters* or *The Citizen of the World*. Though it marks the historical limits of universal reason, it does not halt the dawning of reason over the benighted errors surveyed in the pages of this work. Scott allows that super-naturalism is conceivable—to do otherwise would likely have offended the Christian orthodoxy of his day[17]—but he does not allow it a place in the modern world. In this world, history proves more enchanting than super-natural machinery, as Scott indicated when he eulogized William Pitt and Charles Fox in the Introduction to the first canto of *Marmion:* "Spells of such force no wizard grave / E'er fram'd in dark Thessalian cave, / Though his could drain the ocean dry, / And force the planets from the sky" (*PW,* 91).

This skeptical attitude toward superstition obviously did not lead Scott to think the marvelous had no place in modern literature. He was not a fanatical Puritan, like some of the characters in his books; and though he had studied with a professor of philosophy, Dugald Stewart, who also taught James Mill, he was not a Utilitarian who would banish flowers from the patterns of carpets because in real life one does not tramp atop daisies. The question was the end to which the supernatural would be used in fiction, which by its very nature was kin to superstition, as far as Scott was concerned: "the fairy-land of delusive fiction" (*M* 1:lxxviii). Scott had little doubt "that the doughty chivalry who listened to the songs of the minstrel, 'held each strange tale devoutly true,' and that the feats of knighthood which he recounted, mingled with tales of magic and supernatural interference, were esteemed as veracious as the legends of the monks, to which they bore a strong resemblance." But aside from notations of Protestant orthodoxy, the supernatural in modern fiction was not to be a matter of knowledge or belief. In fact, Scott said, even the period of belief in the legends of romance "must have long past [*sic*] before the Romancer began to select and arrange with care, the nature of the materials out of which he constructed his story" (*SWS* 314).

Scott's modern world is disabused of the fables of earlier generations, and the use of the supernatural in its fiction is entirely a rhetorical problem. The supernatural finds its end in entertainment—in creating a psychological effect—and the only question is in the management of this effect. As Scott writes in his essay on Clara Reeve (1823),

> Where, then, may the reader ask, is the line to be drawn? or what are the limits to be placed to the reader's credulity, when those of common sense and ordinary nature are once exceeded? The question admits only one answer, namely, that the author himself, being in fact the magician, shall evoke no spirits whom he is not capable of endowing with manners and language corresponding to their supernatural character. (*SWS* 97)

He reinforced this judgment in various pieces in which he commented on the Radcliffe school in fiction and criticized its rhetorically unsatisfying and logically inadequate explanations of supernatural mysteries. In his Introduc-tion to *The Bridal of Triermain* (1830), he argued that romantic poetry "neither exacts nor refuses the use of supernatural machinery" (*PW* 586); and he made the same claim for fiction, maintaining that the important distinction was the success or failure of one's effects. His criticism, which is notable for its catholicity of taste, seems to adhere very faithfully to this principle.[18]

This conclusion that the supernatural is simply the subject of rhetorical effects may seem reasonable enough. However, Scott found that it raised a vexing problem in taste. In the Introductory Epistle to *The Fortunes of Nigel*, published two years after *The Monastery*, he argued that the White Lady was a failure "rather in execution than conception" and concluded that his "elementary spirits" were "too fine-drawn for the present taste of the public" (*FN* 1 : xxxvii–xxxviii). Yet this Epistle also suggests that any recourse to the supernatural would have been an error in taste on the part of the author. (So Scott wryly commended *The Fortunes of Nigel* to his readers by saying, "All is clear and above board—a Scots metaphysician might believe every word of it" [*FN* 1 : xxxviii].) When he published his Introduction to *The Monastery* ten years after the original appearance of this novel, the same confusion was evident. Scott defended the conception of the White Lady, justifying it as part of "the indispensable quality of novelty" in the story and further supporting it by references to the Comte de la Motte Fouqué's *Undine*, the *Entretiens de Compte du Gabalis*, the Irish folkore of Banshies, and the Highland legends of spirits.[19] He also took pains to explicate the logic of his spirit's actions, with the aid of references to gnostic and Rosicrucian belief. Nonetheless, he was not sure whether the failure was caused by the indifferent execution of his thoroughly reasoned purpose or simply because "the public did not approve of it" (*M* 1 : xxxi). So he says that though "the introduction of the supernatural and marvellous" has been "the resort of distressed authors since the days of Horace," its "privileges as a sanctuary have been disputed in the present age, and wellnigh exploded" (*M* 1 : xxviii).[20] As the Protestant Reformation appropriated or laid waste to many Catholic monasteries, so it seemed the modern reformation of the novel was obliterating the representation of the supernatural; and Scott was not sure where this change left him.

Scott could explain superstition with great confidence, but he lacked this confidence in discussing the failure of this novel because in reality he was dealing with several objects. One may be called the formal text: the text described by a logic of plot, character, and style. This text shows the author's taste and must maintain regularity and probability even if it trades upon the supernatural. A second object is the public text, which is described by the reactions of readers and against which even the best logic avails nothing. In this regard, Scott wrote, "I care not who knows it—I write for general amusement; and, though I never will aim at popularity by what I think unworthy means, I will not, on the other hand, be pertinacious in the defence

of my own errors against the voice of the public" (*FN* 1:xxxviii). The
uncertainty in Scott's diagnosis of *The Monastery's* failure shows the conflict
between these images of the text. The demands of form, which must be
calculated in terms of the public one addresses, clash with the ultimate
unpredictability of public response in a time of literary change.[21] And then
there is a third object that may remain independent of these other two: the
economic text, which is described by a book's sales and circulation. Scott
noted that *The Monastery* was not a failure in terms of sales,[22] and in the
Introductory Epistle to *The Fortunes of Nigel* he went so far as to boast of the
economic character of fiction:

> I do say it, in spite of Adam Smith and his followers, that a successful
> author is a productive labourer, and that his works constitute as effectual a
> part of the public wealth, as that which is created by any other manufac-
> ture. If a new commodity, having an actually intrinsic and commercial
> value, be the result of the operation, why are the author's bales of books to
> be esteemed a less profitable part of the public stock than the goods of any
> other manufacturer? (*FN* 1:xlix–1)[23]

In itself the battle among these texts may seem unimportant, simply the
price one pays in self-confidence for striving to be a popular writer. Yet it has
the potential for totally upsetting the very idea of taste and thus confronting
the best-selling Author of Waverley with the incompatibility between this
ideology and the desire to work one's rhetoric upon the crowd. Scott recognized this threat when he argued against a proposed Royal Society of Literature in the year after *The Monastery* was published. In literature, he said,
"you will find twenty people entertaining as many different opinions upon
that which is called taste in proportion to their different temperaments habits
and prejudices of education." Therefore, if one brings together "a set of
literary men differing so widely in taste in temper and in manners having no
earthly thing in common except their general irritability of temper and a
black speck on their middle finger what can be expected but all sort of
quarrels fracasseries lampoons libels and duels?" (*L* 6:401, 402).

It seems that an open challenge to taste would lead not only to battling texts
but to fighting men. If this standard were to disappear, even the difference
between natural and supernatural reality might vanish, since in Scott's opinion the vulgar crowd is especially likely to mistake this difference. On more
than one occasion Scott quoted approvingly a liberal maxim from Voltaire—
"tout genre est permis hors les genres ennuyeux"—but the strains of self-
deprecation and self-defense that cross each other in his commentary on *The
Monastery* show his unease over where the desire to entertain might lead him.

The same battle of images appears in Scott's characterizations of himself as
an author. Though he freely announced his desire to please the public and

find economic success, with a candor that disturbed George Eliot's admiration and antagonized others like Frederick Denison Maurice and Thomas Carlyle,[24] he also presented himself as one whose writings were divorced from worldly interests. Like Alexander Pope in his Epistles, Scott would claim that his writings were those of a gentleman and any success they brought him accidental in relation to their origin in disinterested activity. In his Introductory Epistle to *The Fortunes of Nigel,* for instance, he proclaimed his subservience to his audience and his pride in the trade generated by writing but then added this comment:

> But no man of honour, genius, or spirit, would make the mere love of gain, the chief, far less the only, purpose of his labours. For myself, I am not displeased to find the game a winning one; yet while I pleased the public, I should probably continue it merely for the pleasure of playing; for I have felt as strongly as most folks that love of composition, which is perhaps the strongest of all instincts, driving the author to the pen, the painter to the pallet [*sic,*] often without either the chance of fame or the prospect of reward. (*FN*, 1:li)[25]

In passages like this Scott tried to reconcile the image of the author made conventional under the system of patronage with images of the author suggested by the change to a popular market for literature. The traditional tropes came to him easily enough but sort oddly with the conditions he recognized as those of the modern profession of letters, perhaps succeeding only in leading readers to question whether a truly amateur art conducted merely for the pleasure of playing could ever have existed. At the very least, passages like this show a man struggling to maintain an inherited rhetoric of taste in surroundings that he cannot help but notice are hostile to it.

In Scott's essay "On the Supernatural in Fictitious Composition; and particularly on the Works of Ernest Theodore William Hoffmann" (1827), this rhetoric is pressured even more. The confusion of aesthetic standards in his condemnation of Hoffmann is symptomatic of a time of transformations in the institution of literature that have not been fully rationalized in tradition:

> Unfortunately, his taste and temperament directed him too strongly to the grotesque and fantastic,—carried him too far 'extra moenia flammantia mundi', too much beyond the circle not only of probability but even of possibility, to admit of his composing much in the better style which he might easily have attained. The popular romance, no doubt, has many walks, nor are we at all inclined to halloo the dogs of criticism against those whose object is merely to amuse a passing hour. It may be repeated with truth, that in this path of light literature, 'tout genre est permis hors les genres ennuyeux', and, of course, an error in taste ought not to be followed up and hunted down as if it were a false maxim in morality, a delusive hypothesis in science, or a heresy in religion itself. . . . But we do not

desire to see genius expand or rather exhaust itself upon themes which
cannot be reconciled to taste; and the utmost length in which we can
indulge a turn to the fantastic is, where it tends to excite agreeable and
pleasing ideas. (*SWS* 348)

On the one hand, the standards on which the novel was concentrating—
probability and possibility—are mentioned briefly and vaguely. On the other,
the richly elaborated tradition of eighteenth-century criticism leads Scott to
note that tastes are extremely varied, that literature may be permitted to
violate conventions in order to stimulate taste, and that matters of taste are
independent of the more crucial affairs of the world. In the rest of this
conclusion it also leads him to note the allowance due to "capricious" genius
and to a public that may sometimes desire "to look at the wildness of an
Arabesque painting." Scott's capacity for discriminating judgments on the
psychology of artistic creation and appreciation thus outruns his resources for
maintaining the truth of nature, the standard on which he relies in con-
demning what he describes as the complete arbitrariness of Hoffmann's
fiction. One result is the logical incoherence of this passage, which details all
the boundaries taste may overleap and then contradicts this admission of
psychological complexity by simply concluding that taste is a boundary to
itself, characterized by innocuous "agreeable and pleasing ideas." A more
significant result is that Scott is led to define the question of the supernatural
as one that is more than a matter of rhetorical form. Scott does not criticize
Hoffmann, as he had Radcliffe and himself, for an error in execution or
calculation. He condemns him because he goes too far beyond the boundaries
of a community (which is specified, significantly enough, by a classical
allusion, drawn from Lucretius).[26] He even contrasts Hoffmann's writings
with others that follow the traditional forms of the supernatural and so "come
within the legitimate bounds which Glanville [a seventeenth-century writer
on witchcraft] and other grave and established authors, ascribe to the shadowy realm of spirits" (*SWS* 326).

In Hoffmann's work it seems the rhetoric of the supernatural might actually become the supernatural: a "shadowy world, of which our mental faculties are too obscure to comprehend the laws, or corporeal organs too gross
to perceive the inhabitants" (*SWS* 313). By giving Scott such a strong
impression of pathology, Hoffmann's extravagance exposes the limits of his
rhetoric of taste and form. It shows that they make sense only when accompanied by the tacit assumption of a common tradition, like that which Scott
signified by his habitual references to a rationality and a Protestantism
unquestionably shared with his readers. If this assumption vanishes or (what
may be the same case) if a radically conflicting tradition turns up, then a crisis
arises. Rhetoric is no longer a neutral medium for the representation of the

supernatural and fiction no longer an innocent relative of the supernatural: "the province of Utopia" whose "productions, though censured by many (and some who use tea and tobacco without scruple) as idle and unsubstantial luxuries, have nevertheless, like many other luxuries, a general acceptation, and are secretly enjoyed even by those who express the greatest scorn and dislike of them in public" (M 1:lxxiii).

Rather than being a purveyor of mere entertainment, an innocent wizard or magician, in this situation The Great Unknown might be a darker figure. In fact, The Great Unknown might be the darkness of figuration itself: the darkness of rhetoric seen not as an instrument under human control but rather as an unsettling dissonance in language and in the very nature of the human subject. A single author might appear as a battling group of writers wielding incompatible standards and, in place of a genuine work of fiction, issuing a farrago of "quarrels fracasseries lampoons libels and duels."[27] He would be unable to let "parody, burlesque, and squibs, find their own level" (PW 276), as Scott boasted of doing in his Introduction to The Lady of the Lake; for in the absence of a governing tradition the elements of a text are turned toward self-reflexivity and thus tend to appear as parodies or burlesques of themselves.[28] In this context, Scott's oft-expressed worry that he would wear out the interest of the public if he did not introduce sufficient novelty into his work can be seen as the fear of becoming a caricature of himself: of being exposed as rhetoric that does not quicken into story but instead appears as unrelated and pointless effects.

In his essay on Fielding and elsewhere, Scott always defended the novel as an amusement that could be very inspiring and at worst could do little harm—"Excluding from consideration those infamous works, which address themselves directly to awakening the grosser passions of our nature" (SWS 54). Hoffmann's work reveals another danger and so forces onto center stage the image that may be called the proper text, which is described by a work's acceptance within a social tradition. It emphasizes what Fielding had suggested: that the representation of the supernatural could turn out to be a very "dangerous Drug," not a useful tool for conveying an impression of the past and for exciting interest in the reader.

It is interesting in this regard that so many of Scott's novels turn upon conflicting traditions. Even more significant is the fact that his novels often dramatize this problem of textual identity, which can be seen to represent the instability in the institution of literature and the uncertainty in the definition of the novel in his time. In this sense Scott's novels are about the historical conditions of their creation. They involve the conflicting claims to meaning of money, honor, rank, reason, and various other agencies recognized in his culture as bearing some relation to literature; and so it is not fanciful to see Scott's writing discomposed into a number of battling texts that yet are so intermingled that their identities, actions, and purposes become disturbed. Even if an analysis of the heterogeneous discourses in his writing did not bring this recognition, the drama of his novels should.

The Monastery is a case in point. Set in Scotland in the second half of the sixteenth century, when "the picturesque, the beautiful, the sublime, and all their intermediate shades, were ideas absolutely unknown to the inhabitants and occasional visitors of Glendearg" (*M* 1:11), the story involves the consequences of the strife between Scotland and England. One issue is property: the occupation of the Avenel estate by English soldiers and then its usurpation by Julian Avenel, the brother-in-law of Alice Avenel and the uncle of its rightful inheritor, her daughter, Mary. Other issues are rank, romance, and rivalry. Mary and her mother seek refuge at the isolated Tower of Glendearg with another woman widowed by the war, Elspeth Glendinning, whose sons Halbert and Edward fall in love with Mary despite their lower birth. This basic situation might almost be predicted from Scott's previous novels, as might the conflict between the Catholic Church and the forces of Reformation beginning to make their way in the world: a conflict portrayed as having noble and weak characters on both sides. Novelty does appear, however, in the figure of the White Lady. Early in the novel she is seen only by Mary Avenel, while others remain blind to her presence; later, she makes appearances to duck a monk in a river, to spout prophetic verses, and to act in other ways that influence the plot. Her main concern is that the family of Alive Avenel retain possession of the Bible translated into English that Alice has hidden from ecclesiastical authorities. The monk is ducked when he takes the Bible away from the tower, to which it mysteriously returns; the White Lady then retrieves the volume from a second priest while also saving his life:

> . . . he felt a deep anxiety to know whether the volume which he had lost, when so strangely preserved from the lance of the murderer, had again found its way back to the Tower of Glendearg. "It was strange," he thought, "that a spirit," for such he could not help judging the being whose voice he had heard, "should, on the one side, seek the advancement of hersey, and, on the other, interpose to save the life of a zealous Catholic priest." (*M* 1:128–29)

As it happens, Halbert snatches the Bible back from an intense but unconsuming flame in a mysterious grotto to which he has been led by the White Lady, "the extraordinary Being he had seen, half his terror, half his protectress" (*M* 1:149). Eventually, his brother Edward is disappointed in love and sides with the forces of the past by becoming a monk, whereas Halbert gets the girl, the usurped property, and Protestant faith.

In his *Letters on Demonology and Witchcraft*, Scott summarized the sources of superstitious belief as "circumstances and enactments in sacred and pro-

fane history, hastily adopted, and perverted from their genuine reading"
(*LDW* 46); but *The Monastery* shows how hard it is to tell the genuine reading
or the proper text. In his scholarly work, Scott could criticize the way alleged
witches were subjected to trial by water in seventeenth-century England "on
the principle of King James, who, in treating of this mode of trial, lays down
that, as witches have renounced their baptism, so it is just that the element
through which the holy rite is enforced should reject them, which is a figure
of speech, and no argument" (*LDW* 208). He could denounce belief in
witchcraft by saying the Biblical meaning translated by this word "seems
little more than the art of a medicator of poisons, combined with that of a
Pythoness or false prophetess" (*LDW* 61). He noted that the Book of Tobit,
which describes witchery resembling "an incident in an Arabian tale or
Gothic romance," is "imperfect evidence" and an illegitimate text: "the
romantic and fabulous strain of this legend has induced the fathers of all
Protestant churches to deny it a place amongst the writings sanctioned by
divine origin" (*LDW* 62). But *The Monastery* shows that this opposition
between empty rhetoric and meaningful argument can be maintained only by
force.

Scott himself admitted that the catastrophe of his story was brought about
by a "*tour de force*" that "was objected to as inartificial, and not perfectly
intelligible to the general reader" (*M* 1:xxxiv). In the absence of such a
resolution, however, Scott's novels suggest that language will be used by well-
meaning people in utterly contradictory ways. Significantly enough, the
metaphor of the drug turns up in this regard, as if to recall Fielding's warning
about the use of ghosts in fiction or to anticipate Scott's clinical characterization of Hoffmann's writing. Thus, we have the monk who first confiscates the
heretical Bible from the Tower of Glendearg explaining his action to Elspeth
Glendinning:

> "I tell thee, Elspeth, *the Word slayeth*—that is, the text alone, read with
> unskilled eye and unhallowed lips, is like those strong medicines which
> sick men take by the advice of the learned. Such patients recover and
> thrive; while those dealing in them at their own hand, shall perish by their
> own deed." (*M* 1:51)[29]

On the other hand, we have this typical exchange between a Catholic Sub-
Prior and Henry Warden, who has become a Protestant evangelist, though he
was once the Sub-Prior's schoolfellow and close friend:

> "I bless God and Our Lady," said he, drawing himself up, "that my faith
> is already anchored on that Rock on which Saint Peter founded his
> church."
> "It is a perversion of the text," said the eager Henry Warden, "grounded
> on a vain play upon words—a most idle paronomasia." (*M* 1:226)

Given Scott's concern to show well-meaning individuals on all sides of historical conflicts, these disputes leave the impression that "the text alone" exists only as a supernatural power that cannot be fully appropriated by any scheme of reading. The way the White Lady intervenes in the plot of *The Monastery* and symbolizes its Protestant view of historical progress becomes very notable in relation to this battle of texts, for its role resembles and yet mocks the enlightened author's. As the Author of Waverley tries to transcend himself in his inventions, going beyond the boundaries of his place and time in order to identify himself with universal reason, this figure enters into the events of the story and mediates conflicts so as to draw them to the conclusion that is meant to represent historical truth.[30] However, the White Lady also represents the magic of reason: the irrational and arbitrary procedures that define reason as a rhetorical power and so put it into conflict with other forms of rhetoric both inside and outside of particular communities.[31] Using Lukács's terms, one could say this figure represents both the "authentic novel" and its "caricatural twin." The White Lady shows human nature differing from itself or quailing before the failure to recognize itself where it apparently ought to be. As Scott describes Halbert's third encounter with this figure,

> His terror for the moment overcame his natural courage, as well as the strong resolution which he had formed, that the figure which he had now twice seen should not a third time daunt him. But it would seem there is something thrilling and abhorrent to flesh and blood, in the consciousness that we stand in presence of a being in form like to ourselves, but so different in faculties and nature, that we can neither understand its purposes, nor calculate its means of pursuing them. (*M* 1:140)

Despite his concern to justify his conception of the White Lady as one that was reasonable, in this figure the reason of Scott's novels displays its ultimate identity with superstition. It concedes its source in a rhetorical power that exceeds human boundaries. Thus, this figure represents the cultural intervention that can neither be omitted from representation nor wholly controlled within representation by any individual or tradition.

Because the White Lady embodies the attempt to rationalize historical difference, conflict, and change that is carried out in all Scott's novels, her "failure" represents more than an isolated error of conception or composition. It illustrates the vulnerability of Scott's reason to a criticism that would expose the ideological materials—literary, religious, historical, political, and so on—of which it is composed. This figure shows that Scott's attempt to distinguish argument from rhetoric, reason from superstition—as in his characterization of his work as " 'truths severe in fairy fiction dressed' "[32]— cannot be sustained even within his own work. Nor are his other novels any more resistant to such analysis because they do not sport White Ladies in their plots: the spirit of the novel is at work in them too. The difference is that these other novels, by omitting supernatural machinery from the representation of mundane events, offer the modern world its preferred superstition: nature.

Even Scott's scholarly work shows this instability. In his *Letters on Demonology and Witchcraft*, Scott applies his lawyerly mind to "all those that are called accredited ghost stories" and says they "usually fold at the fireside" for a simple reason: "They want evidence" (*LDW* 288). In doing so he contradicts his own historical researches in the book, which show that legal and informal courts alike have often been convinced that there was overwhelming evidence of witchery, and in very recent times, too. Scott also undermines himself when he notes that scientific reformers of the sixteenth and seventeenth centuries were hampered not only by political impediments but also by "articles of philosophical belief which they must have been sensible contained nearly as deep draughts upon human credulity as were made by the Demonologists, against whose doctrine they protested" (*LDW* 159). In the light of this history, his conventional remarks on human imperfection— "every generation of the human race must swallow a certain measure of nonsense" (*LDW* 320)—take on a more disturbing meaning. Like the formulaic comment by "Captain Clutterbuck" at the beginning of *The Monastery*—"that which was history yesterday becomes fable to-day, and the truth of to-day is hatched into a lie by to-morrow" (*M* 1:liv)—they no longer appear as marginal or incidental moments in the unfolding course of reason. Instead they change the very appearance of reason, and "nonsense" appears a very dangerous drug, indeed. It does seem that "our love of the wonderful and the horrible," as Scott says, may prove inconsistent with "the laws of Nature" (*LDW* 286).

It is interesting in this regard that Scott did not place all the blame for *The Monastery*'s failure on the White Lady. He also blamed the Euphuist, Sir Piercie Shafton, whose rhetorical affectations he had intended to divert his readers. The White Lady was meant to be a rhetorical tool, Sir Piercie a rhetorical fool; but his failure also suggests the vulnerability of reason. Though he is meant to be an exceptional case, an unnatural figure, he is also meant to represent a period of history; and his failure to please may show how limited the understanding of history is in relation to the "natural taste proper to the species" (*M* 1:xxxv) that Scott counts on finding in his readers. In other words, it may suggest that the putative "natural" is in fact rhetorical and thus historical and political, not universal and rational. The description of manners and customs was half the art of fiction to Scott, and the case of Sir Piercie suggests that they may be as difficult to translate from one society to another as the text of the Bible has proven to be from one sect to another. Scott tried to escape this implication by arguing that while "the occupations, and even the sentiments, of human beings in a primitive state, find access and interest in the minds of the more civilized part of the species, it does not therefore follow, that the national tastes, opinions, and follies, of one civilized period, should afford either the same interest or the same amusement to those of another" (*M* 1 : xxxv).[33] But there is an inconsistency here, for it was the primitive nature of supernatural belief that was meant to make the White Lady an appealing character but instead was said by Scott to be the cause of her failure. In Scott's conflicting explanations of this matter the romantic image of a primitive text, described by its originative, natural, and universal quality, clashes with the image of the cultured text, which is described by the tastes of particular groups in particular societies. The twin figures of the White Lady and the Euphuist thus exemplify Scott's attempt to rationalize the relation between nature and art even as they reveal his reason to be a tangle of rhetorical maneuvers that represent the cultural struggles of his own day.

Of course, Scott never held reason to be absolutely distinct from irrationality or superstition. As Paul Henderson Scott has pointed out, the philosophical historians who were so important to the Author of Waverley "were under no illusions about the limitations of reason as a guide to human behaviour"[34] and all of Scott's works show this disenchantment. For instance, in the Introduction to the third canto of *Marmion*, addressed to William Erskine, the following passage appears:

> But say, my Erskine, hast though weigh'd
> That secret power by all obey'd,
> Which warps not less the passive mind,
> Its source conceal'd or undefin'd;
> Whether an impulse, that has birth
> Soon as the infant wakes on earth,
> One with our feelings and our powers,
> And rather part of us than ours;
> Or whether fitlier term'd the sway
> Of habit, form'd in early day?
>
> (*PW* 114)

Because reason is a thoroughly qualified figure in Scott's work, the figure of the White Lady does not show that reason has no meaning within these writings. But it does illustrate the complicity of reason with its supposed antagonists. In so doing, it shows that the exposure of language as rhetoric— as discourse representing heterogeneous subjects, sources, interests, and ends—is the greatest danger faced by the conception of reason advanced by Scott and the other heirs of the Enlightenment with which he may be compared. In a distorted but symptomatic way, the nineteenth-century tradition of the novel, as defined by the omission of supernatural machinery, recognizes the need to conceal the cultural apparatus that supports the impression of reality. This is a distinctive lesson of the modern world, of modern reason: that nature must appear to triumph over rhetoric.

This issue of rhetoric raised by *The Monastery* is closely related to Scott's general conception of the novel as a genre. For it was not only the supernatural that Scott tried to distinguish as a matter of rhetoric. In effect, Scott regarded any plot as supernatural machinery. In his Advertisement to *The Antiquary* (1816), Scott characteristically identified the description of manners and the arrangement of "an artificial and combined narrative: as the "requisites of a good Novel" (*An* 1: vii). It was also characteristic of him to confess that he was not especially concerned to tighten and polish his plots, even though he recognized their importance; and his usual apology was the artificiality of plots in relation to the events of ordinary life. As he said in his Introduction to *The Abbot* (1831),

> In life itself, many things befall every mortal, of which the individual never knows the real cause or origin; and were we to point out the most marked distinction between a real and a fictitious narrative, we would say, that the former, in reference to the remote causes of the events it relates, is obscure, doubtful, and mysterious; whereas, in the latter case, it is a part of the author's duty to afford satisfactory details upon the causes of the separate events he has recorded, and, in a word, to account for every thing. (*Ab* 1: xxvi)

In passages like this, the very fact that fiction promises understanding distinguishes it from ordinary reality. Understanding is supposed to be opposed to superstition and yet is described as the subject of rhetorical effects, just like superstition. Scott's frequently voiced opinion that the novel is a relatively unserious thing has often been seen as a sign that he was not a serious or self-conscious artist,[35] but such a view is historically ignorant. In the first place, Scott's apologies for his lack of rigorous planning signify his gentlemanly pose and his recognition that novels such as his are luxury products designed for the genteel; and thus they also serve as ritualistic gestures fending off the supernatural potential of his own rhetoric while soliciting the neutral appearance of language as reason. In this way he symbolically draws walls around his fiction that protect it from the possibility of wandering too far away or of being appropriated by someone from the outside—someone like Hoffmann.

Just as he does in discussing supernatural spirits in fiction, Scott offers additional explanations for his attitude toward art that show the strains he felt in the definition of the literary text. In the Introductory Epistle to *The Fortunes of Nigel* he apologizes for his plots by claiming those that were most labored were criticized as being most feeble, by saying an author must "strike while the iron is hot" if he is not to lose public favor to competitors or arouse outrageous expectations for his next work, and finally by pleading a kind of supernatural compulsion:

> But I think there is a demon who seats himself on the feather of my pen when I begin to write, and leads it astray from the purpose. Characters expand under my hand; incidents are multiplied; the story lingers, while the materials increase; my regular mansion turns out a Gothic anomaly, and the work is closed long before I have attained the point I proposed. (*FN* 1:xliv)

In his dealings with the novel, Scott confronted his expectations of literary tradition but also faced their implications in history, which resulted in clashing images of the text, the author, and the reader. Like George Eliot and Nathaniel Hawthorne, who rejected the spiritualism popularized around the middle of the nineteenth century and yet drew on its terms for *Silas Marner* and *The Blithedale Romance*, Scott tried to adapt the machinery of superstition to the purposes of a rational art of the novel. This use of the supernatural was to be a symbolic assertion of the novel over romance, of literature over folklore, and of reason over superstition. In this project Scott had amazing success according to a number of standards, but he also found writing a demonic activity in more than the light sense with which he toys in the foregoing passage. In his novels, knowledge of superstition often appears as the superstition of knowledge, and not only in the ironic sense conventionally acknowledged in Enlightenment reasoning. The sense is more like Hegel's, in his discussion of "The Struggle of Enlightenment with Superstition": "[T]he new serpent of wisdom, raised on high before bending worshippers, has in this manner painlessly sloughed merely a shrivelled skin."[36] Knowledge appears as superstition in a sense that disrupts the Enlightenment conception of reason, the modern commitment to natural law, and the idea that the novel is a disenchanted literary form, characterized by irony. Ultimately, it becomes impossible to distinguish where Scott uses traditional materials for the purpose of the novel from where he is used by these materials and where abused by the very idea of tradition.

Insofar as it symbolizes the commitment of the novel to natural reality, the omission of supernatural machinery is also an assertion that fiction is fundamentally a vehicle of understanding between author and reader. Although it might have other roles as well—awe-inspiring exhibition, display of taste, means of self-expression, and so on—the basic promise of modern narrative, as Scott said, is that of a form of understanding. Yet one reason the novel is such an unstable genre, a genre so difficult to define, is because the tradition invented in the nineteenth century raised the issue of literary form as truth. In this period the novel became a legitimate representation of life or, to put it more precisely, became that form of representation explicitly based on the distinction between legitimate and illegitimate representation, as in the mid-

Victorian distinction between novel and romance. Insofar as this tradition is maintained, the historical formations and ideological contradictions of knowledge may go unrecognized in literary form or in "the spirit of the novel," just as they may become invisible in the terms, procedures, and principles of legal institutions or in the idealized history of science as the cumulative, inexorable, and neutral progress of truth. Analogies between these three institutions of law, science, and the novel occur in Scott's writings, as in those of later novelists such as Eliot and Thomas Hardy; but more important is the fact that the truth of a literary form should ever have become a question. Before the nineteenth century it had been customary to speak of higher and lower forms of representation, of proper and vulgar forms, or of ancient and modern forms; but the distinction of a *legitimate* form belongs to an age that believes it has lifted a deceiving spell from all humanity. The fact that Scott's appropriation of the supernatural is such a troubled act, then, suggests how much uncertainty entered into the confidence in nature in this age and into the understanding presumed to exist between readers and authors. It also suggests that we understand Scott (and Eliot, Hawthorne, and others) too quickly when we assume we can clearly distinguish the figures they are merely using rhetorically from those that represent their argument or real belief. This assumption may credit the authors with more control over language than they possessed and more even than they believed they possessed. While Scott's novels show that history is made of such distinctions, they also show that these distinctions stem from a power that is neither natural nor supernatural: the urgent, violent, vulnerable power of tradition.

Notes

1. Samuel Richardson, "Preface," *The History of Clarissa Harlow, The Works of Samuel Richardson*, with a Preface by Leslie Stephen, 12 vols. (London: Henry Sotheran and Co., 1883) 4:xiii.

2. See, for instance, Walter Bagehot's description of "a kind of novel" that focuses on romance in his review of Scott for the *National Review* 9 April 1858). "The Waverley Novels," *The Collected Works of Walter Bagehot*, 8 vols. (Cambridge: Harvard University Press, 1965) 2:47.

3. Edward Phillips, *The New World Words* (1706) and Mary Davys, "Preface to *The Works of Mary Davys*" (1725), quoted in *English Theories of the Novel, Volume II: The Eighteenth Century*, ed. Walter F. Greiner, English Texts, 7, ed. Theo Stemmler (Tübingen: Max Niemeyer Verlag, 1970), 37, 12.

4. Sir Walter Scott, "Essay on Romance," quoted in *English Theories of the Novel, Volume III: The Nineteenth Century*, ed. Elke Platz-Waury, English Texts, 9, ed. Theo Stemmler (Tübingen: Max Niemeyer Verlag, 1972), 24. On the history of the distinction between novel and romance, with particular reference to Scott's work, see also Sir Herbert Grierson, "History and the Novel," *Sir Walter Scott Lectures 1940–1948*, with an Introduction by W. L. Renwick (Edinburgh: University of Edinburgh Press, 1950), 31–51; Alexander Welsh, *The Hero of the Waverley Novels*, Yale Studies in English, 154, ed. Benjamin Christie Nangle (New Haven: Yale University Press, 1963), 8–18; Ioan Williams, *The Idea of the Novel in Europe, 1600–1800* (London: Macmillan, 1979), esp. 69–70; Margaret Morshin Criscuola, "Originality, Realism and Morality: Three Issues in Sir Walter Scott's Criticism of Fiction," *Studies in Scottish Literature* 16 (1981): 35–38, 42–43; and Patricia Harkin, "Romance and Real History: The Historical Novel

as Literary Innovation," *Scott and His Influence: The Papers of the Aberdeen Scott Conference, 1982*, ed. J. H. Alexander and David Hewitt, Occasional Papers, 6 (Aberdeen: Association for Scottish Literary Studies, 1983), esp. 162.

5. With the exception of the preceding reference to Scott's "Essay on Romance," citations are given within the text to the following editions of his work: *The Journal of Sir Walter Scott (J)*, ed. John Guthrie Tait (Edinburgh: Oliver and Boyd, 1950); *The Letters of Sir Walter Scott (L)*, ed. H. J. C. Grierson, Assisted by Davidson Cook et. al., 12 vols. (London: Constable and Co., 1932); *Letters on Demonology and Witchcraft (LDW)*, with an Introduction by Henry Morley (New York: Gordon Press, 1974); *The Poetical Works of Sir Walter Scott (PW)*, with the Author's Introductions and Notes, ed. J. Logie Robertson (London: Oxford University Press, 1904); *Sir Walter Scott: On Novelists and Fiction (SWS)*, ed. Ioan Williams (London: Routledge and Kegan Paul, 1968); and *The Waverley Novels*, Border Edition, with Introductory Essays and Notes by Andrew Lang, 48 vols. (London: John C. Nimmo, 1892): *Guy Mannering (GM); The Monastery, (M); The Fortunes of Nigel (FN); The Antiquary (An)*; and *The Abbot (Ab)*.

6. William Hazlitt, "Sir Walter Scott," *The Spirit of the Age, The Collected Works of William Hazlitt*, ed. A. R. Waller and Arnold Glover, with an Introduction by W. E. Henley, 12 vols. (London: J. M. Dent and Sons, 1902) 4:247.

7. Quoted in *English Theories of the Novel, Volume II*, 1.

8. Georg Lukács, *The Theory of the Novel: A Historico-Philosophical Essay on the Forms of Great Epic Literature*, tr. Anna Bostock (Cambridge: MIT Press, 1971), 88.

9. Lukács, *The Historical Novel*, tr. Hannah and Stanley Mitchell (London: Merlin Press, 1962), 36.

10. Mikhail Bakhtin, *Ethétique et théorie du roman*, tr. Daria Olivier, with a Preface by Michel Aucouturier (Paris: Gallimard, 1978), 464.

11. See, for instance, Nathaniel Hawthorne's discussion of romance in the Preface to *The Blithedale Romance*.

12. I have borrowed from the title of a work edited by Eric Hobsbawm and Terence Ranger: *The Invention of Tradition*, Past and Present Publications, ed. T. H. Aston (Cambridge: Cambridge University Press, 1983).

13. Lukács, *The Theory of the Novel*, 73.

14. Lucien Goldmann, *Towards a Sociology of the Novel*, tr. Alan Sheridan (London: Tavistock Publications, 1975), 15.

15. See, for instance, his 1812 letter to Charles Kirkpatrick Sharpe, *Letters* 3:144.

16. Some of the important studies of Scott's conception of history and its relationship to Enlightenment thought, especially the work of the Scottish philosophical historians, are by Duncan Forbes, "The Rationalism of Sir Walter Scott," *The Cambridge Journal* 7 (1953): 20–35; D. D. Devlin, *The Author of Waverley: A Critical Study of Sir Walter Scott* (London: Macmillan, 1971), 34–55; Avrom Fleishman, *The English Historical Novel: Walter Scott to Virginia Woolf* (Baltimore: John Hopkins University press, 1971), 37–101; David Daiches, "Scott and Scotland," *Scott Bicentenary Essays: Selected Papers Read at the Sir Walter Scott Bicentenary Conference*, ed. Alan Bell (Edinburgh: Scottish Academic Press, 1973), 38–60; Graham McMaster, *Scott and Society* (Cambridge: Cambridge University Press, 1981), 49–77; Paul Henderson Scott, *Walter Scott and Scotland* (Edinburgh: William Blackwood, 1981), 58–67; and Harry E. Shaw, *The Forms of Historical Fiction: Sir Walter Scott and His Successors* (Ithaca: Cornell University Press, 1983).

17. On the popularity of supernaturalism even in Scott's time and the diverse reactions to his *Demonology* that resulted from this, see Coleman O. Parsons, *Witchcraft and Demonology in Scott's Fiction: With Chapters on the Supernatural in Scottish Literature* (Edinburgh: Oliver and Boyd, 1964), 1–15.

18. See John Lauber, "Scott on the Art of Fiction," *Studies in English Literature 1500–1900* 3 (1963): 543–54.

19. For the literary, philosophical, and folkloric background of the White Lady, see Parsons, *Witchcraft and Demonology*, 158–63. Also, for Scott's general use of folkloric elements in his fiction, see W. F. H. Nicolaisen, "Sir Walter Scott: The Folklorist as Novelist," *Scott and His Influence*, 169–79; and Nicolaisen, "Scott and the Folk Tradition," *Sir Walter Scott: The Long-Forgotten Melody*, ed. Alan Bold, Critical Studies Series (Totowa, N. J.: Barnes and Noble, 1983), 127–42.

20. Cf. Scott's note on "Second-sight" in his notes on *The Lady of the Lake, Poetical Works*, 279: "But, in despite of evidence which neither Bacon, Boyle nor Johnson were able to resist, the *Taisch*, with all its visionary properties, seems to be now universally abandoned to the use of poetry".

21. On the subject of Scott's relation to his readers, see Parson's comment (*Witchcraft and Demonology*, 263) that "many of Scott's clumsy attempts to warn readers against participating in the beliefs of his characters result from a puzzled distrust of a heterogeneous public which it was his responsibility not to mislead." See also Richard Waswo's discussion of the anxieties Scott confronts "in all the energetic subterfuges of his prefatory masks" in "Story as Historiography in the Waverley Novels," *ELH* 47 (1980): 304–330.

22. Cf. Scott's note that *Rokeby* was not a failure in point of sales (*Poetical Works*, 381) and his similar comment in the Introduction to *The Lord of the Isles* (*Poetical Works*, 474).

23. For Scott's general attitude toward trade, see Lawrence Poston, III, "The Commercial Motif of the Waverley Novels," *ELH* 42 (1975): 62–87.

24. This tradition of finding Scott too mercenary began very early, with Byron's *English Bards and Scotch Reviewers* (1809). Though Byron later repented his charge, it recurred throughout Scott's lifetime and the succeeding age. It is significant as a historical index: writing to sell books could now be seen as an upsetting new possibility perhaps even more dangerous than the practices traditionally seen as degrading to an author, such as selling one's talents to a party or patron without maintaining a respectable image of independence.

25. Like the charge that Scott was mercenary, ths ambivalent representation of himself began early in his career. See, for instance, the exchange of letters with Anna Seward discussed by Edgar Johnson in *Sir Walter Scott: The Great Unknown*, 2 vols. (New York: Macmillan, 1970) 1: 195–96. On Scott's presentation of himself as a gentleman, see also Peter F. Morgan, "Scott as Critic," *Studies in Scottish Literature* 7 (1969): 90–101.

26. Cf. Scott *Journal*, 651: "I have been reading over the *Five Nights of St. Albans* [by William Mudford]—very much *extra moenia flammantia mundi*, and possessed [*sic*] of considerable merit, though the author loves to play at cherry pit with Satan." It is interesting that Scott should employ the same phrase here as in his review of Hoffmann, and yet to a much more neutral effect. If the difference is that between a private and a public utterance, then the problem of his relation to his readers—to the public walls of his community—is highlighted even more.

27. As Scott's prefatory materials to *The Monastery* show, this fate literally occurred to him, as to Cervantes with the false continuation of *Don Quixote*. A London bookseller "printed, as a speculation, an additional collection of Tales of My Landlord, which was not so fortunate as to succeed in passing on the world as genuine" (*The Monastery* 1: lxxxii,n.)—but which did move Scott to announce the death of his narrator, Jedediah Cleishbotham, in an attempt to stave off further impostures.

28. On Scott's use of the supernatural in relation to the self-reflexive nature of his fiction, see Ruth Eller, "The Poetic Theme in Scott's Novels," *Scott and His Influence*, 75–86.

29. Cf. Scott's description of one of Halbert's encounters with the White Lady (*The Monastery* 1: 228): "The whole appearance resembled those faces which the imagination summons up when it is disturbed by laudanum, but which do not remain under the visionary's command, and, beautiful in their first appearance, become wild and grotesque ere we can arrest them."

30. For the conventional treatment of Scott's "relativism," see David Brown, *Walter Scott and the Historical Imagination* (London: Routledge and Kegan Paul, 1979), 202–5.

31. Some critics have noted the "oddness" of the association of a figure of superstition or unreason with Protestantism. See, for instance, Donald Cameron, "History, Religion and the Supernatural: the Failure of *The Monastery*," *Studies in Scottish Literature* 6 (1968): 79. James Anderson's outrage over the compromising effect of this figure on Protestant reason is especially amusing. See "Sir Walter Scott as Historical Novelist: part VI," *Studies in Scottish Literature* 5 (1967–1968): 146:

To the present writer, after a fairly long course of reading in history and literature, there appears to be in Scott only one serious violation of historical plausibility: one thing which really disturbs the "willing suspension of disbelief," and that is the character of the White Lady of Avenel in *The Monastery*. . . . [H]er most objectionable feature to the historian is that she, a fountain-haunting folk-lore sprite or nixie, proves to be an ally of the Calvinists in their struggle against the unreformed church. . . . As a representative of the powers of darkness, she might have been acceptable; even as a champion of the old faith, she might have been made tolerable, with careful handling; but her association with the Geneva gown is the last straw. Yet who can say that this absurdity will be equally evident to future generations?

For a more thoughtful analysis of the White Lady as a figure of the romantic imagination, see Patricia Harkin, "The Fog, the Fairy, and the Genres of Scott's Monastery," *Studies in Scottish Literature* 19 (1984): 177–93. In *Secret Leaves: The Novels of Walter Scott* (Chicago: The University of Chicago Press, 1985), Judith Wilt argues that in *The Monastery*, "language carries its upside down deconstructing element inside it" (107); but her rhapsodic analysis is formulaic and completely ahistorical in its description of "language."

32. The quotation is taken (somewhat loosely) from Thomas Gray's *The Bard*.

33. In his 1830 Introduction to *Rokeby* (*Poetical Works*, 380), Scott gave the same reason for the comparative failure of that work.

34. Scott, *Walter Scott and Scotland*, 64. See also A. O. J. Cockshut's interesting discussion of the relation between reason and irrationality in Scott's novels, which relates it to Scott's conceptions of culture and cultural conflicts, in *The Achievement of Walter Scott* (London: Collins, 1969), 42–62.

35. George Levine's argument is more subtle in *The Realistic Imagination: English Fiction from Frankenstein to Lady Chatterley* (Chicago: University of Chicago Press, 1981). He argues the opposite point: that Scott's "unwillingness to assert the seriousness of his enterprise" shows his self-consciousness, his awareness that it was impossible "to get 'beyond words'" (92). However, Levine's belief in the same spirit of the novel described by critics like Lukács ("Even in Scott realism is an ironic form" [98] leads him to concentrate on an ahistorical "theme of disenchantment" (93) and thus to a portrayal of Scott's assumptions that slights their complexities and disharmonies.

36. G. W. F. Hegel, *The Phenomenology of Mind*, tr. with an Introduction and Notes by J. B. Baillie, with an Introduction by George Lichtheim, Harper Torchbooks (New York: Harper and Row, 1967), 565.

Satire and the Images of Self in the Romantic Period: The Long Tradition of Hazlitt's *Liber Amoris*

Marilyn Butler

Satire is a mode with which we do not as a rule associate the romantic period. Among the trees of the literary forest a few scrubs can still be picked out: minor satirical verse like Mathias's *Pursuits of Literature*, Gifford's *Baviad* and *Maeviad*, the contributions of Canning and Frere to *The Anti-Jacobin*, and the Smith brothers' *Rejected Addresses*. These sold well at the time but have not worn well since, for generations have become convinced that the Spirit of the Age was very different. Symptomatically, the two substantial writers whose bent was unequivocally satirical, Byron and Peacock, are generally represented in the twentieth century as, in one way or another, marginal (though some unease is often expressed, very reasonably, at the demotion of Byron that this entails). As satirists, Byron and Peacock attract similar criticisms. They are irresponsible jesters, without clear satirical aims in view, even to themselvees, and anachronisms, lacking a proper understanding of the age they were born into.

But an age's self-image may not be as distinct as posterity's view of it. The so-called romantics did not know at the time that they were supposed to do without satire. Obvious if sometimes superficial changes in fashion had come about with the passing of time and with the marked growth of the educated reading public. Pope's closed couplet had been under attack since the late eighteenth century, and in the early nineteenth century sophisticated writers could no longer appeal with confidence to a social norm and a moral consensus. But it is easy to exaggerate the break with the recent literary past, or with that portion of it we now designate Augustanism. Swift remained a much-admired writer. Byron's well-known tribute to Pope may have been controversial; Scott's even better-advertised tribute to Dryden was less so. Though the writers of the period are often linked with Shakespeare, partly because it is the era of the brilliant Shakespeare criticism of Coleridge and Hazlitt, in their poetry they are more inclined to draw on Milton, who was probably the most admired classic English writer precisely on account of his intellectuality and his public role. If Peacock is to be dismissed as an eccentric, it may not count for much that in a list of favorite great writers he named Rabelais, Burton, Swift, Fielding, and Sterne. It *is* significant, and typical (but not stereotypical), that Lamb and Hazlitt both defended Restoration comedy against those who wanted comedy without "disagreeables."

Admittedly it became fashionable to announce, as Shelley and Keats did in very similar terms, "didactic poetry is my abhorrence." Satire is not merely didactic, but has to be specifically and pellucidly so, or it cannot be effective. Shelley's poetry remains essentially didactic, and even Keats's seems far more so than he allows; all that these two poets can really be claiming is that their means are generally allusive, fanciful, pictorial, and narrative rather than directly argumentative. Yet even if it is relatively rare for either Shelley or Keats to write formal satires, their sense of the scope and social function of poetry remains in large part traditional. The old questions asked by Jonson in "To Penshurst," by Dryden in *Absalom and Achitophel*, and by Pope in *The Dunciad*—how to judge a good way of life or a good man or a good poet—are also asked by Byron in *Childe Harold* III and IV, by Shelley in *Prometheus Unbound* and *The Triumph of Life*, and by Keats in *The Fall of Hyperion*.

Nineteenth-century readers gradually came to expect good creative writing to be self-referential, and did not cavil if writers took themselves and their problems very seriously. Readers also became less inclined to want, and less inclined to notice, satire, intellectual analysis, debate, and controversy. But in what we now call the romantic period, writing directly about the self was still problematical. On the one hand, the reader seems to demand, and the writer to strive for, a new fullness of self-expression: the qualities prized include sincerity, emotional intensity, and particularity in rendering place, especially the haunts of childhood. On the other hand, as this paper will demonstrate, any work that appears to have self-expression or self-validation as its goal is liable to set up an ethical backlash, a complaint that the individual is not autonomous, that society has claims, and that artists are as much bound by moral law as anyone else. This hostile response is not confined to the reviews, where it would be predictable, since many were written for sections of the public suspicious of the arts and of the increasingly self-important claims of artists. The critique of romantic autobiography, which is also a critique of a growing aestheticism, seems interesting precisely because it occurs within the major poetry and prose of the first three decades of the century. It is the proposition of this paper that some well-known romantic self-portraits are satirical portraits, and even the rest frequently a source of satire in others.

For modern critics, Wordsworth's *Prelude* has a central position in English romanticism. Its innovation is to adapt epic, a genre concerned with society, to the topic of a single private life: an epic about the growth of a poet's mind is, properly, a contradiction in terms. Where Milton's *Paradise Lost* was ornamented with similes that spanned the story of mankind in time and space, in fact and fiction, Wordsworth derives his illusion of depth from "spots of time" that throw out their unexpected lines of sight into the poet's own private experience. Classic antecedents for *The Prelude* are identifiable, not only in Milton but in autobiographers like St Augustine and Rousseau. Citing them normally operates to stress that Wordsworth's treatment is revolutionary not only in his "naturalness" but in his self-absorption, raised to the level of a new metaphysical system.

As it happened, Wordsworth's contemporaries outside the circle of his friends did not know *The Prelude*, but they did know "Tintern Abbey" (1798), that intense exploration of private memory and of the poet's relationship with his sister, and *The Excursion* (1814), in which the poet seems to present himself in the guise of two personae, the Wanderer and the Solitary. The preface and first book of *The Excursion*, firmly declaring its subject to be the inner life, functioned for younger contemporaries as *The Prelude* does for us. The verse preface speaks of "ill sights" among "the tribes / And fellowships of men . . . the fierce confederate storm / Of sorrow, barricadoed evermore / Within the walls of cities" (73–78), and in these circumstances it declares that it is better to muse in solitude:

> Of the individual Mind that keeps her own
> Inviolate retirement, subject there
> To conscience only, and the law supreme
> Of that Intelligence which governs all—
> I sing:—'fit audience let me find though few'.
>
> (19–23)

The quotation from Milton, with his public and universal subject, must have struck alert readers as paradoxical. It was on this kind of evidence that Keats, following Hazlitt's lead, thought of Wordsworth as the Egotistical Sublime.

And yet, other poems by Wordsworth, also well known at the time, themselves ridiculed the notion of the self-satisfied and self-absorbed poet. An unmistakably detached and even satirical attitude to the poet's persona emerges in "Anecdote for Fathers" and "We Are Seven," both of which appeared in *Lyrical Ballads* in 1798, and above all in "Resolution and Independence," first published in 1807, which humblingly contrasts the conceited, absorbed literary man with the leech-gatherer, representative of humanity at one with nature. The curious fact is, then, that Wordsworth himself was a pioneer critic of that notion of the solipsistic poet with which readers of his own day and ours have identified him. And not uninstructed readers alone: Wordsworth's supposedly uncritical image of himself became an important negative inspiration to Shelley and Keats.

Shelley's poem *Alastor* (1816), written the year after *The Excursion* appeared, features a Narrator who tells the story of another idealistic young poet. The latter figure, whom we can distinguish from the Narrator by calling him the Visionary, tries to live by the light of Nature and by an altruism fostered narcissistically within his own mind and imagination; he cuts himself off from sympathy with his own species, and dies. Victorian readers were evidently quick to take the Visionary for Shelley himself, and Mary Shelley in her editorial note on the poem in 1839 contributes to that identification by writing of the bleak autobiographical circumstances in which the poem emerged. But the immediate model for the visionary Poet in *Alastor* is, surely, the Wanderer as a young man, described approvingly by Wordsworth in *The Excursion*, Book 1. The Wanderer's life has been devoted to virtue and to religious idealism, and has apparently been entirely solitary, which means, among other things, celibate:

> There he kept
> In solitude and solitary thought
> His mind in a just equipoise of love.
> Serene it was, unclouded by the cares
> Of ordinary life; unvexed, unwarped
> By partial bondage.
>
> (353–58)

In short, Wordsworth seems to redefine "love" so that it needs no second party, just as he redefines religion so that it needs neither a church nor an independent deity:

> sometimes his religion seemed to me
> Self-taught, as of a dreamer in the woods;
> Who to the model of his own pure heart
> Shaped his belief, . . .
>
> (409–12)

Shelley's poem guys such a creed when the Visionary fails to notice an Arab maiden who offers him "sweet human love." The only sexual experience he proves capable of is a perverse and onanistic one, with a fantasy-woman projected in his dreams; and this figure is, significantly, equated with his own thoughts and his words when making poetry:

> Her voice was like the voice of his own soul
> Heard in the calm of thought; . . .
> Knowledge and truth and virtue were her theme,
> And lofty hopes of divine liberty,
> Thoughts the most dear to him, and poesy,
> Herself a poet.
>
> (153–61)

In the Narrator's introduction to the Visionary's story, and in his summing up afterwards, there are specific quotations from Wordsworth, especially from the "Intimations" Ode: "natural piety" (*Alastor*, 3), "obstinate questionings" (26), and "too deep for tears" (713). It has thus become almost standard to identify the Narrator with Wordsworth; what should follow, and generally does not, is the equally Wordsworthian derivation of the other principal figure, the Visionary. By evoking the lifestyle of the Wanderer, but interpreting his solitariness as narcissistic and doom-laden, Shelley turns the idealization into a critique. The attack is brought home to Wordsworth personally, since Shelley reads the Wanderer as Wordsworth's complacent representation of his decision as a young man to forsake progressivism for a visionary, private, self-nurtured religion. On the contrary, Shelley believes that withdrawal led to Wordsworth's death as a poet, a point he reiterates in the sonnet, "To Wordsworth," which appeared in the *Alastor* volume:

> In honoured poverty thy voice did weave
> Songs consecrate to truth and liberty—
> Deserting these, thou leavest me to grieve,
> Thus having been, that thou shouldst cease to be.

In his "Preface" to *Alastor*, Shelley hints hard that he means us to associate *both* poet-characters with the single figure of Wordsworth. The "Preface" ends with Shelley quoting ironically those lines from *The Excursion*, Book 1, in which the Wanderer really does speak of human love, his own for his "daughter" Margaret: "the good die first, / And they whose hearts are dry as summer dust / Burn to the socket".[1] The "Preface," like the poem, has apparently been about two types of men: the failed imaginative youths, and the delinquents who keep aloof from sympathies with their kind. Wordsworth has been both, which is why his portrait in *Alastor* is a complex one.

Shelley's poem mars its own critical case by conveying a confusing element of sympathy with doomed idealists (even Wordsworth), so that it is perhaps not surprising that it has generally been taken for a classic instance of that poetic indulgence it sets out to satirize. The same fate has met another immature exercise in the same kind, Keats's *Endymion*. The models for Endymion's behavior are, presumably, both the youthful Wanderer and the Visionary in *Alastor*. The clues that Keats is thinking of Shelley's Visionary are that he gives his own hero some of the same adventures, including sexual encounters with two girls, one belonging to the human world (Keats has an Indian maiden where Shelley had an Arab), the other a dream-figure, who in the Keats poem is the moon-goddess Cynthia. True, Keats does not set out with quite the same overtly critical and intellectual intentions as Shelley. He identifies more naïvely and heartily with his hero, who is allowed to choose the right option at each juncture. Endymion goes ahead and makes love to his

Indian girl, as it happens a wise move that earns him his moon goddess after all. This does not alter the fact that Keats in *Endymion* makes the same general point as Shelley in *Alastor:* solitary idealists do no good to themselves or to anyone else, and love as an ideal, though universally professed by literary altruists, can be put into practice only in relationships with others.

What is surprising about Keats's poem is not that it accuses Wordsworth of narcissism and asexuality—these were the commonplaces of the day in critics hostile to Wordsworth—but that it goes out of its way to implicate Shelley too. Keats cannot, it is clear, read the Poet in *Alastor* as a critical portrait. He must think he is setting Shelley straight when he has Endymion make love to the Indian; though the failure of Shelley's hero to make love to his Arab looks now like a distanced ironic way of making the very same point. Here is evidence of a pattern that is to be repeated many times, more frequently with reference to Byron's Childe Harold of Canto III than even to the Wanderer. Writers put forward an unromantic antitype to correct what they see as a too-romantic prototype, each time overlooking an element suspicious of egotism in the first writer. This cannot be thought of as an example of unconscious and virtually satirical locations. The cumulative effect of the practice is to lead us to underestimate the element of skepticism actually present in romantic portraiture of poets.

Given the pattern, one begins to wonder where, if anywhere, a "pure" romantic autobiography is to be had. Byron wrote a number, if he is to be identified with the heroes of a number of his early and middle poems (the Giaour, the Corsair, Lara, Manfred), though for late twentieth-century readers the debunking tone of Byron's journals and letters also makes him an arch-critic of romanticizing. Otherwise, Wordsworth's Wanderer is surely too dramatized and fictionalized a figure to stand in for his creator. Coleridge gives a fillip to the writer's status with his demon-poet in *"Kubla Khan"*, and he supplies copious if abstruse further documentation in *The Lay Sermons* and the *Biographia Literaria;* but the very difficulty and eclecticism of that material is off-putting, and anyone attempting to track Coleridge as an autobiographer (let alone approach him as a biographer) has been inclined to lose heart.

According to some readings, another contender for a "straight" romantic autobiography might be Hazlitt's eccentric "novel," the *Liber Amoris* of 1823, which, as the agonized record of a man in the grip of a sexual obsession, has been commonly regarded as an uncomfortably artless example of the romantic compulsion toward self-expression. But is the hero of the *Liber Amoris* Hazlitt? Is he an emanation of Hazlitt's persona as a writer, being subjected to criticism and mockery? Is he a yet more detached figure, a composite of other characters in life and in books? The divergent possibilities make it a classic instance of the period's skeptical and divided approach to the self.

Hazlitt in February 1822 was forty-four, and in the grip of a mid-life crisis. His first marriage, to Sarah Stoddart in 1808, had broken down by mutual agreement, and Hazlitt now set off to Scotland to obtain a divorce. At Stamford on the way north he began writing first recollections and then a series of letters, some direct to the daughter of his London Landlord, Sarah Walker, most to his friend P. G. Patmore, a few to another friend, J. S. Knowles. Hazlitt was attempting to memorialize, perhaps to exorcize, perhaps even yet to consummate, his passion for the nineteen-year-old Sarah. He agonized to Patmore over the details of her past behavior to him, the conversations they had had, the wording of her brief inarticulate replies. Was she a goddess? Was she a slut? Was she just a coarse, dull teenager? To conform with Scottish divorce law, Hazlitt had to put in three months' residence in Scotland, and he spent the spring, from February to May 1822, at an inn at Tenton, Berwickshire, thirty miles from Edinburgh, composing his increasingly steamy series of letters and, in the act of writing, further intensifying his emotions.

The correspondence as Hazlitt actually penned it has long been known. Indeed one letter from Hazlitt to Patmore was published by a journal hostile to Hazlitt, the Tory *John Bull*, in July 1823, only two months after the publication of an edited 'formal' version of the same letter in the *Liber Amoris*. But the real-life series appeared in its entirety only in 1978, in the Sikes, Bonner, and Lahey edition of the *Letters of William Hazlitt*. The publishers of that edition, faced with the unenviable task of advertising the coldest and most impassive of romantic letter-writers, understandably dwell on the merits of the torrid letters of 1822:

> In an age of self-revealing, "confessional" autobiography, such as that of Rousseau and De Quincey, there is no comparable example of such savagely honest, of such appealing yet unsparingly ruthless self-exposure as appears in Hazlitt's letters which recount the intense struggle of the Romantic temperament with its own violently shifting moods. These letters . . . alone constitute a primary document for the study of the Romantic imagination.[2]

To dwell upon the honesty of the self-exposure is, however, a dubious move. Hazlitt had made a journalistic living variously in the second decade of the century, often with political articles for such liberal papers as the Hunt brothers' *Examiner* and *Yellow Dwarf*, but his métier was probably theater criticism, and the line in his writing between theater and life had long since become indistinct. The "unsparingly honest" letters to Patmore are written in a highly conscious literary manner, full of dramatic cross-references that include "is it not to write whore, hardened, impudent, heartless whore after her name?"; "musing over my only subject (Othello's occupation, alas! is gone)"; "thinking her human and that 'below was not all the fiend's'" (263, 269). From the start he depicts a series of scenes in which he plays, by turns, the parts of Young Werther, Hamlet, Othello, Iago, and Lovelace. The last two roles are significant: Hazlitt's self-image includes the notion of the ingenious contriver who is himself like a stage-manager, or like the author's surrogate within his fiction. It is, then, the most self-conscious, the most continuously literary of love affairs, though some of the sense of contrivance arises because Sarah has scarcely any words of her own, and seems to be waiting, like an actress, for her part to be written. Hazlitt, stage-managing as well as writing and performing, takes all the initiatives and dictates the course of the scenes. He tries Sarah physically by pulling her on to his knee and fondling her; he tests her morally by trusting her with his most prized possession, a little bronze statue of Napoleon. In late May, when he had served his Scottish time but not completed the divorce proceedings, he paid a flying visit to his London lodgings, where he found Sarah chillier than he had hoped for. In his rage he smashed the statue, and thus by a fine symbolic act pronounced the end of the affair.

As if the letters did not reveal an incurable self-dramatizer, they were clearly begun with at least half an eye to publication; by mid-March 1822 Hazlitt was certainly thinking not of a private record but of a book.[3] Henceforth, as he went on wooing Sarah by letter, he did so in the declared knowledge (declared to Patmore but not to Sarah) that he was making copy. The painful feelings were no doubt genuine; the fact that they were stage-managed does not imply that they were under control. Hazlitt at the time was under that compulsion pioneered by the Ancient Mariner, of telling all his friends about his sorrows and, when his friends were not at home, of telling their servants instead.[4] He extended the practice from London to Edinburgh, where he took the professional risk of laying bare his soul to the rather proper and very eminent Francis Jeffrey, editor of the *Edinburgh Review* and one of the leading journalistic patrons of the day.

From its inception as letters to its appearance as a novel, the book is always an inextricable blend of the lover's compulsive self-dramatization and the writer's professional calculation. *Liber Amoris; or, the New Pygmalion* was published anonymously early in May 1823. Each of its three sections is based fairly closely on an original document or group of documents, two of which survive. Part 1, seven fragments of dialogue betwen H—— and S——, derives from a manuscript notebook (now in the Lockwood Memorial Library of the State University of New York at Buffalo); this must be the notebook Hazlitt told Patmore he had begun at Stamford in February 1822. Part II is based on the letters Hazlitt sent Patmore from Renton, with various cuts, rearrangements, and rewriting: the originals survive in various libraries. Part III is made up of the more polished retrospective letters Hazlitt apparently wrote later in the summer to his friend, the Scottish dramatist J. S. Knowles, telling of the closing stages of the affair. But two further passages of "real" material, not used in the novel for, presumably, decency's sake, show

Hazlitt at his most Lovelacean, his most knowingly literary. One is in a letter of 18 June, in which he describes an overheard kitchen conversation between his "goddess," her mother, and her brother in such bawdy terms that to his fevered imagination the lodging house has now taken on the appearance of a brothel. The other is an extraordinary sequence entered in a separate note-book between 4 and 16 March 1823, and thus potentially a fourth episode for the book. The entries record the last and most flamboyantly literary of Hazlitt's contrivances, his procuring of a friend, F——, to test Sarah's virtue by attempting to seduce her. The notebook, which is given as an appendix in the Sikes edition of the *Letters*, consists of Hazlitt's summary of F——'s dealings with Sarah, including a last episode in which they scampered to-gether up the lodging house stairs, "he all the way tickling her legs behind" (388). This last document demonstrates not merely that the "private" mate-rial can be more gripping than what was printed in the edition of 1823; it also shows that, if a clear line ever existed in Hazlitt's mind between living his sotry and making a book of it, this had now broken down. Why was F—— procured? To tell Hazlitt something about Sarah that, nine months after their parting, he still emotionally had to know? It was, surely, to discover some-thing about her that readers of the drama needed to know; though in the end, Sarah, least manipulable of heroines, proved as incommunicable to F—— as she had been to H——.

Ever since the appearance of the *Liber Amoris* in 1823, no clear distinctions between the character H—— and the author Hazlitt, the "novel" and the "real" manuscripts, have ever proved possible to maintain. When the Tory *John Bull* maliciouly printed the unexpurgated letter, it claimed that it did so in the public interest, part of the "truth" having been improperly withheld. Reviewers and columnists immediately identified Hazlitt, no difficult matter when half London was in his confidence, and their descriptions of the *Liber Amoris* show that they thought they were dealing with the truth and nothing but the truth, even if it was not quite the whole truth. Later in the century, the *Dictionary of National Biography* treated the book without demur as an autobiography. Hazlitt, *DNB* supposes, must have been half mad when he wrote it, but "sane enough to get £100 for rivalling Rousseau's *Confessions*."

But in fact the crucial question, "What kind of an autobiography is it?," cannot be settled either by way of the textual evidence (since no text is more private or honest than another) or by biographical speculation. The anecdotes of contemporary literary men tend to support *DNB's* hypothesis that Hazlitt was deranged, and this is a view that fits well enough a reading of the *Liber Amoris* as "the intense struggle of the romantic temperament with its own violently shifting moods." But writers themselves and their families and friends often give very poor evidence about why a book was written, because its significant context need not be the private firsthand experience they have witnessed so much as the books of other writers, the taste of the public, and the state of the market. Viewed with these considerations in mind, the *Liber Amoris* becomes less unaccountable and considerably less insane.

In early 1822 Hazlitt was in difficulties not only with both his Sarahs, but with his journalistic employers and a number of his creditors; he was to be arrested for debt on 12 February 1823. The political polemic that had been one staple of his writing for the past seven years had become unfashionable in the quieter and less controversial times that came with the end of the postwar economic crisis and the temporary slackening of reform agitation. Editors wanted something lighter, more personal, and perhaps profitably titillating— such as both Lamb and De Quincey had in their different styles been achieving during 1821 in John Scott's new *London Magazine*, with the first *Essays of Elia* and the serialized *Confessions of an English Opium Eater*. Of these two new journalistic successes, De Quincey's brilliant impressionistic autobiography must have irked Hazlitt more. While Lamb was a friend of Hazlitt's, De Quincey was an ally and political adherent of the Tory Lake poets. A clear hint that Hazlitt was enviously aware of De Quincey as a journalistic rival came later in 1823, when Hazlitt sent a letter to the *London Magazine* claiming that a recent article by De Quincey against Malthus had used an argument in which Hazlitt had anticipated him.[5]

Above all, the *Confessions* made a target because the book could be read as a classic instance of one of those self-flattering idealizing Portraits of the Artist that stimulated emulation and annoyance in the period. De Quincey adapts the exalted conception of the artist and of his imagination that he has found in the work of Wordsworth and Coleridge, cleverly naturalizing the rather grand concepts by telling a story set in the London streets. Instead of glimpsing a tantalizing Muse, as the younger romantics and their poetic contemporaries had become over-fond of doing, he found and then lost again the haunting young prostitute, Ann, in Oxford Street. The Oriental visions of Beckford, Southey, and Coleridge in "Kubla Khan" become the no less fantastic and lavishly written, but more psychologically explicable, consequences for De Quincey's dream-life of his ten-year addiction to laudanum. But De Quincey has not lost sight of the theoretical potential of the dream-vision, which in the idealist view of art beginning to emanate from Germany, and being popularized by Coleridge, can stand symbolically for another world created and peopled by the artist's imagination. The *Confessions* works as an *apologia pro vita sua* because it isolates the artist again from the common world in which he is placed, elevating him to a special magical category on account of his gift of imagination.

De Quincey himself, in the opening passage of his *Confessions*, complains of *his* most obvious model, the *Confessions* of Rousseau, because it is too self-indulgent. That charge was often leveled against Rousseau's sexually permissive narrative, from an England in the grip of a moralistic religious revival. But when De Quincey is the accuser, the effect conveyed, more strongly than ever, is of the poet calling the kettle black. De Quincey's own *Confessions*, with their exculpatory approach to addiction, their narcissistic descriptions of dreams, their unrelenting egotism, advertise their author at least as provocatively as Rousseau's book does. So flamboyantly is this the case, indeed, that it comes as no surprise to discern in Hazlitt's romantic autobiography of the following year what is in effect a counterexample to De Quincey's.

Countering De Quincey meant feeling for the point at which his approach was specially vulnerable. The generalized ground for complaint against Wordsworth, the leading writer of the Lake school, was, as we have seen, his solipsism; a typical countermove proposed human love, or rather the consummation of the sexual act with one girl, who is explicitly not a mere figment of the fictional poet's fantasy life and so functions as a challenge to his egotism. Though De Quincey has the London street girl in his autobiography, and though he insists that his attitude to her is affectionate and benevolent, he has actually drawn a strangely muted and one-sided relationship. It is not, of course, sexual: that, perhaps, makes a rhetorical point against Rousseau, whose early sexual exploits become the burden of the narrative in his *Confessions*. But if De Quincey describes a mere friendship, bestowing material and physical comfort, the skeptical reader cannot help noticing that it is the waif Ann who gives and the adolescent De Quincey who takes. The key relationship in De Quincey's book thus maintains the asexuality and unsociability that had become a matter of complaint in the work of Wordsworth, De Quincey's main literary mentor. Hazlitt ripostes by taking as the subject of his "memoirs" a common London girl with whom he longs to have sexual intercourse, but whose very nature is hidden by his overintellectualizing.

Where De Quincey admits to an autobiography (and even, by choosing the title *Confessions*, evokes the most notoriously self-indulgent of autobiographies), Hazlitt claims, however notoriously, to be writing a novel. The formal maneuver cannot have been adopted in order to hide the author's identity, or he would have changed initials and place names and other details that made identification certain. Fictionalizing the story is a device for objectifying it, above all for setting up a distance and some measure of control between the author and H——, now formally a character and not Hazlitt himself. Hazlitt was sufficiently conscious of the technical distinction to make a point of it to the painter B. R. Haydon, who passed on to Mary Russell Mitford that the conversations with Sarah and the letters to Patmore were to be published as "a tale of character."[6] It is a critical, not an apologetic, portrait that Hazlitt thinks he is after, and other intellectual novels within his milieu supply a precedent for this. Wiliam Godwin's *Fleetwood* (1805) and *Mandeville* (1817) each make a critical study of an introverted intellectual, through two heroes so neurotically self-absorbed that they are incapable of successfully loving a woman. Godwin's novels fell under the usual curse of books on this topic, of being misread as examples of precisely that complacent misanthropy they were intended to dispel. *Mandeville* becomes one of the satiric targets of Peacock's *Nightmare Abbey*, which borrows its gloomy setting and its misanthropic hero, and lampoons Godwin's novel ("Devilman") as though it is itself uncritical. But *Fleetwood, or the New Man of Feeling* comes nearer to supplying Hazlitt with a useful model, one that its full title, with its revisionist implications, already points to: there is a significant tradition of intellectual novel writing, as we shall see, that uses the debunking subtitle, "or the . . .," followed by a pretentious term for an artist. Fleetwood is a Wordsworthian man who has lived solitarily among the Welsh mountains; in middle age, too late, he tried to find happiness in marriage and is instead consumed by egotism and jealousy. The precedents are thus available for a novel that is apparently autobiographical but in spirit critical, itself introverted in pursuit of a critique of introversion. The precedents are also available to have it misread, but of this Hazlitt may have been unaware.

There is documentary corroboration that in the very month in which Hazlitt began to compile the *Liber Amoris*, he was sketching an outline Portrait of the Artist, one that incorporated the very criticisms which De Quincey's book might have been expected to provoke. The sketch in question appears in yet another letter of an essentially open, public type, Hazlitt's Chesterfieldian "On the Conduct of Life," which was meant from the beginning for inclusion in *Table Talk*.[7] In advising his son what kind of man to be, Hazlitt bitterly advocates that he should not become a writer, since writers do not prosper in that sphere (the sexual) with which Hazlitt equates, apparently both ironically and seriously, success and happiness in life. The passage was so nakedly autobiographical that much of it was cut when the essay was first published in 1825, and only appeared in full when Hazlitt's son himself edited his father's *Literary Remains* in 1836. Hazlitt has just plainly referred to his ill success with Sarah Walker: "There is no forcing liking. . . . Women care nothing about poets, or philosophers, or politicians. They go by a man's looks and manner." But in some profound sense, he goes on to argue, authors bring this rejection on themselves:

> Authors . . . feel nothing spontaneously. . . . Instead of yielding to the first natural and lively impulses of things, in which they would find sympathy, they screw themselves up to some farfetched view of the subject in order to be unintelligible. Realities are not good enough for them. . . . They are intellectual dram-drinkers; and without their necessary stimulus, are torpid, dead, insensible to every thing. . . . Their minds are a sort of Herculaneum, full of old, petrified images;—are set in stereotype, and little fitted to the ordinary occasions of life.
>
> What chance, then, can they have with women. . . . do not, in thinking to study yourself into the good graces of the fair, study yourself out of

them, millions of miles. Do not place thought as a barrier between you and love: do not abstract yourself into the regions of truth, far from the smile of earthly beauty. . . . should you let your blood stagnate in some deep metaphysical question, or refine too much in your ideas of the sex, forgetting yourself in a dream of exalted perfection, you will want an eye to cheer you, a hand to guide you, a bosom to lean on, and will stagger into your grave, old before your time, unloved and unlovely. . . .

A spider, my dear, the meanest creature that lives or crawls, had its mate or fellow: but a scholar has no mate or fellow. For myself, I had courted thought, I had felt pain; and Love turned away his face from me. I have gazed along the silent air for that smile which had lured me to my doom. And as my frail bark sails down the stream of time, the God of Love stands on the shore, and as I stretch out my hands to him in vain, claps his wings, and mocks me as I pass![8]

The significance of this extraordinary passage is that it both reflects Hazlitt's obsession with Sarah Walker and objectifes it, so that it becomes the basis for a satirical view of the modern artist as an impotent and marginal figure. There is a possible allusion to De Quincey in the phrase, "they are intellectual dram-drinkers." There is a much clearer anticipation of the entire plot and theme of the *Liber Amoris*, with an emphasis that points up the full implications of the subtitle of that work: *the New Pygmalion*. Aesthete, narcissist, Pygmalion fell in love with the statue he had made, an icon of his own creation. Inserting the word "new" has the effect of updating the portrait, and of debunking it further. Really, Hazlitt seems to sigh, no matter how up-to-the-minute the cult of the artist, there is nothing new under the sun.[9]

The power and fascination of the *Liber Amoris*, most underrated of romantic autobiographies, derives precisely from the interplay between what is personal to Hazlitt, genuinely obsessive, and what has a generalized reference to the lives of all artists. H—— has two icons, which correspond to Hazlitt's in real life: Sarah herself, sometimes goddess and sometimes whore; and the little bronze statue, or bust, of Napoleon. The presence of these two successive passions in Hazlitt's life is a matter of record, and was already publicly on record by 1823. Hazlitt had even told the public that he saw a continuity between his old veneration for Napoleon, itself an extension of his youthful revolutionary idealism, and the passionate love he now felt for Sarah Walker. In an essay entitled "On Great and Little Things," written in January 1821 and printed in the *New Monthly Magazine* (n.s. 4, 1822), he first alludes unmistakably to his unhappy love affair ("to see beauty is not to be beautiful, to pine in love is not to be loved again") and then, in an upsurge of hope, imagines both love and the political hopes of earlier days restored to him: "The sun of Austerlitz has not set. It still shines here—in my heart; and he, the son of glory, is not dead, nor ever shall, to me." (Hazlitt admittedly appended the footnote to the paragraph: "I beg the reader to consider this passage merely as a specimen of the mock-heroic style, and as having nothing to do with any real facts or feelings.") Within the *Liber Amoris*, Sarah too makes the statue stand for her unrequited sexual desires, since Bonaparte's face reminds her of a man with whom she has been in love. In the stage-direction with which Hazlitt completes the final dialogue of Part I, "The Reconciliation," H——and Sarah appear precariously at one in their con-templation of the statue:

> I got up and gave her the image, and told her it was hers by every right that was sacred. I pressed it eagerly, and she took it. She immediately came and sat down, and put her arm around my neck, and kissed me, and I said, "Is it not plain we are the best friends in the world, since we are always so glad to make it up?" And then I added, "How odd it was that the God of my idolatry should turn out to be like her Idol, and that it was no wonder that the same face which awed the world should conquer the sweetest creature in it!" How I loved her at that moment! (82)

So long as the bust survives, it can be used, even if ominously, to symbolize their different sexual fantasies. When H——smashes it on his last visit to Southampton Buildings in May 1822, the crash involves not just the icon he has made of Sarah, and thus the current love affair, but the old, thwarted, superseded passions of both, and thus, by implication, the human comedy implicit in the making and breaking of icons.

But if here the *Liber Amoris* generalizes, elsewhere it particularizes. No autobiographical document of the period, and certainly not the novels with which the *Liber Amoris* was compared by an admiring reviewer, Rousseau's *Julie* and Goethe's *Werther*, in fact delved so minutely into the psycho-pathology of frustrated sexual love.[10] Sarah's behavior is almost as intriguing to the reader as it was to Hazlitt, for she copes erratically with his long campaign of sexual harassment, sometimes by avoiding her persecutor, most often by a discouraging reserve, but sometimes with passive acquiescence. Hazlitt grows almost delirious with joy when he fancies himself encouraged, as he does when Sarah's younger sister says that Sarah prizes his books; he is then plunged into deeper torment as it becomes plain in the course of the next week that Sarah is keeping out of sight (155). He fully recognizes the humiliating spectacle he must make to others, a man of rich inner resources the slave to a girl without conversation, in whom most of his friends do not even see good looks. In the unpublished parts of the letters, still more than in the *Liber Amoris*, he moans over the pleasure, even in memory, of fondling her body, even through clothes, and he moans too at his own abject depen-dence on her.[11] When *John Bull* alludes to the hero of the muted published version as a "disappointed dotard" and an "impotent sensualist," it has the text(s), read unironically, on its side.

Powerful and extraordinary though it is on its own, Hazlitt's Portrait of the Artist seems incomplete until we have contemplated it superimposed upon other portraits. Along with his fellow writers, Hazlitt was caught up in a collective enterprise in which the notion of the stereotypical intellectual was explored, corrected, given Identikit features, one contribution fitting over and losing itself in the last. Hazlitt's sorrowing and ridiculous Pygmalion gains from his dialogic relationship with De Quincey's tormented but vindicated Dreamer. Together, moreover, these two books advance the stereotype and show up how thin, sentimental, and bombastic it was before. De Quincey with his sluttish Muse in Oxford Street, Hazlitt with his in Southampton Buildings, Holborn, are both modern literary men, aeons away from the idealizations of the poets or from the canvasses of historical painters. For its full revisionist impact, the work of De Quincey and Hazlitt should be seen in the context of the craze, at its height across Europe in the first two decades of the nineteenth century, for a mythologized pantheon of artist-heroes: Homer, Tiresias, Dante, Tasso, and Milton recur, victimized but also resplendent, in the poetry of Byron and Shelley, Goethe and Foscolo, and in the paintings of late neoclassical artists, particularly in France.[12] The figures of Ann and Sarah need comparing, too, with the poets' impressive idealized meetings with their Muses, who for Foscolo are the Graces, for Keats Greek divinities and Queens of the Underworld.

Yet, even though De Quincey and Hazlitt are like one another and unlike the poets in their realistic treatment of detail and setting, they cannot be compared with one another as iconoclasts: it is only Hazlitt who pits literary realism against literary idealism. The *Examiner's* reviewer hailed the *Liber Amoris* as a very philosophical book, in the tradition of Bishop Berkeley and Sir William Drummond, the skeptical thinker admired by Shelley: these comparisons are not clearly explained, but it is possible to see why a sympathetic fellow-liberal made them.[13]

Since that time the *Liber Amoris* has not received much recognition, and certainly not the *Examiner's* kind of intellectual recognition. Today copies of it are hard to find, and even readers of Hazlitt have often never heard of it. Nevertheless the book represents a crucial breakthrough in Hazlitt's career. He was not only working Sarah, the real girl, out of his system; by interpreting their story symbolically, he was defining his position in relation to some extreme contemporary versions of the doctrine of the Imagination, which, in Hazlitt's rendering, kills. The book is of key importance for him because it marks the final transition from his activities in the second decade of the century, when he was a critic and a political journalist, to his final phase as an autobiographical essayist. Oddly, Hazlitt exclaimed with relief to his publisher Colburn as, on 3 March 1822, he finished the second volume of his *Table Talk:* "I have now done with essay writing for ever" (*Letters*, 238). What he was really achieving was an extension and enrichment of his life as an essayist, since henceforth these fragments could be seen against a larger project, a critical, intellectual, and generalized portrait of himself. The essayist who wrote "On Going a Journey," "The Indian Jugglers," and "On the Pleasure of Hating" remained an autobiographer, as he remained the author of dramatic monologues and the manipulator of real-life experience. The persona and the voice is developed in the *Liber Amoris;* so is the train of critical thinking that contextualizes the portrait, without which Hazlitt's career as a whole would lack an intellectual dimension.

But then the same point might be made about romantic autobiography, and about most English romantic writing as we habitually represent it: without its critical element, its corrections, critiques, parodies, and satires, it lacks an intellectual dimension apparent (if uncertainly) to writers and readers of the age. With the passing of time, critics seem to have become less, rather than more, aware of the satirical and intellectualist strain in romantic writing. The problem is that all modern professional persons of letters are romantics, in one way or another, and the premises on which most of our procedures rest are biased in favour of aestheticism. Biographers, psychobiographers, editors, textual critics, deconstructionists, critics of the poem or the poet in isolation, take, as a matter of course, the specialized, narrowly restricted view that in the early nineteenth century was still encountering intelligent criticism. The sympathetic portrait of the solitary artist, lifted by his calling above the ordinary obligations of life, initially aroused resistance because it demanded to be read on its own terms, which put aesthetics above ethics. The satirical counterportrait is hard to read (and was already hard when it first appeared) because it refuses "romantic" self-sufficiency. The meaning of a work remains incomplete until it is read alongside another work: *Alastor* alongside *The Excursion,* Book I; the *Liber Amoris* alongside *The Confessions of an English Opium Eater.*

For some tastes, the case for aestheticism was proved philosophically by Kant, Schelling, Hegel, and their adherents (there is a philosopher's equivalent of the Whig Idea of Progress). If this is the case, the gestures of the English younger romantic generation were a futile rearguard action, soon overtaken by history, or by revelation. From a more skeptical point of view, the sudden prestige of aestheticism around 1800 is itself a historical phenomenon, no more above criticism than any other movement of ideas, and certainly not immune from the observation that the intellectuals and artists who fostered it had an interest. From that angle of vision, it is pleasant to see romantic aestheticism meeting, at the outset, some pockets of resistance.

Notes

1. Shelley's version of line 501 in the "Preface" to *Alastor* reads: "And those whose hearts are dry as summer's dust."

2. *The Letters of William Hazlett,* edited by Herschel Moreland Sikes, assisted by Willard Hallam Bonner and Gerald Lahey (New York: New York University press, 1978; London: Macmillan 1979): publisher's advertisement on dustjacket. References to Hazlitt's letters are to this edition. Though floridly written, this description is not otherwise untypical. Compare the extended "romantic" accounts in Catherine M. Maclean, *Born Under Saturn: A Biography of Hazlitt* (London, Collins 1943), pp. 415–99; Cyril Connolly, "Hazlitt's *Liber Amoris,*" *London Magazine,* November 1954; Ralph M. Wardle, *Hazlitt* (Lincoln: University of Nebraska Press, 1971), 300–365.

3. *Letters,* 246. A postscript to the letter reads: "I have begun a book of our conversations (I mean mine and the statue's), which I call *Liber Amoris.*" The text of this letter becomes Letter 1 of Part 2 of the published *Liber Amoris.*

4. The amusing account of Hazlitt's communicativeness by B. W. Procter (the writer "Barry Cornwall") is quoted in Richard Le Gallienne's privately printed edition of the *Liber Amoris* (London, 1894), xiv. References are to this edition.

5. *London Magazine,* November 1823. De Quincey writes on the subject in October and (replying to Hazlitt) December 1823. See *Letters,* 329–32.

6. *Diary of Benjamin Robert Haydon,* edited by Willard B. Pope, 5 vols (Cambridge: Harvard University Press, 1960–63), 382, cited by Robert Ready, "The Logic of Passion: Hazlitt's *Liber Amoris,*" *Studies in Romanticism* 14 (1975); 41–57. This article is one of the few discussions to take seriously the claims of the *Liber Amoris* as a work of art: Ready sees it as a carefully fashioned, if eccentric, novel.

7. "I had a letter from my little boy the other day, and I have been writing him a long essay in my book on his conduct in life" (Hazlitt to Sarah Walker, 9 March 1822), *Letters,* 243–44.

8. *Letters,* 233–35. Though the 'Letter' was included in *Table Talk* (1825), the entire passage quoted here was omitted.

9. One precedent for Hazlitt's full title, Godwin's *Fleetwood, or the New Man of Feeling,* has already been noted. But Godwin's daughter, Mary Shelley, also wrote an admonitory fable about the intellectual life: *Frankenstein, or the Modern Prometheus* (1818). The themes of Hazlitt's and Mary Shelley's books have much in common. Frankenstein, too, is a creative figure, purportedly a scientist but allegorically, surely, an artist, who sets out with exaggerated notions of the benefits that he, like the fire-bearer Prometheus, is bringing to mankind. What he actually succeeds in bringing is a murderous Monster, an intensely lonely creature who is the mirror-image of Frankenstein's own egotism. For *Frankenstein's* link with *Alastor* and with the critique of Wordsworth's *Excursion,* see my *Peacock Displayed* (London: Routledge and Kegan Paul, 1979), 72.

10. *Examiner,* No. 798 (11 May 1823): quoted in *Liber Amoris,* xxiii. It is interesting that even this sympathetic reviewer remarked on the resemblance neither to Godwin's novels (for which see text) nor to Benjamin Constant's *Adolphe, and the Red Notebook* (1816), which anticipates the *Liber Amoris* in that it purports to be the edited manuscript of a lover now dead.

11. Hazlitt, to P. G. Patmore [31 May 1822], *Letters,* 263–65.

12. See Jon Whitely, "Homer Abandoned: A French Neoclassical Theme," in *The Artist and the Writer in France,* edited by F. Haskell, A. Levi, and R. Shackleton (Oxford: The Clarendon Press, 1974), 40–51. Whitely estimates that no fewer than sixteen French painters before 1830 used mythical themes from Homer's life, further amplified in modern times to suggest that the blind artist was peculiarly neglected and unfortunate.

13. *Examiner,* No. 798 (11 May 1823), quoted in *Liber Amoris,* xxiii.

Part 3
Romantic Literary Practice: Politics and Gender

History and Apocalypse in Blake's *The Four Zoas:* The Final Nights

G. A. Rosso

The final nights of *The Four Zoas* prepare for and present Blake's apocalypse, a subject well researched but not exhausted by Blake scholars, most of whom describe it as a purely internal event.[1] While an emphasis on the internal and individual apocalypse is correct, it is incomplete, for Blake's version of apocalyspe is both individual and collective and, in *The Four Zoas*, retains an historical basis. This basis allows Blake to invoke the "End" without calling for an end to the human project; his narrative would compel his audience to "reverse" history without annihilating it. Blake thus mediates apocalypse through poetic structure, challenging readers to work through the "imagery" of violence rather than apply a literal interpretation conducive to corporeal war. In the final nights of *The Four Zoas*, Blake symbolically reverses the cyclical violence of history embodied in the so-called "Orc Cycle": first, by exposing the sociopolitical roots of his own apocalyptic moment in the 1790s; and second, by imagining the revolutionary future in terms that exemplify the passage from individual to collective transformation.

While Blake scholars emphasize the personal and transcendental elements of apocalypse, others argue that "apocalytpic" becomes a way of reading contemporary history and taking a stance toward it. D. S. Russell, for example, underscores the historical basis of the genre: "It is true . . . that in the apocalyptic literature prominence is given to the destiny of the individual and to personal salvation in the age to come; but the overall perspective is still that of the community . . . and the objective of salvation is the creation of a new society. . . . not just in some far-off time or place, but in the struggles of contemporary life."[2] The Book of Revelation adopts the political perspective of pre-Christian apocalyptic because it too addresses contemporary social struggles. Although opinions differ as to the political content of Revelation, "no one would want to deny," says Bernard McGinn, "that the Apocalypse was a call to decision in a time of trial."[3] The cosmic "trial" in Revelation between the forces of light and darkness thus is rooted in the politics of Christian persecution in Asia Minor late in the first century A.D. Adela Yarbro Collins further contends that Revelation's first readers would search the book for "a program of action" advocating either militant violence or peaceful resistance against foreign aggression.[4]

That transcendence is the far goal of apocalypse cannot be denied. But since the predetermined course of apocalyptic history implies the literary unity of a "total form," the transcendental dimension is linked inextricably to its narrative presentation. The end point of time can be rendered only in the narrative, a fact that returns apocalyptic to its historical roots in prophecy. We must distinguish between an actual "End" of time and the "end-time" (which could last indefinitely). In other words, because eternity is experienced in the narrative, or *in time,* apocalyptic history retains an orientation toward the future. The narrative end functions as a prelude to the communal realization of the promised "kingdom." Christ's proclamation in the Gospel is itself apocalyptic: "The time is fulfilled, and the kingdom of God is at hand" (Mark 1 : 15). Yet Christ's incarnation represents an initial stage in the end-time. For the full or communal arrival of the kingdom is expected in the still future Second Coming. Thus, because of the delay of the Parousia, the transcendental perspective of apocalyptic is crossed by an historical one, which keeps anticipatory history, or prophetic typology, central to the genre. And as Paul Korshin argues, "the types of the Apocalypse can only refer to antitypes in history *since the writing of that book.*"[5]

Blake adapts the historical perspective of Revelation along with its narrative strategies, especially its figural typology. He uses Revelation typology for the symbolic compression it affords, for its encyclopedic compass, which can contain the evolving "consolidations of error" that, for him, characterize the historical process. Joseph Wittreich argues that what Blake derives from Revelation is an organic or "Living form" that encompasses movement in time: this organic structure is actually a shaping principle "characterized first by an 'elegant *Simultaneum,*' then by a pattern of gradually sharpening antitheses."[6] These "antitheses" are Blake's consolidations; they represent contending worldviews or ideologies that underpin the movement of history. Blake does not use Revelation as a sanction to abolish history in the name of visionary transcendence. Rather, as Wittreich argues:

> A model like the Book of Revelation suggests that form is a means to an end, which may "contradict . . . form and even deny it"; the final objective of form is not, then, to "prevail us . . . 'timeless designs' or eternal paradigms" but to effect liberation.[7]

Blake retains the political objective of Revelation even as he develops the dramatic structure of "epic-prophecy," the drama of contending perspectives that raises corporeal into spiritual war, a drama enacted through what Northrop Frye calls the "Orc Cycle."

In Frye's formulation, the "Orc Cycle" symbolizes the movement of history within an even larger cosmological scheme that Blake names the Circle of Destiny. This larger cycle, however, is guided by a "providential" vision sealed in Blake's "seven Eyes of God" construct, derived from the Persian apocalyptic idea of a cosmic World Week, each week representing a thousand-year period. In Blake, the "Eyes," the seven ages of history, are associated with the Urizen-Orc struggle that never reaches culmination despite the potential for apocalypse, or finality, in each period. But while Blake adopts the sevenfold structure of Revelation, he interweaves it with his own scheme of nine nights. Frye concludes that Blake's historical cycles thus are not sequential, but rather a "seven-times-recurring phenomenon" that contains the three stage Orc-Urizen struggle.[8] I would agree that Blake disrupts linear narrative patterns and strives for a kind of simultaneity of reference. But I would also contend that Blake's nine nights contain three broadly *historical* stages; Frye's three stages are structural and occur within each of the seven frames. If we historicize Fry's archetypal construct, we can clarify Blake's obscure narrative history in *The Four Zoas*. Like his millenarian seventeenth-century forerunners, Blake compresses all previous historical stages within the "end-time" of his own age, an age that exceeds its forerunners in apocalyptic urgency.

For Blake, the revolutionary situation in late eighteenth-century England opens with the Reformation, particularly with the civil war of the mid-seventeenth century. This moment of apocalypse, however, was deferred by what Blake chooses to call "Deism, or Natural Religion," a moderate form of worship championed by such theologically minded scientists as Robert Boyle and Isaac Newton. By claiming that natural law provides a more certain model of religion than revelation (without, of course, denying revelation), Boyle and Newton, among others, helped the Anglican Church distance scripture from history and so defuse the socially radical message of the Puritan sects.[9] This distancing is the target of Blake's critique of natural religion and underlies his vision of history in *The Four Zoas*.

In Blake's typological view of history, Anglican natural religion repeats the ancient "error" or abstracting moral law from prophetic vision, or of reifying imaginative into institutional forms of worship, thereby undermining the potential for apocalypse.[10] As Blake sees it, the Hebraic priesthood turns the thundering visions of prophecy into a legalistic morality, and this strategy is replicated by the Roman Church, which transposes the "poetic tales" of Jesus into Christian doctrine. Blake attempts to make this point by juxtaposing "typical" events from Old Testament, New Testament, and contemporary British history, which he condenses into a symbolic "moment" capable of being transformed by his readers. That is, there is a "kerygmatic" force in the text that turns the poem over to the community of readers, who must grasp their own age as part of a single, repetitive "error."[11] Once they reverse that

error, turning abstract moral law back into vision, Blake's readers free
themselves from the compulsive repetitions of the "Orc Cycle" and ready
their society for apocalyptic reversal.

But a problem remains. For if each age exceeds the previous one in
apocalyptic urgency, *and* if apocalypse is deferred continually in each age,
then how can history be said to move toward a definitive reversal? Blake
solves this logical difficulty by an imaginative strategy that Frye calls the
"consolidation of error."

> Blake . . . postulates a historical process which may be described as the
> opposite of the Hegelian one. Every advance of truth forces error to
> consolidate itself in a more obviously erroneous form, and every advance of
> freedom has the same effect on tyranny. Thus history exhibits a series of
> crises in which a sudden flash of imaginative vision (as in the French
> Revolution) bursts out, is counteracted by a more ruthless defense of the
> *status quo*, and subsides again. The evolution comes in the fact that the
> opposition grows sharper each time, and will one day present a clear-cut
> alternative of eternal life or extermination.[12]

Augustine developed this idea of a progressive revelation by crossing pagan
historiography with scriptural history: he transformed the Greco-Roman
pattern of growth and decline by recasting the notion of recurrence into an
expanding spiral. In this view, the exodus out of spiritual bondage championed by Christ is greater than the exodus out of Babylon, which, in turn, is
greater than the exodus out of Egypt; by extension, the exodus at the Last
Judgment will surpass all these liberations. Blake too employs the spiraling
sevenfold structure of Revelation, but he crosses this symbolism with the
ninefold period of human gestation in order to ground the roots of apocalyptic in human history.

In what follows I ask the reader to enter the mighty maze of Blake's most
difficult but, I believe, most powerful and interesting work. To complicate
matters, I am choosing to explicate Blake's final two nights of *The Four Zoas*,
nights left in draft state by Blake, and whose meanings in themselves, let
alone as parts of the poem, are debated vociferously by scholars.[13] But these
nights offer a unique glimpse not simply of a great poet struggling with his
material, but one struggling to extricate himself from the individualist net
that critics recently have deemed the "Romantic Ideology."

Night VIII

In Night VIIb, Los, Blake's prophetic hero, struggles to grasp the apocalyptic meaning of Orc's crucifixion on Urizen's Tree of Mystery. This Tree
functions as the symbolic center of a series of "births" that underpins the

narrative action of Night VIII. Several characters resurface from earlier nights and take on meanings obliquely hinted at before. The "male" characters include Orc's serpent and "eternal" forms—the latter being Luvah, one of the four zoas—as well as the seminal "Lamb," depicted as suffering within "Luvah's robes of blood"; the "Spectre of Urthona," or Los's eternal form; and "Satan," who replaces the Spectre once Los achieves his integration in VIIa. The "female" characters all derive from Vala, originally the titular spirit of the epic, and include the complex "Shadow of Enitharmon" (Enitharmon being Los's female counterpart who, with Los's Spectre, gives birth to the seminal figure of "Rahab"). Blake identifies Rahab with Revelation's "Whore of Babylon," but her narrative function is elusive and multivalent, related both to Vala and one "Shadowy Female," whose activities in VIIb are incorporated into Rahab's in Night VIII. My aim is not to decode the labyrinth of Blake's narrative strategies, but to offer a thread that ties these strategies to Blake's apocalyptic vision of history.[14]

Night VIII, for all its complexity, prepares for Blake's apocalypse through a series of consolidations that condense the activity of previous nights. The consolidations identify, on the one hand, Urizen, Orc, and Blake's Satan with Revelation's "great red dragon," and, on the other hand, Los, Luvah, and Blake's Jesus with John's symbolic "Lamb." As Orc "organizes" his serpent form—historically in Napoleon's wars of conquest—Urizen "in self-deceit his warlike preparations fabricated," "Communing with the Serpent Orc in dark dissimulation/And with the Synagogue of Satan in dark Sanhedrim/To undermine the world of Los & tear bright Enitharmon."[15] Blake uses the imperialistic French aggression and British reaction to consolidate the "Orc Cycle," exposing each side to be a version of the other. His narrator embodies this exposure or "revelation" in the figure of Satan and shows that the providential or evolutionary process of consolidation lies beyond any individual zoa's control.

> Terrified & astonished Urizen beheld the battle take a form
> Which he intended not a Shadowy hermaphrodite black & opake
> The Soliders namd it Satan but he was yet unformed & vast
> Hermaphroditic it at length became hiding the Male
> Within as in a Tabernacle Abominable deadly. . . .
>
> (E 374)

The soldiers' naming the war "Satan" presages a decisive turning point in the epic: for they are the "spectres of the dead" whose salvation, like that of the slain martyrs in Revelation, the "Lamb," Los, and Enitharmon make their primary concern. More particularly, the soldiers indicate their awareness of Urizen-Orc's (England-France's) dual complicity in the war. For while they do not seem to recognize Rahab's role—the hermaphrodite is "yet un-formd"—Satan, Blake's Antichrist, is comprised of Rahab and the combined serpent forms of Urizen and Orc.

The term "Antichrist" appears only in the Letters of John, but traditionally it has been attributed to the Beast-Whore symbol in Revelation. 2 Thessalonians offers an interesting perspective in that it concerns the exposure of error that precedes the revelation of Jesus as Christ. The Geneva Bible identifies Antichrist with the "son of perdition" of 2 Thessalonians, a figure who sits in the temple opposing and exalting himself "above all that is called God." Blake grounds this apocalyptic figure in the revolutionary-reactionary struggle of late eighteenth-century Europe:

> The war roard round Jerusalems Gates it took a hideous form
> Seen in the aggregate a Vast Hermaphroditic form
> Heavd like an Earthquake labring with convulsive groans
> Intolerable at length an awful wonder burst
> From the Hermaphroditic bosom Satan he was namd
> Son of Perdition terrible his form dishumanized monstrous
> A male without a female counterpart a howling fiend
> Forlorn of Eden & repugnant to the forms of life
> Yet hiding the shadowy female Vala as in an ark & Curtains
> Abhorrd accursed ever dying an Eternal death
> Being multitudes of tyrant Men in union blasphemous
> Against the divine image. Congregated Assemblies of wicked men.
>
> (E 377)

The political context emerges more clearly than usual—Erdman, for example, sees the congregated assemblies as "the armies and war councils of Britain, France, Prussia, Russia, Austria, and Spain" in 1804.[16] But in linking the assemblies with the "ark & Curtains," Blake includes both Old and New Testament allusions to make his point about the collusion of Church and State in repressing vision. That is, as his Revelation source makes clear, when prophetic vision ("Jerusalem's Gates") is institutionalized into a state church, religion turns into yet another "morality" that excuses tyranny and imperial conquest.

Blake names this historical phenomenon "Deism, or Natural Religion" because in his age Anglican reformation has repeated the contradiction that Revelation exposes and denounces in the dragon-whore symbol: the aggressive collusion of the state and religion in the name of "Law." Adhering closely to his Revelation source, Blake situates Rahab within the assemblies—"The Synagogue created her from Fruit of Urizen's Tree"—where she functions as the motive for war, ancient and modern, but now "vegetated," like Orc, into her most delusive manifestation: "The Synagogue of Satan Clothd her with Scarlet robes & gems / and on her forehead was her name written in blood Mystery" (E 378). Blake takes us both backward, to Old Testament legalism (Rahab descends from Urizen's Tree), and forward to his own age, using Revelation as a clarifying point of departure. The Anglican-Whig state, incorporating and yet containing the millennial thrust of radical Protestantism, spills blood in the name of natural religion. That is, in Blake's view, Anglican "natural religion" combines a "druidic" worship of natural law with an expansionist economic and social policy, a conjunction of religious and civil power that legislates the construction and defense of the British empire, with the countless deaths that go with it. Blake thus appropriates and updates the political perspective of Revelation, drawing particularly on those chapters (17 and 18) that are focused centrally on the "Mystery" of Roman imperialism, on the "Whore of Babylon," which helps him to integrate the various contexts of the epic into a "Living Form."

Blake expands his Revelation typologies both backward and forward in the section on the Lamb's crucifixion, which is the ultimate scene of consolidation. In Blake's antinomian view, natural religion functions as the state church's ideology because its obsession with moral law blocks the realization of apocalyptic desire. The contradictory nature of this law is exposed when Los sees the Lamb descend to judgment "thro Jerusalem's gates . . . to put off Mystery time after time" (E378). Perhaps *because* "all his words were peace," the Lamb is condemned to death "as a murderer & robber," as a threat to law and order. Yet, when the Lamb suffers crucifixion in "Luvah's robes of blood," the desire for apocalypse is raised to a symbolic level: Luvah-Orc's serpent form is "cut off" and the Lamb rends the veil or net of morality, revealing the impotence of natural law in the process. The apocalyptic moment has arrived that not only exposes the beast (of monarchical tyranny) and the whore (of natural religion), but transmutes Luvah-Orc into the Lamb of peace:

> But when Rahab had cut off the Mantle of Luvah from
> The Lamb of God it rolld apart, revealing to all in heaven
> And all on Earth the Temple & Synagogue of Satan & Mystery
> Even Rahab in all her turpitude. . . .
>
> (E 379–80)

The Lamb's "posthumous presence," as Mark Bracher calls it, simply contravenes the mortal law of nature and sets up the potential for contravening moral law as well. For belief in the posthumous presence can affect individuals in society, "freeing them from the fear of death and even encouraging self-sacrifice." And once self-sacrifice spreads in the body politic, then compassion and forgiveness can render morality obsolete. But individuals must accept self-sacrifice over sacrifice of others, for if they "realize that such perishing is ultimately a creative transformation of their own being and that of other individuals which they influence, the very being of the Shadowy Female (Rahab) will vanish."[17]

Blake's hope is that, once his audience (re) learns to read history as *figurative* history, the power of Rahab, or the whole system of natural religion, will self-destruct. Blake depicts this self-destruction at the conclusion of Night VIII. When Rahab is exposed "in all her turpitude," Urizen undergoes his ultimate transformation into the biblical Leviathan, equated in Revelation with "the dragon, that old serpent . . . and Satan"—i.e., with Antichrist. Rahab goes to Urizen and the "Prince of Light beheld / Reveald before the face of heaven his secret holiness"; he feels her "stupor" while "sitting in his web of deceitful Religion" and "(f)orgetful of his own Laws pitying he began to embrace / The Shadowy Female" (E 381). This embrace symbolically enacts the contemporary consolidation of error into "Deism, or Natural Religion."

In the historical allegory, the Anglican state church, complicitous with liberal and revolutionary forces, promulgates a religion of nature that degenerates into a lawless parody of Christian community. This is an inevitable result, according to Blake, of its literalist worldview. Orc has already transposed himself into this "satanic" state by declaring revolutionary war in the name of the Supreme Republic and *Vertu*. Blake consolidates this "error" by showing how Urizen, as rational monarchical state, and Orc, his irrational revolutionary counterpart, become one "state" through Rahab, the harlot of nature who draws them both into corporeal war. Based on a self-righteous sacrifice of others—whether in the name of English or French "virtue"—the architects of natural religion carry on a campaign against revelation as religious mystery while, Blake shows, instituting yet another form of mystery in its place.

> Satan divided against Satan resolvd in open Sanhedrim
> To burn Mystery with fire & form another from her ashes. . . .
> The Ashes of Mystery began to animate they calld it Deism
> And Natural Religion as of old so now anew began
> Babylon again in Infancy Calld Natural Religion.
>
> (E 386)

This exposure and critique in Night VIII prepares for the internalized apocalyptic reversals of Night IX. Natural religion has been placed in its historical context: the rest is up to the reader.

Night IX

After consolidation, transformation. The agent of this transformation is the Lamb in Luvah's robes of blood, a figure Blake equates with "the spirit of prophecy," a figure that can sublimate the literal revolutionary violence of Orc. The mediating charge of this sublimation, however, falls to Blake's "eternal prophet," Los. As Wittreich suggests, Los must respond to history like the two witnesses of Revelation, who "testify to the spirit of prophecy and . . . embody it; they witness to the truth of a new birth . . . and thus precipitate a revolution that reforms the world."[18] Reformation, however, is not equivalent to individual conversion. The Lamb's "posthumous presence" or spiritual agency must spread through the community. Thus, to instill a desire to reverse the "fallen" ideology of Rahab's natural religion, Blake depicts in Night IX the very process he would inculcate: the integration of the individual into the collective form Blake calls the "Universal Humanity."

The Lamb bears crucially on the transvaluation of war, or division, that lies at the center of the epic. Of particular importance is, again, the Lamb's victory over natural law, the visionary force that nullifies death and the power of the literal sword. Night IX exhibits the fundamental prophetic principle that the higher heroism lies in intellectual war. In the opening lines of Night IX, the Lamb teaches Los and Enitharmon to separate the body (ideology) of nature from that of vision and pulls them off the battlefield into the prophetic workshop. In effect, they enter narrative space and take control of the action, tearing down the poetic world erected in the first eight nights. Perspectives rather than human beings are doing battle: Los "burns" mystery and "cracks" Urizen's cosmology, his "Mundane Shell," by the hammer of his imaginative faith. His aim is to free Orc from Urizen's branches, which also entangle Los, by first freeing himself. He must clarify the historical problematic in individual terms, showing that Orc's hatred of tyranny and injustice, while based on honest indignation, is crossed by a debilitating emotional fury. But we should not forget that Los's regenerative embrace of Urthona's Spectre in Night VIIa was meant not only to cleanse Los's vision but "to comfort Orc in his dire sufferings." Los preserves or refines Orc's revolutionary wrath by self-sacrificing the Spectre, the Urizen, within himself. In effect, Los's task is to transform wrath, Luvah's robes of blood, into a symbolic form of warfare: "and the remnant were slain with the sword of him that sat upon the horse, which sword proceeded out of his mouth" (Revelation 19:21).

Blake attempts to draw readers into the field of his symbolic war by "rouzing" their faculties, testing their responses to his apocalyptic imagery. Signs of violence are everywhere. But ample clues are provided for understanding the signs *as* signs: Blake underscores the *written* nature of the Urizenic, Newtonian cosmos and its reversal in Night the Ninth's conflagration:

> Then fell the fires of Eternity with loud & shrill
> Sound of Loud Trumpet thundering along from heaven to heaven
> A mighty sound articulate Awake ye dead & come
> To Judgment from the four winds Awake & Come away
> Folding like scrolls of the Enormous volume of Heaven & Earth
>
> Rahab and Tirzah wail aloud in the wild flames they give up themselves to
> Consummation

The books of Urizen unroll with dreadful noise the folding Serpent
Of Orc began to Consume in fierce raving fire his fierce flames
Issud on all sides gathring strength in animating volumes

(E 386–87)

Blake can give Orc full vent of his rage within the imaginative space of Los's narrative, for symbolism undercuts a literal interpretation. One could argue that Blake's apocalypse is wish fulfillment of a particularly gruesome kind; indeed, Blake could see a terrible beauty in the violence of the French Revolution. But the symbolic nature of the warfare is continually emphasized, as when the linchpin of the Anglican state church, the accusatory morality embodied in the Tree of Mystery, is burned by "living flames winged with intellect," and which "march in order flame by flame" until all priests and kings, all "Mysterys tyrants are cut off & not one left on Earth" (E 388). Obviously, the final overthrow of these tyrants has occurred within the mind of our eternal prophet. Los's activity, however, while paradigmatic of the individual reader's internalization, must be integrated with the other zoas and emanations to effect a communal liberation. Blake thus finally awakens the "hero" of his epic, Albion (England), the composite being of Los, Urizen, Orc, and all the rest, whose speech to Urizen constitutes one of the key exchanges in the poem.

Albion's first speech since Night II focuses on the war theme. Hearing "Mystery" howl in the flames, he demands to know "Whence is this sound of rage of Men drinking each others blood" and, suspecting Urizen, commands: "Shake off thy cold repose . . . great opposer of change" (E 389). Two more commands follow, indicating Albion's (England's) repossession of his powers. Enlightened by Los's activity within him, Albion separates Urizen from the unreasonable satanic state he has generated in history. "Lie down before my feet O Dragon let Urizen arise," Albion says, and he then gives the solution to the nightmare of the "Orc Cycle": "Let Luvah rage in the dark deep even to Consummation / For if thou feedest not his rage it will subside in peace" (E 389).

Albion here penetrates to the psychosocial roots of Urizen's preoccupation with war. Blake's particular target is the internal repression by moral law whose external correlative, the exploitation of nature's energies, is sanctioned by the ideology of natural religion, which, for Blake, has fueled the social upheavals of the late eighteenth century. Vowing unending war on Urizen if he refuses to unite with Orc, Albion threatens him with his own "self-destroying beast formd Science," the scientific religion of Newtonianism that defers and distances the promise of apocalypse from its personal and historical realization.

My anger against thee is greater than against this Luvah
For war is energy Enslavd but thy religion

The first author of this war & the distracting of honest minds
   Into confused perturbation & strife & honor & pride
Is a deceit so detestable that I will cast thee out
If thou repentest not & leave thee as a rotten branch to be burned
With Mystery the Harlot & with Satan for Ever & Ever

                                                                    (E 390)

The whole Newtonian cosmos must be dismantled, both within the individual and, subsequently, in the society—not because Newtonian physics is wrong per se, but because the Newtonian "synthesis" has been used to legitimate imperial war and domestic oppression.

Los's activity in Night IX reverses the cosmic construction of Night II. It depicts a process of ideological decomposition and reconstruction, translating the literal war of nations into a war of contending perspectives. But Los's reconstruction is not enough: Urizen's ruined world cannot be remade until the other zoas and emanations integrate into a collective body. That is why Albion cannot "Enter the Consummation" with Urizen: communal work must still be done to bring the apocalyptic harvest.

Thus Albion's first policy decision is to reverse the war production that has plagued the nine nights of Blake's history. "The noise of rural work" resounds as Albion's children alter their former activity: "They sing they seize the instruments of harmony they throw away / The spear the bow the gun the mortar they level the fortifications / They beat the engines of destruction into wedges," which Urthona's sons use to forge rollers that "break the clods to pass over the nations" (E 393). History has ripened for the harvest—"The field is the world . . . the harvest is the end of the world" (Mark 13:38)—which signals Blake's communal apocalypse. Yet, as ever, Blake sustains the symbolic nature of his narrative action: "Then follows the golden harrow in the midst of mental fires," and Urizen announces dramatically, "Times are Ended" (E 400).

On the brink of apocalypse, Blake inserts a feast between harvest and vintage that repeats essential motifs from his entire narrative history. Only in this eschatological context are the alternatives between literal and symbolic war, between extermination and eternal life, finally clear-cut.

The "Feast of the Eternals" separates harvest and vintage, the treading of the winepress of wrath that "consumes" six thousand years of toil. It also sets up the zoas' integration with each other and their emanations, manifesting the collective unity toward which the poem proceeds. The coherence of Blake's epic design is indicated also by the feast. On the one hand, it offsets the violent feast of Los and Enitharmon in Night I, which celebrated Orc's struggle with Urizen. The "nervous wine" of the first feast is replaced by the "wine of eternity" of the second, and the "Bloody sky" is replaced by Luvah's "flames" as the source of activity. "Clearly," James Evans writes, "the feast in Night I is a feast honoring a false semblance of victory in corporeal battle; the feast in Night IX is a feast of the victory of mental harmony."[19] On the other hand, the feast in Night IX provides a setting for one of the "Eternals" to proclaim the principles of unification. This proclamation enables not just the zoas and emanations to integrate in the risen Albion, but for Albion himself to unite with *his* family, the Eternals.

In what, for my purposes, is the definitive speech in the poem, an "Eternal" rises and recasts the story of the first eight nights in the apocalyptic context of Night IX ("Being the Last Judgment"). The situation calls for a reversal of the history put in motion by the two seminal symbolic figures, Tharmas and Enion, the "parental powers" of humanity who create the "Circle of Destiny," the tormenting warp and woof of time that generates the "Orc Cycle." The Eternal consolidates and then unpacks the "error" of earthly life, uniting the psychological, social, and cosmological perspectives of Blake's narrative.

> Man is a Worm wearied with joy he seeks the caves of sleep
> Among the Flowers of Beulah in his Selfish cold repose
> Forsaking Brotherhood & Universal love in selfish clay
> Folding the pure wings of his mind seeking the places dark
> Abstracted from the roots of Science then inclosed around
> In walls of Gold we cast him like a Seed into the Earth
> Till times & spaces have passed over him duly every morn
> We visit him covering with a Veil the immortal seed
> With windows . . . we cover him & with walls
> And hearths protect the Selfish terror till divided all
> In families we see our shadows born. & thence we know
> That Man subsists by Brotherhood & Universal Love
> We fall on one anothers necks more closely we embrace
> Not for ourselves but for the Eternal family we live
> Man liveth not by Self alone but in his brothers face

>   (E 401–2)

The solution of selfless brotherhood, witnessed earlier by Los seeing the Lamb in Luvah's robes of blood, is buttressed in this passage by a marginal allusion to Ephesians 3 : 10. The only other glosses in the poem appear on the title page, and one in particular (it introduces the poem) forms a counterpart to the Ephesians' gloss. Blake in fact ties them closely together: the title page epigraph about spiritual wickedness in high places is reversed by the passage on page 133 of Blake's text. In Ephesians 3 : 10, Paul tells his audience that he has been blessed with grace to preach "fellowship," but with the radical "intent that now unto the principalities and powers in heavenly places might be known by the church the manifold wisdom of God." The primitive Christian "church" is the spiritual agency of this direct challenge to the authorities. Its anger, however, has coupled with the visionary courage inspired by the Lamb, so that a new composite arises: the Eternal then embraces Albion "the New born Man" as part of the "Eternal family," an embrace that completes the individual integration of Los with his Spectre in Night VIIa.

The Eternal's speech shows a firm grasp of the function of prophetic narrative. In Blake's conception of prophecy, as in the "fourfold" hermeneutic scheme of the medieval church, the figural movement from prophetic types to apocalyptic antitypes occurs but is not completely contained within the "polysemantic" space of the narrative. There is a "kerygmatic" dimension to prophecy that encourages its audience to take direct action on a text, to make a dialectical turn from text to history, which Albion does when he embraces the Eternal following the proclamation of brotherhood. This dialectical turn begins in individual readers, but it also opens the internalized apocalypse to the larger community. As in the medieval scheme of four levels, Blake's narrative shifts gears from the literal to the typological through the "tropological" (moral) levels of meaning, so that the destiny of the people (Israel) is rewritten in terms of individual biography (Christ). But, with Fredric Jameson, I believe that the "tropological" level of individual moral biography "is clearly insufficient by itself, and at once generates the fourth or anagogic sense, in which the text undergoes its ultimate rewriting in terms of the destiny of the human race as a whole."[20] Although Blake's narrative does not need the medieval scheme to make sense, his multivalent text does move from the individual trajectory of Los to the collective destiny of Albion.

Once Albion embraces the Eternal, the epic is poised for its narrative consummation, which Blake dramatizes as the vintage that turns the grapes of wrath into the wine of spiritual communion. Luvah's "robes of blood," the garments of war, undergo a symbolic transformation into the Lamb's "vesture dipped in blood," a garment John of Patmos identifies with the "Word of God" (Revelation 19:13). Blake presents the vintage as an inherently social event, a fulfillment of the Second Coming anticipated in Christ's first incarnation in the individual. Adapting a passage from *America a Prophecy*, Blake places it into the more fully realized context of Night IX to highlight the political perspective of his apocalypse. The passage begins "Let the slave grinding at the mill run out into the field" and concludes: "Are these the Slaves that groand along the streets of Mystery / Where are your bonds & task masters are these the prisoners / Where are your chains. . . . The good of all the Land is before you for Mystery is no more" (E 402–3).

The reference to the conclusion of *Paradise Lost* is apt, particularly in the collective context under discussion. For Adam and Eve's departure from Eden points to the extratextual dimension of Milton's poem, or to the fact that Milton's protagonists do not fulfill Michael's prophecy in the narrative space of the epic. And if, as Milton scholars argue, Adam and Eve somehow represent Milton's readers, then one could argue that these readers do not fulfill prophecy in the space of the narrative either. Individual readers enact the kerygmatic demand of prophecy when they become part of the larger community trying to implement the divine plan of liberation. Once this

collective goal is grasped, the divisions of war can vanish, and Blake's prophet
of rage (Luvah-Orc) can be released from the burden of sacrifical atonement
for others.

Luvah's liberation is precisely what is accomplished in Night IX of *The
Four Zoas*. As he drinks the "wine of ages" and sings a new song, "his crown
of thorns fell from his head" (E 403). Luvah has ceased to define himself in
opposition to Urizen; he has realized that Urizen is a "Man" and not a
"God," for the mysterious, abstract deity of natural religion embodies a
fundamental error: "Attempting to be more than Man We become less said
Luvah." With Luvah and Urizen now regenerated, Tharmas and Urthona
(the regenerated Los) resume their ancient partnership at the controls of
history. They take over the harvest and vintage, creating bread and wine from
Urizen's thresher and Luvah's wine presses.

The communal transformations of Night IX correct the errors instigated
by the Urizen-Luvah conspiracy, the "Orc Cycle," and the subsequent attempts at domination by each of the zoas. As the most creative zoa, Urthona
becomes the key figure: indeed, it is his "fall into Division & his Resurrection
to Unity" that Blake announces as his epic theme in the opening pages. As
Urthona (re)emerges as the hero of the final pages, the narrator depicts his
activity as reversing the insidious social effects of the Urizenic philosophy.
And in a difficult but suggestive passage, the narrator says: "Urthona made
the Bread of Ages. . . . then took his repose . . . in the night of Time."
Harold Bloom sees an apocalyptic reversal taking place between lines 19 and
20 of page 406, between Urthona's "night of Time" and the "Morning" of
Albion's resurrection into unity (E 967). Whether or not Bloom is right, the
signficiant gap between night and morning effectively turns the poem over to
its readers. Urthona does not reverse the world *for* Blake's audience; he
attempts to inculcate a mode of perception that, if adopted, can effect a
reversal of perspective that leads to "vision." Readers then become responsible for realizing vision in act, for becoming witnesses to imaginative truths
that can transform a war-torn world into a community.

We thus return to the problem of an individual and social apocalypse and
the concommitant issue of literalism. The romantic poets, unlike their pre-
Enlightenment forerunners of the seventeenth century, tend to stress the
symbolic nature of apocalypse to avoid the literal closure of history. But they
do so in the subjective terms that Frye and M. H. Abrams have reiterated.
Wittreich, building on Frye and Abrams, anchors the romantic apocalypse
more securely in this world, and he makes the astute observation that "Blake
is the only Romantic poet to present a united vision of apocalypse in the mind
and in history."[21] But when we move from theoretical to "actual" history in
The Four Zoas, from the seven-phase eschatological frame to within the frame
where the wars are being fought, we see that history eludes Los the prophet's
individual control. Los relies on the Lamb's providential power, on the
"Universal hand" (E 376), when he despairs of arresting the cycles of blood-

shed. There is no need to deny the essential role of individual conversion, the paradigmatic experience of self-examination the prophet undergoes. For the solution to the "error" of literal apocalyptic lies in the kerygmatic conception of apocalypse that requires passage from individual to collective conversion.

If conversion is traditionally a matter of vision or perception and is related to how we see, we should also realize that perception itself is determined by the ideological constraints blocking vision. Blake does not argue that apocalypse annihilates the external world; he wants to suggest that the "external world," in addition to its materiality, is a construct of human experience with social ramifications. Blake does want to induce, or at least encourage, his readers to alter their perceptions of reality. That is why we get the same objects, the Urizenic cosmos, in Night IX as in earlier nights, only from an entirely different epistemological perspective. Again, those who stress the individual apocalypse make a crucial but, I believe, partial contribution to understanding Blake's idea of apocalypse, particularly (and perhaps primarily) in *The Four Zoas*, where Blake is still trying to drag history with him into the Last Judgment. War will continue to drive the wheel of history unless both the mental constructs *and* their social correlatives are broken. While the individual is responsible for breaking his or her own "mind-forg'd manacles," spiritual wickedness in high places requires the collective opposition of "Brotherhood & Universal Love."

With Blake, then, we must come to terms with the forceful illogic of his position, the paradox of summing up history in an eschatological narrative while keeping the future open for collective conversion. The point lies in the fundamental and enabling gap between fiction and the world, between narrative and its audience, a gap that enables the audience to assimilate the idea of apocalypse without literally seeking to annihilate history. Hence the importance of poetry as a mediation between history and "the End." Blake's apocalypse operates in the gap between fiction and the world and opens into history by virtue of its transactive focus. His radical narrative thus reveals a truth about all narrative: that it is constituted by the interaction of an internal form and a kerygmatic force.[22] If *The Four Zoas* is not a perfect poem, it remains a powerful one. It is the prophetic workshop where Blake matures his epic vision, where he forges his "spirits of fire" to challenge and admonish readers to carry that vision into the community. "For Man liveth not by Self alone but in his brothers face."

Notes

1. Many of Northrop Frye's works touch on the internalized apocalypse: see *Fearful Symmetry: A Study of William Blake* (Princeton: Princeton University Press, 1947), 305–9; and "The Keys to the Gates," in *The Stubborn Structure: Essays on Criticism and Society* (Ithaca: Cornell University Press, 1970); see also M. H. Abrams, "English Romanticism: The Spirit of the Age," in *Romanticism Reconsidered*, ed. Northrop Frye (New York: Columbia University Press, 1963); and Joseph A. Wittreich, *Angel of Apocalypse: Blake's Idea of Milton* (Madison: University of Wisconsin Press, 1975).

2. D. S. Russell, *Apocalyptic: Ancient and Modern* (Philadelphia: Fortress Press, 1978), 27.

3. Bernard McGinn, "Early Apocalypticism: the ongoing debate," in *The Apocalypse in English Renaissance Thought and Literature*, ed. C. A. Patrides and Joseph A. Wittreich (Ithaca: Cornell University Press, 1984), 23.

4. Adela Y. Collins, "The Political Perspective of the Revelation to John," *Journal of Biblical Literature* 96 (1977): 242.

5. Paul Korshin, *Typologies in England, 1650–1820* (Princeton: Princeton University Press, 1982), 334.

6. Joseph A. Wittreich, *Visionary Poetics: Milton's Tradition and His Legacy* (San Marino, Calif.: Huntington Library, 1979), 44.

7. Ibid.

8. Frye, *Fearful Symmetry*, 211.

9. The creators of natural religion achieved their greatest influence through the Boyle Lectures (1692–1714), which gave them a public forum to connect their interests in natural philosophy, social policy, and morality. Newton's *Principia* (1687) supplied them with the "single law" that explained the harmonious operation of all earthy and heavenly movement, a "law" that underpinned their philosophical rationale for social and political "order." The coherence of their ideas, coupled with their ability to popularize the *social* meaning of Newtonian natural philosophy, helped forge an "ideology" that assured the Anglican Church's survival in the post-1688 social order, which they showed to be both providentially guided by God and mathematically validated by Newton's physics.

10. Following the Enlightenment critique of typological thinking, Blake could not return unself-consciously to the biblical model. I believe, with Paul Korshin (*Typologies in England*, 349–50), that Blake practices an "abstracted" version of typology: "Blake mentions *types* infrequently, but so pervasive is his effort to explain the hidden meanings of the biblical myths that he introduces the traditional typological characters . . . with clear prefigurative import. . . . The sweeping generality of Blake's typological equation testifies to the central position that prefigurative structures occupy in his poetry."

11. I borrow this theological concept to emphasize the transactive nature of Blake's narrative strategies. "Kerygma" refers to the "proclamation" of the Gospels; it indicates the historicity of the biblical text, its call for an "existential commitment" by readers to "Go thou, and do likewise."

12. Frye, *Fearful Symmetry*, 260.

13. For the thorny debate over the final nights of *The Four Zoas*, see *Blake: An Illustrated Quarterly* 12 (Fall 1978), and Paul Mann, "The Final State of *The Four Zoas*" in *Blake: An Illustrated Quarterly* 18 (Spring 1985).

14. For a detailed analysis of these characters and their complex relations to each other and to *The Four Zoas* narrative per se, see Donald Ault's challenging book, *Narrative Unbound: Revisioning William Blake's "The Four Zoas"* (Barrytown, N.Y.: Station Hill Press, 1987).

15. David V. Erdman, *The Complete Poetry and Prose of William Blake*, rev. ed. (Berkeley: University of California Press, 1982), 373–74. All citations are taken from this edition and henceforth are cited parenthetically as "E" followed by page number from the text.

16. David V. Erdman, *Blake: Prophet Against Empire: A Poet's Interpretation of The History of His Own Times*, 3rd ed. (Princeton: Princeton University Press, 1977), 401.

17. Mark Bracher, *Being Form'd: Thinking Through Blake's "Milton"* (Barrytown, N.Y.: Station Hill Press, 1985), 93.

18. Wittreich, *Angel of Apocalypse*, 227–28.

19. James Evans, "The Apocalypse as Contrary Vision: Prolegomena to an Analogical Reading of *The Four Zoas*," *Texas Studies in Language and Literature* 14 (Summer 1972): 320.

20. Fredric Jameson, *The Political Unconscious: Narrative as a Socially Symbolic Act* (Ithaca: Cornell University Press, 1981), 30–31.

21. Joseph A. Wittreich, "'The Work of Man's Redemption': Prophecy and Apocalypse in Romantic Poetry," in *William Wordsworth and the Age of Romanticism*, ed. Kenneth Johnston and Gene Ruoff (New Brunswick, N.J.: Rutgers University Press, 1987), 59.

22. See Donald Marshall, "Plot as Trap, Plot as Mediation," in *Horizons of Literature*, ed. Paul Hernadi (Lincoln: University of Nebraska Press, 1982), 82.

No Face Like the Human Divine?: Women and Gender in Blake's Pickering Manuscript

Catherine L. McClenahan

Blake's attitude toward gender, women, the body, and sexuality is being increasingly debated, especially with respect to his later poetry, which some readers have long seen as evidence of a shift to religious and political conservatism.[1] Blake's treatment of gender and sexuality is a crucial issue because the poems after 1795 persistently represent the structure of gender and its concomitant battles for priority and power as the primary embodiment of his society's fundamental structure of unequal division and domination.[2] In the major prophecies, the female characters serve a complex double function both as individual characters (women) and as emanations (forms of Woman produced by male consciousness). Thus it may be easier to begin considering the later Blake's treatment of this issue with the poems of the Pickering Manuscript, where men and women are depicted more "straightforwardly," though of course not simply.

There are other reasons to turn to the Pickering Manuscript. The poems there were composed during the same period that Blake was working on *Vala* (later *The Four Zoas*) and perhaps even *Milton* and *Jerusalem*.[3] Indeed—apparently due in large part to the increasingly repressive climate—Blake did not actually publish any poetry between 1795 and 1810; nevertheless, though Blake never engraved this group of Notebook poems, he did copy them for some unknown friend or patron. And certainly some of this group have long attracted serious critical attention, most notably "The Mental Traveller," as well as "Auguries of Innocence," "The Crystal Cabinet," and even "The Golden Net." This makes it all the more curious that other poems in this group dealing directly with women and gender have remained unnoticed in the debate over Blake's later views on these subjects. Of the five poems I will consider, "Mary" and "William Bond" are particularly important examples of how acutely the later Blake understood the social construction of gender and, even more, of why a poet struggling to find a voice in those troubled times may have learned from women how to exploit the contradictions and loopholes of a "feminized" position.

Like the earlier *Songs*, the ballads of the Pickering Manuscript dramatize particular, limited, and changeable *states* of vision and desire in their characters and narrators.[4] Blake's verbal or visual techniques also represent these states as embodying internal contradictions and thus multiple interpretations. These contradictions are painful; at the same time, however, they preserve— even as they mean to repress or marginalize—discursive and conceptual bases from which to interrogate, subvert, or construct changes in the power relations of social reality. Most of the Pickering Manuscript poems thus dramatize aspects of the state of Experience (the exception being "Auguries of Innocence"), and only one, "William Bond," directly represents the beginning of a way to transform the frustration and helplessness characteristic of this state to more positive action, both individual and social.

As David Aers argues, Blake's work continuously develops "an original and profound understanding of the dialectics of sexual conflict" and of the internalizing of social relations within individual consciousness. In the Pickering Manuscript, however, Blake presents women who not only, as Aers says, propagate "the very ideology which oppresses them and their male counterparts" but who also challenge and resist it, despite the very real limitations under which they labor.[5]

By the late 1790s, British women existed in a society in which the separation of home and workplace, and hence the restriction of women's roles, were increasing. Socially defined only in relation to men (as daughters, sisters, wives, mothers, widows, spinsters), women were assigned to the private sphere as nurturers and rewards of men, as bearers of men's wealth and objects of their exchange. As a result, women had no political and very few legal rights over their persons, their property, or their children. As Mary Poovey points out, women's nature was correspondingly defined as a kind of absence. Women were held to have an "emotional responsiveness" that made them on the one hand morally superior (thus fit guardians of family moral education and cultural values), but especially vulnerable to sexual appetite on the other. Indeed, because women's indulgence of *any* appetite could lead to dangerous sexual desires, moralists and writers on women's propriety enjoined women to the complete suppression of any assertive "self" at all. Chastity could thus be displayed only by women's silence and inaction. Paradoxically, however, the very insistence on women's modesty as the guardian of their chastity made modesty itself "provocative," "an advertisement for—and hence an attraction to—[their] sexuality."[6]

When Blake wrote the Pickering Manuscript poems, the pressure of war with France and fear of invasion as well as of revolution at home had led both to legal reprisals against public meetings and public speech or writing critical of King or government and to successful propaganda campaigns. The corresponding identification of the family as the foundation and security of the state only intensified fears about any change in established ideas about women's nature, rights, roles, and proper behavior. As a result, most English men and women now equated the nascent liberal feminism of thinkers such as Condorcet and Wollstonecraft with atheism, revolution, and sexual immorality—in other words, with social chaos.

The sympathetic allusions to Wollstonecraft's life and work in a number of the Pickering Manuscript poems is all the more pointed given the intense outcry against Wollstonecraft after her death in 1797, which had further contributed to the discrediting of any debate over issues related to women in England. In 1798, Joseph Johnson had published her husband William Godwin's *Memoirs of the Author of A Vindication of The Rights of Women,* which "freely discussed her love affairs, suicide attempts, and pregnancies, and praised her (not altogether accurately) for her rejection of Christianity."[7] At the same time, Godwin and Johnson brought out four volumes of posthumous works that included her letters to her former lover Gilbert Imlay and the fragments of her last novel, *Maria, or The Wrongs of Woman.* Their "tribute" damaged her reputation and the respect that her two *Vindications* had received. Soon after this, all political reform movements in England died or went underground with the passage of the Combination Acts in 1799 and 1800. In France, Girondin feminists, male and female, had died in prison or by the guillotine. In 1803, the man or woman who still hoped for peaceful revolution in England had even more reason to feel an almost total absence of social support and power than they did ten years earlier.

In short, what Sheila Rowbotham says of Wollstonecraft when she published *A Vindication of The Rights of Woman* back in 1792 is even more true of Blake in 1800: that they were trying to consider the condition of and the possibilities for women *before*

> . . . there was either the possibility of a radical and socialist movement from below, to which the revolutionary feminist could relate, or a movement like that of suffragettes, of privileged women for equal rights with bourgeois man.[8]

Not until 1825, two years before Blake's death, did changes in England allow Owenite socialist thinkers like William Thompson to articulate and *publish* practical plans for an alternative society that large groups of men and women could actually struggle to achieve instead of merely appealing to bourgeois society to change itself.[9]

Under these conditions, the female characters of Blake's Pickering Manuscript, and especially the two Marys of "Mary" and "William Bond," are shown to be in a more complex situation than a choice between simple dependence or domination can describe. Their struggles to shape a desire of their own, like everyone's, "can only be carried on by alienated and tormented human beings, immersed in contradictions which are at once intimately personal and social, pressing forward in a painful, thoroughly dialectical movement."[10] In the poetry after 1795 (the beginning of his hiatus in publishing poetry), Blake is working out two distinct questions. One is what men and women can do under the specific conditions of this time and their particular situations in it to "*keep* the Divine Vision in time of trouble" (*Jerusalem* 44[30].15 and 95.20; emphasis added), with the understanding that "keep" carries the idea of limiting vision as well as the idea of preserving a potentially liberating form of vision from destruction. The other question is what kind of conditions could allow a conscious "human form divine," individual or social, to emerge and how that human form would act/speak. Blake's answer to this second question is explicit in the narrator's role (on the individual level) and in the conclusions of *Milton* and *Jerusalem* (on a social level); the poems of The Pickering Manuscript deal primarily, but not exclusively, with the first.

One of these, "The Land of Dreams," dramatizes Poovey's description of the eighteenth- and early nineteenth-century "woman as desiring subject": a " 'blackness,'. . . a negative that comes into view only when it interferes with the ideal woman, who cannot be seen at all."[11] Here the imaginations of two males, a father and child, have condensed their desires into the image of a dead woman, a wife and mother, whom they can see only in the land of dreams. The father tries to keep the child from crying in his sleep with the assurance that "Thy Father does thee keep" (4) but has no such comfort for his own mourning. Accepting the limitation of vision and frustrated desire characteristic of Experience, he can only admit that even in his own dream, "I could not get to the other side" (16) of the stream that bars him from possessing his desire. Once awake, however, the child questions his father's closure of desire. Characterizing the father's world as a "Land of unbelief and fear," he asks why they remain in it ("what do we hear"?). This question seems to imply more than a death wish, because, even more important, the child questions the adequacy of their shared image of desire: "O what Land is the Land of Dreams/ What are its Mountains and what are its Streams"? (17–18; 5–6). But the child's vision seems to fade in a final acceptance of the vision he inherits from his father since the child closes with the statement that he accepts all the potential range of desire as merely a "Land of Dreams," which is "better far" than his father's but unattainable, "Above the light of the Morning Star" (19–20).

In answer to the child's questions, what we do here in experience is first of all to constrict desire to sexual forms only, and secondly to deny or restrict our desire in social and moral codes of chastity and modesty that, as Wollstonecraft often observed, enforce deceit and selfishness. In "The

Golden Net," the young male speaker is entrapped—but only by females already entrapped themselves. The three Virgins who lure him are "clothd in flames of fire. . . in iron wire. . . in tears and sighs" (5–7). Their unsuccessfully repressed desire persists as torment, constrained or dampened by the garments or man-made constructs that forbid them to express desire except through the passive gesture of appearing weak and in need of chivalrous assistance and to speak it only through tears and simple utterances of emotion, "Alas for woe." The young man's answering tears ("Pitying I wept to see the woe / That Love and Beauty undergo") merely enmesh him in the net of socially constructed restraints upon the desire for "Love and Beauty"; he becomes a victim like the Virgins, reduced to their tears of "intreating." But the poem reveals that all the range of desire that "Love and Beauty" might signify has been condensed to something even more fundamental than the sexual: that sexuality itself has become the expression of a desire for conquest or the assertion of power over another. And here it is important to remember that it is the male speaker who locates this desire in women. The fact that the Virgins are themselves already entrapped indicates that this construction of feminine desire simply reflects the masculine, and can be expressed only by its apparent negation, wordless tears of helpless woe that can achieve no more than luring companions into women's misery as the enforced embodiment of "Love and Beauty."

A similar double bind occurs in "Long John Brown and Little Mary Bell," but here Blake shows the differing structures of male and female desire as originating in a specifically masculine point of view. It is Long John Brown who states that "Love is a Sin" (6).[12] This declaration simultaneously defines "Love" as sensual desire and projects that desire, the "Fairy," onto the woman, dissociating it from himself. His desire is thus shaped as a "Devil": a Devil that inevitably beholds itself as being drawn into the very desires it tried to deny and suppress as "Sin." And it is John, not the woman, who tries to gratify the other bodily appetites, eating and drinking, as a substitute; but as men argued was the case with women, he finds that the expression of any appetite only increases sexual desire, and grows thinner and thinner from frustration until he dies. Mary Bell survives physically, but the culturally enforced repression of sexual desire in women at last succeeds. The fairy of sensual desire abandons her, leaving her possessed by the devil of frustration actuated by the man's equation of love-woman-sin and the gender-based codes of behavior that result from it.

"The woe that Love and Beauty undergo" once these become names of Woman, or what is done here in Experience to women's desire, is also the subject of the longer narrative in "Mary," unmentioned by critics of the later Blake's alleged sexism.[13]

The story of "Mary" is as interesting for what it isn't about as for what it is. It is not, as one might expect, the simple reverse of the "young man trapped by a woman" scenario (so often highlighted in discussions of poems like "The Crystal Cabinet" or "The Golden Net"), i.e., not the story of a passive woman who is seduced and abandoned by a man. Mary's problem, and the counterpossibilities the problem implies, are more radical than the standard gender-determined story. Mary is neither exploiter nor exploited. She is a young woman condemned for openly expressing both sexual *and* other kinds of love, for her pleasure in giving as well as getting what her "Merit" or individual talents make possible. Her troubles arise not because she assumes a masculine role but because she desires to take on a role that is different from the sexual and social patterns assigned to either men or women. (How it is that she might have been given such a "liberated" consciousness will emerge later.)

The story is this. "Sweet Mary" goes to her first ball (an unusually explicit social setting for Blake, and one that marks her as middle- or upper-class), where her beauty, her innocent pleasure, and what she later describes as her generous behavior immediately attract both "young Men and Maidens" to "throng" around her (stanzas 1–2). She moves frankly "in soft beauty and conscious delight . . . nor once blushes" with consciousness of her own attractiveness of person and behavior and her pleasure at the companions it attracts (stanza 3).

But Mary's self-image and desires are already being interpreted differently by those around her. The codes of modesty and chastity do not allow her to be seen as just a human being or even as just an innocently frank young woman. The "words on every tongue" first frame her as other than human and as sexless: "An Angel is here from heavenly climes" (5).[14] Because Mary's behavior does not conform to the rules for "angelic" maidens, she is quickly re-categorized. When she continues to try to define herself differently, going out the next morning with the intent "Among Friends[15] to be free" (15), she finds, of course, that "Some calld her proud, some calld her a whore" (17): guilty of breaking commandments about feminine social and sexual modesty, but also of refusing her legitimate roles as chaste spinster or prospective wife, and thereby challenging male systems of family and property.

Mary is older than the child in "The Land of Dreams," but she persists in her questions, though she cannot frame answers. When she asks, "Why was I born with a different Face" and "bountiful hand" in the middle of "an Envious Race" and "envious Land" (stanza 6), she recognizes that the very beauty and generosity that should (according to the rules) win acclaim for these specifically feminine virtues in fact condemn her to envy and dislike: both from the men who fail to win her, or resent the "power" of her attractiveness, and from the women whose role demands that they compete with her for masculine favor. Moreover, Mary's wish to interact with others without possessing or being possessed is resented by both men and women whose desire has already been successfully condensed into those two alternatives. As she says, "if you raise Envy your Merit[']s to blame / For *planting* such spite in the weak and the tame" (stanza 7; emphasis added).

But when Mary tries adapting to these rules, the results are far worse than name-calling and social snubs. She renounces fine dress and balls; she determines that her "Eyes will not shine" with open pleasure and that she will refuse "any girls lover" who "forsakes her for me" (stanza 8).[16] When she goes out again "in plain neat attire," even the "Child in the Street" has learned enough of class and gender rules to reject this change: "Proud Mary's gone Mad" (stanza 9), and her unalluring dress still ends up "bespattered with mire" (36). Mary's community can presumably read several potential and contradictory "sins" into the gesture of her attire: dressing as though she is not an object of masculine desire and does not by nature love fine clothes[17] could indicate a deceitful pretense or even "monstrous" denial of her feminine nature; an immodest display of excess (and lower-class) religious enthusiasm; or even radical political notions. Thus Mary is in truth made mad by the impossibility of satisfying her own, or anyone's, desire. She is mad not only because "she trembled and cried / She forgot it was Night she forgot it was Morn," but also because she can no longer keep from internalizing the condemnation of her different desires and their expression: "Her soft Memory imprinted with Faces of Scorn" (38–40). Because the "Faces of scorn" and "Eyes of disdain" become "Like foul fiends inhabiting Mary's mild Brain," Mary "remembers no Face like the Human Divine" (41–43).[18]

It is not Mary but the narrator who generates this last phrase, an image of the desire that overflows the natural and customary[19] categories used by the boy and father in "The Land of Dreams." Instead of imaging desire as woman, the narrator conceives a less restricted, nongender-specific, form of human desire: without a barrier between human and divine, visible to imagination but not to a reason that has "naturalized" social mores. Yet the narrator does not elaborate on this vision, nor explain the way to get from disillusioned experience to an actualization of this new form of desire. Instead, the conclusion of "Mary" simply redefines the lineaments of Mary's beauty that attract this speaker's different kind of love:

> And thine is a Face of sweet Love in Despair
> And thine is a Face of mild sorrow and care
> And thine is a Face of wild terror and fear
> That never shall be quiet till laid on its bier.
>
> (45–48)

The narrator's final line speaks of more than Mary's actual death. Noting that modesty will naturally dispose women to silence in company, the highly influential Dr. Gregory assures them in *A Father's Legacy to His Daughters* (1774) that they can take part in conversation simply by " 'the expression in the countenance.' "[20] Thus the final ironic twist is that Mary cannot even be modestly silent, for her expressive face cannot stop signifying, whatever her intent. Yet even if readers of that face find there a message that calls for social change, the narrator leaves any hope or plan of reform that could prevent or heal Mary's trauma to their imagining (why he does so is discussed in my conclusion).

The reason for Mary's unusually radical ideas and behavior seems to be her connection with Mary Wollstonecraft, whose significance in Blake's work is becoming a matter for renewed attention.[21] When the narrator states that Mary "remembers no Face like the Human Divine," Blake seems to be quoting Wollstonecraft quoting Milton's phrase "human face divine" (*Paradise Lost* 3.44). In *A Short Residence in Sweden* (published by Joseph Johnson in 1796), Wollstonecraft wrote,

> I like to see animals sporting, and sympathize in their pains and pleasures. Still I love sometimes to view the human face divine, and trace the soul, as well as the heart, in its varying lineaments.[22]

What is notable here is that "Mary" is the *only* poem in which Blake keeps the terms of Milton's phrase: Blake's own characteristic and revisionary formulation is "human form divine," from "A Divine Image" in the *Songs of Innocence* (1794) to late works like *Jerusalem* and *The Everlasting Gospel*.

Moreover, the scene at the ball in "Mary" echoes the passage in the *Vindication of The Rights of Woman* where Wollstonecraft cites Dr. Gregory's advice that a young girl should

> give the lie to her feelings, and not dance with spirit, when gaiety of heart would make her feel eloquent without making her gestures immodest. (*VRW,* 28)

Wollstonecraft does not remark that a girl's "eloquence" must be nonverbal as well as restrained, but she comments on the reading strategies of the girl's audience: ". . . why, to damp innocent vivacity, is she darkly to be told that men will draw conclusions that she little thinks of?" These are "indecent cautions," Wollstonecraft adds, where only the girl's capacity for "exercise" should be the issue (*VRW,* 28), a sign of how women can only *mean* sexuality and thus be something less than human—although they are punished, at least, as if they were fully human and thus morally responsible for their acts. She also notes Dr. Gregory's advice for a married woman "never to let her husband know the extent of her sensibility or affection" (*VRW,* 30), supposing that she is still able to experience conscious physical desire or pleasure after years of being trained to deny or repress it. In phrases that sometimes resonate with Blake's address "To The Christians" in *Jerusalem's* fourth chapter, Wollstonecraft counters Rousseau as well as the British authors of conduct books for women in her argument that

> the woman who strengthens her body and exercises her mind will . . . become the friend, and not the humble dependent of her husband; and if she, by possessing such substantial qualities, merit his regard, she will not find it necessary to conceal her affection, nor to pretend to an unnatural coldness of constitution *to excite her husband's passions.* (*VRW*, 29; emphasis added)

Wollstonecraft points to what Blake dramatizes in several of these poems: that women's very modesty, their trained pretense to the absence of sexual feeling, becomes to male observers the very feature that makes them attractive and a necessary stimulus to masculine desire—i.e., it "plants" desire in men.

An incident in Wollstonecraft's life seems to be quoted in another poem from the Pickering Manuscript, "William Bond," discussed below. In the 1790s, Wollstonecraft had formed what she interpreted as an emotional and intellectual passion for Blake's friend Henry Fuseli, which the latter certainly encouraged. After Fuseli married, Wollstonecraft proposed that she join the household, though only as his spiritual partner. Not surprisingly, the suggestion was angrily rejected by Mrs. Fuseli.[23]

The allusion to Wollstonecraft in "William Bond" as well as the links between Blake and Wollstonecraft in "Mary," make it all the more interesting that Blake also applies his Mary's question, "Why was I born with a different Face?" to himself. In a letter to William Butts of 16 August 1803 describing the incident with the soldier that led to his upcoming trial for uttering "Seditious words," Blake closes by writing:

> I have been very much degraded and injuriously treated. But if it all arise from my own fault I ought to blame myself
>> O why was I born with a different face
>> Why was I not born like the rest of my race
>> When I look each one starts! When I speak I offend
>> Then I'm silent and passive and lose every Friend
>>
>> Then my verse I dishonor. My pictures despise
>> My person degrade and my temper chastise
>> And the pen is my terror. the pencil my shame
>> All my talents I bury, and dead is my Fame
>>
>> I am either too low or too highly prizd
>> When Elate I am Envy'd, When Meek I'm despisd.
>>   (Erdman, 733)

Blake's construction in both poem and letter of a link between himself and Wollstonecraft after her death and the furor over Godwin's *Memoirs* clearly points to a profound difference as well as a fundamental likeness between them. In the poem, Mary's "different face" is most obviously her female gender and her beauty; in Blake's letter, the "different face" has nothing to do with gender or physical appearance. Yet for Mary, Wollstonecraft, and Blake, the different face is also a matter of having ideas and modes of behavior that do not fit social, moral, and intellectual norms. As Wollstonecraft, Mary shares with Blake the double problem of their own and others' censure. If they escape self-censure by exercising their "merits" in speech, writing, or deed, they earn public hostility or neglect. Yet the link itself highlights Blake's awareness of the profound difference that gender makes in public response. Blake is depressed because his ideas offend; Wollstonecraft was vilified and her ideas ignored because her sexual behavior as a woman offended. The Mary of the poem is outcast and made mad because all her behavior, indeed her very being as woman, is read as sexual, and therefore offends. Both Marys fail to meet the separate standard enforced on women so that their desire and creativity can be shaped and reserved for acceptable masculine use. This connection with Wollstonecraft may be one reason that the narrator of "Mary" sees no possibility of peace in her face "until laid on its bier."

When Wollstonecraft died in 1797, Blake's public silence as a poet had already begun. But while the Napoleonic Wars and English Reaction continued, a man or woman who, like Blake, still hoped for peaceful revolution in England would necessarily have to look for modes of resistance and change on a smaller scale than collective social movements. The Mary in "William Bond" is indeed a woman enmeshed in painful personal and social contradictions but struggling to exploit them creatively. Her example demonstrates the way in which the ideologies that we internalize do not just *limit* but also *enable* thought and action.[24] This Mary follows some aspects of the codes for feminine propriety but breaks others. If woman's nature is defined as "love," she exploits that definition and its contradictions to break the bans on woman's consciousness of desire and on her expression of it. Because she does, William Bond is moved to transform his desire and the narrator to transform his vision, keeping and expanding a form of the Human Divine in time of trouble.

This third Mary thus has several face(t)s. One suggests Blake's acknowledgement that both the life and work of Mary Wollstonecraft helped to focus his own analysis of the politics and psychology of gender. Another suggests both a parallel and contrast with Wollstonecraft. In Blake's eyes, Wollstonecraft's reliance on reason and her retention of arguments for chastity in the *Vindication* (Chapter 7) could not have given her an adequate means of recognizing her own sexual desire in the case of Fuseli.[25] Nor in the case of Gilbert Imlay (for whom she made the journey to Sweden) could reason provide a way to avoid being trapped by an awakened sexual desire for a man who could or would not share her uncustomary views or feelings. From this angle, the William who learns from her example to alter his own vision and desire would make a positive contrast to Fuseli and Imlay, sharing Wollstonecraft's capacity for a social and political form of desire (not only "William Bond," then, but also a William Blake who has himself struggled with the bonds of sexual anxiety and conflict). But still another Mary Green simply suggests a more "ordinary" woman without Wollstonecraft's talents and circumstances and whose life must still be conducted within the confines of customary female roles.

The narrator of "William Bond" opens with standard male indictments of females:

> I wonder whether the Girls are mad
> And I wonder whether they mean to kill
> And I wonder if William Bond will die
> For assuredly he is very ill.
>
> (1–4)

The balladlike form and the tone of this stanza at first suggest an authoritative and unproblematic narrator. If we take his account at face value, we are led to see Mary Green as we do the three Virgins in "The Golden Net," a victim whose need for help ironically makes her the victimizer of a man. Yet the narrator's own tale gives evidence that his location of the problem in "the Girls" is an inadequate account of cause and effect, demonstrating that the narrator's state of vision is limited by the learned social assumptions of experience. The tale in fact suggests three socially constructed "bonds" that make William a sick man: both as a "diseased" incarnation of "the Human Divine" and as literally sick from frustration. First, William's illness begins in church, where "the Angels of Providence" drive out his "Fairies" of sensual desire (stanza 2). Deprived of private gratification, William ignores his public responsibilities and takes to his bed "in a Black Black Cloud" of "Misery" caused by his own internalization of demands for male as well as female chastity, with the Angels at his head and feet to forbid thoughts or acts of desire (8–16). But the second and third causes of William's suffering are the very codes of modesty and chastity imposed far more strenuously on women.

We discover that William loves an unnamed woman who may be the second cause of his inability to have what he thinks he needs to be healthy. This woman's nonappearance in the poem, and especially the narrator's question about whether the girls mean to kill, may suggest that William's desire for her is unrequited. Perhaps the Other Woman is too chaste and modest to respond to his overtures (whatever these may be). On the other hand, perhaps she too is out to "bind" him, psychologically or legally. As we have seen, the denial of power to women is simultaneously the attribution of power to them (they "plant" desire in men, to use the other Mary's term). A woman's chaste and modest silence can thus be read as a weapon (of attraction or refusal) that can bind a man to her or bind his desire either through rejection or through confining it to "legitimate" social relations.

A third bond is connected with Mary Green, who weeps by William's bedside with his sister Jane.[26] William and Mary have an already established relationship that may also give her a claim or bond on him: the very violence of William's rejection of her (see below) implies a guilty sense that he has given a social or moral bond to her as lover or future husband.

This bond is also implied by Mary's specific act of relinquishing any claim that is not mutually desired, in an offer that echoes, if more submissively, Wollstonecraft's offer to Fuseli:

> O Wiliam if thou dost another Love
> Dost another Love better than poor Mary
> Go take that other to be thy Wife
> And Mary Green shall her Servant be.
>
> (21–24)

This act is one of two turning points in the course of William's illness and recovery. Like the other Mary's behavior, it may mean one thing to her and another to her audience, and even more than one thing to her. In the discourse and roles available to her, the words "poor Mary" may voice selfish desire and jealousy as well as the customary feminine lure of pity for her virtuous self-abnegation. But her offer also tries to articulate an alternative to the either-or choice between male tyrant-as-victim and female victim-as-tyrant.

Nevertheless, William still accepts the bo[u]nds of that choice. From the perspective of a male-dominated society that marginalizes women and denies their desire, the difference that Mary is trying to express is at first simply incomprehensible to William. All he perceives is, first, a female object that he has no desire to "take." Second, her meaning for him does not reside in her words but in her position in relation to his desire: and despite his lack of desire, he sees her as an object that literally embodies a claim or bond on it (though of course she has no power of enforcement). In short, her existence makes him feel guilty as well as frustrated; hence his only desire toward her is the desire to assert his power, to punish:

> Yes Mary I do another Love
> Another I Love far better than thee
> And Another I will have for my Wife
> Then what have I to do with thee.
>
> (25–28)[27]

Note that whatever form of socially legitimate "Love" William feels for a prospective "Wife," it is still not attended by the "Fairies" of genuine sensual desire: William passively reflects middle-class social constructions of "good" masculinity even in the violence of his rejection of Mary's "illegitimate" offer. Indeed the talk of wives adds the possibility that Mary and her offer are also "illegitimate" because she and William did have a sexual relationship before guilt drove him to thoughts of marriage. So the eloquence of Mary's words is not enough to cure William of the sickness of his desire for vengeance and of a desire that he wants to repress (i.e., sexual desire in general and/or a desire for Mary persisting in the comparative statement that he loves another "far better").

Recognizing that her words cannot convince, Mary is left with no means of expression except the other kind of "discourse" said to be "natural" to women, the wordless eloquence that William, like Dr. Gregory, is trained to read into a girl's bodily movements: she trembles and falls into a swoon. Of course this language is not as subject to her direction as words, unless it is merely simulated and used to lie. In this sense her swoon is like William's illness, the expressiveness of the body when effective speech or action seem inaccessible. Nevertheless, her "illness" is not an exact analogue of his. William became ill when he encountered social prohibitions of his desire but "rallied" when he accepted a "legitimate" substitute; moreover, this accept-ance gave him access to "legitimate" structures of masculine author-ity and their discourse. Thus he felt enabled to express a sense of "self" and choice (however illusory) by negating Mary's through his words. Mary Green does not swoon at the point when she finds that she cannot have her initial desire (William's love). She accepts that fact and *uses* the self-sacrificing discourse assigned to women both to reconstruct her desire and to propose an alter-native. That alternative is considered below. The point for now is that Mary is driven back on a purely unconscious "eloquence" only when William's violent words assert that as far as he's concerned, she has no existence, much less the power of effective words. She may seem, then, to obey what William has in effect told her to do: drop dead, Mary.

In the poem's second and surprising turn, however, and without explana-tion, the narrator next tells that Mary has been "Laid / On the Right Hand of her William dear" in his bed—not as a fellow victim of the Angels of Providence, however, for they have disappeared. In their place, "the Fairies that fled from William Bond / Danced around her Shining Head" (37–42). Their return indicates that Mary's desire remains conscious, and their dance that it has been gratified; but the light that she now emits also indicates that she can somehow illumine the "Black Cloud of misery that a moment ago had engulfed William, Mary, and narrator.

The "I" who then speaks in the poem's last two stanzas seems to combine William Bond and the narrator, since the revision of love and desire in these stanzas would explain how William must have made some response to Mary that returned her to life and joy and also express the narrator's final comments on his tale.

> I thought Love livd in the hot sun shine
> But O he lives in the Moony light
> I thought to find Love in the heat of day
> But sweet Love is the Comforter of Night
>
> Seek Love in the Pity of others Woe
> In the gentle relief of anothers care
> In the darkness of night and the winters snow
> In the naked and outcast Seek Love there.
>
> (45–52)

Because William's description of the Other Woman contains imagery that Blake often uses positively ("ruddy and bright as day / And the sun beams dazzle from her eyne"), whereas his description of Mary Green contains imagery that Blake often uses negatively ("Melancholy Pale / And on thy head is the cold Moons Shine"), Hazard Adams argues that the conclusions of the last two stanzas are false: evidence that William simply falls into the bonds of customary constructions of desire and female wiles, needlessly restricting his own desire.[28] This is one possibility: it would, among other things, reflect Blake's own fear and the shame it causes when wrath and pity for others' woe seem incapable of translation into open speech or act.

But it is a William Bo[u]nd who generated these opposed descriptions of the two women and believed (like the narrator at the beginning) that choosing the desire he sees embodied in one woman must negate the desire embodied in the other. In contrast, the multiple speaker who redefines "love" in the closing two stanzas incorporates a voice like William/Bard's in *The Songs of Experience*, "Calling the lapsed Soul" of humanity in its individual and social forms to recognize and exert its power to "renew" the "fallen fallen light" of customary perception and desire ("Introduction," 6,10). Like the Bard, or the narrator of "Mary," this voice persuades not by outlining a reformer's plan but by shifting the focus of the perceiving "I" outside the self to identify with "others Woe": to desire the relief of others' cares and imagine how it might be done. William Bard, after all, is an active, imaginative, working state of the same William Blake whose hand in other states is bound by fear and shame as well as circumstance.[29]

A "history," as a more exuberant Blake wrote in *The Marriage of Heaven and Hell* (Plate 5), can be "adopted by both parties": as the "his-story" of William Bond is also the "her-story" of Mary Green, and both are adaptable to reactionary or radical vision. Within the specifics of her personal situation and this period of British history, what might Mary Green have achieved, and how?

Mary's offer to be a servant may reflect a sense of "illegitimacy" and women's training to be of use and to "love" selflessly, options disquieting to twentieth-century readers. But Mary Green breaks more rules than she keeps because she literalizes some of those rules and exploits the contradictions and possibilities of the discourses they provide. Arguments for women's moral superiority and responsibilities empower her to imagine and openly assert her offer of freedom to William and of service not only to him but to another woman: an offer that breaks down and restructures the limits of the family on which her nation rests so much of its security. Such arguments for her special feminine capacity to love also enable her to defy the bans on her recognition and assertion of sexual desire and to defy as well the hidden suspicion that she is capable of nothing else.

Mary Green's innovations thus give rise to far more than her own satisfaction, though only because what she communicates through her verbal and physical eloquence moves the men in this story to see that it is her story as well as theirs—and so to conceive new possibilities. What the multiple male speakers of the last two stanzas (narrator, protagonist, and author) can get from her story, if they will see it, is a way to begin freeing themselves from the bonds of selfish fear and desire. In effect, Mary's example appears to start a social movement, however small in scale, that goes beyond woman's "proper" family influence.[30]

Both narrator and William began by focusing on purely private satisfaction and trying to ignore a reality they found frustrating: "to reject experience in hopes of capturing a dazzling illusion"[31]—the illusion of some ideal "day" or "sun" or "spring" that they cannot stop pursuing even as they assume it is unattainable. The new vision and desire that these multiple male speakers express in the final stanza have expanded to the social instead of the merely personal and sexual, to gratifications that come from solidarity with the suffering and hope of others, recognized as equal in importance with one's own. These new values could be read as part of the spiritual and moral responsibilities especially enjoined on women, socially marginalized in the private sphere, but in England they also could be read as "hysterical" politics in the public sphere, like the cry of the disenfranchised for "Liberty, Equality, Fraternity." But Mary Green's struggle to put into action the ideologies she's been trained to internalize, to be a model of women's difference, and the effect she has on her male readers demonstrate how a political and ideological structure can hold open a set of differences even where it intends to deny or repress them.

From these social possibilities, like the slim chance of any Mary's successful influence, a poet marginalized by class and politics, if not by gender, constructs his own artistic strategies of resistance and revolt. During a period of war and political repression, he is forced, like Mary Green, to find a legally acceptable form of discourse that can still be adapted to radical designs: such as the language of Christianity (implicit in Mary Green's offer but explicit and central in the later prophecies), which had been adapted to radical as well as conservative politics in England since the Civil War.[32]

In addition, Blake's poems build on the culturally "feminized" possibility that "positive" example, however limited, can persuade instead of tyranniz- ing. On the one hand, the Pickering Manuscript poems repeat the Bard's strategy in *Experience,* relying for the most part on negative examples of men's and women's anger, pain, fear, and confusion. Note, however, that only the powerful characters (males, crowds) openly display anger, and then only to vulnerable ones (women); author and female characters do not. This absence may simply reflect the fact that the current laws of England and rules for women are framed to deny or repress the existence or expression of anger. Yet this absence may also reflect the counterproductive results of merely individual anger. Until and unless it can be harnessed to social ends, individ- ual anger (selfish or not) repeats the either/or choice of tyrant and victim. Blake offers his negative examples to evoke that shared anger at shared woes which in itself begins to connect anger and "love" and to motivate the desire for collective labor and social change.

On the other hand, as we have seen, Blake includes examples that remain positive even if they fail (like Mary) or make small progress (like Mary Green). Yet (as is typical of all Blake's work) the poet's own practice becomes his most positive example. The textual strategies of the Pickering Manuscript poems open still more space in which his readers can recognize their freedom and exercise it, *if* we will; further, they imply our authority, ability, and potential willingness to do so.[33] Blake's choice of words and framing of propositions exploit the gaps and contradictions established by the polysemy of language itself in order to let us see difference customarily repressed. By omitting causal connections in narratives or authoritative explanations by narrators, by including questions that remain unanswered unless by a reader, by representing contradictions in behavior and conflicts without resolution, Blake shapes a radically democratic reader-text exchange. The poems restore a form of labor to us, making room not only for our own wrath or compassion but also our own dissent. Yet they also remind us of the social sphere where such exchanges are seldom possible.

The content of these poems mostly shows how "Divine Vision" is kept down, or at best its precarious survival in the acts of Mary Green and the men who are willing to imitate and extend her example. But their strategy aims for the release of "Divine Vision" in author and reader, a free and equal but collaborative labor of individual men and women. If it succeeds, not just a Face but a form like the Human Divine already acts and speaks. On the individual level, such private literary labors practice certain modes of seeing, wanting, and exchanging that can rehearse for public action on the social level.

How insistently Marys recur in these poems. When Blake's texts call the real Mary Wollstonecraft into play—where they suggest anger and compassion for her particular difficulties as woman and writer or admiration for what she attempted and achieved—it reminds us again to look carefully at his "stereotyped" women and those who tell tales of them. His tales point to the social construction and enforcement of gender stereotypes. The fact that his culture demands that women be role models does not mean they cannot or should not be. If in these poems Blake sometimes depicts what women suffer under the constraints they must live with, he also demonstrates how he found reason to honor and imitate women's example.

Notes

1. In the twentieth century, arguments for Blake's increasing religious and political conservatism go as far back as Mark Schorer's *William Blake: The Politics of Vision* (New York: Henry Holt and Co., 1946) and persist as recently as Marilyn Butler's *Romantics, Rebels and Reactionaries* (Oxford: Oxford University Press, 1981). The debate over Blake's attitude to women was reopened with Susan Fox's argument that Blake's females are "inferior and dependent (or, in the case of Jerusalem, superior and dependent) or . . . unnaturally and disastrously dominant" in "The Female as Metaphor in William Blake's Poetry," *Critical Inquiry* 3 (1977): 507–19. This argument is accepted and extended by Anne Mellor in "Blake's Portrayal of Women," *Blake: An Illustrated Quarterly* 63 (Winter 1982>-83): 148–55. In the same issue, Alicia Ostriker's "Desire Gratified and Ungratified: William Blake and Sexuality" (156–65) argues for four different "sets of Blakean attitudes toward sexual experience and gender relations" that "were with him always . . . in varying proportions," although she also believes that Blake eventually shifts from "a love of nature . . . to a growing and finally absolute rejection of nature and all fleshly things; and from an immanent to a transcendent God" (156, 165). The views of Fox and Mellor find parallels in the psychoanalytic criticism of Brenda Webster, *Blake's Prophetic Psychology* (Athens: The University of Georgia Press, 1983), and Diana Hume George, *Blake and Freud* (Ithaca: Cornell University Press, 1980).

2. See Catharine A. MacKinnon, *Feminism Unmodified: Discourses on Life and Law* (Cambridge: Harvard University Press, 1987), 8–9.

3. David V. Erdman in the textual notes to *The Complete Poetry and Prose of William Blake* (Berkeley and Los Angeles: University of California Press, 1982), 859, suggests that the Pickering Manuscript belongs "to the late Felpham period" and cites Bentley for 1800 to 1804 as the date of composition. (The latter year also saw the design of the title pages to *Milton* and *Jerusalem*.) Erdman's edition will be used to refer to all Blake quotations appearing in the text, with line numbers given parenthetically.

4. As a check of the *Concordance* will show, the word/concept of "states" becomes far more prominent in Blake's work after 1795.

5. See David Aers, "William Blake and the Dialectics of Sex," *ELH* 44 (1977): 500; and "Blake: Sex, Society and Ideology," in *Romanticism and Ideology: Studies in English Writing 1765–1830*, ed. David Aers, Jonathon Cook, and David Punter (London: Routledge and Kegan Paul, 1981), 33. For a similar approach, see also David Punter, "Blake, Trauma and The Female," *New Literary History* 15 (Spring 1984): 474–90.

6. Mary Poovey, *The Proper Lady and The Woman Writer* (Chicago: University of Chicago Press, 1984), 18–19, 21–22, 23-24; see chap. 1 generally.

7. Claire Tomalin, *The Life and Death of Mary Wollstonecraft* (New York: New American Library, 1974), 225. See also Regina M. Janes, "On The Reception of Mary Wollstonecraft's *A Vindication of The Rights of Woman*," *Journal of The History of Ideas* 39 (1978): 293–302.

8. Sheila Rowbotham, *Women, Resistance and Revolution* (New York: Pantheon Books, 1972), 45. See below for Blake's comparison of his isolation with Wollstonecraft's.

9. On Thompson's "Appeal of one half of the Human Race, Women, against the pretensions of the other Half, Men, to retain them in Civil and Domestic Slavery," see Rowbotham, 47–50 and Barbara Taylor, *Eve and The New Jerusalem: Socialism and Feminism in The Nineteenth Century* (New York: Pantheon Books, 1983), especially chap. 2.

10. Aers, "William Blake and the Dialectics of Sex," 512.

11. Poovey, *The Proper Lady*, 22.

12. David Erdman relates this statement to William Wilberforce, the spokesman for the Abolition Society in Parliament but also the promoter of "the Vice Society, based on the proposition that woman's love is Sin and democracy is Blasphemy," in his discussion of *Visions of The Daughters of Albion*, pointing out Blake's connection of slavery, the oppression of women, and the defense of political inequality. See *Prophet against Empire*, 3d ed. (Princeton: Princeton University Press, 1977), 235. In regard to the same poem, Nelson Hilton suggests that when Blake concluded the Annotations to Lavater's *Aphorisms on Man;* by saying that the "mistake in Lavater and his contemporaries, is, They suppose that Womans Love is Sin, in consequence all the Loves and Graces with them are Sin" (Erdman, 601), he was including Lavater's "best friend" and translator, Henry Fuseli; see "An Original Story," in *Unnamed Forms: Blake and Textuality*, ed. Nelson Hilton and Thomas Vogler (Berkeley and Los Angeles: University of California Press, 1986), 75.

13. See n. 1.

14. Poovey notes (*The Proper Lady*, 22) that the other side of women's theoretically "angelic" nature is that a woman risked "being designated a 'monster' " both by defining herself outside "the paradox of sexuality/chastity" which was held to be her nature and by defining herself openly in terms of sexuality. See also David Punter, "Blake, Trauma and The Female" (483, 485–86), on the "trauma" he suggests Blake underwent at the recognition of *women's* trauma: that women had been culturally "figured as simultaneously disabled and 'angelic' "; "His fear was about what women had become due to the pressure of ethical codes: dehumanized, unreal, in the literal sense monsters."

15. Note that "Friends" eschews both gender distinctions and hierarchical social differences.

16. Mary's formulation of this resolve leaves it open whether she would reject the man out of compliance with propriety or out of solidarity with the girl whose lover has proved faithless or out of resistance to the rule that restricts desire to one object.

17. Wollstonecraft cites Dr. Gregory's instructions that girls should "cultivate a fondness for dress" because that "is natural to them": *A Vindication of The Rights of Woman*, ed. Carol H. Poston (New York: W. W. Norton and Co., 1975), 28. Further citations to *VRW* are indicated in the text.

18. Cf. Jerusalem, who can only "faintly" see the Divine Lamb and "Insane . . . raves upon the winds hoarse, inarticulate," even though (or because) she knows "I am deluded by the turning mills. / And by these visions of pity and love because of Albions death" to the life of the "Human Divine" (*Jerusalem* 60.39, 44, 63–64). The two objects of "deluded" indicate that the nature of her "insanity" depends on whether the point of view is Albion's or the Divine Humanity's: from the latter point of view, she is "insane" or "deluded" by seeing Jesus the sacrifical lamb instead of the human form divine—although at the same time she is "keeping" a form of divine vision in time of trouble.

19. "Customary" is a charged word in Blake's time and I use it deliberately. The authority that is increasingly attached to "custom" in British political, social, and even aesthetic theory throughout the eighteenth century and into the nineteenth is an essential feature of the politicalization of the family and any issue connected with women. See in particular John Barrell, *English Literature in History 1730–80: An Equal Wide Survey* (New York: St. Martin's Press, 1983).

20. Cited by Poovey, *The Proper Lady*, 24.

21. Mark Schorer is confident that this poem is about Wollstonecraft (142), though Hazard Adams does not consider this connection. The most illuminating and best documented argument for Blake's treatment of her work and life (especially the Fuseli episode) earlier in his career is Nelson Hilton's discussion of *Visions of The Daughters of Albion* in "An Original Story," cited above.

22. Mary Wollstonecraft, *A Short Residence in Sweden* and William Godwin, *Memoirs of The Author of "The Rights of Woman"* (Hammondsworth, England: Penguin Books, 1987), 84.

23. See Tomalin, *Life and Death of Wollstonecraft*, 115.

24. Poovey, *The Proper Lady*, xiv. Like Poovey, I am not using "ideology" to mean "false consciousness" but the set of beliefs and assumptions that comprehend political, economic, and social relations as well as internal psychological structures.

25. See Hilton's "An Original Story."

26. Jane then disappears from the poem, demonstrating the unimportance of the sisterly relation to men. We cannot be sure of her relation to Mary Green. They do work together in their efforts to ease William's pain, though they have only the power of their "emotional responsiveness," which in itself cannot help them to alter the causes of their own.

27. The final question, "Then what have I to do with thee," also ends the first and last stanzas of "To Tirzah," a late addition to *The Songs of Experience* and perhaps from the same period as the Pickering Manuscript (see Erdman, 800). William is sure that the answer is "Nothing." Do we agree? The question seems even more urgent to the unidentified speaker in "To Tirzah," yet why, when all the other songs teach us to question the speaker's state of vision, should we assume that the same answer comes straightforwardly and without irony from the author's mouth?

28. For example, Hazard Adams, *William Blake: A Reading of The Shorter Poems* (Seattle: University of Washington Press, 1963), 146.

29. John Sutherland reads this poem much as Hazard Adams does, arguing that Blake really was bound by his marriage bonds and Catherine's jealousy from enjoying another lover and thus retains his bond with William in giving up on sexual love. See "Blake: A Crisis of Love and Jealousy," *PMLA* 87 (May 1972): 424–31. Again, the personal crisis and this reading remain possible, though I do see it as an advance in Blake's thinking that he focuses with increasing rigor on the social construction of desire in all its forms, rejecting any naive belief that the joys of "happy copulation" are "natural" or simple.

30. For a similar argument about the positive significance of female characters' actions in *Milton*, see W. J. T. Mitchell's "Blake's Radical Comedy" in *Blake's Sublime Allegory*, ed. Stuart Curran and Joseph Anthony Wittreich, Jr. (Madison: University of Wisconsin Press, 1973), 281–307.

31. Adams, *William Blake*, 146.

32. Like every party of his time, Blake adopted the cherished belief in and rhetoric of "the free-born Englishman." In Blake's case, the myth becomes the ground on which to protest against England's systems of oppression and call for their reform. See Barrell, 119–21 and *passim;* E. P. Thompson, *The Making of The English Working Class* (New York: Vintage Books, 1963), chap. 4.

33. Olivia Smith's discussion of Thomas Paine's prose strategies and their effects in *The Rights of Man* presents suggestive parallels to Blake's poetic techniques. See *The Politics of Language: 1791–1819* (Oxford: Clarendon Press, 1984), chap. 2.

The Meaning of The Ancient Mariner

Jerome J. McGann

What does "The Rime of the Ancient Mariner" mean? This question, in one form or another, has been asked of the poem from the beginning; indeed, so interesting and so dominant has this question been that Coleridge's poem now serves as one of our culture's standard texts for introducing students to poetic interpretation. The question has been, and still is, an important one, and I shall try to present here yet another answer to it. My approach, however, will differ slightly from the traditional ones, for I do not believe that we can arrive at a synthetic answer until we reflect upon the meaning of the question itself. I will begin, therefore, by reconsidering briefly the history of the poem's criticism.

The Critical History

From its first appearance in *Lyrical Ballads*, the "Rime" was an arresting, if problematic, work. Though well known to readers during the first two decades of the nineteenth century, no early consensus about the meaning or value of the poem was reached. Readers might praise Coleridge's imitation of "the elder poets"—which is what Francis Wrangham, Wordsworth's friend, had done—or they might, like Robert Southey, ridicule the act of imitation';[1] in either case, most early readers found the poem difficult to understand, mysterious, strange.[2] This response itself divided into two judgmental camps: on the one hand, those who, like Charles Lamb, valued the poem for its ability to keep "the mind . . . in a placid state of wonderments"; and, on the other, those who, like the anonymous *Analytical* reviewer, compared it to "the extravagance of a mad German poet." Dr. Charles Burney's conflicted set of remarks is entirely typical of the situation:

> The author's first piece, the *Rime of the Ancyent Marinere,* in imitation of the *Style* as well as the spirit of the elder poets, is the strangest story of a cock and a bull that we ever saw on paper: yet, though it seems a rhapsody of unintelligible wildness and incoherence, there are in it poetical touches of an exquisite kind.[3]

The "Rime" was the opening poem in the first edition of *Lyrical Ballads*, and these troubled reactions of the book's first readers were a serious worry to Wordsworth:

> From what I can gather it seems that The Ancyent Marinere has upon the whole been an injury to the volume, I mean that the old words and the strangeness of it have deterred readers from going on. If the volume should come to a second edition I would put in its place some little things which would be more likely to suite the common taste.[4]

In the end the poem was not replaced, but its position was changed, its title was altered, and its archaic style was drastically modernized. All this was done at Wordsworth's insistence, but not every reader was pleased with the result. Lamb was dismayed because the alterations had the effect of rationalizing the strange beauty of the poem:

> I am sorry that Coleridge has christened his *Ancient Marinere,* a *Poet's Reverie;* it is as bad as Bottom the Weaver's declaration that he is not a lion, but only the scenical representation of a lion. What new idea is gained by this title but one subversive of all credit—which the tale should force upon us—of its truth.[5]

Lamb was right, of course, but then so was Wordsworth: each simply had a different way of responding to the poem's "obscurity." Coleridge, typically, had his own special response: to expound at length with "metaphysical elucidations" the profound "mysteries" of his ballad imitation. Coleridge's interlocutor on this occasion—in Germany, from 1798 to 1799—was Clement Carlyon, who did not find Coleridge's commentary much more lucid than the ballad and who later poked fun at Coleridge's explanations when he was recollecting the events.[6]

During Coleridge's lifetime the poem was recognized to have an intellectual or allegorical import, even—witness the essay by J. G. Lockhart—a religious or visionary significance.[7] These impressions remained inchoate until the mid-century, however, when critics first began to develop explicitly symbolic and allegorical interpretations. Those mid-Victorian readings established the hermeneutic models that have dominated the subsequent history of the poem's interpretations. Though details and emphases have changed and shifted, and though the commentaries have become more extended, the fundamental interpretive approach has not altered significantly since that time.[8] Those who have veered away from such interpretations do so not by developing alternative hermeneutic methods but by rejecting the approach at more fundamental levels. Thus E. E. Stoll and Elisabeth Schneider deny that Coleridge ever "intended" his poem to be read symbolically or allegorically; on the other hand, Irving Babbitt, William Empson, and David Pirie reject

the entire Christian-symbolic schema not because it is unintended but because it is trivial.[9] Rather than simply dismiss the poem, as Babbitt does,
Empson and Pirie go on to solve the problem by substituting one (trivial) text
for another (important) one: that is to say, they argue the necessity of reading
the poem in its 1798 rather than in its 1817 version.

This brief analytic summary of the poem's interpretive tradition is necessary if we are to come to grips with the problem of the "Rime" and its
meaning; for meaning, in a literary event, is a function not of "the poem
itself" but of the poem's historical relations with its readers and interpreters.
As we shall see, when the history of the "Rime"'s hermeneutics is traced to
the ballad's point of origin, we begin to understand how the work developed
under the dominion of Coleridge's own hermeneutic models. To see this last
point in its full historical particularity is to arrive, finally, at a *critical* vantage
on the poem. For not until we see that our dominant interpretive tradition has
been licensed and underwritten by Coleridge himself will we be able to
understand the meaning of that tradition, and hence the meaning of the
meanings of the "Rime." Richard Haven has said that the poem "seems to
rule out few of the interpretations which have been offered" during the past
one hundred and eighty years; and his further argument—that modern
interpretations represent variant rather than alternative versions of nineteenth-century commentaries—is a point equally well taken.[10] The full significance of Haven's findings emerges when we come to see the relation of
these facts to Coleridge himself and to the hermeneutic traditions that he
helped to establish in the academy.

Early Textual History: The Formal Significance

Everyone knows that the "Rime" underwent a series of major textual
alterations between 1798, when it first appeared in *Lyrical Ballads*, and 1817,
when Coleridge all but completed his revisions in the *Sibylline Leaves* collection of his verse. These revisions included additions, subtractions, and
changes in the verse text; changes in the poem's title and prefatory material;
and, most dramatic of all, the addition of the prose gloss in the textual
margin.

Let me begin with the gloss, which to this day most readers take to
represent at least one level of Coleridge's own interpretation of his poem.
M. H. Abrams, for example, takes this view for granted: "Coleridge added
[the gloss] to assist the bewildered readers of the first published version" in
interpreting the poem's symbolic Christian narrative.[11] Even critics who,
unlike Abrams, dislike the gloss share his view of its function and status.
Pirie's comments, for instance, illustrate the sort of problems that arise when
the status of the gloss is misconceived in this way. The following passage

appears in Pirie's longer argument for taking the 1798 rather than 1817 version as the base reading text:

> The most serious attempt to distract the reader from the poem in the *Sibylline Leaves* version is of course the addition in the margin of the ageing Coleridge's own interpretation of his poem. Partly just a feeble literary joke, this must have always been intended to confuse the unwary as indeed it continues to do. Whether Coleridge was optimistic enough to hope that the marginalia would be regarded as much as part of the poem proper as they now are is debatable. But the marginalia are by their very nature perverting. They are a third-person, and thus by implication objectively true, account of a story whose essence is that it is a first-person narrative. Its full title, its narrative framework of the hypnotized listener, its disturbing vividness, all stress that it is at once event and account. The poem breaks through simplistic distinctions between "subjective feeling" and "objective reality." It concentrates by its very form on the fact that the mariner is condemned to recurring moments of "total recall" of which this is but a single example, condemned to experience again all that he felt alone on the wide, wide sea. The marginalia turn the speaker into a specimen. Worse, they lie. It is clearly not true, nor ever could be, that "the curse is finally expiated" and the very real creature that the mariners fed on biscuit-worms cannot become "a pious bird of good omen" without being ludicrous. To tell the reader in the margin that it is a good omen, when the succeeding stanzas demonstrate how impossible it is until too late to tell whether it is of good or bad omen, is to make nonsense of the poem at its very core. Coleridge claimed that Walter Scott's handling of superstition put the writer in a damagingly superior position to his story: "that discrepance between the Narrator and the Narrative chills and deadens the Sympathy." The narrator in the marginalia puts a similarly cold distance between the reader's sympathy and the story as experienced by the mariner.[12]

First, some preliminary explanations. Pirie speaks of the gloss as "a feeble literary joke" because he recognizes its antique character. When he calls it a "third-person" account, he points toward an important fact about the gloss, but he seems to miss the significance of that fact. Finally, his discussion of the gloss's "lies" also registers an important fact whose function Pirie seems once again to overlook.

We may begin to unravel the problems raised by Pirie (and preserved as well in nearly all contemporary interpretations) if we return to the poem's initial publication. The "Rime," as noted above, was the opening poem in Wordsworth and Coleridge's *Lyrical Ballads*. This 1798 version tries to adhere so closely to the conventions of ancient balladry, which Coleridge adapted from Thomas Percy, that the work sometimes approaches pastiche. This quality in the early "Rime"—its status as an imitation or literary ballad—sets it quite apart from all the other ballad-influenced poems written for *Lyrical Ballads*. The others are not literary ballads but lyrical ballads, a very different thing altogether.

When a second edition of *Lyrical Ballads* was called for in 1800, Wordsworth, as we have seen, urged Coleridge to make some alterations. His views carried the day, and the result was a conscious attempt, acutely registered by Lamb, to make the "Rime" appear less a literary ballad and more a lyrical ballad. Archaisms were removed from the verse text, but the most important alterations came at the beginning. The title was changed from "The Rime of the Ancyent Marinere" to "The Ancient Mariner: A Poet's Reverie," and the 1798 Argument, which was archaic and slightly mysterious,

> How a Ship having passed the Line was driven by Storms to the cold Country towards the South Pole; and how from thence she made her course to the tropical Latitutde of the Great Pacific Ocean; and of the strange things that befell; and in what manner the Ancyent Marinere came back to his own Country,

became more descriptively straightforward:

> How a Ship, having first sailed to the Equator, was driven by Storms, to the cold Country towards the South Pole; how the Ancient Mariner cruelly, and in contempt of the laws of hospitality, killed a Seabird; and how he was followed by many and strange Judgements; and in what manner he came back to his own Country.

The former, archaic in style, is appropriate to a literary ballad; the latter, on the other hand, remains in a contemporary idiom that perfectly marries with the new, self-conscious title. Lamb did not like the distance that the 1800 changes enforced between the "mariner's ballad" and "Coleridge's poem." Changes like these broke the spell under which Lamb's belief, in 1798, had been willingly suspended.

Pirie's (and Empson's) discussion of the "Rime" is fundamentally akin to Lamb's: all three prefer the work in its most primitive character and appearance. This is a poem in which Coleridge *in propria persona* seems most thoroughly removed from his own work. When Empson and Pirie object to the further changes introduced into the work in 1817—and principally to the addition of the gloss—they argue that these alterations represent a further, and even worse, modernization ("the ageing Coleridge's own interpretation of his poem"). In fact, however, Coleridge's 1817 additions were a complex effort to represent (if also to methodize) his poem as a literary ballad. In this he worked on two fronts especially: first, to strengthen the original archaic aspect of the work; and second, to carry even further the process, begun in 1800, of distinguishing as it were "levels of authority" or points of view in terms of which the poetic events were to be experienced and narrated.

When Pirie called the gloss a third-person account, he drew attention to the distance between the attitude represented in the gloss and that represented in the verse text conceived as imitation archaic ballad. For the truth is that the verse narrative and the prose gloss present themselves in Coleridge's poem as the work of two distinct (fictional) personages. The verse narrative appears as one "received text" of an early English ballad, a type that Percy called an "old minstrel ballad" and that Scott, later, called a "romantic ballad."[13] When Coleridge printed his poem in 1817, however, he added the prose gloss, which is to say he added to his work a fictive editor of the (presumptively) ancient ballad text. In an important and much neglected article, Huntington Brown demonstrates very clearly the distinctive character of these two figures in Coleridge's poem, and he shows that (*a*) the minstrel's ballad is meant to be seen as dating from the time of Henry VII or thereabouts—in any case, certainly after the voyage of Columbus but prior to the age of Shakespeare—and (*b*) the editor is a later figure still, a scholar and an antiquarian whose prose indicates that he lived sometime between the late seventeenth and the early eighteenth centuries.[14]

As Brown has shown, this fundamental distinction between the verse text and the gloss has two principal effects. First, it "serves to emphasize the remoteness of the story and its teller by setting them off at two removes" from the contemporary reader. Second, it calls attention to the multiple points of view that are embedded in the total work. Brown distinguishes "the personality of the Mariner who reports [the voyage], . . . the Wedding-Guest who listens [to the story], . . . the minstrel [who authors the verse] and, finally, . . . the pious antiquarian [who edits the ballad]."[15] As we shall see, Coleridge's "Rime" in fact presents yet another point of view—that is, Coleridge's, or the contemporary author's—which operates in a determining way, controlling all the others.

The textual changes that the "Rime" underwent between 1798 and 1817 tell an important story about Coleridge's developing purposes toward his poem. These changes, in fact, highlight the formal poetic terms within which all interpretations of the poem must take place. Before we can take up the hermeneutical problem, however, we must elucidate more clearly the historical significance of the textual events. Empson and Pirie regard the process of revision as a reactionary movement in which a daring and radical poem is transformed into a relatively tame work of Christian symbolism. For them, the textual changes tell the story of Coleridge's scandalous ideological retreat from his radical views of the 1790s to his later Christian orthodoxy. Their position eventually places the poem's entire interpretive tradition of criticism under an inquisition;[16] for this tradition, in their view, has merely carried forward into our own day symbolic Christian interpretations sanctioned by "the ageing Coleridge."

As I shall try to show in the next section, Pirie and Empson have accurately represented the historical relation between Coleridge's developed theory of hermeneutics and the later, dominant tradition of interpretation. Important as it is, however, their attack upon the established critical tradition needs to be revised historically. That is to say, we must look again, much more carefully than Empson and Pirie have done, at the sorts of continuities that exist between the "radical" Coleridge of the 1790s and the Sage of Highgate. Not only do Empson and Pirie misrepresent Coleridge when they characterize the history of his religious convictions; what is worse, they fail to see the relation of his religious ideas to the "Rime" either at the poem's point of origin in the late 1790s or at its later stages of revision up to 1817.

Coleridge's Hermeneutic Models: 1792–1834

At his death in 1834, Coleridge left his manuscript treatise *Confessions of an Inquiring Spirit* in which he set forth his most mature and coherent thoughts "on the Inspiration of the Scriptures." Indeed, the essay sums up the developed state of Coleridge's ideas from their first emergence in the early 1790s to their latest—and in many ways most radical—form. Coleridge's marginal glosses on J. G. Eichhorn, Gotthold Lessing, and Johann Gottfried von Herder, his *Lay Sermons*, the *Aids to Reflection*, and all of Coleridge's scattered commentary on the issues of the Higher Criticism are gathered together and summed up in the *Confessions*.

In the *Aids to Reflection*, Coleridge condemned "the pretended right of every individual competent and incompetent, to interpret Scripture in a sense of his own, in opposition to the judgment of the Church, without knowledge of the originals or of the languages, the history, the customs, opinions, and controversies of the age and country in which they were written."[17] The *Confessions* explains Coleridge's view more clearly when he rejects the conservative theological position that insists upon the immediate divine authority for every word and line in the Bible:

> Why should I not believe the Scriptures throughout dictated, in word and thought, by an infallible Intelligence? . . . *Why* should I not?—Because the doctrine evacuates of all sense and efficacy the sure and constant tradition, that all the several books bound up together in our precious family Bible were composed in different and widely distant ages, under the greatest diversity of circumstances, and degrees of light and information, and yet that the composers, whether as uttering or as recording what was uttered and what was done, were all actuated by a pure and holy Spirit, one and the same—(for is there any spirit pure and holy, and yet not proceeding from God—and yet not proceeding in and with the Holy Spirit?)—one Spirit, working diversly, now awakening strength, and now glorifying itself

in weakness, now giving power and direction to knowledge, and now taking away the sting from error! (AC, 305–6)

Coleridge's view is that the Scriptures are, as it were, a living and processive organism, one that comes into existence in human time and continues to develop in that "fallible" and limited sphere. This view leads him to affirm that the Bible is indeed the Word of God, but that its Word is uttered by God's mortal creatures:

> Every sentence found in a canonical Book, rightly interpreted, contains the *dictum* of an infallible Mind;—but what the right interpretation is,—or whether the very words now extant are corrupt or genuine—must be determined by the industry and understanding of fallible, and alas! more or less prejudiced theologians. (AC, 316)

Such a historical view of the Scriptures leads Coleridge along a radical path to a relatively conservative stance as regards the authority of the Church. Each new generation, and every new reader of the Bible, must listen to the assembled "panharmonicon" which is the Church's authority, that is, its recorded history of those who read and interpreted the Scriptures in the enthusiasm and the faith that was peculiar to their age and circumstances. The faith of the historical Church must be the model for the contemporary faithful. God's eternal Word is expressed and later reexpressed through commentary, gloss, and interpretation by particular people at different times according to their differing lights. The sting is taken out of whatever error they may introduce by the existence of their faith, by their enthusiasm for the Word and the diffusion of the Word, and by their participation in the continuous historical process of incarnation.

As Elinor Shaffer has shown, these views represent Coleridge's particular reformulation of the Higher Critical approaches of men like C. G. Heyne, J. D. Michaelis, Alexander Geddes, Lessing, F. A. Wolf, Herder, and Eichhorn—that is, of the leading figures in the new approaches to textual criticism that were being most radically pursued in Germany. The theoretical foundations of this movement were laid by the mythographic, philological, and historical exegetes of the eighteenth century who studied various sorts of ancient texts and cultures—classical, oriental, biblical, and national. In her discussion of this movement, Shaffer has shown that Coleridge was not merely influenced by its work; he himself emerged as one of its principal and most important representatives.[18]

Like the other founders of the Higher Criticism, Coleridge was not trying to use its methods to destroy religion but to salvage it. The program resulted in what Shaffer calls "a new form of history" as well as a mythological hermeneutics that dominated Western thought for over a century and continues, to this day, to exercise considerable authority, especially in the literary academy.[19] Shaffer describes very well the originary circumstances in terms of the famous problem of the "authenticity" of the Scriptures:

> Coleridge's argument reflects a long struggle of the new criticism with the idea that an eye-witness account must be of special value. If, by their own critical endeavour, it became clear that none of the Gospels was an eye-witness account, the status of the "event" therein recounted must, on the old view, be diminished, its credibility undermined; but if there are no such privileged accounts, if all event is interpretation, then the Gospels need not suffer. Indeed, as we shall see, their value as literature is increased. For Coleridge, "event" and "mystery" must be expressed with equal delicacy, obliquity, and restraint. The miracle becomes the paradigm of reported historical event; the historical events reported by eye-witnesses represent instantaneous mythmaking. "Erkennen ist mythologisieren." [20]

Such a view of experience (it is to this day a prevalent one) carries with it a wholly revised sense of "tradition" and "authority":

> It is neither the unquestioned authority of the Church nor the unquestioned authority of the Biblical text on which tradition rests, but the perpetually shifting sense within the Christian community of what has the power to persuade its members and strengthen them in the faith. Coleridge was to develop these two, still embryonic, approaches into one in his later writings: whatever the literal, documentable truth might be found to be, the historical experience of conviction within the Christian community was in itself a form of validation, and this experience could be maintained and reawakened through an imaginative grasp of what that experience had been.

As Shaffer goes on to remark, "These concerns were, of course, at the centre of romantic aesthetics."[21]

Coleridge's explicit, extended prose discussions of the leading figures and ideas dealt with by the Higher Critics were not made until after he went to Germany in 1798. Nevertheless, that he was earlier thoroughly familiar with the general approach and with the work of Heyne, Michaelis, Lessing, and Geddes is absolutely certain.[22] Shaffer dates Coleridge's acquaintance with this critical tradition from the late 1780s, but her estimate may be too early. Still, by 1792 Coleridge was fully aware of these important scholarly developments, though his own views were, at that point, still fairly traditional. In 1795, for example, Coleridge was still arguing that Moses had authored the Pentateuch.[23] By 1796 his views had begun to show some considerable alterations, however, for in his "Essay on Fasts" we find him arguing that the "coincidence of the number of days [between Elijah's and Pythagoras's forty-day fastings] seems to cast a shade of doubt on the genuineness of the beginning of the fourth chapter of Matthew and Luke: in which the same miraculous circumstance is related of our Savior." Coleridge's method of reasoning here plainly follows a Higher Critical line:

> It was the policy of the early Christians to assimilate their religion to that of the Heathens in all possible respects. The ceremonies of the Romish church have been traced to this source by Middleton, the miraculous conception is a palpable imitation of the story of Romulus, the son of a vestal virgin, by the descent of a Deity; and so, I suppose, because Pythagoras fasted forty days, the Interpolators of the Gospels must needs palm the same useless prodigy on Jesus. Indeed the conversion of the Heathens to Christianity, after the first century, does very much resemble Mahomet's miracle: as the mountain would not come over to him, he went over to the mountain.[24]

The set of Coleridge's mind revealed in this passage differs very little from what is to be found later in his annotations to Herder and Eichhorn, in the *Lay Sermons*, and in the *Aids* and *Confessions*. The only marked difference is a tonal one: for the later Coleridge would not have permitted even the suggestion of jocularity in his discussion of such weighty matters. Interpolations and glosses in the text of Scripture by later writers, redactors, and scribes was a matter for the most serious thought and analysis.

The plainest evidence for the continuity of Coleridge's thought lies, however, in the coincidence of ideas between his 1796 "The Destiny of Nations" (see especially lines 13–126) and his later prose writings. Coleridge says in his early poem, for example, that the highest form in which "Freedom" appears is the following:

> But chiefly this, him First, him Last to view
> Through meaner powers and secondary things
> Effulgent, as through clouds that veil his blaze.
> For all that meets the bodily sense I deem
> Symbolical, one mighty alphabet
> For infant minds;
>
> (15–20)

This theory of symbolism is well known from "The Aeolian Harp" and *The Statesman's Manual*.[25] In "The Destiny of Nations," Coleridge develops his thought in some detail:

> So by a strange and dim similitude
> Infinite myriads of self-conscious minds
> Are one all-conscious Spirit, which informs
> With absolute ubiquity of thought
> (His one eternal self-affirming act!)
> All his involved Monads, that yet seem

With various province and apt agency
Each to pursue its own self-centering end.

(42–49)

Implicit in both these passages is Coleridge's further range of thought,
which he expands upon later in the poem: that God's self-revelation through
the "apt agency" of finite, historical beings is a processive event. When
Coleridge presents his example from primitive Lapland culture (lines 60–
126), his point is that the "Wild phantasies" of Greenland's epic lore are full
of deep import. Not only is such primitive lore symbolic; it illustrates the
developing historical operation of the One Life:

> For Fancy is the power
> That first unsensualises the dark mind,
> Giving it new delights; and bids it swell
> With wild activity; and peopling air,
> By obscure fears of Beings invisible,
> Emancipates it from the grosser thrall
> Of the present impulse, teaching Self-control,
> Till Superstition with unconscious hand
> Seat Reason on her throne.

(80–88)

The "legends terrible" (line 90) teach, immediately, certain fundamental
human virtues, but ultimately they operate as part of a vast, worldwide,
spiritualizing scheme:

> Till from Bethabra northward, heavenly Truth
> With gradual steps, winning her difficult way,
> Transfer their rude Faith perfected and pure.

(124–26)

The "Beings of higher class than Man"—God and his angels—"choose their
human ministers" (lines 127, 130) to carry out a providential economy; and
each historical period raises up its ministers of this continuous revelation.
When Coleridge writes "The Destiny of Nations," he reveals himself to be an
important functionary in the scheme he himself is articulating.

These ideas coincide fundamentally with what Coleridge says later in the
work already cited. A repetition of this important point, however, is not out
of order. In the *Confessions*, for example, Coleridge argues at length that the
Scriptures are not an unmediated and fixed biblical text but an evolved and
continuously evolving set of records that include the Church's later glosses on
and interpretations of the earlier documents. The entire project of textual
transmission and elucidation is a symbolic, revelatory act: "all the intermediate applications and realizations of the words are but types and repetitions—

translations, as it were, from the language of letters and articulate sounds into the language of events and symbolical persons?" (AC, 303). As a result, Coleridge goes on to argue that every person should approach the Scriptures with a double understanding. First, readers must see that the received documents—primitive texts, interpolations, commentaries—report historically mediated materials and hence must be "examined each in reference to the circumstances of the Writer or Speaker, the dispensation under which he lived, the purpose of the particular passage, and the intent and object of the Scriptures at large" (AC, 320). Second, the reader must also understand that he is, as a reader, equally subject to time-specific cultural limitations: "the conflicts of grace and infirmity in your own soul, will enable you to discern and to know in and by what spirit they spake and acted,—as far at least as shall be needful for you, and in the times of your need" (AC, 320).

This is Coleridge's version of "a man speaking to men." Having a more explicitly historicized theoretical view than Wordsworth, however, Coleridge is able to see that the communication involves contact between what we would today call ideologically committed beings—between individuals whose humanness seems complete because they appear so thoroughly involved in their social and cultural milieus. As Coleridge had said earlier in *The Statesman's Manual:*

> And in nothing is Scriptural history more strongly contrasted with the histories of highest note in the present age than in its freedom from the hollowness of abstractions. While the latter present a shadow-fight of Things and Quantities, the former gives us the history of Men, and balances the important influence of individual Minds with the previous state of the national morals and manners, in which, as constituting a specific susceptibility, it presents to us the true cause both of the Influence itself, and of the Weal or Woe that were its Consequents.[26]

This sure grasp that the concreteness and particularity of an individual is a function of his ideology ("national morals and manners") is an important aspect of Coleridge's thought to which I shall return later.

The "Rime" and the Critical Tradition

As far as the "Rime" is concerned, we have to note the special importance of certain aspects of this body of thinking. I refer specifically to the idea, which Coleridge explicitly endorsed, that the biblical narratives were originally bardic (oral) poetry that gradually evolved into a cycle of communal literary materials. Embedded in primitive and legendary saga, the Scriptures grew by accretion and interpolation over an extended period of time. They do not represent a "true" narrative of certain fixed original events; rather, they are a collection of poetic materials that represent the changing form of "witness" or testament of faith created by a religious community in the course of its history.[27] The function of the Higher Criticism, as a method, was to reveal the various "layers" of this poetic work by distinguishing the Bible's different religious/poetic styles, or forms of expression, from the earliest and most primitive to the latest and most sophisticated.

This general approach toward historically transmitted texts produced two specific theories that bear particularly on the "Rime." Geddes's "Fragment Hypothesis" argued that the Pentateuch "was put together by an editor out of a collection of independent and often conflicting fragments."[28] Coleridge accepted this interpretation but modified it by arguing that the conflation of the disparate fragments was a communal process rather than a unique event.

The second theory, put forth by Wolf in his *Prolegomena ad Homerum* (1795), argued that the *Iliad* was a redaction of different lays which had been passed down through a bardic tradition. Wolf's ballad theory of the epic partly drew its inspiration from the scholarship developed in the writings of the ballad revival. The argument in Percy's influential "Essay on the Ancient Minstrels of England" which introduced his *Reliques*, is paradigmatic. According to Percy, England's ancient poetic traditions from the pagan skalds to the old Christian minstrels was a continuous one; and although "the Poet and the Minstrel early with us became two persons," "the ancient minstrels" preserved in their ballad and song traditions a profound continuity with the old pagan skalds. Indeed, the common practice of the ancient minstrels—in contrast to the new, developing line of leisured poets—was not to compose new works but to adapt and extend the older ones that descended through the tradition from primitive pagan times.[29]

The foregoing is the ideological framework for the following remarkable passage. The quotation is Coleridge's marginal gloss in his copy of Eichhorn's *Einleitung in das alte Testament* and is itself a theory, or explanation, of the meaning of glosses and textual interpolations. Commenting on Genesis 36:31, Coleridge writes:

> But why *not* consider this as a gloss introduced by the Editors of the Pentateuch, or Preparers of the Copy that was to be layed up in the Temple of Solomon? The authenticity of the Books would be no more compromised by such glosses, than that of the Book before me by this marginal Note of mine.[30]

Coleridge means that, given a coherent cultural tradition, the text that exhibits marks of its historical passage (in the form of later interpolations, glosses, and other textual additions and "impurities") retains its ideological coherence despite the process of apparent fragmentation. Such a text is, in truth, a Book of Revelation by itself, an apocalypse of its evolved and interconnected poetic/religious coherences.

When Coleridge applies these critical views to non-Scriptural texts, as he does in "The Destiny of Nations," his idea is that the pagan bards of Greenland initiated a body of poetic material whose traditions culminated in the Christian revelation. Ancient "superstition," in these poetic repositories, will eventually "Seat Reason on her throne" through the processive movement of spiritual history. The textual history of primary epic and ballad materials exhibits in a concrete way the process of continuous spiritual revelation.

The "Rime" is presented as just this sort of text, and its own bibliographical history illustrates *in fact* what Coleridge fictively represents his poem to be *in imagination*. The special significance of the gloss, as far as the "Rime" is concerned, lies in its (imagined) historical relation to the ancient ballad that Coleridge has represented through his poem. By the time Coleridge has "evolved" his 1817 text, we are able to distinguish four clear layers of development: (*a*) an original mariner's tale; (*b*) the ballad narrative of that story; (*c*) the editorial gloss added when the ballad was, we are to suppose, first printed; and (*d*) Coleridge's own point of view on his invented materials. This last represents Coleridge's special religious/symbolic theory of interpretation founded upon his own understanding of the Higher Critical analytic.

From Coleridge's viewpoint, the "Rime" is a poem that illustrates a special theory of the historical interpretation of texts. In its earliest state (1798), the theory is not easy to deduce, though it is certainly in operation; when the glosses are added, however, Coleridge has extrapolated fully, and thereby made explicit, his religious theory of interpretation, which has its roots in the Higher Critical tradition.

Like all literary ballads, the "Rime" is a tour de force, for Coleridge built it according to theories of the ballad (and of other historically transmitted works) that he had studied and that he expected his readers to know and to recognize. Certain stylistic facts about the poem demonstrate—on the authority of Percy—that the text has material which "dates back" to the early lays of the ancient minstrels.[31] On the other hand, other stylistic aspects of the text, including the gloss, show that its "date" is relatively late, certainly after Columbus, but perhaps before Magellan's voyage to the Pacific. In general, Coleridge means us to understand that the ballad narrative dates from the sixteenth century, that the gloss is a late seventeenth-century addition, and, of course, that Coleridge, at the turn of the nineteenth century, has provided yet another (and controlling) perspective upon the poetic material. Indeed, Coleridge certainly intended his more perspicuous readers—that is, those read in the theory and practice of the new historical criticism—to see that the "Rime" was an imaginative presentation of a work comprising textual layers of the most primitive, even pre-Christian, sort. No one schooled in the new German textual criticism could fail to "see" that the opening portions of part 6 represented a textual survival of the most ancient kind of pagan lore.

Coleridge's final (Broad Church) grasp of the "Rime" demonstrates his great theme of the One Life.[32] Like the Bible, the *Iliad*, and all great imaginative works possessed and transmitted by different cultures, the "Rime" is Coleridge's imitation of a culturally redacted literary work. The special function of the poem was to illustrate a significant continuity of meaning between cultural phenomena that seemed as diverse as pagan superstitions, Catholic theology, Aristotelian science, and contemporary philological theory, to name only a few of the work's ostentatiously present materials. The "Rime," in its 1798 or its 1817 form, reconciles many opposite and discordant qualities.

A well-known passage from *The Table Talk* sets out the structural and thematic foundation of the "Rime" in its most general philosophic formulation:

> My system, if I may venture to give it so fine a name, is the only attempt I know, ever made to reduce all knowledges into harmony. It opposes no other system, but shows what was true in each; and how that which was true in the particular, in each of them became error, *because* it was only half the truth. I have endeavoured to unite the insulated fragments of truth, and therewith to frame a perfect mirror. I show to each system that I fully understand and rightfully appreciate what that system means; but then I lift up that system to a higher point of view, from which I enable it to see its former position, where it was, indeed, but under another light and with different relations; so that the fragment of truth is not only acknowledged, but explained. Thus the old astronomers discovered and maintained much that was true; but, because they were placed on a false ground, and looked from a wrong point of view, they never did, they never could, discover the truth—that is, the whole truth. As soon as they left the earth, their false centre, and took their stand in the sun, immediately they saw the whole system in its true light, and their former station remaining, but remaining as a part of the prospect.[33]

The "Rime" is structured around three fundamental ideologies: pagan superstition and philosophy, Catholic legend and theology, and Broad Church Protestantism. As noted, the poem's formal layering reflects this material. The pre-Coleridgean "fragments of truth" represent "a wrong point of view" on the material of human experience. The "events" treated in the poem actually represent interpretations of events carried out in terms of certain fragmentary "systems"of human thought, and the purpose of the poem is to "lift [these systems] to a higher point of view" whence they will be open to a critical, self-conscious, but sympathetic valuation. This "higher point of view," which *The Table Talk* passage represents as a final (divine) one, is Coleridge's own "system" where "the whole truth" adumbrated by the (historically relative) fragments of truth is discovered. *What* that whole truth constitutes is (*a*) that there is a whole truth which justifies and is the ground of all the fragments of the truth; and (b) that this whole truth is in a perpetual process of becoming—indeed, that its being is *the process of its being*.

Coleridge's system, then, is justified in the continuous and developing history of human thought. In terms of the "Rime," Coleridge's ideological commitment to a preconditioned ground of processive truth sanctions in its readers a diversity of interpretations based upon their particular lights. Because "the whole truth," recognized or not, subsumes a priori all the interpretions, readers are encouraged to formulate their particular expressions of the truth. Coleridge's much-discussed symbolic method in the poem is nothing more (or less) than his rhetorical machinery for producing such interpretive results. In Coleridge's terms, the symbolically grounded interpretations are acts of witness rather than definitions, human events that dramatically testify to the desire to know and continuously create the truth that has always set men free.

In this context, when Haven shows the congruence between nineteenth- and twentieth-century interpretations of the "Rime," we are able to extrapolate the significance of his research. The basic continuum of thought comprising the poem's many interpretations testifies to the power of Coleridge's own poetic project. Although a few critics have attempted to resist the tradition outlined by Haven—I will return to them in a moment—the vast majority follow the model set forth in Coleridge's own comprehensive hermeneutic system established through the poem itself. The interpretive tradition licensed by the "Rime" corresponds to the network of ideological institutions (the clerisy) that Coleridge's ideas helped to create. Before Coleridge, the Church for centuries had been the principal ideological state apparatus, but *On the Constitution of Church and State*, among other works, marks the change that Coleridge was promoting. With him we witness the retreat of the Church and the emergence of the educational system, the academy, as Western society's principal ideological institution. As John Colmer recently remarked, in referring to educators in today's secular world, "We are the clerisy."[34] To measure the influence of Coleridge's program one need but recall the dominant ideologues in Anglo-American culture during the past one hundred and fifty years: from Coleridge, through Arnold, Emerson, Leavis, and Eliot, to Trilling, Abrams, and the contemporary apologists for English and American romantic thought.

The complex cultural problems related to the hegemony of this tradition appear again, in miniature form, when we approach Coleridge's great literary ballad. The history of the poem's criticism reveals, for example, that readers have not found it easy to escape the power of Coleridge's hermeneutics. From Babbitt to Empson and Pirie, a few critics have struggled against the dominant tradition of readers. Their characteristic method is to attack either the romantic-symbolical readings—ridiculed by Empson and Pirie, for example—or Coleridge himself and the entire project ("split religion") that generated such readings. Sometimes, as in Empson's case, a distinction is drawn between the "early," "secular" Coleridge—author of the 1798 "Rime"—and the late, Christian dodderer—author of the 1817 revisionist piece. This antithetical tradition is important chiefly because it corroborates, from a hostile position, the basic ideological uniformity that underlies the dominant symbolic tradition initiated by Coleridge.

The problem with such antithetical readings is that they are at war with the differentials they themselves emphasize and corroborate. Babbitt and Empson are married, by antithesis and anxiety, to the positions they are attacking. The rules for such relationships, which have been laid down in the theoretical works initiated by *The Anxiety of Influence*, produce what can well be called "the fate of reading." What this means—I merely state the basic problem in another form—is that a historical process begins to appear as a fatal one; specifically, the act of literary criticism comes to seem so repetitional that drastic evasive measures begin to be taken. Babbitt's and Empson's violence succeeds to the play of differences in poststructuralism because acts that make a difference, in the mind as well as in the world, begin to seem difficult if not impossible to achieve. When traditional human activities seem as unimportant as academic criticism has grown to seem in this period of our culture—when it appears to make no difference what, if any, literary criticism you read or write—movements begin (deconstructionism in this period, aestheticism and naturalism at the end of the nineteenth century) that throw into relief the crisis line of an ideological tradition.

In terms of the critical history of the "Rime," antithetical critics like Babbitt and Empson seem to violate the past of its treasures, while the traditional line seems to have exhausted its future and left us with nothing to follow. At such moments a historical analysis becomes a cultural imperative, for it is through such an analysis that we can recover what the past has sent to us and redefine the future of our own work. Such a method demands that differences be sharpened and clarified historically. The resources made available through the "Rime" and its critical history will not be recovered until we begin to specify clearly the ideological gulf that separates us from them both. A poem like the "Rime" dramatizes a salvation story, but it is not the old story of our salvation *in* Christ; rather, it is the new story of our salvation *of* Christ. Coleridge would have us believe that the latter story is the latest expression of the former and hence that the former retains its cultural truth. To the critical view of a contemporary materialist and historical consciousness, however, the "Rime"'s advanced Christian machinery represents a view of the world only qualitatively less alien to ourselves than the ideology which supports the *Iliad* or the writings of Confucius. These works, we must come to see, transcend their particular cultural circumstances not because they contain unchanging human truths but rather because their *particular* truthfulness has been so thoroughly—so materially—specified.

Like the *Iliad* or *Paradise Lost* or any great historical product, the "Rime" is a work of transhistorical rather than so-called universal significance. This verbal distinction is important because it calls attention to a real one. Like *The Divine Comedy* or any other poem, the "Rime" is not valued or used always or everywhere or by everyone in the same way or for the same reasons. Poetical and artistic works have chequered critical histories that testify to their discontinuous power and employment. The study of a work's critical history is imperative precisely for that reason: the analysis reveals to us, in yet another form, the special historical life that a work has been living in the dialectic of its processive career. Historical analysis uncovers, therefore, a paradox of thought that yet contains a fundamental human truth: that the universal or transhistorical significance of any ideological product is a function of the specific limits of place and circumstance that are inscribed, and therefore "immortalized," in those works we call poems which are created and re-created over time. The importance of great art is that it has always made a difference.

Anyone who has taught ancient or culturally removed literature has experienced the difficulty of transmitting historically alienated material. Nor does it help much to assume or pretend that what Bacon says in "Of Education," what Sophocles dramatizes in the *Oedipus*, or what the Jahwist has presented in his Genesis can be appreciated or even understood by an uneducated student or reader. Of course, the problem can be solved if the teacher avoids it altogether and asks the student to deal with the work in its present context only, that is, to supply it with a "reading." Alien works may be, as we say, "interpreted." But we must understand that such exercises, carried out in relative historical ignorance, are not *critical* operations. Rather, they are vehicles for recapitulating and objectifying the reader's particular ideological commitments.[35] To "read" in this way is to confront Ahab's doubloon, to read self-reflexively. The danger in such a method is that it will not be able to provide the reader with a social differential that can illuminate the limits of that immediate interpretation. The importance of ancient or culturally removed works lies precisely in this fact: that they themselves, as culturally alienated products, confront present readers with ideological differentials that help to define the limits and special functions of those current ideological practices. Great works continue to have something to say because what they have to say is so peculiarly and specifically their own that we, who are different, can learn from them.

Though the "Rime" is not nearly so removed from the present as the *Oedipus*, we must not allow its alienation to escape us. The force of a line like "It is an ancient mariner" comes from one's sense that an ancient minstrel did *not* write it but that Coleridge did. This is an awareness that was, and was meant to be, available to audiences from the poem's first appearance. But with the passage of time other perspectives become both possible and necessary. *We* see, for example, that the minstrel represented to us here is *not* the figure known to Child or Gummere but the one specifically available to a reader and admirer of Percy. To see this fact, even in so small an event as that line, is to be able to read the line *in* its own terms but without being made *subject* to those terms. We willingly suspend our disbelief only when disbelief, or critical distance, is the ground of our response. Such critical skepticism (it is not an attitude but a method) is especially important for a work like the "Rime," since the poem itself seeks to break down a sense of ultimate discontinuity through the structure of its artistic illusions. Criticism must penetrate those illusions and specify what is involved in the particular uses to which they have been put. The meaning of the "Rime" emerges through the study of the history of its illusions.

The "Rime" and the Meaning of Symbol

In his introduction to the *History of the Russian Revolution,* Trotsky defends himself against the charge that he is a biased reporter by attacking the concept of "objective history." No historian's presentation can ever be free of tendentious and ideological elements, Trotsky argues. His position is not, however, subjectively relativistic. On the contrary, one judges the adequacy of a historian's work by its value as an explanation of the phenomena, by its congruence and comprehensiveness in relation to the objective circumstances. But the explanation must be constructed, Trotsky says, from an ideological vantage of some sort, and in his own case Trotsky argues that he is both more objectively correct in his vantage and analysis and more subjectively honest and clear about his methods. Trotsky, that is to say, makes every effort not to disguise his ideological position behind a specious appeal to objectivity but instead builds and objectifies his bias into the very structure of the analysis and keeps the reader aware of it at all times. Trotsky does this because, in his view, the ideology is a crucial part of the analysis, as much a part of his historical subject as it is the basis of his historical method.

Trotsky's ideology corresponds to what Coleridge called "first principles," except that the former is a structure of scientific thought and the latter a theological, or what Coleridge termed a metaphysical, system. The general argument in *The Statesman's Manual*—that the Bible is the most reliable guide for secular statecraft—is based upon a view wholly analogous to Trotsky's: that history, whether lived or narrated, is not a sequence of atomized moments or facts but a structured phenomenon, the praxis of a living and related set of commitments. For Coleridge, the crucial importance of a work like the Bible lies in its continuous historical existence. Because it must be read through the mediation of its transmitters, that is, through the Church, readers cannot receive its words except through acts of faith or, as we should say, through tendentious interpretations, acts of conscious commitment to the received materials. The Bible comes to us bearing with it the history of its criticism; it is a writing that also contains its own readings and that generates the cumulative history of its own further retransmissions and reinterpretations.

As already seen, Coleridge's views on the Bible were merely paradigmatic of his views on all literary texts. A committed Christian, he necessarily saw the Bible as the world's central literary event; but, like his contemporaries, he understood very well that other non-Christian cultures had their equivalent of the Western Bible. Indeed, as Coleridge argued in "The Destiny of Nations," the West's central pre-Christian documents, for example, the saga literature of the skaldic bards, were important scriptural events not merely in themselves but in relation to the general development of mankind's religious cultures. German biblical critics were revealing the non- and pre-Judaic strands in the Scriptures, and the new philologists of primitive and classical texts were at work on similar projects.

The "Rime," as readers have known all along, is an imitation or literary ballad modeled on works like those contained in Percy's *Reliques* or on translations of Gottfried Bürger's imitation ballads. What has not been so clear is Coleridge's ideological motive in producing the "Rime." The context of his religous and critical thought shows quite clearly, I believe, that the poem is, as it were, an English national Scripture; that is to say, the poem imitates a redacted literary text that comprises various material extending from early pre-Christian periods through a succession of later epochs of Christian culture, and the ultimate locus of these transmissions is England. We must also understand, however, that for Coleridge each redaction specifies and calls attention to the series of distinct epochal (that is, ideological) interpretations through which the poetic material has been evolving.

By re-presenting not merely a text but an evidently *mediated* text, Coleridge provided both a spur and a model for later readers, who have been encouraged to elucidate for themselves and their own special needs the meaning and significance of the poem's symbolic statements. Ultimately, however, although Coleridge's project aimed to generate an unlimited number of readings, it was equally committed, by its own hermeneutic ideology, to a certain sort of reading. These are the interpretations that Haven has synthesized for us. Coleridge's theory of symbolism is a Western and a Judeo-Christian theory, and the hermeneutics of the "Rime" has always been governed by this general frame of reference and set of, what Coleridge called, "facts":

Christianity is especailly differenced from all other religions by being *grounded* on *facts* which all men alike have the means of ascertaining, the same means, with equal facility, and which no man can ascertain for

another. Each person must be herein querist and respondent to himself;
Am I sick, and therefore need a physician?—Am I in spiritual slavery, and
therefore need a ransomer?—Have I given a pledge, which must be re-
deemed, and which I cannot redeem by my own resources?[36]

Such facts are, of course, what we call ideology. The important thing to see,
however, is that Coleridge knew perfectly well that these facts were "interpreted facts," faith-determined and faith-constitutive. To read the "Rime"in
such a "redemptive" frame is, as Coleridge maintained (and as we must
agree), to reduplicate its determinative, a priori ideology. In this way does the
"Rime" assume into itself its own critical tradition.

Through works like the "Rime," Coleridge successfully sustained his
theistic and Christian views about nature and human history in the institutions of Western education. Hence the literary criticism of the "Rime" has
never been, in the proper sense, *critical* of the poem but has merely recapitu-
lated, in new and various ways, and not always very consciously, what
Coleridge himself had polemically maintained. To a *critical* view, however,
what Coleridge re-presents in the "Rime" is a historically and culturally
limited set of ideas. Readers have not always found it easy to see this fact
when they interpret the poem's "symbols" because they characteristically
regard their interpretations as something that *they bring to* the preexistent
"text." The "Rime" is one thing, and its interpretations are something else,
separated by time, place, and person. But Coleridge's own poem, as well as
his involvement in the German critical tradition, ought to remind us that an
act of interpretation may be assumed a priori in the materials to be interpreted. In the case of a poem like the "Rime," hermeneutics is criticism's
grand illusion.

A properly critical view of the "Rime" can only begin with the recognition
that what needs criticism and interpretation is not simply the work's set of
symbolic paraphernalia (albatross, mariner, spectre-bark, water snakes, rain,
sun, moon, etc.); these are "in" the poem and therefore the objects of our
analysis, but they are only in the poem *as symbols.* That is to say, they enter
the reader's horizon as objects-bearing-meaning, as already significant (or
preinterpreted) phenomena. A critical analysis of the poem's poetic materials,
therefore, cannot be carried out by erecting a thematic elucidation of albatross, sun, moon, water, and so on but only by erecting an analysis of the
meaningful albatross, the *significant* sun, moon, stars, water. The materials
dealt with by the "Rime" are not—indeed, never were—mere "secular" or
"natural" facts; they are predesigned and preinterpreted phenomena. We
may, indeed must, read the poem's symbols, but what we must critically
elucidate are the meanings of the symbols. Readers of the "Rime" generate its
meanings; critics set out and explain the meaning of its meanings.

The albatross, for example, is an interpreted phenomenon *ab initio:* the bird is part of the mariner's superstitious preconceptions. So too the mariner himself: by virtue of his association with the Wandering Jew, for example, he has been incorporated by the poem into a special structure of signification. In each case the reader is reading meaning not of the bird or mariner in isolation but of bird and mariner as they represent or locate certain superstitious (and, ultimately, religious) forms of thought. Similarly, the terms "Bridegroom" and "Wedding-Guest" are delivered to and through the Western, nineteenth- and twentieth-century reader in terms of their Christian frame of reference. These are not words from an innocent, "natural" language, as it were, but from a particular symbolic and religious context of discourse.

In general, what Coleridge does in his poem is present us, via an imitation ballad, with a wide variety of culturally and historically mediated material; and he arranges this material, formally, according to philological rules that governed the constitution and transmission of ancient texts and that were just then being formulated in the circles of the Higher Critics. This formal procedure empowers Coleridge to produce a wide variety of poetic effects. It enables him, for example, to achieve the wit of lines like "We were the first that ever burst / Into that silent sea" (lines 105–6), where the contemporary reader encounters an "explanation" of how the Pacific Ocean (*Mare Pacificum*) may originally have received its name (see also line 110). More significantly, the Higher Critical model gave Coleridge a structure in which various materials apparently alien to each other could be reconciled and harmonized. Different sorts of superstitious phenomena are held in a significant relation with various Christian ideologies. We are enabled to "interpret," for example, the originally pagan Polar Spirit in terms of a redemptive Christian scheme because the philological model tells us that the two are historically related via the operation of processes of textual transmission and interpolation. One important function of Coleridge's Polar Spirit, therefore, is to remind us that such superstitious phenomena retain their power of signification in history even after their ideology has ceased to play a dominant role in the institutions of a culture; that they retain this power by virtue of their incorporation precisely because they are, originally, *interpreted* rather than merely natural phenomena.

Creating this sort of poem required Coleridge to imitate a transmitted ballad. He had to establish a text that displayed several textual "layers," as we have already seen, and the poem's lexicon is the ultimate carrier of this set of textual layers. The "Rime" cannot work if it does not contain words the reader will associate with diverse historical periods. Attention has always been drawn to the archaic diction of the ballad, but equally important is the modern diction. "Bassoon" and "lighthouse" are seventeenth-century words, and their appearance in the text indicates (fictively, of course) "late interpolated passages." In general, the archaic diction is only significant in its relation to the more modern dictions; the poetic system that holds them together is using both as the formal foundation for its work of symbology.

Coleridge takes it for granted that an "Enlightened" mind of his or a later period will not believe that the spectre-bark ever had a concrete and objective existence or that the creatures called Death and Life-in-Death ever did what the poem reports or ever existed in the ordinary sense. The Enlightened mind will recognize such phenomena to be mental projections of the mariner's delirium; indeed, it will see all the fabulous events in this way, that is, as phenomena mediated either by the mariner, or by the balladeer(s), or by some still later editor or scribe, like the writer of the gloss. All of these are pre-Enlightenment minds. But to Coleridge's (post- and anti-Enlightenment) mind, this Enlightened view is itself a limited one. The Enlightenment (Higher Critical) attitude sees (a) that all phenomena are mind-mediated and (b) that these mediations are culturally and historically determined. What it does not see, in Coleridge's view, is that the entire system (or history) of the mediations is organized a priori and that the history of the mediations is an evolving process whereby the original (God-instituted and redemptive) system is raised up into human consciousness by the processive acts of human consciousness itself.

This Coleridgean view of the poem is what has licensed its traditions of symbolic interpretation. But this view must itself finally be laid aside as a determinative one. Coleridge's appeal to historical process and his insistence that symbolic interpretation (the meaning of symbols) is a function of specific cultural and historical factors ultimately overtake his own poetic ideology. For his is a sacramental and Christian view of symbols in which history itself is revealed as a sacramental Christian symbol. The "Rime" imitates or re-presents a process of textual evolution, and the symbolic meaning of that process—which is the poem's dominant symbolic event—is that the process *has* a symbolic value and meaning, that is, a religious, a Christian, and ultimately a redemptive meaning. In this we can see very clearly the living operation of processive historical events. At the outset of the nineteenth century and in reaction to the revolutionary intellectual developments of the Enlightenment, Christian ideas find a new birth of freedom, not in the *fact* of Christ's resurrection, which is the traditional Pauline view, but in the symbol of the resurrection, in its *meaning*.

Pre-Raphaelite Symbolism: A Critical Differential

We can specify the peculiar (historically determined) character of Coleridge's form of symbolism if we juxtapose it briefly with some alternative symbolic modes. The limits of the Coleridgean view would be quite apparent if we were to compare it with, for example, Mallarmé's or Rimbaud's *symboliste* programs, which represent a very different set of cultural determinants and limitations. But this cross-cultural comparison will not illuminate Coleridge's position nearly so well as a comparison drawn from within the English poetic tradition. I have in mind here the programmatic symbolism developed through the Pre-Raphaelite movement, by Dante Gabriel Rossetti in particular.

M. H. Abrams has rightly said of High English Romanticism that it sought to reformulate and save the "traditional concepts, schemes, and values" of the Christian heritage. Abrams believes, wrongly I think, that this was the program of all forms of romanticism; however that may be, his thesis is perfectly exemplified in Coleridge's work.

> *The Ancient Mariner* is neither an allegorical fable nor a symbolist poem. The persistent religious and moral allusions, however, both in the text and in the glosses . . . , invite us to take the Mariner's experience as an instance of the Christian plot of moral error, the discipline of suffering, and a consequent change of heart. The Mariner's literal journey, then, is also a spiritual journey. . . . [37]

The commentary is right on the mark, though one would wish to add that Coleridge's glosses were a brilliant addition to his poem because they emphasized a slight sense of historical discontinuity. Abrams is correct to say that the poem is neither *symboliste* nor allegorical because this discontinuity exists. The "Rime" presents us with an obviously "Christian" plot, but it insists that we "read" the plot in a highly personal and unorthodox way. Though its meaning is not so extensive or open as the meaning of a *symboliste* poem, the "Rime" relaxes the allegorical urgency of its materials just enough to permit "personal" interpretations that will yet not violate the poem's essentially Christian structure of concepts and values.

As we know, the Pre-Raphaelites and their circle were devoted to the literary ballad, which in fact achieved the rank of an important genre in the hands of the romantics. The "Rime" is the best early representation of this highly romantic form. But with the Pre-Raphaelites, veri-similitude of historical detail, both substantive and formal, became so central an issue that England produced, in the person of Swinburne, her greatest master of the literary ballad. Paradoxically, or so it might seem, this demand for a literalness of imagination resulted in poems that did not draw close continuities with the spirit of the past and its traditional forms of order, but rather heightened one's feeling of the separation between past and present. The medieval worlds evoked by Morris and Rossetti and Swinburne were interesting precisely because that famous Pre-Raphaelite detail distanced their material, made it appear remote and strange. The reader of "The Blessed Damozel" is placed in a forest of symbolic detail so dense that correspondences become unmanageable. Yet the situation is neither symbolic (in the Coleridgean mode) nor *symboliste*. Pre-Raphaelite detail does not put the reader on the threshold of a fresh openness, of extensive new sets of possible relations, but shocks him with the realization that his traditional romantic accommodations with past symbolic orders do not serve the actual truths of those orders, which are in fact much more mysterious than had been realized. The "Rime" draws continuities with the past; Pre-Raphaelite ballads enforce separations.

The relevance of these observations for Coleridge's use of a Christian symbolic mode will become clearer if we extend this analysis into a few more Pre-Raphaelite commonplaces. Pre-Raphaelite art and literature reproduce Christian iconography in great quantity, but anyone familiar with this pivotal movement knows that, despite its religious substance and even the religious convictions of at least some of its practitioners, Pre-Raphaelitism is not a religious art. The inheritors of Pre-Raphaelitism—the Vienna Sezession and art nouveau—are the logical extensions of a Pre-Raphaelite attitude; and though a true religious mood is discernible in these later movements, it is a religious mentality doing conscious battle with forms of romantic orthodoxy, as the work of Gustav Moreau and Stefan George makes very plain.

Pre-Raphaelitism, on the other hand, represents a return to certain basic romantic principles. It is a movement that did not want so much to elaborate a revision upon traditional romantic forms—which is what Tennyson ended up doing—as to return romantic perception to its *raison d'être*. The Pre-Raphaelite insistence upon careful realistic detail, so apparently unromantic, is in fact one of the two essential features of its romanticism. The other is the inclination to deal with very traditional subjects, and in particular with Christian subjects. These two qualities, operating together, opened another revisionist phase wherein Pre-Raphaelite art at last discovered a usable aesthetic medium for the viewpoint of a wholly secularized, and therefore non-Coleridgean, form of the Higher Criticism.

But the whole matter is best discussed in an example. Rossetti fixed the following sonnet to his painting "The Girlhood of Mary Virgin":

> These are the symbols. On that cloth of red
>   I' the centre is the Tripoint: perfect each,
> Except the second of its points, to teach
>   That Christ is not yet born. The books—whose head
>   Is golden Charity, as Paul hath said—
>   Those virtues are wherein the soul is rich:
>   Therefore on them the lily standeth, which
> Is Innocence, being interpreted.
> The seven-thorn'd briar and the palm seven-leaved
>   Are her great sorrow and her great reward.

Until the end be full, the Holy One
Abides without. She soon shall have achieved
Her perfect purity: yea, God the Lord
Shall soon vouchsafe His Son to be her Son.

In an older context, this sonnet might not seem so strange. Its force here comes from the fact that, though the interpretation he gives to the details of the painting is quite traditionally grounded, it is an interpretation without any essential religious import precisely because it is so literal. The details of poem and painting are precise enough, and their Christian context is sufficiently complete to allow an allegorical action; yet the poem forbids a religious response. For if Rossetti's allegorical pattern is exact, it is also consciously recovered, and thus presents itself to us not as a religious insight but as an antiquarian discovery. The result is that all the details in the painting and the poem, though "interpreted," have an even greater phenomenological innocence than they would have had in a medieval context. One is suddenly faced with a world (Christianity) that one thought one knew but whose spirit is in fact now seen to be profoundly remote.

Unlike the "Rime," this poem is no vehicle back to the essential religious significance of the Christian myth. Rather, it transports us back further still, to the essentially secular, or aesthetic, significance of that myth. The poem shows us that Christian iconology can have a significance, its beauty, that is even more radical than the most profound allegorical interpretation. It also tells us that allegorical interpretation can retain its own importance even after the withdrawal of the sea of faith, for such interpretations still possess the beauty of their design. The very details of Rossetti's "Christian" interpretation acquire a physique comparable to the details of the painting. Rossetti forces the interpretation to stand apart from us, forces us to view it is an object of delighted curiosity. What ought to be a definitive interpretation of the picture is discovered to be not an intellectual but a purely sensational, or perhaps anthropological, experience.

When Pre-Raphaelites return to an extremely detailed reproduction of traditional forms, it is always to work for effects like this. Indeed, when Rossetti writes upon some work of a painter from an earlier culture—one of his numerous sonnets for pictures—he not only repeats the technique of "The Girlhood of Mary Virgin" and its pendant sonnet; he tends to make his purposes even more explicit. His sonnet "An Allegorical Dance of Women," for example, is written on Mantegna's "Parnassus," in the Louvre, which seems to represent the triumph of Venus over Mars. But Rossetti opens his sonnet with the observation: "Scarcely, I think; yet it indeed *may* be / The meaning [of his own work] reached him." Rossetti is doubtful that Mantegna knew the full meaning of his own picture because Rossetti knows that, while meaning and allegorical constructs multiply, the essential character of art and life alike is their ability to generate human creations which are forever escaping the ideologies that made them possible. Of the Mantegna "Parnassus," then, he concludes:

> Its meaning filleth it,
> A secret of the wells of Life: to wit:—
> The heart's each pulse shall keep the sense it had
> With all, though the mind's labour run to nought.

That is, though the cultural gap between Mantegna and Rossetti is complete—a situation that is distinctly *not* the case with the historically diverse materials re-presented through Coleridge's "Rime"—Rossetti is yet able to join hands with Mantegna across the gulf of their differences. What the two share, according to Rossetti, is not a mutual commitment, symbolically maintained, to a religious ideology but a common devotion to the practice of art. In this case symbolism is material and technological rather than conceptual. The atheist Rossetti keeps company with the Catholic Mantegna, and with Christian traditions generally, by seeing hermeneutics not as a process of interpretaion but as a history of changing style. In the Pre-Raphaelite movement appears, for the first time unmistakably, the polemical deposition: no ideas but in things.

Conclusion

What, then, is the meaning of the "Rime"? Coleridge tried to guide his early readers to an answer in his famous *Biographia Literaria* pronouncement on the poem and the entire *Lyrical Ballads* project:

> In this idea originated the plan of the *Lyrical Ballads* in which it was agreed that my endeavours should be directed to persons and characters supernatural, or at least romantic; yet so as to transfer from our inward nature a human interest and a semblance of truth sufficient to procure for these shadows of imagination that willing suspension of disbelief for the moment, which constitutes poetic faith. (Chap. 14)

If we examine this passage carefully—assisted, perhaps, by our knowledge of its critical history—we will see that the famous dictum about the "willing suspension of disbelief" is being used in two senses. In the first instance the phrase refers to Coleridge's use of legendary, "supernatural," "romantic" materials, that is, to what is "contained" in the "Rime" when we see it as an ancient tale or, as we might now say, as a "myth." This sort of material is recognized to be a "delusion" by Coleridge, and his work shows that similar delusions can be found at the level of the ballad narrative as well as at the level of the gloss. The spectre-bark, Life-in-Death, the Polar Spirit, and the "grace of the Holy Mother" are not, to use Coleridge's term, "real" except under the deluded eye of the beholders of such phenomena. The art of the "Rime" persuades us to suspend our disbelief in such matters; indeed, when Coleridge speaks of a "*willing* suspension of disbelief," we understand that he is presuming in his readers a shared consciousness of the superstitious character of his primitive (mainly pagan and Roman Catholic) materials.

But Coleridge imitates a more comprehensive understanding of the willing suspension of disbelief when he says that it "constitutes poetic faith." From this vantage the statement can be seen, and of course has been seen, as a locus classicus for the romantic ideology of the creative imagination. "To transfer from our inward nature a human interest and semblance of truth" to the "Rime"'s superstitious materials is to psychologize reality and to suggest that the "true" reality of all external phenomena, whether "real" or "delusion," is inward and subjective. In this case, the willing suspension of disbelief does not apply to a poetic tour de force but to an imaginative construct that offers limitless opportunities for symbolic interpretation. In the first case the reader is willing to suspend his disbelief—which he nonetheless remains conscious of and attached to—whereas in the second he is willing to gain a poetic faith. When the latter occurs, the "Rime" enters upon its symbolic history and becomes the object of romantic hermeneutics.

From our present vantage, what we must do is inaugurate our disbelief in Coleridge's "poetic faith." This romantic ideology must be seen for what it is, a historical phenomenon of European culture, generated to save the "traditional concepts, schemes, and values" of the Christian heritage. To interpret the "Rime" at all, without a prior historical analytic, is necessarily to reify the romantic concept of the creative imagination. But that concept must become for us the same sort of "superstition" and "delusion" that "the grace of the Holy Mother" was to Coleridge. Only then will the poem become available once again to a (new) tradition of interpreters. Indeed, only then will Coleridge's own "poetic faith" become possible, for such a faith depends upon the hypothetical suspension of a prior, and presumed, disbelief.

To inaugurate such a disbelief in the "Rime"'s ideology of symbolism, we must historicize every aspect of the work. This is a procedure that the poem's own method has initiated. The mariner interprets his experiences by his own lights, and all subsequent mediators—the ballad transmitters, the author of the gloss, and Coleridge himself—represent their specific cultural views. In such a situation we must read the poem with the fullest possible consciousness of its poetically organized "historical layerings." The spectre-bark is seen as such by the mariner and is accepted *literatim* by the fictive textual transmitters. But if the poem assumes these superstitious attitudes into itself, it also presumes the presence of Enlightened readers. The latter will of course recognize the ship to be a hallucination, perhaps with no basis in physical reality at all, perhaps an imagined structure created by the mariner's fevered brain out of some whisps of sea fog. Because Coleridge has an Englightened mind as well, he knows that "In a distempered dream things & forms in themselves harmless inflict a terror of anguish."[38] But his mind is also Christian and symbolist, so even as he asks us, in the "Rime," to disbelieve in the phenomenal reality of the spectre-bark, he also asks us to suspend that disbelief:

> The excellence aimed at was to consist in the interesting of the affections by the dramatic truth of such emotions, as would naturally accompany such situations, supposing them real. And real in this sense they have been to every human being who, from whatever source of delusion, has at any time believed himself under supernatural agency.

What may be seen as a "delusion" in one point of view may be usefully regarded as a spiritual truth in another. Meaning replaces event, and word replaces fact as the real gives way to the symbolic.

When Newman watched Coleridge replace the Truth with the Imagination of the Truth, he concluded that Coleridge had "indulged a liberty of speculation which no Christian can tolerate, and advanced conclusions which were often heathen rather than Christian."[39] Newman's analysis, like his orthodox fears, were both correct and farsighted, for Coleridge's own method would necessarily place his interpretive scheme beneath the critical razor he first employed. Interpretation of the spectre-bark is analogous to the interpretation of every facet of the poem, including its general theme and structure: interpretation, including the author's interpretation, falls subject to those historical limitations that critical analysis can explicate. The fictive writer of the gloss gives a long and beautiful commentary on the stars of line 266. The best gloss on such a gloss is a passage like the following from *The Statesman's Manual:*

> The great PRINCIPLES of our religion, the sublime IDEAS spoken out every-where in the Old and New Testament, resemble the fixed stars, which appear of the same size to the naked as to the armed eye; the magnitude of which the telescope may rather seem to diminish than to increase. At the annunciation of *principles*, of *ideas*, the soul of man awakes, and starts up, as an exile in a far distant land at the unexpected sounds of his native language, when after long years of absence, and almost of oblivion, he is suddenly addressed in his own mother-tongue. He weeps for joy, and embraces the speaker as his brother.[40]

This is not the meaning of the poem's text, but it is the meaning that perhaps best clarifies what kind of poem we are dealing with. Coleridge might associate the meaning of this passage with his text, but it is a special reading, peculiar to Coleridge. In such matters, as Coleridge had said, "Each person must be . . . querist and respondent to himself."[41]

A poem like the "Rime" encourages, therefore, the most diverse readings and interpretations. Since this encouragement is made in terms of the Christian economy, the interpretations have generally remained within the broad spiritualist terms—"heathen" terms, in Newman's view—that Coleridge's mind had allowed for. The historical method of the "Rime," however, had also prepared the ground for a thoroughly revisionist view of the poem, in which the entire ideological structure of its symbolist procedures would finally be able to be seen in their special historical terms. When this happens, the meaning of the "Rime" emerges as the "dramatic truth" of Coleridge's intellectual and religious commitments. In the event, the poem suffers no loss of power or significance; on the contrary, at that point we begin to see quite clearly the true extent of its power and the immense significance it has had, just as we also begin to see how these things come to pass. When the entire poetical work—including, perhaps especially, its verbal forms and its symbolic procedures—is scrutinized through the lens of a critical rather than a hermeneutic method, the "Rime" will once again begin to discover its future. It will cease to be an object of faith—whether romantic or Christian—and become, instead, a human—a social and a historical—resource.

Notes

1. Wrangham's review appeared in *The British Critic* 14 (October 1799), Southey's in *The Critical Review* 24 (October 1798); both are quoted in *Wordsworth and Coleridge: The Lyrical Ballads*, ed. R. L. Brett and A. R. Jones (London: Barnes and Noble, 1963), 317–20, 313–14. For a good selection of early reviews, see *Coleridge: The Critical Heritage*, ed. J. R. de J. Jackson (London: Barnes and Noble, 1970).

2. See Richard Haven, "The Ancient Mariner in the Nineteenth Century," *Studies in Romanticism* 11 (1972): esp. 365–68.

3. *The Analytical Review* 28 (December 1798); Burney's review was in *The Monthly Review* 29 (June 1799); see *Wordsworth and Coleridge*, ed. Brett and Jones, 314–17.

4. Wordsworth to Cottle, 24 June 1799, *The Letters of William and Dorothy Wordsworth*, ed. Ernest de Selincourt, rev. Chester Shaver, 5 vols. (Oxford: Clarendon Pres, 1967), 1:264.

5. Lamb, *The Letters of Charles Lamb*, ed. E. V. Lucas, 3 vols. (London: J. M. Dent and Sons, 1935), 1:240.

6. See Clement Carlyon quoted in *Coleridge: The Critical Heritage*, 197–204.

7. J. G. Lockhart, "Essay on the Lake School," *Blackwood's Magazine* 6 (1819); see also the anonymous reviews of *Sibylline Leaves* in *London Magazine* (July 1820) and *The Monthly Review* (January 1819).

8. See Haven, "The Ancient Mariner in the Nineteenth Century," 370–74.

9. See E. E. Stoll, "Symbolism in Coleridge," *PMLA* 63 (1948): 214–33; Elisabeth Schneider *Coleridge, Opium, and "Kubla Khan"* (Chicago: University of Chicago Press, 1953), 252–55; Irving Babbit, "Coleridge and Imagination," *On Being Creative and Other Essays* (Boston: Houghton Mifflin Company, 1932), 116–120; and William Empson and David Pirie, eds., *Coleridge's Verse: A Selection* (New York: Faber, 1973).

10. See Haven, "The Ancient Mariner in the Nineteenth Century," 361. The general uniformity of approach to the poem's formal and thematic aspects is illustrated quite clearly in the

various contemporary handbooks and student guides: see esp. *Twentieth-Century Interpretations of "The Rime of the Ancient Mariner,"* ed. James D. Boulger (Englewood Cliffs, N. J.: Prentice-Hall, 1969) and *"The Rime of the Ancient Mariner": A Handbook,* ed. Royal A. Gettmann (Belmost, Calif.: Wadsworth, 1966). The point is also nicely illustrated in John Beer's excellent *Coleridge the Visionary* (London: Chatto and Windus, 1959), chap. 5.

11. M. H. Abrams, *Natural Supernaturalism* (New York: W. W. Norton, 1971), 272.

12. Pirie, *Coleridge's Verse,* 214–15.

13. See Thomas Percy, *Reliques of Ancient English Poetry,* ed. J. V. Prichard, 2 vols. (London: G. Bell and Sons, 1905), 1:xliii, and Walter Scott's introduction to *Minstrelsy of the Scottish Border,* ed. Thomas Henderson, 3 vols. (Edinburgh: W. Blackwood and Sons, 1902), 1:168–73); see also Scott's "Modern Imitations," ibid., 1:173–76), and his "Essay on Imitations of the Ancient Ballad," ibid., 4:1–52.

14. Huntington Brown, "The Gloss to the Ancient Mariner," *Modern Language Quarterly* 6 (1945): 319–20.

15. Ibid., 322, 324.

16. J. R. Ebbatson's "Coleridge and the Rights of Man," *Studies in Romanticism* 11 (1972): 171–206, contains an interesting discussion of some of the poem's historical intersections; it consciously follows the line opened by Empson in his 1964 *Critical Quarterly* essay, "The Ancient Mariner," in which his view on the poem initially appeared.

17. Coleridge, *Aids to Reflection and The Confessions of an Inquiring Spirit* (London: G. Bell and Sons, 1893), 200n; all further citations to this work, abbreviated as *AC,* will be included in the text.

18. See Elinor Shaffer, *"Kubla Khan" and the Fall of Jerusalem* (Cambridge: Cambridge University Press, 1975), esp. chaps. 1–3. This is a work of real importance for students of romanticism as well as for Coleridge scholars.

19. Ibid., 32

20. Ibid., 46–47.

21. Ibid., 85–86.

22. For Geddes, see ibid., 24–34; Coleridge's 1795 "Lectures on Revealed Religion" were written with Michaelis in hand; and Coleridge refers to Heyne—who was, indeed, a giant figure in scholarly circles—in his *Notebooks* of 1796 (see *The Notebooks of Samuel Taylor Coleridge,* ed. Kathleen Coburn, 3 vols. [New York: Pantheon, 1957], 1:no. 278).

23. See Coleridge's *Lectures 1795 on Politics and Religion,* ed. Lewis Patton and Peter Mann (Princeton, N. J.: Princeton University Press, 1971), 118.

24. Coleridge, *The Watchman,* ed. Lewis Patton (Princeton, N. J.: Princeton University Press, 1970), 52.

25. For *The Statesman's Manual,* see *Lay Sermons,* ed. R. J. White (Princeton, N.J.: Princeton University Press, 1972), 29–31 and 70–73.

26. Ibid., 28.

27. See Shaffer *"Kubla Khan" and the Fall of Jerusalem,* 75–79.

28. See ibid., 78.

29. See Percy, *Reliques of Ancient English Poetry,* xxiii–xxvi and notes.

30. Coleridge quoted in Shaffer, *"Kubla Khan" and the Fall of Jerusalem,* 79.

31. See Percy's discussion in *Reliques of Ancient English Poetry* (xlii–xliii) of the diction of the ancient minstrels (e.g., the accentuation of words like Coleridge's "countree," 1:407).

32. See Charles Sanders, *Coleridge and the Broad Church Movement* (Durham, N.C.: Duke University Press, 1942), and James D. Boulger, *Coleridge as Religious Thinker* (New Haven: Yale University Press, 1961).

33. Coleridge, *The Table Talk and Omniana,* ed. T. Ashe (London: G. Bell and Sons, 1923), 138–39.

34. John Colmer *Coleridge: Critic of Society* (Oxford: Clarendon Press, 1959), 32.

35. This result lies in the nature of hermeneutics itself, at least as presently understood. See, for example, Heinrich Ott's "Hermeneutics and Personhood," where he states the basic principle of this interpretive method: "In my first knowledge of the subject matter I already know implicitly all that which I later learned in addition" (from *Interpretation: The Poetry of Meaning,* ed. S. R. Hopper and D. L. Miller [New York: 1967], 17).

36. Coleridge, *Lay Sermons,* 55.

37. Abrams, *Natural Supernaturalism,* 272. The following section of my essay is a revised portion of a review essay, "Romanticism and the Embarrassments of Critical Tradition," which appeared in *Modern Philology* 70 (February 1973): 243–57.

38. Coleridge, *Notebooks,* 1:no. 205 (the entry is dated 1796–97).

39. John Henry Newman, "The Prospects of the Anglican Church," *Essays Critical and Historical* (London: Longmans, Green, and Co., 1897), 268.

40. Coleridge, *Lay Sermons,* 24.

41. Ibid., 55.

Historical Amnesia and Patriarchal Morality in Keats's *Ode on a Grecian Urn*

Daniel P. Watkins

1

The period from late 1818 to mid-1819 was one of rapid intellectual development for Keats. His thinking about the imagination, religion, politics, and history matured significantly, providing an important intellectual groundwork for the great poems that would be written over much of this same period. This was a time, as he remarked to Woodhouse in December 1818, when he had "a new leaf to turn over": "I must work—I must read—I must write" (*LJK* 1:412).[1] Or, as he put it to George and Georgiana Keats three months later, he was striving "to know myself" (*LJK* 2:81). The extent to which he was aware of his own intellectual development, and the extent of his modesty in the face of it, are suggested by his comment to Benjamin Robert Haydon that he was "moulting,"[2] beginning to "see by little and little more of what is to be done, and how it is to be done, should I ever be able to do it" (*LJK* 2:32). Such remarks were accompanied during this period by his reading of Voltaire and William Robertson (*LJK* 2:100), by his studious effort to work through what he considered the limitations of Christianity (*LJK* 2:103), and, in August 1819, by his decision to move to Winchester so that he might have access to a library (*LJK* 2:137, 139).

One hope that Keats nourished as he gave himself up to intellectual pursuit was that he might put himself in a position of someday "doing the world some good" (*LJK* 1:387), a hope that is implicit in his many comments on history and on the politics of his age. Always "rather inclined to the liberal side of things" (*LJK* 2:14), during this period he voiced his distress over the institutions of British government, lamenting that "There is of a truth nothing manly or sterling in any part of the Government," and his belief that "Politics . . . are . . . only sleepy because they will soon be too wide awake" (*LJK* 1:396). His interest in politics is also manifested in the fact that he read the *Examiner* regularly and wrote in his letters about Cobbett, Hobhouse, and the Westminster elections; spent time with his radical friends the Snooks, with whom he "used to have over a little Religion and politicts [*sic*] together almost every evening" (*LJK* 2:60); expressed his concern—derived as much from his reading of the *Examiner* as from his conversations with Charles Brown—that there would be "a national Baknruptcy" (*LJK* 2:62); and on occasion during this period saw his radical friend David Lewis, who, Keats remarked after one visit, "is going on as usual among his favorite democrat papers—we had a chat as usual about Cobbett" (*LJK* 2:63). He also spoke frequently in his letters about Hazlitt, quoting extensively from that writer's essays in the *Examiner* and expressing great admiration and respect for his political-literary writings (see, for instance, *LJK* 2:74–76). His dislike for contemporary political authority was accompanied by his dislike for contemporary religious authority. On more than one occasion he voiced his contempt, in no uncertain terms, for "Men interested in the pious frauds of Religion" (*LJK* 2:80). In short, in his view he had become a virtual "infidel" (*LJK* 2:116), staunchly opposed to the structures of authority that ruled Regency England and that he believed worked against human betterment.

Such comments as these, which convincingly establish Keats's interest in world affairs, are supported by Keats's friends, who frequently described his liberal and republican attitudes (see, for instance, *KC* 2:185, 2:261, 2:264, 2:291–95), and they provide one basis for Clarence DeWitt Thorpe's argument, made long ago, that Keats's life was marked by an intelligent sense of the politics of his age, and for June Koch's more recent argument that Keats's political interests inform his poetry in significant and positive ways.[3] Certainly it is important to recognize and to acknowledge Keats's expressed intentions in such matters, and, moreover, there is a need to take direction from such scholars as Thorpe and Koch and to elaborate more fully the ways Keats's reading and knowledge of history and politics are embodied and projected in his poetry; such a line of critical investigation would surely find that the utopian dimension of his poetry is not to be explained so much by the poet's spiritual and religious temperament (as Earl Wasserman and others claim[4]) as by his sincere desire to formulate an alternative model of hope for a world weighed down by "money-getting" (*LJK* 2:14) and entrapped by political contradiction and oppression.

At the same time, however, even as Keats's progressive and sympathetic position on such matters as politics and religion is elaborated, and even as his poetry is reinterpreted in political and historical ways as an expression of desire for human betterment, the extent to which his thought and writing are implicated in and controlled by certain facts of oppression during the romantic period must not be overlooked. For in a very real and important sense, many of the oppressive features of Keats's world that he desperately sought to push out of his poetic vision come back to haunt that vision. To put the matter somewhat differently, his work is politically and historically significant not only for its utopian dimension, for its dream of a better world, but also for the way it is saturated in the loneliness, tension, contradictions, and struggles that characterize the bourgeois culture of which it is a part.

The extent to which Keats's poetry remains implicated in—and thus helps us to know—historical and social contradiction can be illustrated by a materialist analysis of *Ode on a Grecian Urn*, one of his most beautiful and problematic works. Despite this poem's expressed and laudable desire for something of permanence and beauty behind the turmoil and mutability of everyday life, it duplicates ideologically a form of oppression that Keats and his age never escaped—even when they situated themselves knowingly and firmly against political and religious tyranny, as Keats clearly did—namely, the oppression of women. As in the work of many other romantic poets, gender is an ideological blind spot, and by investigating and documenting its role in the *Urn*, it is possible to show how even the most sincere utopian impulses during the romantic period inevitably are marked by elements of oppression and sometimes even by violence—by the very disturbing elements that the romantic poetic vision would avoid.

The argument I wish to make takes its point of departure from Tilottama Rajan's excellent and important book, *Dark Interpreter: The Discourse of Romanticism*, which sets as its task to demonstrate the anxiety present in romantic texts. This anxiety is vividly expressed in the *Urn*, Rajan argues, as "the poem seeks to project on the urn [a vision] that is constantly challenged and disrupted by the vision of art that emerges from the urn itself—in all probabilty a funeral urn." Emphasizing the conflict between the flat surface of the urn, which constitutes a "figured curtain of art," and the depth of the urn, which "contains the ashes of the dead, of a civilization that is past," Rajan charts the poetic attempt to contain, enclose, or overcome this conflict by creating "a fictitiousness that excludes the urn's real function." Although Keats recognizes the existence of the "depth and ambiguity" suggested by the urn's interior, he does not give them full expression, because "To search beneath the surface, by seeking the historical Greece underlying the Arcadian fiction, would be to ask what becomes of the abstractions of idealism when they are incarnated in the real world and made the property of real men and lovers. In the fourth stanza Keats almost does this. But at the crucial moment he draws back from excavating too deeply in the archaeology of the idealizing consciousness, fearing a complete dissolution of the surface." Thus, Rajan concludes, "irrespective of who speaks them, the last lines of Keats's poem reaffirm the rhetoric of the surface and reduce questions to the flatness of statement and the urn itself to its merely decorative appearance."[5]

While it is certainly correct and even necessary, as Rajan urges, to see the funeral urn as a reminder—for us, as for Keats—of past civilizations now dead, it is also important to understand that history is not simply that which must die. To imply, as Rajan does, that history is represented only by the ashes in the funeral urn and by the poet's sense of his own mortality, while arguing that the figures and images on the urn and in the poem represent fictions, or qualities that would resist or overcome this history, is to posit a static dualism between the individual imagination and historical reality:

history equals mortality, while art (hopefully) equals the enduring power of the individual imagination. Such a formulation limits historical explanation by obscuring the fact that the figures and images on the surface of the urn are no less historical than the ashes contained within the urn. Indeed, the conflicts and tensions in the poem that Rajan considers are not so much a product of the irreconcilable differences between historical (mortal) and fictional (enduring) properties, or of the difficult relations between surfaces and depths, as they are of a single, complex historical reality, which defines both. In other words, the textual anxiety that Rajan describes is also an expression of historical anxiety. In this view, history is not simply depth, or that which is curtained over by the products of the imagination; it is, rather, the ontological ground that encompasses and gives rise to all human activity and that therefore necessarily limits, empowers, and defines poetic practice.

To situate poetic practice within this framework of ideas is to acknowledge that it cannot be explained in purely textual terms. In the *Urn* Keats is not simply meditating on and recording the details inscribed on a perfectly cloistered museum piece; he is committing a historical and political act, *using* the urn to formulate the past. This act also formulates and discloses the historically specific system of values and beliefs of Keats's own historical situation, characterized by social fragmentation, alienation, and loneliness, all of which intensified and became culturally pervasive with the rise of a nonagricultural economy and population, and which helped to produce subjectivity as a culturally dominant ideology. That the *Urn* never escapes these social contradictions—and in fact is constituted by them—is seen most impressively in the fact that while truth and beauty are clearly uppermost in the poet's mind, and are formulated and articulated in moving poetic language, their integrity is bought at a very dear price. The values underwriting the poetic vision of beauty and truth derive from one of the most powerful supports of capitalism during Keats's day, namely patriarchy, which takes for granted the masculine nature of creativity, the passive nature of femininity, and the definitional role of the father. These values, though never stated explicitly, are pervasive, and they movingly expose the tendency in romantic poetry to flatten certain issues of human oppression and human struggle into a natural conflict between the desire for immortality and the fact of mortality. I want to trace this patriarchal morality through the poem as a necessary, though submerged, ingredient, illustrating its historical and political role in Keats's poetic imagination and, more generallly, in the romantic ideology.[6]

2

The intensity with which patriarchal morality is drawn in the poem can be accounted for, partially, in biographical terms.[7] (I should stress, however, that I do not wish to reduce the issues in the *Urn* to Keats's personal eccentricity; I take for granted that the contradictions in Keats's life and in his poetry are also at least partly the contradictions of his age.) In a letter to Benjamin Bailey, written less than a year before the *Urn*, Keats remarked:

> I am certain I have not a right feeling towards Women—at this moment I am striving to be just to them but I cannot—Is it because they fall so far beneath my Boyish imagination? When I was a Schoolboy I though[t] a fair Woman a pure Goddess, my mind was a soft nest in which some one of them slept though she knew it not—I have no right to expect more than their reality. I thought them etherial above Men—I find then [*sic*] perhaps equal—great by comparison is very small—Insult may be inflicted in more ways than by Word or action—one who is tender of being insulted does not like to think an insult against another—I do not like to think insults in a Lady's Company—I commit a Crime with her which absence would have not known—Is this not extraordinary? When among Men I have no evil thoughts, no malice, no spleen—I feel free to speak or to be silent—I can listen and from every one I can learn—my hands are in my pockets I am free from all suspicion and comfortable. When I am among Women I have evil thoughts, malice spleen—I cannot speak or be silent—I am full of Suspicions and therefore listen to no thing—I am in a hurry to be gone. (*LJK* 1 : 341)

Five months later (in a letter in which he also discusses his views on beauty and truth[8]), he remarked to his brother about the "inadequacy" of women (*LJK* 2 : 19). The anxiety evident in these comments attends one of the poetic impulses behind many of Keats's poems. In *La Belle Dame Sans Merci*, he depicts woman both as the highest object of masculine desire and at the same time as the victimizer of men; in *The Eve of St. Agnes*, he describes the young Madeline as the object of a Peeping Tom's prurience, and as a person who benefits from subjecting herself to the Peeping Tom's will; in *Lamia*, he portrays woman as a beautiful yet witchlike creature who attempts to isolate man from the public world, where he supposedly belongs; and in the *Fall of Hyperion*, he portrays woman (in the character of Moneta) as a cold, blind goddess, directly connected to money, whose willingness to serve poetic man exacts a very high price.[9] Such examples from his life and poetry suggest that the portrayal of the feminine in the *Urn* is not an exception but a tendency in his poetic practice.

Before sketching the specific way the *Urn* defines and structures femininity in erecting its vision of beauty and truth, it might be helpful to ask what, exactly, is feminized in the poem, and what use is made of those things that are feminized. First, the urn itself is presented as a "still unravished bride of quietness" (1), and it is worth recalling that the urn is stationary and silent throughout, not only described and defined by the poet but also serving as the still object of his contemplation and as the receiver of his anxieties, hope, desire, and despair: just as the interior of the urn is said to be the repository of the ashes of the dead, the exterior is the repository of and inspiration for the poet's imaginings. Second, the figures on the urn themselves mirror the relation between poet and urn/object. The male figures are likened to "men or gods" (8), whereas the women, like the urn, are presented as stationary, frozen in time ("She cannot fade," 19). Moreover, the male figures engage in "mad pursuit" while the female figures "struggle to escape" (9). Without arguing that the poem's description of these figures approaches a description of rape, it should be emphasized that the masculine aggression is presented as a "wild ecstasy" (10), although literally nothing in the descriptions of the female figures (who are described as "loth" [8]) suggests even desire, and certainly not ecstasy. Third, the sacrifice described in the penultimate stanza also appears in masculine and feminine terms. In a religious ritual, a priest leads to death a "heifer lowing at the skies, / And all her silken flanks with garlands drest" (34–35). Again, we need not insist that the description here is of a literal woman—though it is worth noting that in Keats's day, as in our own, "heifer" was a common term used to describe not only cows but women, and also that in most rituals, such as the one described, it was typically a bullock and not a heifer that was sacrificed—to see that the violence being enacted, and religiously sanctioned, is gender specific.

Put differently, poetics and ideology in the poem are inextricably entwined. Poetic activity involves the structuring of quite real power relations, as well as the definition of these power relations as noble and as the source of virtue, integrity, and morality; it transforms oppression into an acceptable, even laudable, form of social existence. To recognize this active value-producing function in the poem is to understand, with Michele Barrett, that gender has less to do with biological difference than with political reality; it must be identified in terms of "division, oppression, inequality, internalized inferiority for women,"[10] that is, in terms of specific and controlling forces and relations that emerge from social practice, of which poetry is one form.

The production of this masculine ideology in the *Urn* follows a very clear path, one that Rosemary Radford Ruether's theory of the struggle against the mother, or the feminine, helps to illuminate. According to Ruether, the suppression of women is a historically explicable phenomenon, in which "the female person, possessing a different but strong body and an equal capacity for thought and culture, was subverted and made to appear physiologically and intellectually inferior." Ruether charts the process of this subversion through three diachronic stages, which she labels the Conquest of the Mother, the Negation of the Mother, and the Sublimation of the Mother. "The stages of this history," Ruether says, "are . . . reflected in the changing ideology or symbolization of the 'feminine' in (male-defined) culture."[11]

In her discussion of the Conquest of the Mother, Ruether notes that this first phase originated when the center of economic life shifted out of the family. Two central developments contributed to this shift:

The first is the transition from tribal or village to urban life. The urban revolution originally affected only a small segment of society, with most of society remaining agrarian and family-centered handicraft economies. But it created a new elite group of males whose power was no longer based on the physical prowess of the hunter or warrior, but on the inherited monopoly of political power and knowledge. Females were equally capable of entering into this kind of power on equal terms, but instead they were excluded from it and consigned to an ornamental role—with occasional exceptions.[12]

This urban revolution was followed by "the development of mass industrialization, which diffuses urbanization over more and more of the world and shifts economic production increasingly from the family to a work place separated form the home. For the first time women as a group became marginal to production and economically dependent on male work for survival."[13] This account, which focuses primarily on the economic realities underlying the historical development of gender relations, draws very heavily on Engels's *The Origin and History of the Family,* and it entails a critically significant ideological dimension, in which women are seen in purely passive terms. Situated outside the world of public power, women become "restricted to a sheltered sphere": "Dress, confinement, lack of physical development, direct bodily repression through corsets, footbinding, or veils mold women . . . into an unnatural physical weakness and psychological timidity."[14] At the same time "a male-identified consciousness [is elevated] to transparent apriority."[15]

According to Ruether, the elevation of masculine consciousness leads to the second historical stage, the Negation of the Mother.

Creation is seen as initiated by a fiat from above, from an immaterial principle beyond visible reality. Nature, which once encompassed all reality, is now subjugated and made into the lower side of a new dualism. . . . Consciousness is abstracted into a sphere beyond visible reality, including the visible heavens. This higher realm is the world of divinity. The primal matrix of life . . . is debased as mere "matter" (a word which means "mother"). . . . Maleness is identified with intellectuality and spirituality; femaleness . . . with lower material nature. This also defines the female as ontologically dependent and morally inferior to maleness.[16]

The third phase involves the idealization of women, which arises "as the corollary of the repression of physical sexuality and procreation. The Virgin Mary was the antetype of spiritual femininity over against 'carnal femaleness.' However, it was only in the romantic reaction following the French Revolution that this concept of spiritual femininity became secularized and generalized as a myth about the superior nature of women."[17] The reason for this, she argues, is that "In the aftermath of the French

Revolution, when the very fabric of Western civilization seemed to be undermined, European thinkers went scrambling to recover bits and pieces of a threatened social order. . . . Romanticism sought, simultaneously, to renew human sensibilities through contact with the mystical depths of nature, from which rationalistic man had become alienated, and to compensate for the depersonalized world of industrialism and democracy that threatened the house of patriarchal society." This development is socially and historically pervasive, incorporating under its power the institutions of marriage, religion, family, sexuality, and aesthetics, and producing, finally, in Ruether's opinion, "the dehumanization of society."[18]

This is a condensed description of Ruether's theory, but it illustrates, I think, her basic points, which are that masculine morality and value, as exercised under patriarchy, depend fully on active oppression and conquest; that the conquered is woman; and that the hierarchy of values resulting from this conquest prevents "reciprocity." The masculine "view of what is over against itself is not that of the conversation of two subjects, but of the conquest of an alien object. The intractability of the other side of the dualism to its demands does not suggest that the 'other' has a 'nature' of her own that needs to be respected and with which one must enter into conversation. Rather, this intractability is seen as that of disobedient rebellion."[19] The feminine, in being conquered, is not only silenced but also transformed, denied all human complexity and made into the passive repository of masculine desire. The purity and morality that come to be associated with this silenced femininity derive from the masculine ability to *use* the feminine— just as it uses the world—to its own ends. In effect, the feminine is cherished because its subordination serves the masculine ego's carefully constructed sense of itself.

Ruether's argument may be seen as representing homologically the general pattern of Keats's *Urn*. That is, while the poem does not address thematically the problem and nature of the historical development of patriarchy into its present form under capitalism, its portrayal of the feminine follows symbolically, and with remarkable force, the historical pattern described by Ruether. And though the poem does not of course present an account of the hard economic conditions upon which Ruether grounds her theory, it does reveal the form that gender relations take under those conditions. In its intense struggle to avoid or suppress all matters of historical consequence (note Rajan's argument, above), the *Urn* presents itself finally as a near-perfect articulation of the process by which patriarchy establishes its authority, and of patriarchal morality as it existed in Keats's day.

A more direct concern involves the function of poetic practice as a function of history. In describing above the place of the feminine in the poem, it was noted that the urn itself, especially the presentation of the figures on it in stanzas 1 and 2, and the presentation of the sacrifice in stanza 4, constitutes

the important gender-specific references. It now should be noted that the
conflict described in stanza 1 ("What men or gods are these? What maidens
loth? / What mad pursuit? What struggle to escape?" [8–9]) is not simple love
play. The maidens are described as "loth"—a word that means more than
reluctant and certainly more than coquettish[20]—and their struggle is shown
to be quite desperate, just as the movement of the male figures is characterized by a sort of Dionysian ecstasy. What is more, the scene is described in
terms of the masculine effort to hypostatize the conflict, and in fact the final
scene is one of masculine victory, in spirit if not in body, as the maidens are
"frozen" as objects of masculine desire:

> Bold lover, never, never canst thou kiss,
> Though winning near the goal—yet, do not grieve;
> She cannot fade, though thou hast not thy bliss,
> For ever wilt thou love, and she be fair.
>
> (17–20)

This hypostasis, which allows the "bold lover" ever to behold women as
"fair," generates in the poem a virtual madness of ecstacy (stanza 3): love,
happiness, and song weigh the lines down as the poet attempts to articulate
the pleasures that he imagines are "still to be enjoy'd" (26), until the prospect
of such extreme sensual delight overwhelms him, producing the consideration of religious ritual.

The sacrifice that occupies stanza 4 is traditionally seen as a discovery by
the speaker of figures on the urn previously overlooked, a discovery that calls
the poet's attention from the beauties that had occupied him to the truth that
is expressed in even the most inspiring works of art.[21] This view is essentially
correct *in terms of the poetic voice controlling the poem*, but it is incomplete in
terms of the social relations working themselves out through the poem's
larger ideological structures. Certainly the tone is somber as the poet describes the "little town" with its silent streets, its emptiness, and its general
desolation; but the somberness comes with the religious ritual of sacrificing
the heifer, that is, in Ruether's terms, of negating the feminine, not only
through physical violence (the sacrifice), but also by "lowering" or "debas-
ing" the feminine (see Ruether's comments, above) by presenting it in
animalistic terms (heifer). Further, not only is the event presided over by a
priest; the town itself sits under the watchful eye of the "peaceful citadel," a
distinctly military image recalling the struggle of the preceding stanzas,
which is now completed, having been followed first by celebration and now
by ritual. Even as the scene reflects seriousness and sincerity—recalling
Ruether's account of the development of a masculine religion—the physical
resources of the masculine world stand by as a certain reminder of the specific
power behind the ritual.

Conquest and negation are accompanied by a sublimation of the feminine, implicit in the poem's opening lines describing the urn as the "still unravish'd bride of quietness" (1), as a pure resource of the highest imaginable values. While the scenes on the urn tell the story of the triumph of men over women, the urn itself remains quiet and pure, giving the struggles inscribed on its borders the gloss of a "flowery tale" (4). The urn is a "Sylvan historian" (3), one that quietly and in appealing tones tells the version of history that patriarchy wants to hear, and for this reason it is spiritualized and revered, seen to carry forth to subsequent ages eternal and incontestable truths. It is a "Cold Pastoral" (45) not because it is deceitful but because it is cleansed of the hot pursuits and struggles of material history. Its coldness, in fact, is directly connected to its perceived embodiment of things eternal and to its claimed friendship to all humanity:

> Thou, silent form, dost tease us out of thought
> As doth eternity: Cold Pastoral!
> When old age shall this generation waste,
> Thou shalt remain, in midst of other woe
> Than ours, a friend to man.
>
>   (44–48)

Thought is subordinated to belief; history is transformed into mortality; the urn is presented as a constant that endures, providing humanity with the structures of belief that are not to be questioned: all real human struggles are naturalized and idealized, taken out of the domain of history as conflict, and the feminized object made to carry this message of the imaginative beauties that overarch the truth of mortality is revered no less than the Virgin, of whom we are reminded by the description of the urn as an "unravish'd bride" who bears forth those qualities that (so the poet seems to think) offer a grace to humanity:

> Beauty is truth, truth beauty,—that is all
> Ye know on earth, and all ye need to know.
>
>   (49–50)[22]

Applying Ruether's theory to the *Urn* reveals an extreme ethical violence, in which the beliefs of one group (in this case, symbolized in the statement "beauty is truth, truth beauty") are made possible by the violation and domination of another. This domination is exemplified not only in the poem's structure but in the act of poetic production itself; the poem *appropriates* the urn, even as the urn appropriates certain historical phenomena by transforming into art—and thus sanctifying—a specific view of human relations and values. In this view, stanza 4 does *not* offer an unsettling recognition that disrupts the illusion of beauty, as Rajan argues; rather it naturalizes and sanctifies sacrificial acts. Sacrificial death and natural death, in fact, become one, and they are equally accepted and revered. The mediations that define death in terms of specific realities—the conflict described in lines 8 and 9; the "other woe" hinted at in line 46; the poetic use made of the feminine—are transformed and frozen, made to serve the final vision of beauty and truth, terms that are discussed in the same letter in which Keats describes his own gynephobia (see the letter to Bailey, quoted above). What Simone de Beauvoir says of the oppression of women generally bears directly on the process described in the *Urn:* "Now, what peculiarly signalizes the situation of woman is that she—a free and autonomous being like all human creatures— nevertheless finds herself living in a world where men compel her to assume the status of the Other. They propose to stabilize her as object and to doom her to immanence since her transcendence is to be overshadowed and forever transcended by another ego *(conscience)* which is essential and sovereign."[23] The effect of the speaker's comments in the *Urn* is to stabilize the urn, thereby stabilizing the masculine view of history by flattening the urn to single significance (i.e., "Beauty is truth," etc.).

One consequence of the poem's unfolding vision is the production of sheer sterility under the title of beauty. The ashes in the funeral urn of course are not written into the poem itself, but are present by implication. They do not simply challenge or disrupt the figures drawn on the surface of the urn, but emphasize a reality that is shown repeatedly to constitute the surface itself as well as the poetic depiction of this surface. The urn is a "Cold Pastoral"; the "little town" is "emptied" as "good folk" leave, presumably to participate in a sacrifice; struggle defines the first two stanzas; "other woe," which implies present woe as well, is projected for the future, long after the speaker has perished. This is not to deny the spiritual and transcendental impulses that critics have rightly noted as motivations for poetry, but to argue that in this case the impulse both arises from and promotes sterility; it describes beauty under the conditions of its human impossibility, presenting hope (much as Blake does, though ironically, in the *Songs of Innocence*) that is grounded in hardship and sacrifice. This throws an important light on the final lines of the poem. Far from being a statement of a dialectical relationship—which, for instance, might be rendered as "beauty leads to truth, and truth leads back once again to beauty"—these lines express a masculine *equation*, one that identifies domination of the feminine with transcendental beauty and value. The point is not that the truth of our mortality causes us to cherish a hope for something—in this case art—that will endure, but rather that what we hold dearest is covered over with the blood of others; the sacrifice of stanza 4 and the ashes contained within the urn are a constituent part of the value scheme articulated in the poem, and these surely are the sacrifice and ashes of women, a point that is illustrated by the developing and sharpening focus of the poem. Throughout the *Urn*, men and maidens are described in tandem until the final lines, when Keats moves toward the statement about beauty and truth, at which time woman is written out of the poem, present now only in the hypostatized form of the urn, which remains as "a friend to man" (48). The spiritual and the aesthetic are conflated, and their credibility comes at the expense of the feminine.

3

One important feature of the poem that helps to elucidate its historical dimension is silence, which I have mentioned earlier and which I would now like to consider in more detail. It is common to interpret the many references to silence in the poem as a sign of purity, as an indication that Keats is concerned with matters of the soul or spirit. The spirit, according to this argument, hears what the flesh cannot, a point symbolized in this poem, as well as elsewhere in Keats, by the emphasis on stillness and silence.[24] The difficulty with this perspective is not that it stresses matters of spirit and soul—these *are* important concerns in the *Urn*, and certainly bear critical investigation—but rather that it begins from idealist assumptions which prevent awareness of the fact that silence is always feminized. The conquest, negation, and sublimation of the feminine entail a violation of feminine expressive capacity, much as Tereus (to use a particularly brutal example), after raping Philomela, rips out her tongue in the belief that her forced silence will assure his continued power and ostensible integrity within the family.[25] The denial of the feminine voice both enables and emboldens the masculine voice, allowing the poet's mind and imagination to run freely over the images on the urn, interpreting and defining them at will.

If silence is meant to suggest spirituality and transcendence in this poem, clearly Keats assumes that spirituality and transcendence are wholly masculine. The silence that is described in such compelling and beautiful language is the silence of the Other, and it is a sign of the denial of power; like the urn itself, it is interpreted as the speaker sees fit. One way the poem deflects attention from this fact is by alluding to its own aesthetic medium and stating that the power of language possessed by the poet is in fact not real power. When the poet asserts that the urn's stillness and "quietness" actually "speak" a purer language than poetry ("Sylvan historian, who canst thus express / A flowery tale more sweetly than our rhyme," 3–4)—a self-effacing statement of reverence that, in terms of Ruether's theory, must be seen as sublimation—he suggests that a major focus in the *Urn* is on the difference between visual and verbal art forms, and that the medium of sculpture is superior to that of poetry because it is quieter and hence purer. This effectively draws attention to aesthetic and, by extension, to spiritual matters, eliding not only the gender issues involved in these distinctions but also the fact that it is masculine poetic language that is able to claim its own inferiority, a claim that is also a subtle and magnificent display of power. The emphasis on voice and silence articulates once again the conflicts in the poem between the passive feminine and the active masculine, pointing to a hierarchy of values that, even as it *claims* superiority for the silent, feminine urn, *reveals* superiority for the masculine poetic voice.

Another way of considering the role of silence in the poem is to recognize that the suppression of the feminine is also a suppression (or at least a limiting) of knowledge of historical process. To put it crudely and reductively, history is a very noisy, human affair, and the poetic act in this case sets about to contain and silence it, to "freeze" it into a "flowery tale," forgetting not only that even in Arcady death figures prominently *(et in Arcadia ego)* but also that both death and life are historically and socially mediated. In this view, the determinant power of patriarchy transforms art itself into a handmaiden of tyranny. The poet does not want to *hear* the death cries of history inscribed everywhere on the urn, as well as contained within it, but prefers instead to celebrate those "unheard" melodies—idealizations of human experience— that allow the illusion of harmony, an illusion that betrays the fact of oppression. To silence the Other, and to celebrate this silence as spiritually and poetically inspirational, limits severely our knowledge of history.

The politics of silence that I am describing can be seen clearly in the opening two lines, which establish the patriarchal voice controlling the remainder of the poem. By portraying the urn first as the "unravish'd bride of quietness" and as the "foster-child of silence and slow time"—that is, in terms of the institutions of marriage and the family—and by identifying the feminine position with respect to these entirely in terms of silence, these lines securely position the urn as an object of masculine desire. More important, however, is the visible manipulation of the images, which suggests the poetic refusal to allow the urn its historical status within a network of market—and gender—relations. Especially in line 2 silence is not necessarily natural; in fact, it has been fostered onto the urn. Again like the silent Philomela in the nightingale myth, the urn seems to be "still unravished" because it is inextricably bound to quietness and silence, controlled and defined by these in the "slow time" of historical process, which has made wives and daughters into so much property to be tended and shaped by masculine desire. Or, to put the matter somewhat differently, Keats's description of the urn as a "Sylvan historian" may be a lament for a preindustrial world of agrarian bliss, but even in such an imagined world the patriarchal negation of the feminine remains intact.

4

I want now to consider briefly the role of desire in the *Urn* in an attempt to show that this is not an innocent category, even when it is understood as a desire for beauty. In her reading of the poem, Rajan argues that "Keats seeks in the urn a closed, Apollonian form. . . . Certain elements in the initial description of the urn appear to correspond to this desire."[26] While this certainly describes Keats's own self-representation of the situation, it is incomplete in historical terms because it assumes that this desire is the product of Keats's own "refusal to consent to incompleteness" (136); it individualizes and subjectivizes the term and in so doing elides the context within which it arises. In a very real sense, the desire upon which the poetic vision is built is both a product and a reflection of unsatisfactory and repressive social relations: the expression of desire is also a sign of the denial of desire. This does not contradict—and in fact confirms—the argument above about the masculine oppression of the feminine, for that oppression makes social and therefore human wholeness impossible, and thus the desire for completeness of being intensifies in proportion as oppression intensifies.

The point is that poetic desire is neither transcendental nor purely subjective but social and historical, firmly caught up in the relations that are articulated everywhere in the poem. This desire is a signature of and a contribution to human inequality, for in its radically individualistic cast it assumes that a superior domain of value will be gained not by changing the world but by transcending it. In this view, poetic desire is, to borrow Lukác's phrase, a "negation of history,"[27] or what Christopher Caudwell calls, in describing Keats's poetry, "a flight *from* reality."[28] This is not to question the *sincerity* of Keats's desire; rather, it is simply to insist on its historicity. A comment by G. V. Plekhanov, though not about Keats, states explicitly the position I wish to advance: "The ideal of beauty prevailing at any time in any society or class of society is rooted partly in the biological conditions of mankind's development—which, incidentally, also produce distinctive racial features—and partly in the historical conditions in which the given society or class arose and exists. It therefore always has a very rich content that is not absolute, not unconditional, but quite specific. He who worships 'pure beauty' does not thereby become independent of the biological and historical social conditions which determine his esthetic taste; he only more or less consciously closes his eyes to these conditions."[29] I do not think that Keats is consciously ignoring the material conditions that underlie his poetic practice; I certainly do not believe that he is engaged in malicious deception; but I do think that his poem participates in a system of social values that structurally excludes the feminine from history, just as it removes collective intervention from the realm of possibility.

5

A final set of remarks about historical developments at the conjunctural level should be made because they both elucidate the anxiety in the *Urn* and provide an important context for understanding the patriarchal assumptions in the poem. In March 1817, Keats wrote two sonnets about the Phidian Marbles that Lord Elgin had brought to England, and it is clear that from the beginning he shared the enthusiasm for and admiration of the Marbles expressed by many of his friends. As Clarence DeWitt Thorpe says in an editorial note to the two sonnets written to Haydon on the occasion of seeing the marbles, "After a long and bitter controversy Haydon had convinced the sceptics that the Elgin Marbles were genuine works of the Phidian school, and had been largely instrumental in their purchase by the government (though at a price which netted Lord Elgin £16,000 less than the £51,000 they had cost him). The sonnets show Keats's state of mind after seeing these new wonders: he is stunned, dizzy with swirling ideas, and unable to bring his crowding impressions into order. Later he is to achieve perfect expression of his experience with Greek art in the *Ode on a Grecian Urn*."[30] Haydon, who introduced Keats to the Marbles, was similarly impressed, noting that "In the Elgin Marbles, the Composition, that is the arrangement of objects, to express the end in view as a whole, is perfect. The science of the parts that compose these objecs individually [is] profound, and the execution of these parts to express the conceived Idea, of the end of the object, particularly as referring to the said whole [is] easy, vigorous, & powerful. The whole, the result of genius in the conception, arrangement, & industry & perseverance of execution."[31] Hazlitt too said of the Marbles that "their forms are ideal, spiritual. Their beauty is power. By their beauty they are raised above the frailties of pain or passion."[32]

The actual beauty of the Marbles notwithstanding, there was a great deal of controversy in Keats's day about their presence in England, a controversy in which Keats did not participate, but about which he must have known, especially since Haydon was an avid supporter of Lord Elgin (see, for instance, Haydon's *Diary* 2:12–13). Byron was especially bitter in his condemnation of Elgin's raids on Greek culture and art, attacking the antiquarian both in the second canto of *Childe Harold* and in *The Curse of Minerva*. In a letter of 1811, also, Byron noted to Hobhouse that "Lord Elgin has been teazing to see me these last four days, I wrote to him at his request all I knew about his robberies, & at last have written to say that as it is my intention to publish (in Childe Harold) on that topic, I thought proper since he insisted on seeing me to give him notice, that he might not have an opportunity of accusing me of double dealing afterwards."[33]

This controversy is important because it points explicitly to the political context within which Keats wrote poetically about questions of beauty and truth. The ravaging of Greece for artifacts of great beauty to be sold to the British government, which in turn put the artifacts on display as a sign of British culture and power, and the suppression of the political realities of these acts are material signs of the system of values controlling Keats's world. Not to acknowledge the absolute and determining significance of England's possession of the Marbles is to suppress this context and thus to distort and redefine aesthetic concerns presented in the *Urn*, diverting attention from the specific historical acts of violence and political power of which the feminization of the Other is a part.

In this view, the exercise of imperialist power (i.e., Elgin's exploits in Greece, as well as England's involvement in India and the New World) and the debasement of women are equally forms of political oppression, inextricably entwined within a single social situation that helps to explain the anxiety, even neurosis, in the *Urn*. That Keats chose to present as self-evident the power and beauty of the Marbles and to feminize the object of his poetic musings suggests that the poem does more than display textual "ambiguity" arising from the relation of poem to urn,[34] or the tension between art and reality[35]; it displays acute historical anxiety arising from actual human struggles and atrocities that it has repressed and forgotten, but that will not remain completely submerged.[36] What Phyllis Chessler says against Freud's theory of hysterical amnesia provides an important gloss on the historical amnesia that I believe is present in the *Urn*:

> The headaches, fatigues, chronic depression, frigidity, paranoia, and overwhelming sense of inferiority that Freud recorded so accurately about his many female patients was never *interpreted* in any remotely accurate terms. Female 'symptoms' were certainly not viewed by Freud as the indirect communications characteristic of slave psychologies. Instead, such symptoms were viewed as 'hysterical' and neurotic productions, as underhanded domestic tyrannies manufactured by spiteful, self-pitying, and generally unpleasant women whose *inability to be happy as women* stems from unresolved penis envy, unresolved Electra (or female Oedipal) complexes, or from general, intractable, and mysterious female stubbornness.[37]

Accepting Freud's general *description* of neurosis in women, Chesslar takes strong issue with his *interpretation* of it. Where Freud tended to see it in purely individual and private terms, Chessler recognizes it as a product of social relations, that is, as a product of the specific difficulties women have long experienced at the hands of patriarchy. The anxieties present in the *Urn* are vulnerable to exactly this explanation. To historicize Keats's portrayal of the feminine is to expose the political underpinnings of his seemingly transhistorical vision, which is ostensibly inspired only by sculptural beauty.

To approach the poem from this direction—that is, from the assumption that it is historically implicated and that its vision of beauty and truth is fundamentally patriarchal—is to commit oneself to critically questioning Keats's poetic articulation of value, belief, and social relations. It is not a matter of attempting to let the poem speak for itself; it does speak *for* itself, unrelentingly, in strong patriarchal language. Rather it is a matter of engaging in historical critical excavation to expose the bones of the dead and the blood of the beaten that are essential to this poetic expression, in the hope that just as the poem appropriates the urn for patriarchal purposes the poem itself can be appropriated for purposes of exposing human atrocity. To subject the *Urn* to the fires of a materialist feminist critique is not to say that it should be dismissed as just another display of patriarchal one-sidedness—simply to dismiss articulations of patriarchy without investigation and critique is to assure its ongoing power—but rather to argue that its poetic expression is also a historical expression and, thus, of absolute importance to understanding a specifically patriarchal form of social existence. It is to see that Keats's attempt to develop an alternative model of hope outside the military aggression, ideological conflict, and economic hardship of his own day entailed significant elements of social domination: the valorization of the agrarian past in the *Urn* is at the same time the valorization of patriarchal values that prevailed in Keats's world. That he was never able to escape these values entirely is seen by even the briefest glance at his other poems, ranging from *Endymion*, which envisions the feminine as the solution to masculine alienation, to *Lamia*, which presents the feminine in serpentine form capable of destroying a well-meaning and innocent masculine ego. Given this fact, what is needed is a full-scale feminist reevaluation of Keats's goddesses and his portrayal of gender relations, one capable of finding a productive and positive way of using his work to excavate and articulate the way those relations function under capitalism.

In historicizing and politicizing the *Ode on a Grecian Urn*, I have not sought to denigrate the considerable beauty and achievement of Keats's poetry, his ambition "of doing the world some good," or his individual integrity; to the contrary, I believe that his struggles and contributions must be honored by all who come after him. Rather, my purpose has been to argue that Keats's poetry is vitally important in our history and still has a great deal to teach us, even if it may not teach us exactly what Keats had in mind, because it provides glimpses of the power relations with which people must struggle, and expressions of hope that endure through history and that can and should be recognized as a hope for a better world. The importance of his work is not that it allows us to see beyond history, but that it provides us with a means of resisting historical amnesia.

Notes

1. All quotations from Keats's letters are taken from Hyder Edward Rollins, ed., *The Letters of John Keats, 1814–1821* (Cambridge: Harvard University Press, 1958), and are cited in the text as *LJK*. All quotations from the poetry are taken from Jack Stillinger, ed., *The Poems of John Keats* (Cambridge: Belknap Press of Harvard University Press, 1978), and line numbers are cited in the text. References to Hyder Edward Rollins, ed., *The Keats Circle* (Cambridge: Harvard University Press, 1965) appear in the text as *KC*.

2. Note also his comment in July 1819 to Reynolds that "I have of late been moulting: not for

fresh feathers and wings: they are gone, and in their stead I hope to have a pair of patient sublunary legs" (*LJK* 2:128).

3. Clarence DeWitt Thorpe, "Keats's Interest in World Affairs," *PMLA* 46 (1931):1228–45; June Koch, "Politics in Keats's Poetry," *Journal of English and Germanic Philology* 70 (1972): 491–501. See also J. Philip Eggers's interesting essay "Memory in Mankind: Keats's Historical Imagination," *PMLA* 86 (1971): 990–98. Although Eggers does not draw political conclusions, he establishes clearly the importance of historical subjects and processes to Keats's poetic imagination.

4. In addition to Earl Wasserman's *The Finer Tone: Keats's Major Poems* (1953; reprint, Baltimore: Johns Hopkins University Press, 1967), see Ronald A. Sharp's *Keats, Skepticism, and the Religion of Beauty* (Athens: University of Georgia Press, 1979).

5. Tilottama Rajan, *Dark Interpreter: The Discourse of Romanticism* (Ithaca and London: Cornell University Press, 1980), 133–35.

6. That is, I am concerned with the role patriarchal morality plays in the imaginative, or poetic, reconciliation of real social contradiction. I leave unexamined the question of *why* it is women who are oppressed in Keats's vision, seeking rather to document the *fact* of oppression. A thorough study of the objective conditions of women in the romantic period would be necessary to elaborate the precise material grounds of Keats's portrayal of women. Two essays on the *Urn* have been particularly influential on my thinking about this topic, though their emphasis is quite different from my own: Philip Fisher, "A Museum with One Work Inside: Keats and the Finality of Art," *Keats-Shelley Journal* 33 (1984): 85–102, and Stuart Peterfreund, "The Truth about 'Beauty' and 'Truth': Keats's 'Ode on a Grecian Urn,' Milton, Shakespeare, and the Uses of Paradox," *Keats-Shelley Journal* 35 (1986): 62–82—Fisher's essay particularly in its emphasis on the past and on the way history produces art on "an emergency basis" (87), and Peterfreund's in its emphasis on Keats's handling of the feminine.

7. I am aware that "patriarchy" is a controversial and perhaps unsatisfactory term for the sort of analysis I am offering in that it runs the risk of being established as a universal rather than a historical category. I use it simply as shorthand for the stratification along gender lines that can be found in the *Urn*. For a discussion of the debates surrounding this term, see Annette Kuhn and AnnMarie Wolpe, eds., *Feminism and Materialism: Women and Modes of Production* (London: Routledge and Kegan Paul, 1978), 11–67; Zillah R. Eisenstein, *The Radical Future of Liberal Feminism* (Boston: Northeastern University Press, 1986), 14–26; and Ellen Carol DuBuois et al., *Feminist Scholarship: Kindling in the Groves of Academe* (Urbana and Chicago: University of Illinois Press, 1985), 145–46.

8. The relevant portion of the letter reads as follows: "The more we know the more inadequacy we discover in the world to satisfy us. . . . This same inadequacy is discovered (forgive me little George you know I don't mean to put you in the mess) in Women with few exceptions—the Dress Maker, the blue Stocking and the most charming sentimentalist differ but in a Slight degree, and are equally smokeable—But I'll go no further—I may be speaking sacriligiously—and on my word I have thought so little that I have not one opinion upon any thing except in matters of taste—I never can feel certain of any truth but from a clear perception of its Beauty" (*LJK* 2:18–19).

9. I am aware that this description of Moneta in the *Fall* conflicts with most if not all considerations of this goddess. Building on K. K. Ruthven's excellent essay, "Keats and *Dea Moneta*," *Studies in Romanticism* 15 (1976):445–59, which discusses Moneta as the goddess of money, I have in a forthcoming book on Keats attempted to show her as the matriarch of commodity culture, to whose power all human activity—including the making of poetry—is subjected. While there are many positive descriptions in the poem of Moneta, she is also, like so many of Keats's other female characters, made to carry a heavy load of negative characteristics and to serve a secondary or subordinate role to the masculine perspective.

10. Michele Barrett, *Women's Oppression Today: Problems in Marxist Feminist Analysis* (London: Verso, 1980), 83. Barrett is here striking a blow against those French feminists who present the body as the site of difference, and who argue that women must assert the liberating power of this difference. As Ann Rosalind Jones succinctly poses the key question that feminism must answer: "Does female sexuality exist prior to or in spite of social experience?" See "Writing the Body: Toward an Understanding of *l'écriture Feminine*." In Judith Newton and Deborah Rosenfelt, eds., *Feminist Criticism and Social Change: Sex, Class and Race in Literature and*

Culture (New York and London: Methuen, 1985), 91. Barrett's position, and the position I am attempting to argue in this essay, is that it does not. To use the catch phrase of materialist feminism: gender is not born but produced.

11. Rosemary Radford Ruether, *New Woman New Earth: Sexist Ideologies and Human Liberation* (New York: The Seabury Press, 1975), 5.

12. Ibid., 7. It should be noted that Ruether's account refuses to accept the notion of a primitive matriarchal culture (which many feminists take as the necessary starting point in investigating patriarchal culture), for, in her view, such a notion uses myth as the basis for analysis, and thus is ahistorical (5–6). She begins, rather, with a consideration of a historically definable "village culture" (6) and traces the historical developments from this sociocultural arrangement to later ones.

13. Ibid., 8.

14. Ibid., 10.

15. Ibid., 195.

16. Ibid., 14.

17. Ibid., 19.

18. Ibid., 19–23.

19. Ibid., 195–96.

20. It is worth noting the definitions of this term included in the *OED*, if only to provide a defense against those critics who would see the poem in purely innocent terms as a depiction of pastoral bliss. The first definition given by the *OED* is "Hostile, angry, spiteful"; the second is "Repulsive, unpleasant, hateful"; the third is "Ugly"; the fourth is "Averse, disinclined, reluctant, unwilling." Only the fourth definition is listed as being current through the nineteenth century, but the others were prominent well into the Renaissance, the literature of which Keats knew virtually by heart.

21. See, for instance Jack Stillinger's comments in *"The Hoodwinking of Madeline" and Other Essays on Keats's Poems* (Chicago: University of Illinois Press, 1971), 108.

22. Tellingly, however, even as these lines are spoken—either by the urn or by the poet—limitations are placed upon knowledge ("that is all ye *need* to know"), once again discouraging too close a scrutiny of the conflicts and struggles that purchase the wisdom in these concluding lines. The urn is unravished, it represents purity, but it is also limiting.

With respect to the punctuation of these final lines, the textual difficulties that for years have occupied critics are not thematic difficulties within the frame of reference that I am trying to establish. That is, whether it is the urn or the poet who speaks these lines, the value system is masculine, falling fully within the parameters of patriarchal belief. Under patriarchy, women no less than men express masculine values, just as in a bourgeois culture both the middle and working classes express the values of the ruling elite. Note, on this topic, Marx's famous comment that "the ruling ideas of every age are the ideas of the ruling class." For an excellent discussion of these final lines of the poem, see Stillinger's essay in *Hoodwinking*, 167–73.

23. Simone de Beauvoir, *The Second Sex*, trans. and ed., H. M. Parshley (1952; reprint, New York: Vintage, 1974), xxxiii–xxxiv.

24. Note, for instance, S. R. Swaminathan's comment that the reference to the "ditties of no tone" in the poem "is obviously a finer music heard only by the soul." *The Still Image in Keats's Poetry* (Salzburg, Austria: Institut Für Anglistik und Amerikanistik, Universität Salzburg, 1981), 329.

25. I do not intend here to offer a feminist critique of Keats's *Nightingale* poem, but I do mean to suggest that the gender issue is vital in this poem as well, as the myth of Procne, Philomela, and Tereus suggests.

26. Rajan, *Dark Interpreter*, 133.

27. Lukács is speaking of Heidegger, but the phrase applies equally to Keats. See *Realism in Our Time: Literature and the Class Struggle* (1964; reprint, New York: Harper and Row, 1971), 21.

28. Christopher Caudwell, *Illusion and Reality: A Study of the Sources of Poetry* (1937; reprint, New York: International Publishers, 1973), 108.

29. G. V. Plekhanov, *Art and Social Life* (1912; reprint, Moscow: Progress Publishers, 1977), 30.

30. Clarence DeWitt Thorpe, ed., *John Keats: Complete Poems and Selected Letters* (New York: Odyssey Press, Inc., 1935), 78.

31. Willard B. Pope, ed., *The Diary of Benjamin Robert Haydon* (Cambridge: Harvard University Press, 1960), 1:434–35.

32. P. P. Howe, ed., *The Complete Works of William Hazlitt* (London and Toronto: J. M. Dent and Sons, Ltd., 1930–34), 4:79.

33. Leslie A. Marchand, ed., *Byron's Letters and Journals* (Cambridge: Belknap Press of Harvard University Press, 1973–82), 2:65–66. Further references to this edition are cited in the text as *BLJ*. Marchand states in a note to this letter that "Hobhouse took a more favourable view of Elgin's work than did Byron, contending that preservation of the Greek marbles in London would benefit 'an infinitely greater number of rising architects and sculptors.' . . . Byron's reply to this in his first letter on Bowles was: 'I opposed, and will ever oppose, the robbery of ruins from Athens, to instruct the English in sculpture (who are as capable of sculpture as the Egyptians are of skating)' " (66).

34. David Perkins, *The Quest for Permanence: The Symbolism of Wordsworth, Shelley, and Keats* (Cambridge: Harvard University Press, 1959), 238–39.

35. Rajan, *Dark Interpreter*, 133–36.

36. While I have not been very specific about these actual human struggles and atrocities, they are not difficult to find. The most cursory glance at the *Examiner* during 1817–19 on the fear of national bankruptcy, or at the writings of Cobbett on the plight of the working people, illustrate these matters vividly. Note too the uncertainty and general despair pervading Europe and England after the defeat of Napoleon, exemplified clearly in Byron's remark that "Every hope of a republic is over, and we must go on under the old system. But I am sick at heart of politics and slaughters; and the luck which Providence is pleased to lavish on Lord [Castlereagh] is only a proof of the little value the gods set upon prosperity" (*BLJ* 4:302).

37. Phyllis Chessler, *Women and Madness* (New York: Avon Books, 1972), 79.

The Political Prometheus

Stuart Curran

A long time back, or so it seems, I spent the free spaces of a half-dozen years in quixotic pursuit of the multiple avatars of Prometheus among the students of comparative myth, religion, and anthropology in the late eighteenth and early nineteenth centuries. Without question, the prominence of Prometheus among the numerous theorists or apologists or disputants in some cause or other went beyond his relative importance in classical mythology and served in some large manner to explain the appeal of the figure throughout the romantic period, and particularly within the British tradition of Shelley and Byron. And yet, paradoxically, what I learned from this investigation was that Prometheus, for all intents and purposes, might as well have been Proteus. The language Newman Ivey White once used to subtitle an essay on Shelley's lyrical drama—"or Every Man His Own Allegorist"—is essentially characteristic of the titan of syncretic mythology: the brunt of this massive scholarship is that Prometheus always stands for something else—character, principle, idea—never for himself.[1]

By the time, a few years later, I began to share the confidence of Thales in Part 2 of *Faust* that I could catch this Proteus as well as anyone, fortunately I was finishing my chapter on representations of Prometheus among syncretic mythographers and, in recognition of having just escaped becoming what I beheld, borrowed an ironic chapter title from Casaubon's unfinished magnum opus in *Middlemarch*, "The Key to All Mythologies."[2] Without belaboring the false etymologies, the slipshod and selective learning, and the hidden but still fervent ideological tendentiousness that contributed to a reduction of all myths into one another, we can leave it to George Stanley Faber (one of the lucky divines to receive a copy of "The Necessity of Atheism," on the strength of his having preached rather often to the adolescent edification of Shelley's co-conspirator, Thomas Jefferson Hogg, in the family's parish church at Norton), Faber, who came at the very end of the prescientific study of syncretic mythology, to represent its practices in their full luxuriance of offhand invention:

> Suffice it to say . . . that, according to the orphic poet, Protogonus or the
> first-born, Planes, Priapus, Titan, Helius or the Sun, Jupiter, Pan, Her-

ades, Cronus, Prometheus, Bacchus, Apollo, Pean, Adonis, and Cupid, are all one divinity: according to Sophocles, Titan or the Sun is the same as that Prometheus, whom the Orphic poet declares to be Cronus.

In sum, "both Prometheus, Cronus, and the Orphic Jupiter, are all most certainly the great-father; that is to say, Adam reappearing in the character of Noah."[3] Assuredly, the various legends surrounding Prometheus—as creator, prophet, educator, benefactor, and self-sacrificing savior—implicate major religious themes spanning time and cultures, and thus it is probably inevitable that the titan should be drawn into a syncretic harmony with Judeo-Christian scriptures.

Yet in the timeless abstraction of this mythic distillation, where names are construed as representing attributes of a structural paradigm of human thought (even if one that at this time was considered a solemn truth of revelation lost through the dispersal of Noah's family), there is discernible a fundamentally conservative impulse. The protean reformations in Faber's catalog, like all typological constructions, simply lend variety to an inherent sameness; they are roles for a single actor who always ends up playing himself. All religions are one, which in Faber's case speaks with the voice of angels (that is to say, the Book of Common Prayer) and sings to the tune of the Anglican hymnal. Although such a formulation is intrinsically laughable, the efforts of the syncretic mythographers, at least as they involve the figure of Prometheus, do reinforce major attributes of the literary portrait we can extract from Shelley's *Prometheus Unbound*, in, for instance, their acknowledging a oneness of human experience and desire, but even, more narrowly, in Prometheus' representation (through his links with Noah and thus, in the etymological cognate insisted upon by Jacob Bryant and all who followed him, with Nous) as the One Mind.[4] Yet, what is absent from such formulations is arguably more important as a basis for understanding the romantic Prometheus: the resolute humanism of Goethe's conception or the defiant and universal refusal of Byron's or the anarchist liberation inscribed in Shelley's. Looking back at this investigation from the vantage point of many years, I see the clear paradox that escaped me in its fascinating midst, which is that, however the syncretic mythographers contributed to a climate of mythmaking and even accentuated the character of Prometheus as an exemplary figure within it, at least in England their instincts were directly opposed to those of Byron and Shelly, who saw not an august patriarch but a spokesman for the oppressed, not an agent in God's design for the earth but a revolutionary denier of all divine right to it. The romantic Prometheus is a fundamentally political icon. And as the example of Goethe a generation earlier indicates, the Younger Romantics in England did not fabricate it out of air.

Syncretic mythology may have provided this culture an atmosphere of remythologizing, a renewed awareness of the values and uses of allegory, and certainly an expanded gazetteer of place names with mystified associations and volumes overflowing with curious divinities, but the political context for the figure of Prometheus had to come from elsewhere. Although I will endeavor here to indicate some of the forms it took, forms well known in their time and with distinct political resonance, and to suggest in all but one case the presence of associations soon to be adopted as well in Shelley's *Prometheus Unbound,* I do not want my effort here construed as a mere identification of direct sources. To narrow one's sights to a question of an indisputable source is to reduce to a mechanical relation what is a far subtler operation, for it ignores why the relation should exist in the first place, what gives the purported source its residual power, what in the culture pronounces it worthy of being appropriated. It also reduces to a question of personal authorial choice a decision that is an aspect of a larger cultural determination, what Hans Robert Jauss has termed the "horizon of expectations" within which any author first lives and then, secondarily writes.[5] But on the other hand, I am confident in using *Prometheus Unbound* as my reference point for political contexts independently raised by other writers of the romantic period, including Byron, since its form is by nature syncretic and it aspires to be inclusive in its symbolic applications. Also, and perhaps most important, Shelley was raised in a household professionally committed to political causes of a liberal bent and attuned, whatever Sir Timothy's own unadventurous tastes, to the oratorical and propagandistic application of classical authority to those causes. *Prometheus Unbound* is unrivaled in conceiving its subject as a reservoir into which pour numerous cultural tributaries, and they converge from low as well as high. Although it also bears the distinctive ideological imprint of its author, one that runs directly counter to Byron's conception of Prometheus, Shelley's approach was more systematic than Byron's, more scrupulous in its scholarship and use of authorities, even (as the activities of his Marlow circle would indicate) more dependent on the broad knowledge and at times quirky conceptions of his friends.[6]

1

The most obvious place to locate the inherent political dimensions of the figure of Prometheus is in its major classical embodiment, the *Prometheus Bound* of Aeschylus. Mythographers could placidly assimilate Prometheus to the Orphic Jupiter, constituting some super-divinity who merged the generations of titan and god, but in Aeschylus there remains only an implacable and primary opposition. Moreover, not even those accustomed to a scholarship of apologetics could easily dismiss the dual focus on unmerited pain and victimization summed up in Prometheus' ringing last cry: "See how unjustly I suffer." More precisely, the necessity of having to beg the questions attributable to traditional apologetics made the very exercise seem specious. In the romantic period there is no repetition of Thomas Morrell's claim, in the introduction to his 1773 translation, that "many extraordinary passages will occur to the Christian reader, if at all acquainted with the Scriptures; relating to the destruction and renovation of mankind, [and] the fall of Lucifer and his angels."[7] If silence on that ground may be presumed as a recognition that it little served the cause of theology to present Aeschylus's Jupiter as a gentile redaction of Jehovah, there is, one supposes, ample reason for silence to prevail on another count as well. Forty years later, it would have been imprudent for any author in the British Isles to interpret Aeschylus' purposes with the candid language represented by Charlotte Lennox in 1759: "It is not impossible but that the subject, which, to use Dacier's expression, appears monstrous to us, is an allegory upon kings, and perhaps upon Xerxes or Darius, which must necessarily be extremely pleasing to a republic."[8] Yet, leaving questions of prudence to the side, it is equally hard to imagine that this conception of the tragedy's political implications was not almost universally shared in the romantic period.

One reason it is so is that Aeschylus for the first time became widely available to a British readership. Fielding's endearing portrait of Abraham Adams forever lost in the intricacies of his Aeschylus depends for part of its effect on a general ignorance of Greek drama among all but the most highly educated of his readers. Lennox's translation of Brumoy nearly two decades after *Joseph Andrews* made available the plots of the seven surviving tragedies, but Morrell's *Prometheus in Chains* of 1773 is actually the first appearance of an Aeschylus drama in English. He was followed by Richard Potter, who in 1777 presented the whole of the corpus in prose. In the four decades intervening before Shelley decided to supply the lost final play of the trilogy, the reputation of Aeschylus shifted diametrically: within a generation the notoriously difficult and obscure primitive had become the crowning glory of the Athenian stage. As is indicated by its being the first of the plays to be translated, *Prometheus Bound* held a privileged position. In dedicating his translation to David Garrick, Morrell saw it as particularly fitting that he inscribe to "Indisputably the *First* Actor in this (perhaps in any) Age, the Translation of this the *First* Play Extant." Potter neatly conjoins tragedian and tragic hero in an encomium typical of the veneration of the later eighteenth century: "like his own Prometheus, [Aeschylus] not only gave [tragedy] being and form, but animated it with the brightest ray of ethereal fire; leaving posterity to admire the force of his genius, and to doubt whether he was ever excelled, or even equalled, till our Shakespeare arose blessed with an happier invention and more extensive powers."[9] On such a lofty pinnacle had Aeschylus been raised that between 1795 and 1825, as Christian Kreutz notes, there were seven collected editions of his surviving works made available in England, as well as fourteen editions of individual dramas.[10]

But such numbers scarcely indicate the dimensions or the import of this reconception of Aeschylus. It peaked at the end of the first decade of the nineteenth century, about the time the adolescent Shelley finished his tutelage at Eton College and transferred to University College, Oxford, where he immediately met Hogg, more moonstruck with Greek classics than with Humean skepticism.[11] In 1809 and 1810 Great Britain was inundated by Aeschylus, with the unannotated text of C. G. Schütz being printed in Oxford both years, the first half of Samuel Butler's effort to revivify the antiquated seventeenth-century text of Thomas Stanley being issued from Cambridge in 1809, reprints of the Potter translation in both 1808 and 1809, and Charles J. Blomfield's attempt to establish a new text of *Prometheus Bound*, aided by the notes of his mentor Richard Porson who had died in 1808, being published at Cambridge in 1810. Before Blomfield's edition appeared, it was used by a close associate, Peter Elmsley, to savage Butler's recension of a useless text in two numbers of the *Edinburgh Review*, which in turn prompted a lengthy defense by Butler, *A Letter to the Rev. C. J. Blomfield . . . containing Remarks on the Edinburgh Review of the Cambridge Aeschylus*, a pamphlet of seventy-eight blustering pages. However much this duel of pedants may have reduced to what the *Gentleman's Magazine* characterized as a "comédie larmoyante," the hapless Reverend Butler was no match for Porson's successor in British classical scholarship.[12] Blomfield's emergence on the scene was heralded with an enthusiasm hard to imagine today. His edition of *Prometheus Bound*, for instance, was a major subject of the newly formed *Classical Journal*, where it was meticulously reviewed in five issues over three years. Some indication of its felt importance can be gleaned from the reviewer's remark that "Mr. B. has enjoyed an honor, we believe unprecedented in the annals of English editors of Greek authors, of finding such a demand for his publication, as to warrant a re-impression in the course of twelve months."[13]

Ancient textual debates, with both sides stoutly defending spurious principles, are, of course, not the point here. What matters is that a work already privileged in the canon of Aeschylus and, indeed, of world drama as first even among equals should, through endeavors to establish a more secure text, attain such an unusual intensity of popular interest. In such an atmosphere it seems not only natural, but almost inevitable, that in 1810, when the newly matriculated Shelley reported to his tutor at University College, Oxford, the first work recommended for his reading was *Prometheus Vinctus*.[14] There were other, and to our purposes perhaps more significant, representations of Prometheus in these same years, ones in which the political implications of the figure are directly emphasized. In contrast to these, to which we now turn, the scholarly editions no less than the commentary on them avoid introducing any vulgar topicality upon those apparently sempiternal concerns of textual emendation, indeed, appear to take refuge from contemporary realities of tyranny and suffering in the problematic syntax of their representation. Still, however resolutely scholarly authorities might look the other way, the unparalleled interest in *Prometheus Bound* cannot help but signal a relation to those geopolitical realities, whether in the test of European systems being waged in the Napoleonic Wars or as a reflection of a dogged national perseverance through long years of painful adversity. The recommendation of Shelley's tutor, "a little man [with a] small voice," is in this sense emblematic of the process of cultural transference, as his "almost inaudible whisper" in later years became, in Shelley's voice, "to unawakened earth / The trumpet of a prophecy."[15]

2

It is an observation of professor Schütz, that the objects which Æschylus appears to have had in view when he wrote his patriotick tragedy of Prometheus, were to confirm the Athenians in the ardent love of that liberty which they so enviably enjoyed, and to inspire them with an utter detestation of despotism, and a determined resistance to oppression. In the voluptuous monarchy of Persia the poet saw enough to disgust him with tyranny; and the contrast exhibited between the miseries attendant upon such a form of government, and the happiness arising from Athenian freedom, was a cause sufficiently powerful to raise to an exertion almost more than human the genius of the Shakespeare of Greece. Such too is the object of the author of the present work.

These might be thought unexceptionable sentiments with which to begin a preface, except that the title of the work—*Washington, or Liberty Restored*—shifts the context sharply from the pious verities of the schoolroom to an implicit analogy between England and the decadent despotism of ancient Persia and between George Washington and the unflagging political commitment of Prometheus.[16] The analogy between Washington and Prometheus is openly broached before the end of the first book of Thomas Northmore's ten-book epic:

> Not jealousy, nor envy, nor defeat,
> Nor rancorous malice, nor unjust abuse,
> Not traitorous friendship, nor internal foes,
> Not misery itself in every shape,
> Famine, disease, and pestilence, and feuds,
> Can shake his soul's fix'd purpose; e'en his evils
> Serve but to raise him in the people's love,

> And for their liberties, Prometheus-like,
> He'd stand unmov'd amid the wreck of worlds.
>
> (1.264–72)

Northmore claimed that the enthusiasm of his celebration of Washington was "if not caused, yet aggravated by the proclaimed increase of the influence of the crown, and the gigantick strides of modern corruption" (iv). It is, however, not an easy task to trace such themes through his epic, partly because he would have faced a legal risk in pursuing them openly and therefore concentrates on Washington's virtues rather than Britain's vices, partly too because he drives his epic machinery with reckless abandon. The main agent in denying independence to the Americans, it appears, is not the British army but Satan, who is discovered at one point squatting by the ear of Cornwallis and giving him what turned out to be very bad advice. The attention Northmore lavishes on his Satanic crew is worthy of Milton in a different (and obviously better) epic poem, and it results in something of a confusion of ideological purposes. Almost two hundred lines in the eighth book, for instance, are devoted to a set piece, following Homer, describing Satan's shield. The conflict between Jupiter and Prometheus, "the benefactor of mankind" (8.223), is recalled at length, without, however, discriminating between them (as Shelley feels called upon to do in the preface to his lyrical drama) in motivation or morality.[17] Yet, if Northmore is less refined in his distinctions than Shelley will be a decade later, he does share, and uniquely as far as I can see in the history of mythography, an essential conjunction with Shelley. The description of Satan's shield begins thus:

> On its huge boss, a vast and solid rock,
> Sat dreaded Demogorgon; and around
> Pursuit and Flight, and Fear, and Uproar wild,
> And dire Confusion, mix'd with fiends from hell,
> Whose name the Muse disdains to bring to light.
>
> (8.169–73)

At the center of Shelley's lyrical drama, in line count no less than conception, is the same raw and revolutionary power.

There is, of course, no record of Shelley's ever having read Northmore's epic, and certainly it is an unlikely item to have been lying about Maria Gisborne's house in Livorno, or even the Palazzo Mocenigo Byron rented in Venice. And it goes without saying that it is not the kind of book that Sir Timothy would have recommended to his head-strong son. But on the other hand, it is by no means beyond credibility that such a poem could be encountered by an intellectually ambitious student in his final year at Eton or in his even more radical incarnation a few months later at Oxford. The very excesses of Northmore's gothic machinery would have appealed to this devil-ridden adolescent, and the celebration of Washington would certainly have been congenial to the author of polemical poems like "To the Republicans of North America." A direct connection to the side, Northmore's association of Prometheus with political liberation should be seen as the development of a stereotype, and it is one with attendant linkages of imagery that the mature Shelley would exploit over and over again. The final lines of *Washington, or Liberty Restored*, a parting tribute to the Spirit of Liberty, resonate with the same image patterns, the same association of liberty with Promethean fire, with poetic creation and social love, that permeate poems like "Lines Written among the Euganean Hills" or the "Ode to Liberty":

> Hail! Spirit divine! All hail! nor 'deign to hear
> The voice of gratitude. To thee the Muse
> Owes her best fires; to thee all nature owes
> Her varied blessings; for where thou art not
> Nothing is good, or beautiful, but all
> A dreary wilderness, where vice and sin
> Sport with the human feelings. But no more
> Shall these pollute the earth; thy sacred orb
> Shall far dispel them into outer dark;
> And in their stead shall mirth and love abound
> With virtue ever pure; the vales and hills
> Impregn'd by thee, shall teem with new delights,
> And e'en the depths of ocean laugh with joy.
>
> (10.762–74)

This entire complex, extended and refined, and even more directly centered on the mythical base of Prometheus, appears in the same year and the same form as Northmore's epic. And in the case of Joel Barlow's *Columbiad*, it is hard to believe that Shelley did not silently claim a pronounced debt.[18] Any British reader could be forgiven for missing Northmore's perverse attempt to rub his country's nose epically in its political failings, but Barlow's poem was of a far different order, and it was hard to avoid contact with it. The most elegant book printed in America to this point (1807), its sheets were transferred to London, where *The Columbiad* was published under the imprint of Richard Phillips in 1809 and reviewed with customary condescension by Jeffrey in the *Edinburgh Review*. Its impact is almost immediately discernible in a poem like Samuel Rogers's *Voyage of Columbus*, published in 1810. Given Barlow's extensive contacts with the Aristocratic Whigs in the 1790s and his renewed diplomatic activity as a representative of the United States, it is even conceivable that such a work might have found its way into the library of Field Place. With its visionary projection of a new world order established on libertarian principles, it is unquestionably the kind of poem that would have attracted Shelley.

Barlow's opening invocation to liberty touches the same chords as North-

more's paean and implicitly raises the Promethean paradigm it will later
return to exploit.

> Almighty Freedom! give my venturous song
> The force, the charm that to thy voice belong;
> Tis thine to shape my course, to light my way,
> To nerve my country with the patriot lay,
> To teach all men where all their interest lies,
> How rulers may be just and nations wise:
> Strong in thy strength I bend no suppliant knee,
> Invoke no miracle, no Muse but thee.
>
> (1.23–30)

America, in Barlow's striking conception, is a world waiting to be invested
with myth. The ancient paradigms, with their attendant theological thrust,
do not fit its lineaments:

> Celestials there no sacred senates hold;
> No chain'd Prometheus feasts the vulture there,
> No Cyclops forges thro their summits glare,
> To Phrygian Jove no victim smoke is curl'd,
> Nor ark high landing quits a deluged world.
>
> (1.346–50)

Through the logic of fit analogy Barlow returns to the figure of Prometheus as
bestower of the "holy fire" which is "The sense of liberty" (4.439). As a figure
for the self-educating force of the human intellect, Prometheus is originally
engaged in the accumulation of scientific knowledge (4.443–70). But in the
context of the reformulation of human ends that is America, the role of
Prometheus in human development is itself reconstituted, as Hesper, the
guardian spirit of America, testifies in Columbus's dream of the visionary
future.

> But when he steps on these regenerate shores,
> His mind unfolding far superior powers,
> FREEDOM, his new Prometheus, here shall rise,
> Light her new torch in my refulgent skies,
> Touch with a stronger life his opening soul,
> Of moral systems fix the central goal,
> Her own resplendent essence. Thence expand
> The rays of reason that illume the land;
> Thence equal rigors proceed, and equal laws,
> Thence holy Justice all her reverence draws;
> Truth with untarnish'd beam descending thence,
> Strikes every eye, and quickens every sense,
> Bids bright Instruction spread her ample page,

To drive dark dogmas from the inquiring age,
Ope the true treasures of the earth and skies,
And teach the student where his object lies.
        Sun of the moral world! effulgent source
Of man's best wisdom and his steadiest force,
Soul-searching Freedom! here assume thy stand,
And radiate hence to every distant land.

                                                    (4.471–90)

These Enlightenment couplets have something of a deadening effect on our realizing Barlow's underlying import. He saves one implication for the next book of his epic, where Lafayette and Kosciusko are seen as harbingers of the unavoidable revolution in European states, bearing the flame of freedom "Prometheus-like" (5.675) to France and Poland. But even more directly Barlow is marking the kind of distinction Shelley will later embed in the complementary monologues of Asia in Demogorgon's cave and Prometheus in describing the regenerate cave of the human mind in which he and Asia serve as united impulses, between the gathering of knowledge to serve basic human needs and the moral responsibility for its uses. It is less refined, perhaps, than the memorable formulation of the *Defence of Poetry*, but essentially congruent.

> We want the creative faculty to imagine that which we know; we want the generous impulse to act that which we imagine; we want the poetry of life: our calculations have outrun conception; we have eaten more than we can digest. The cultivation of those sciences which have enlarged the limits of the empire of man over the external world, has, for want of the poetical faculty, proportionally circumscribed those of the internal world; and man, having enslaved the elements, remains himself a slave. (502–3)

Even clearer is the link with the intellectual colonizing of the universe envisioned in the fourth act of Shelley's lyrical drama: "We will take our plan / From the new world of man / And our work shall be called the Promethean" (4.156–58).

The larger significance of Barlow's employment of Prometheus in *The Columbiad* should not be lost in remarking specific extensions of the figure as an exemplar for intellectual and political revolutions. Barlow's initial attempt to cast these materials, *The Vision of Columbus* of 1787, had systematically demythologized the New World, conceiving its primary virtue as residing in its very freedom from the constraints of traditional European paradigms. *The Vision of Columbus* is a fervent, even dogmatic, embodiment of Enlightenment rationalism. But its reconception is in remarkable accord with a shift in Zeitgeist, and the representation of Prometheus is its surest indication. It is not enough to see through the old superstitions, the outmoded institutional facades, the inherited shells of ideologies. They must be replaced with a new mythology, one invested with a libertarian ethos, a form without constraint or closure that energizes rather than tyrannizes the mind. It is this spirit that empowers the sublime propaganda of *Prometheus Unbound*, which in its conceptual reach beyond the vision of *Queen Mab* may be said similarly to outdistance *The Columbiad*. Barlow's epic is assuredly a cultural document of genuine significance, for Britain as well as America, but its mythology is ultimately only Jeffersonian, and the contradictions of its model, even in its own time, made it suspect—perhaps even itself a facade for tyranny like the traditional myths it would replace.

It is possible, indeed, that in 1809 the time was propitious, despite a wary British censorship, for publishing two epics celebrating American liberty from a repressive monarchy. America's fatal flaw was all too obvious to Great Britain, which in 1807 had climaxed a parliamentary struggle of at least a generation by abolishing the slave trade in its dominions. To celebrate that achievement and particularly the perseverance of its leading agitators, Thomas Clarkson, Granville Sharpe, and William Wilberforce, a memorial volume, as grandly done up as Barlow's *Columbiad*, was published in 1809.[19] *Poems on the Abolition of the Slave Trade*, with lengthy contributions from three poets identified with the liberal Dissenting tradition—James Montgomery, James Grahame, and Elizabeth Benger—was organized by the publisher Robert Bowyer, dedicated to the Duke of Gloucester, and clearly intended for a readership of means and political commitment. One such candidate on both scores would have been Sir Timothy Shelley, who clearly cast his vote in the Commons on behalf of Abolition. Again, it is tempting to picture his son, in the summer hiatus between his graduation from Eton and his matriculation at Oxford, reading through this volume in the library at Field Place. And again it is just as likely that, if not at home, he would have encountered it during his early months at Oxford, if only through the booksellers Slatter and Munday.[20] Wherever Shelley might have come upon this volume, he would have opened it to a remarkable mythological vignette by Robert Smirke (fig. 1), depicting the British Hercules freeing the African Prometheus from his long durance. Turning the page, he would have read the following poem, which one presumes was written by Bowyer:

Lines explanatory of the Vignette in the Title-page
PROMETHEUS DELIVERED
'COME, Outcast of the human race,
'Prometheus, hail thy destined place!
'This rock protects the dark retreat,
'Unvisited by earthly feet;
'We only shall thy mansion share,
'Who haunt the chamber of despair!
'The vulture, here, thy loathed mate—
'Rapacious minister of fate!

'Compels life's ruddy stream to part
'With keenest torture from thy heart.
'Yet not to perish art thou doomed,
'Victim unspared, but unconsumed;
'Death shall not sap thy wall of clay,
'That penal being mocks decay;
'Live, conscious inmate of the grave,
'Live, outcast, captive, victim, slave!'
　　　The Furies ceased; the wrathful strain
Prometheus hears, and, pierced with pain,
Rolls far around his hopeless gaze,
His realm of wretchedness surveys;
Then maddening with convulsive breath,
He moans or raves, imploring death.
Thus hours on hours unnumbered past,
And each more lingering than the last;
When lo! before his glazed sight,
Appears a form, in dauntless might.
'Tis he! Alcides, lord of fame!
The friend of man, his noblest name!
Swift from his bow the arrow flies,
And prone the bleeding vulture lies.
He smites the rock, he rends the chain,
Prometheus rises man again!
　　　Such, Africa, thy suffering state!
Outcast of nations, such thy fate!
The ruthless rock, the den of pain,
Were thine—oh long deplored in vain,
Whilst Britain's virtue slept! at length
She rose in majesty and strength;
And when thy martyr'd limbs she viewed,
Thy wounds unhealed, and still renewed,
She wept; but soon with graceful pride,
The vulture, Avarice, she defied,
And wrenched him from thy reeking side;
In Britain's name then called thee forth,
Sad exile, to the social hearth,
From baleful Error's realm of night,
To Freedom's breath and Reason's light.

Only within a literary atmosphere as momentarily dominated by Aeschylus as this was, it might be argued, could there be conceived such a remarkable conflation of *The Eumenides*, with this black Orestes assaulted by vengeful Furies, and *Prometheus Bound*. The fact that Shelley makes the same conflation in the first act of *Prometheus Unbound*, though obviously remarked, has, as far as I can determine, essentially never been queried in the numerous commentaries on Shelley's uses of Aeschylus. But the coincidence that he there invokes the Aeschylean Furies to a more extensive exposition of a similarly interiorized dynamics of despair strongly suggests that this vignette and poem were seen by him at some point and made an indelible imprint on his mind. The supposition is materially strengthened by two other elements in the characterization, the repeated identification of Prometheus as a human rather than immortal figure and the concentration on what Shelley calls "the wingless, crawling Hours" (1.48) of his torture. On the other hand, the self-congratulatory portrait of Britain as Hercules, in line with an early liberal ideology of British imperialism, is not, one presumes, the way the youthful Shelley conceived his world. Certainly, the endnotes to *Queen Mab* are clear in their notion of imperialism as an extension of capitalism into domination by the state.

That, too, is Blake's vision of the imperial mission, even when invested within a nominal independence on the part of the colonists. His representation of a female Prometheus being tortured by the male American eagle in *Visions of the Daughters of Albion* (fig. 2) is a striking instance of his use of illuminations to establish oblique contexts for his poetry. Even so early in his career (1793) Blake has already abandoned a poetic reliance on traditional forms of mythology, but the iconography of Prometheus serves pictorially to invoke the negative connotations of the later Promethean figures we have just surveyed. The "soft American plains" (1.20) are equally a virgin land being converted to ownership, a native people transported from primeval freedom into capitalist slavery, and a gender systematically denied freedom through a double standard of sexual morality. Oothoon's vision of free love, though couched within an impassioned rhapsody, is the lament of a prisoner denied freedom under multiple charges and without hope for parole. And it is small comfort, as Blake represents this complex, to see her as distanced by an intervening ocean and blatant American hypocrisy. She is a "Daughter of Albion," her condition the product of British civilization and an extension of its imperial values. Those sisters who lament her state reside in England, and the world they decry is as manifest in Jamaica as in the Carolinas—even, through a slight transmutation of terms into the subtler extensions of this morality, in the "London" of the *Songs of Experience*, where the alternatives for woman, marital submissiveness and sexual exploitation, are simply mirror images of each other.

In the case of Blake, undoubtedly, it would stretch credence to suggest that his multivalent icon was in any way available to Shelley. And yet it is at least fitting that "Visions of the Daughters of Albion" is an implicit tribute to Mary Wollstonecraft and the feminist publications of Joseph Johnson.[21] There is, however, one further extension of the Promethean myth into the political consciousness of England's Regency, and it too is more an allegorical icon of despair than an avatar of liberation. Byron easily embraces it in the final stanza of his "Ode to Napoleon Bonaparte," as well as later in "The Age of Bronze," but a fuller exposition of its terms, if obliquely expressed, is better discerned in a work by an author Shelley much admired, *France* (1817) by Sydney Owenson, Lady Morgan. This is her description of the vanquished Napoleon on St. Helena:

> Alone, in his desolate dwelling; deprived of every solace of humanity; torn from those ties, which alone throw a ray of brightness over the darkest shades of misfortune; wanting all the comforts, and many of the necessities of life; the victim of the caprice of petty delegated power; harassed by every-day oppression; mortified by mean, reiterated, hourly privation; chained to a solitary and inaccessible rock, with no object on which to fix his attention, but the sky to whose inclemency he is exposed; or that little spot of earth, within whose narrow bounds he is destined to wear away the dreary hours of unvaried captivity, in hopeless, cheerless, life-consuming misery! Where now is his faith in the magnanimity of England? his trust in her generosity? his hopes in her beneficence?[22]

Behind this passage is Lady Morgan's contemporary recognition that the Bourbon Restoration was dependent on the units of the British army that remained in France to prevent any attempts to return Napoleon to power. The implicit equations are between Napoleon and Prometheus, his jailors and the vulture, petty bureaucrats and the sycophant Mercury, between Great Britain and Jupiter. The terms are shifted diametrically from those informing the "Prometheus Delivered" of the *Poems on the Abolition of the Slave Trade*. They remind us, however, if we have strayed too far in reading Shelley's lyrical drama from Prometheus' despairing vision of the French Revolution, or Kenneth Neill Cameron's forceful representation of the entire work as a sustained allegory on it, that Shelley had in the still-living figure of Napoleon a contemporary representation of the failed Promethean, one of arresting power.[23] To look at the hopes with which the Revolution began, to see them then transformed into the Roman trappings of Napoleon replete with martial eagles as icons, and then to watch them dashed on the rocks of St. Helena, that is to contemplate Prometheus and discover in his image the Phantasm of Jupiter. In turn, it is to confront, on a specific and living contemporary plane, the rationale for despair enunciated with such chiseled rhetoric by the First Fury (1.618 ff). It is small wonder that all Prometheus can muster by way of answering her syllogisms is pity.

3

Mary Shelley's commentary on *Prometheus Unbound,* first published in the four-volume collected edition of 1839 and then frequently thereafter, notes that Shelley first contemplated the subject of his drama in April 1818 during their month-long stay in Milan. The passage through the Alps was sufficient, as the Shelleys' journal indicates, to bring Aeschylus' drama to mind, but we can surmise that something beyond mere scenery, sublime though it was, prompted the poet's further reflections.[24] Paradoxically, it is likely that the chief influence came from a wholly opposite experience, one not of wild natural landscapes but of civilized refinement. On the evening of 5 April, the day after their arrival, the Shelleys and Claire Clairmont attended La Scala. The opera was Joseph Weigl's *Il rivale di sé stesso*, which they found indifferent. The effect of the ballet that followed it, however, was wholly opposite. All three wrote of its powerful impact: "infinitely magnificent," said Mary; "the most splendid spectacle I ever saw," was her husband's verdict. The group was so impressed that they returned for the twinbill three weeks later.[25] The ballet was *Otello, ossia Il Moro di Venezia*. The choreographer was Salvatore Viganò, at the height of his fame as the founder of a new school of romantic dance-drama. So celebrated was he that only a few months before the Shelley party arrived in Milan, a bronze medal had been struck to commemorate his ballet of *Prometeo* (fig. 3). Is it possible that these English tourists, stage-struck by a new artistic experience—the very type of "arts, though unimagined, yet to be" (*Prometheus Unbound*, 3.3.56)—did *not* see this medal? Indeed, it is more than likely that it was on display in the Teatro alla Scala itself, perhaps with momentos of the production, including at least a cast list, and that the libretto for the ballet was likewise widely available, if not in the theater then in its immediate precincts.[26]

Viganò had first tried his hand at this subject under truly illustrious circumstance, choreographing Beethoven's *Die Geschöpfe des Prometheus* for the Hoftheater, Vienna, in 1801. There were fifteen performances the first year, another thirteen in 1802. Returning to Italy and establishing himself as the resident choreographer at La Scala, a decade later Viganò recast the narrative and greatly enlarged his conception of the ballet. Premiered on 22 May 1813, *Prometeo* was in six acts, with music drawn from the Beethoven production, as well as from Gluck, Haydn, Mozart, Weigl, and Viganò himself (Luigi Boccherini was his uncle). It was proclaimed his masterwork: "Non ballo, ma poema, opera divina."[27] The prima ballerina was Antonia Pallerini, the same dancer whom the Shelley party admired as Desdemona. Some idea of the scale of the ballet may be gathered from the fact that it had thirteen principals and thirty-eight identifiable characters within the chorus. A grand pantomime, representing the marvels of heaven at the beginning of the second act, suggests an even larger corps de ballet. *Prometeo* was conceived in every sense as a spectacle, and if Shelley were aware of nothing more than that Viganò had earlier rendered such a piece, the experience of this new dramatic ballet might have been sufficient to spark his own imagination toward a "sublime spectacle" based on the Prometheus myth.

But there are correspondences between the two works that suggest a more intimate acquaintance with Viganò's conception. The second-act pantomime

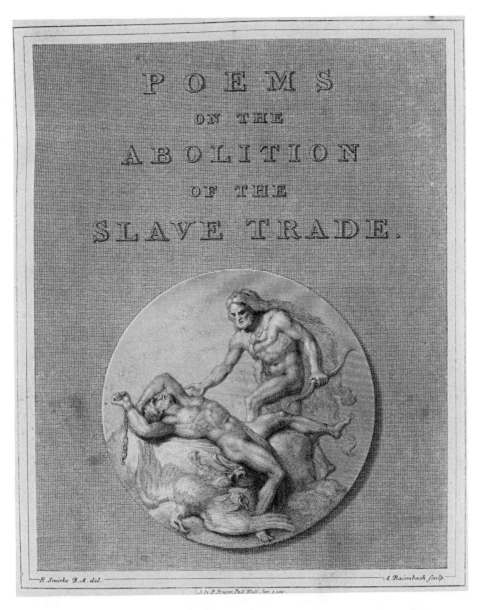

Fig. 1. *Poems on the Abolition of the Slave Trade* (1809)—title page vignette.
(Reproduced courtesy of Henry E. Huntington Library.)

And none but Bromion can hear my lamentations.

With what sense is it that the chicken shuns the ravenous hawk?
With what sense does the tame pigeon measure out the expanse?
With what sense does the bee form cells? have not the mouse & frog
Eyes and ears and sense of touch? yet are their habitations.
And their pursuits, as different as their forms and as their joys:
Ask the wild ass why he refuses burdens: and the meek camel
Why he loves man: is it because of eye ear mouth or skin
Or breathing nostrils? No. for these the wolf and tyger have.
Ask the blind worm the secrets of the grave, and why her spires
Love to curl round the bones of death: and ask the ravnous snake
Where she gets poison: & the wing'd eagle why he loves the sun
And then tell me the thoughts of man. that have been hid of old.

Silent I hover all the night. and all day could be silent.
If Theotormon once would turn his loved eyes upon me;
How can I be defild when I reflect thy image pure? (woe
Sweetest the fruit that the worm feeds on. & the soul prey'd on by
The new washd lamb ting'd with the village smoke & the bright swan
By the red earth of our immortal river: I bathe my wings.
And I am white and pure to hover round Theotormons breast.

Then Theotormon broke his silence. and he answered.

Tell me what is the night or day to one oerflowd with woe?
Tell me what is a thought? & of what substance is it made?
Tell me what is a joy? & in what gardens do joys grow?
And in what rivers swim the sorrows. and upon what mountains

Fig. 2. William Blake, *Visions of the Daughters of Albion* (plate 3). (Reproduced courtesy of Henry E. Huntington Library.)

Fig. 3. Bronze medallion struck in 1817 to commemorate Salvatore Viganò's *Prometeo* (7.4 cm). (Author's private collection.)

in heaven, for instance, involves a succession of allegorical figures representing Darkness, Dawn, the Hours, Phoebus Apollo, the Year, the Seasons, and
the Months, the stuff of allegorical painting, particularly that of Salvatore
Rosa, transposed to the stage. But it is clearly the semblance of this stage on
which the fourth act of *Prometheus Unbound* also opens, with dawn replacing
night, and a double chorus of Hours who "bear Time to his tomb in eternity"
(4.14) passing successively across it. As Ronald Tetrault has convincingly
argued, a number of devices in *Prometheus Unbound*, particularly its spirit
choruses, seem to derive from balletic practice, but his supposition that this
reflects Shelley's admiration for Mme. Melanie, the principal ballerina in
London before his departure for the continent, tends to privilege performance over choreographic conception.[28] The libretto for Vigano's ballet reveals
a decided preference for dramatic spectacle over mere dance, which was,
indeed, his legacy to the development of the art of nineteenth-century ballet.
The finale of the second act is indicative. From Phoebus Apollo's sun-chariot,
Prometheus, aided by Minerva, lights a torch to transport the heavenly fire to
earth. "Jove, apprized of this great theft, burns with anger. The burst of a
lightning bolt announces the divine vendetta; a dark mist envelops the chariot
of the sun, Minerva vanishes, and the wretched Prometheus falls to earth in
the midst of whirlwinds and whistling storms."[29]

Beyond the nature of the mythic conception itself, there are as well specific
details reminiscent of Shelley's drama: for example, a chorus of ten Loves
(Amorini) who arise from the sparks of Prometheus' falling torch at the
beginning of Act 3 and begin the process of raising humanity from its state of
savagery, or the three Graces, who are summoned to the Temple of Virtue in
the fifth act to surround the representative human couple whom Prometheus
has raised to a state of civilization and whose subsequent nuptials are celebrated with an allegorical epithalamial dance.[30] Most striking is the name of
the exemplary woman, danced by the prima ballerina, Palladini: Eone.
Inasmuch as Shelley's Ione seems to fulfill a similar role, being the closest to
the human state of Shelley's three immortal women, his adoption of the name
may have a simpler provenance than his commentators have been able thus
far to discover. Even if Shelley were simply following an Italian (or Latin)
rendering of the name of Aeschylus' representative human, Io, which is the
solution I argued in *Shelley's Annus Mirabilis* (49), an Eone derived by an
Italian dramatist to exactly the same purpose would at least suggest precedent.

Beyond what Vigano's *Prometeo* portends for the history of dance, however,
it has a further historical import, one whose ideological thrust is in this time
uniquely congruent with that of Byron and particularly Shelley. The title
page for the libretto, quite understandably, misrepresents the actual circumstances of Vigano's production. His *Prometeo* did not take place in the "R.
Teatro alla Scala," the Royal Theater of La Scala, but in the free Milan of the

late Napoleonic Empire. By the time the medal was struck and the Shelleys spent their month in Milan, Lombardy had been ceded, as part of the settlement of the Congress of Vienna, to the Hapsburg empire of Austria.[31] It is ironic that the only treatment of the ideological currents underlying Viganò's ballet should have got them exactly wrong. Raymond Trousson, apparently reading one sentence from the libretto, characterizes the work as reactionary, counseling man's duty as total submission to the will of God.[32] On the contrary, Viganò's *Prometeo* is written in the spirit of the Napoleonic mythos and, independent of whether Shelley knew anything beyond its mere existence, its ideological import has bearing on the radical, if refined, politics of Shelley's own drama.

In fairness to Trousson, there are obvious hermeneutic problems involved in interpreting the libretto of a ballet. It is difficult to ascribe irony to a situation wholly dependent for our understanding on a pantomime we can never observe. Still, when after Prometheus is seized his human dependents burn with resentment and Virtue teaches them submission to the divine will and propitiation through prayers and sacrifice, it is also difficult not to see such counsel, which of course cannot be articulated, as heavily tempered by its surroundings. The humanity that originally submitted, without knowing better, to the divine will was in a state of savagery: they are described as "le umane belve," wild, ferocious humanity (12), in the libretto. Asia describes the same abject condition depicted in the first act of Viganò's ballet:

> And Jove now reigned; for on the race of man
> First famine and then toil and disease,
> Strife, wounds, and ghastly death unseen before,
> Fell; and the unseasonable seasons drove,
> With alternating shafts of frost and fire,
> Their shelterless, pale tribes to mountain caves
> And in their desart hearts fierce wants he sent
> And mad disquietudes, and shadows idle
> Of unreal good, which levied mutual war,
> So ruining the lair wherein they raged.
>
> (2.4.49–58)

Viganò's ballet begins as "Prometheus contemplates the human species, and seeing it coarse, weak, defenceless, deprived of expedients and of reason, and inferior to the brutes themselves, is saddened and laments over it, yet nonetheless he resolves in his great mind by what means to raise the species above all other living beings."[33] The opening act ends in a general melee as the apple given to Eone by the personification of Agriculture precipitates among her fellow humans a brutal struggle for its possession and Prometheus is ready to abandon his plans for their redemption. It is an ugly and naturalistic scene, a remarkable departure from the conventions of classical ballet, and it posits a myth of human development opposed to the Christian fall and implicating the will of Jove, to which Virtue will later counsel submission, in the degradation of humanity.

The final act opens with several Cyclops binding Prometheus to a mountainside, impaling him with a diamond rivet, and summoning the vulture to lacerate his abdomen, while Virtue and her now submissive humanity vainly pray for Jove's intercession. Suddenly there enter on stage Hercules and a group of his followers, for which we may, I think, rightly read Napoleon and the French army. Indignant at the spectacle of this undeserved torture, Hercules does not hesitate, but climbs the mountain, kills the ravaging bird, and liberates Prometheus, who by now is on the verge of death. Such stress on Prometheus' mortal condition may be construed as Italian theatrical sentiment, but it assuredly places a strong accent on the linkage of Prometheus with humankind, and on the responsibility taken by a human, Hercules, for freeing their savior. At last, out of love for his son Hercules, which may be interpreted as an acceptance of human rights in the world, Jove relents and descends to crown Prometheus with eternal amaranth. Neither chronology nor characterization are exactly consistent here, but what is unquestionably so is the responsibility of humanity for its own elevation and preservation. The Jove of this ballet is a monarch of the ancien régime, content in his heavenly palace and wholly indifferent to the state of the proletariat left in deprivation on earth. Prometheus the encyclopedist gives humanity knowledge by which to better itself, but it only avails when invested in deeds, when placed into action. This is not so much the abstraction of Faust's "In the beginning was the Deed" as it is an enforcement of human will and power. So Hercules, in his only speech (three and a half lines) of Shelley's drama, greets the regenerate Prometheus:

> Most glorious among spirits, thus doth strength
> To wisdom, courage, and long suffering love
> And thee, who art the form they animate,
> Minister, like a slave.
>
> (3.3.1–4)

Shelley's accents fall on the subservience of force to wisdom, courage, and love, which after a quarter-century of warfare is highly understandable, but in every other sense his lyrical drama reinforces the ideology of Viganò's "choral drama."[34] Human reason, which dislodges false gods from idolatry, employs its best arts to liberate humanity from degradation. Love socializes this individual reach for excellence. A collective strength ensures the assertion of human rights. If there are gods left at this point—whether a reeducated Jove or a dark power named Demogorgon—they are at last operating in the service of the people. But if they do not serve humanity, they (and the institutions that are their support) must be superseded. Viganò's humanist ballet, written in the shadow of Napoleon's waning fortunes, is a testament to the revolutionary ethos of contemporary Europe before it disappeared in the reaffirmation of feudal legitimacy in 1815. *Prometheus Unbound*, written on the other side of that great divide, is a similar testament, a keeping of the old and still burning faith.

As I suggested at the beginning of this essay, it is easily conceivable that Shelley was familiar with every example cited here except for that of Blake. Yet even if he were not, or if he came across a political representation of Prometheus long before he planned his drama and it therefore did not truly register, the large certainties that motivate this argument remain. Prometheus, in these representative examples from Britain's romantic period, is an avatar of revolution against specific oppressions: civil, racial, sexual, and religious. He stands for a humanity bound to an undeserved state and no longer acquiescent in its degradation, a humanity with the will to be free and the power to dictate the terms of that freedom. From his association with mental growth this Prometheus assimilates the psychological threats that come from within—despair, inanition, and a loss of moral authority—to the external political repression he would overthrow. They are equal dangers, the legacy of the *ancien régime* and of the Napoleonic Empire alike. *Prometheus Unbound*, acknowledging that legacy, therefore adds another integer to the equation—patience. "Methinks we have survived an age of despair," Shelley wrote in the preface to *The Revolt of Islam*, contemplating the wreck of Europe's revolution shortly before he set forth from England. *Prometheus Unbound*, his next major poem, may be a great artistic advance, but it testifies to essentially the same faith. It is at once a manual for survival against that despair and a memorandum of the grievances yet to be assuaged.

Notes

This essay was written during tenure as a fellow of the Henry E. Huntington Library, San Marino, California. I wish to express my gratitude to its incomparable staff; to the knowledgeable proprietors of the Numismatico Todori, Florence, Italy; and to Nancy Shawcross of the Dance Collection, New York Public Library at Lincoln Center

1. White's essay was directed toward critical quarrels over Shelley's drama long before we might suppose there were any: *PMLA* 40 (1925): 172–84.

2. I am referring to chap. 2 of *Shelley's Annus Mirabilis: The Maturing of an Epic Vision* (San Marino, Calif.: Huntington Library, 1975).

3. George Stanley Faber, *The Origin of Pagan Idolatry ascertained from Historical Testimony and Circumstantial Evidence* (London: Rivington, 1816) 2:214; 1:267. Not only is Hogg's father listed as a subscriber, but so is a supposed member of the parish simply identified as "Peacock, Esq. Norton." It is very likely that this is Thomas Love Peacock through the agency of the younger Hogg, who by this time was his frequent correspondent and fellow enthusiast for Greek classics.

4. Bryant, *A New System, or an Analysis of Ancient Mythology* (London: Payne, White, and Walter, 1774–1776) 2:202–3. Earl Wasserman argues at great length for the definition of

Prometheus as the One Mind, a rubric derived from Shelley's philosophical speculations but even there conditioned by notions of contemporary mythography, in *Shelley: A Critical Reading* (Baltimore: Johns Hopkins University Press, 1971), esp. 256–66, 275–77, 359–73.

5. Jauss, *Toward an Aesthetics of Reception*, tr. Timothy Bahti (Minneapolis: University of Minnesota Press, 1982), 23–26.

6. On Shelley's conception of Prometheus as answer to Byron's, see Charles E. Robinson, *Shelley and Byron: The Snake and The Eagle Wreathed in Fight* (Baltimore: Johns Hopkins University Press, 1976) chap. 6. It is apparent that Peacock's refined neo-Hellenism was a constant impetus to Shelley's thought and writing: how hermetically sealed, even precious, this world could be can be gleaned from the correspondence of Peacock and Hogg contained in *The Athenians, Being Correspondence between Thomas Jefferson Hogg and His Friends Thomas Love Peacock, Leigh Hunt, Percy Bysshe Shelley, and Others*, ed. W. S. Scott (London: Golden Cockerel, 1943). Who in this circle earned the nickname Demogorgon it is unlikely we will ever discover, but it suggests the level of intellectual play within the circle as well as the existence of coterie referentiality in the writings, including *Prometheus Unbound*, of its members.

7. *Prometheus in Chains, Translated from the Greek of Aeschylus* (London: Longman, 1773), sig. A3. Indicative of the problems confronted by apologetics, an exactly opposite view of the drama as a foreshadowing of the martyrdom of Christ is contained in a serially printed essay, "On the Prometheus Vinctus of Aeschylus," *Gentleman's Magazine* 66 (1796): 66, 188–90, 306–7, 397–98, 490–91; signed E. E. A.

8. *The Greek Theatre of Father Brumoy*, tr. Charlotte Lennox (London: Millar, Vaillant, Baldwin, 1759) 2:136. This conclusion is Pierre Brumoy's and not Charlotte Lennox's interpolation.

9. R. Potter, Preface (1777) to *The Tragedies of Aeschylus* (Oxford: Bliss and Baxter; London: Rivington, Longman's, 1812), xv.

10. *Das Prometheussymbol in der Dichtung der Englischen Romantik, Palaestra*, no. 236 (Göttingen: Vandenhoeck and Ruprecht, 1963), 20–31.

11. One presumes some prior acquaintance on Shelley's part with Thomas Morrell's textbook of PROMETHEUS DESMOTES. *cum variis lectionibus, Stanleiana versione . . . in usum studiosae juventutis*, published at and for Eton by M. Pote and E. Williams in 1798.

12. The attack on the Butler edition was published in the *Edinburgh Review* 15 (1809–10): 152–63; 315–22; the bemused account of the scholarly controversy may be found in the *Gentleman's Magazine* 80, ii (1810): 241–43.

13. Edmund Henry Barker, *Classical Journal* 5 (1812): 299; see also: 3 (1811): 271–85; 4 (1811): 209–222; 425–36; 5 (1812): 299–309; 6 (1812): 197–201; 7 (1813): 169–71. There was as well a review of the Butler recension in the first issue of the *Classical Journal* I (1810): 16–36, and an account of the recent history of Aeschylus editions, with particular attention to *Prometheus Bound*, in the second: (1810): 461–72.

14. See Thomas Jefferson Hogg, *The Life of Percy Bysshe Shelley*, ed. Humbert Wolfe (London: Dent, 1933) 1:70. There is no evidence that Shelley did as he was told. Two years later Aeschylus was one of the Greek authors Shelley ordered, in original and translation, from Clio Rickman: see *Letters of Percy Bysshe Shelley*, ed. Frederick L. Jones (Oxford: Clarendon, 1964) 1:344.

15. "Ode to the West Wind," lines 68–69. All quotations from Shelley are from *Shelley's Poetry and Prose*, ed. Donald H. Reiman and Sharon B. Powers (New York: Norton, 1977).

16. Thomas Northmore, *Washington, or Liberty Restored* (London: Longman's [alternate title-page, Clarke, Westley and Parrish, Miller and Pople, and Anderson], 1809), [iii].

17. The association of Satan with Prometheus is as obvious as it is traditional, and by their very silence on the subject clearly a main impetus to the attempts of Christian apologists to shift the typological values they endeavored to extract from Aeschylus' play. Like Shelley, Elizabeth Barrett, in the preface to her translation of Aeschylus' tragedy, argues that the superficial resemblance conceals a profound difference: "Prometheus stands eminent and alone; one of the most original, and grand, and attaching characters ever conceived by the mind of man. That conception sank deeply into the soul of Milton, and, as has been observed, rose from thence in the likeness of his Satan. But the Satan of Milton and the Prometheus of Aeschylus stand upon ground as unequal, as do the sublime of sin and the sublime of virtue. Satan suffered from his

ambition; Prometheus from his humanity: Satan for himself; Prometheus for mankind: Satan dared perils which he had not weighed; Prometheus devoted himself to sorrows which he had foreknown"—*Prometheus Bound. Translated from the Greek of Aeschylus. And Miscellaneous Poems, By the Translator* (London: Valpy, 1833), xiv–xv. This was Barrett's first publication, a woman's daring, if anonymous, entry into the male classical kingdom, intended to be the first poetic translation of the Aeschylus drama in English. The honor was, however, snatched from her by no less than Shelley's cousin, Thomas Medwin, who, claiming in his preface an exemplary education in Greek at the hands of Shelley and Prince Mavrocordato, published his inferior verse translation the previous year with William Pickering.

18. I suggest the evidence for the impact of this work on *Queen Mab* in particular, as well as its importance for the romantic libertarian epic at large, in *Poetic Form and British Romanticism* (New York: Oxford University Press, 1986), 171–72.

19. *Poems on the Abolition of the Slave Trade; written by James Montgomery, James Grahame, and E. Benger. Embellished with Engravings from Pictures Painted by R. Smirke, Esq. R. A.* London: Printed for R. Bowyer . . . by T. Bensley, 1809. This is the date of imprint, but the illustrations bear an 1810 date. I have not found a copy with a subscription list and therefore assume that none existed.

20. There can be no doubt that Byron, whose departure for his eastern tour appears to have just predated publication of this volume, would on his return and entry into Lord Holland's Whig establishment in the House of Lords have become familiar with it.

21. The figure of Prometheus does not, as far as I can determine, otherwise appear in this feminist literature, probably because the legendary associations are themselves so lodged within a male system of values. Occasionally, especially among the syncretic mythographers, we are reminded that Prometheus overreached himself in creativity by bringing Pandora into the world.

22. *France*, 3d American ed. (Philadelphia: Thomas, 1817), 327. The passage is quoted in full in the infamous *Quarterly Review* attack on Lady Morgan's *France*, which was well known and widely censured (17 [1817]:280). In the same guise and even more directly, but from a twenty-year retrospect, is Edgar Quinet's representation of Napoleon: "Du nouveau Prométhée ils ont ouvert le flanc: / Le vautour d'Albion boit lentement son sang" (*Napoléon* [1836], XLVIII, "Sainte-Hélène"). For further examples of this contemporary icon, consult Raymond Trousson, *Le thème de Prométhée dans la littérature européenne* (Geneva: Droz, 1964) 2:335–42: "L'échec d'un destin titanique: le prométhée de Saint-Hélène."

23. Cameron, *Shelley: The Golden Years* (Cambridge: Harvard University Press, 1974), 485–88, 499–501, 539–40.

24. 26 March 1818: "The scene is like that described in the 'Prometheus' of Aeschylus; vast rifts and caverns in granite precipices"—*Mary Shelley's Journal*, ed. Frederick L. Jones (Norman: University of Oklahoma Press, 1947), 94–95.

25. *The Letters of Mary Wollstonecraft Shelley*, ed. Betty T. Bennett (Baltimore: Johns Hopkins University Press, 1980) 1:64: Shelley, *Letters* 2:4; Claire Clairmont's Journal entry for 25 April 1818, which documents the return to La Scala, can be found in *Shelley and His Circle*, ed. Donald H. Reiman (Cambridge: Harvard University Press, 1973), 5:452. The music for the ballet was derived from Rossini's opera, *Otello*.

26. *Prometeo. Ballo Mitologico, inventato e posto sulle scene del R. Teatro alla Scala da Salvatore Viganò nella primavera dell'anno 1813.* Pp. 30. The medal is inscribed on the rear as follows: "A Salvatore Viganò impareggibile coreografo che colla rappresentazion del Prometeo data l. an MDCCCXIV nel Regio Teatro di Milano immortalatosi tanta gloria nella Mirra e nel Psammi brillante tuttavia sostiene gli ammiratori del bello sacravano meritamente nel MDCCCXVII" (To Salvatore Viganò, incomparable choreographer, who having immortalized himself with his production of Prometheus, given the year 1814 in the Royal Theater of Milan, still brilliantly sustains so much glory in Myrrha and Psammi, the admirers of the beautiful deservedly dedicated [this medal] in 1817).

27. "Not a ballet, but a poem, a divine creation": I quote from what is presumably a contemporary reaction reported in the article on Viganò in the *Enciclopedia dello Spettacolo* 9:1678–79. Stendhal drew a comparison between Viganò's *Mirra* and productions of Shakespeare in *Rome, Florence, and Naples* (entry for 22 November 1816), which was elevated by Lady Morgan to the claim that Viganò "is the Shakespeare of his art; and with such powerful

conceptions, and such intimate knowledge of nature and effect, as he exhibits, it is wonderful that, instead of composing ballets, he does not write epics": *Italy* (London: Henry Colburn, 1821), 1:98.

28. "Shelley at the Opera," ELH 48 (1981): 144–71, esp. 161–65.

29. "Giove, accostosi del gran furto, arde di sdegno. Lo scoppio d'un fulmine annunzia la divina vendetta; buja caligine s'avvolge intorno al cocchio del Sole, Minerva sparisce, e il misero Prometeo precipita sulla terra in mezzo al roteare de' turbini ed al fischiare delle procelle" (*Prometeo*, 17).

30. Spirits of Love succeed the Furies in *Prometheus Unbound*, 1.664 ff.; on the three Graces as models for Asia, Panthea, and Ione, see Wasserman, 364–66, and Curran, *Shelley's Annus Mirabilis*, 50; the epithalamial duet of Asia and the Voice in the Air (customarily interpreted as Prometheus) at the end of Act 2 is enlarged and extended in the love duet of the Earth and Moon in Act 4.

31. It is at least conceivable that the elegant tributary medal for Viganò memorialized a state of mind and of polity, the titan of Milanese freedom crushed by the tyranny of this new Jupiter. At the very least, a celebration of Italian artistic genius, in these circumstances, had decidedly nationalistic overtones.

32. *Le thème de Prométhée dans la littérature européenne*, 2:305.

33. "Prometeo contempla la specie umana, e vendendola rozza, debole, inerme, priva d'accorgimento e di ragione, ed inferiore agli stessi bruti, se ne rattrista, ne geme, e volge nella sua gran mente i mezzi coi quali sollevarla nondimeno al di sopra di tutti gli altri esseri viventi" (*Prometeo* 2).

34. Shelley used this term, so highly suggestive of his generic designation for *Prometheus Unbound*, in a letter to Peacock the day after seeing Viganò's *Otello* (*Letters*, 2:4).

Notes on Contributors

MICHAEL LÖWY lives in Paris and is currently Research Director of Sociology at the National Center for Scientific Research. He is the author of numerous aritcles and books, including *Georg Lukács—From Romanticism to Bolshevism* (1979) and, most recently, *Verdinglichung und Utopie: Ernst Bloch und Georg Lukács* (1987).

ROBERT SAYRE lives in Paris and teaches English at the University of Leon. He has written several articles on English and American romanticism and is author of *Solitude in Society: a sociological study in French Literature* (1978).

MICHAEL FERBER is an Associate Professor of English at the University of New Hampshire. He has written *The Social Vision of William Blake* (1985) and many articles on literature, politics, religion, and the arms race.

DAVID SEBBERSON is Assistant Professor of Rhetoric and Composition, Department of English, St. Cloud State University. For a number of years he was a consultant at The World Bank.

MICHAEL SCRIVENER teaches in the English Department at Wayne State University in Detroit. Author of *Radical Shelley* (1982), Scrivener has been working on an anthology of verse from the periodicals of the English democratic movement (1789–1850) and a critical study of the movement's literary culture.

DANIEL COTTOM is Professor of English at the University of Florida. His previous works include *Social Figures: George Eliot, Social History, and Literary Representation* (1987) and *The Civilized Imagination: A Study of Ann Radcliffe, Jane Austen, and Sir Walter Scott* (1987). His most recent publication is *Text and Culture: The Politics of Interpretation* (1989).

MARILYN BUTLER teaches at St. Hugh's College, Oxford. She has published widely on romantic literature and is the author of *Jane Austen and the War of Ideas* (1975) and *Romantics, Rebels, and Reactionaries* (1982).

CATHERINE L. MCCLENAHAN is Assistant Professor of English at Marquette University. She has published several articles and reviews on speculative fiction and is now completing a book on Blake's *Jerusalem*.

JEROME J. MCGANN is Commonwealth Professor of English, University of

Virginia. He is editor of the Oxford Byron and author of many articles and books, including *The Romantic Ideology* (1983) and, most recently, *The Literature of Knowledge* (1989).

STUART CURRAN is Professor of English at the University of Pennsylvania and editor of the *Keats-Shelley Journal*. He is the author of many articles and books, including *Poetic Form and British Romanticism* (1986). He is currently writing a critical study of women poets of the romantic period.

Index